A GREAT AND TERRIBLE WORLD

The Pre-Prison Letters 1908–1926

A GREAT AND TERRIBLE WORLD

The Pre-Prison Letters 1908–1926

Antonio Gramsci

Edited and translated by
Derek Boothman

Haymarket Books • Chicago, Illinois

First published by Lawrence and Wishart Limited
in the United Kingdom in 2014.

This edition published by Haymarket Books in 2014

Haymarket Books
PO Box 180165,
Chicago, IL 60618
773-583-7884
info@haymarketbooks.org
www.haymarketbooks.org

ISBN: 978-1-60846-393-0

Trade distribution in the United States, Canada and all current US territories, including Samoa, Guam, US Virgin Islands, Northern Marina Islands, and Puerto Rico, and bookshops servicing the US military through Consortium Book Sales and Distribution, www.cbsd.com.

Special discounts are available for bulk purchases by organizations and institutions. Please contact Haymarket Books for more information at 773-583-7884 or info@haymarketbooks.org.

This book was published with the generous support of Lannan Foundation and the Wallace Action Fund.

Printed in Canada by union labor.

Library of Congress CIP data is available.

10 9 8 7 6 5 4 3 2 1

Contents

30 giugno 1924

Mia carissima Iulca,

hai ricevuto la mia lettera della settimana scorsa? Ho pensato molto a te in questi giorni: ho riletto molte tue lettere, riandavo col pensiero a tutti i ricordi della nostra vita comune, dal primo giorno che ti ho visto a Serebriani Bor e che non osavo entrare nella stanza perché mi avevi intimidito (davvero, mi avevi intimidito e oggi sorrido ricordando questa impressione) al giorno che sei partita a piedi e io ti ho accompagnato fino alla grande strada attraverso la foresta e sono rimasto tanto tempo fermo per vederti allontanare tutta sola, col tuo carico da viandante, per la grande strada, verso il mondo grande e terribile e poi e poi tutto il nostro amore: oggi tu stai per essere madre e le nostre vite sono legate, ma noi siamo lontani l'uno dall'altro.

Cara, ho sofferto molto in questi giorni pensando a te che sei lontana. Lavoravo, ma appunto perciò soffrivo, perché avrei voluto che anche tu avessi lavorato insieme a me, vicino a me: non riesco più a vedermi solo, mi pare di essere diminuito e di non poter fare tutto ciò che vorrei: una parte della mia volontà è lontana da me. E poi, da più di un mese non so più nulla della tua vita. So che devi avermi aspettato; ma cosa hai pensato e fatto in tutto questo tempo oltre all'aspettarmi? E la tua salute è rimasta salda? Di tante piccole cose vorrei essere informato: tante cose vorrei fare per te e l'impossibilità in cui mi trovo mi immalinconisce.

Forse fra una settimana partirò per Mosca: con la prossima posta potrò dirti definitivamente qualcosa in proposito. La situazione si è stabilizzata, ma rimane tesa. Essa è tale per cui da un momento all'altro può nuovamente inasprirsi. Entro questa settimana si potrà deliberare se una mia assenza sia possibile. Scrivimi e mandami notizie per mezzo di Bianco. Ti potrò riabbracciare solo quando sarai una buona mammina o mi sarà possibile esserti vicino anche quando il nostro bambino nascerà? Ti voglio tanto bene, Iulca e ti abbraccio forte forte

G.

Letter from Gramsci to Julia, 30 June 1924 (see p311).
Facsimile courtesy Gramsci Institute.

Acknowledgements

Many people generously gave of their time to help and advise on various aspects of this book. In particular the translator would like to thank Caterina Balistreri, Joseph Buttigieg, Alessandro Carlucci, Colin Chambers, Ben Fontana, Emilia Kosterina, Alessandra Marchi, Adam David Morton, Jeni Nicholson, Luigi Matt, Giuseppe and Luigi Manias, Luca Paulesu (literary executor for the family), Rossana Platone, Angelo Rossi, Giancarlo Schirru, Regan Scott, Jonathan Smith and Anita Weston. In addition to these, two people no longer with us, Roger Simon in Britain and Antonio A. Santucci in Italy, were for many years of great help on all things related to Gramsci, while, during the preparation of this volume, the translator has been grateful for the great patience and support that has been shown by Sally Davison, managing editor of Lawrence and Wishart.

A word of special thanks goes to all the staff of the Fondazione Istituto Gramsci in Rome, in particular to Anna Bodini, Giovanna Bosman, Leonardo Pompeo D'Alessandro, Francesco Giasi, Eleonora Lattanzi, Dario Massimi, Cristiana Pipitone and Maria Luisa Righi, and to its president, Giuseppe Vacca and director Silvio Pons. The Gramsci Institute is thanked especially for its permission to reproduce various illustrations relating to the letters, as is the Casa Gramsci museum in Ghilarza.

A collective 'thank you' goes to fellow-members of Rome's Gramsci Seminar, held under the auspices of the Italian section of the International Gramsci Society. Libraries and archives whose staff helped greatly include London's Marx Memorial Library, the Istituto Universitario Europeo at Fiesole (Florence), the Russian State Archive for Social and Political History (RGASPI) in Moscow, for consultation of the Comintern Archives, the Sraffa Archive (Trinity College, Cambridge), and, as ever, the British Library. Past and present colleagues and former students of what is now the University of Bologna's Department of Interpretation and Translation (DIT) who advised on problems in different languages, sometimes without knowing it, include Elio Ballardini, Francesca Biagini, Andrew Cresswell, Margherita De Michiel, Francesca Gatta, Marco Mazzoleni, Lisa Orsato, Michele Prandi, Diana Roberts, Simona Sangiorgi, Lucia Scardapane, IraTorresi, and Daniela Zorzi. Not least, the translator's thanks go to Alessandra Giovagnoli and Stefano Boothman for their forbearance during the book's preparation.

The quotation from Pascarella's Romanesque dialect poem *The Discovery of America* (letter of 16 April 1924 to Jul'ka) is reproduced by kind permission of the translator John DuVal and his publisher, the University of Arkansas Press, while the report of Gramsci's speech at the XII Conference of the Russian Communist Party is based on Caterina Balistreri's Italian translation, published in *Belfagor* (see Carlucci and Balistreri in the Select Bibliography) of the original article in *Izvestija*.

IN MEMORIAM

During the latter stages of the long gestation of this book, the community of Gramsci scholars lost five important people who, each in their own way, had contributed as authors or translators to making known and using Gramsci's thought originally and constructively: Giorgio Baratta (Italy), Carlos Nelson Coutinho (Brazil), Francisco Fernandez Buey (Spain) and John Cammett and – as the book was going to press – Frank Rosengarten (United States). This volume is dedicated to their memory and their work.

General Introduction

A collection of letters is also essentially a biography – here of a man recognised as one of the twentieth century's leading thinkers. Despite the long crisis afflicting the left in the traditional industrialised world, Gramsci's reputation has remained unscathed and indeed has been enhanced. Concepts he developed in prison, often encountered in this selection in their first formulations, have been taken up and applied to effect by many outside the bounds of the left, sometimes in areas of the world and in fields that would not have been guessed at in his time. The present volume fleshes out what the English-speaking world knows of him, both politically and personally, through the widely available *Prison Letters*, Fiori's standard, but by now rather old, biography and Davidson's intellectual biography.[1]

A wide selection of Gramsci's pre-prison letters – around two thirds of those currently known – is here offered, covering the period up to his arrest by the fascist regime in November 1926. Since the publication of Antonio A. Santucci's Italian edition of the pre-prison letters that were known in the early 1990s (Gramsci 1992), and even since the first two volumes of correspondence in the prestigious ongoing Italian *National Edition of Antonio Gramsci's Writings* (Gramsci 2009 and 2012), further letters and documents have emerged from various archives, and are still emerging (though those that are still of uncertain attribution are not included here). Some letters are published here either for the first time in any language or shortly after their first Italian appearance.[2] When there is an overlap of content with others previously known, precedence has been given to these newly-found letters; and unnecessary duplication has also been avoided elsewhere in the selection, while at the same time all letters are published in the fullest text available, excepting that Party and Comintern protocol numbers have been omitted.

Unlike the *Prison Letters*, Gramsci's pre-prison correspondence discusses events then happening. This introduction and the endnotes to each chapter are designed to aid readers in further understanding these events and locating them within their historical context.

A factor that comes strongly into play in Gramsci's letters is the intertwining of personal and political themes in his overall development. This is immediately apparent: his family circumstances and the general conditions of life in his native Sardinia show up very early on, and feed into in the writings and theorisations that we begin to see regarding the 'South'. The term 'South', on the surface seeming to denote a merely geographical area, increasingly takes on metaphorical connotations that bring into play uneven and under-development, overexploitation and countryside-city relations. In the letters dating from the latter stages of his schooling in Sardinia, there is a marked political element which, even when not explicit, tends to hover in the background. Later on, the personal and political factors converge and merge in a different way, for example in his relations with Party comrades, and in particular in his relations with three of the Schucht sisters – relations that went deep for all concerned and, as transpires from the letters, were more complex than has been thought up to now. One of the sisters, Julija (Julia in English and Giulia in Italian, usually known by her Russian diminutive, Jul'ka) became Antonio's partner and mother of their two sons.

One phrase that is frequently used in the letters between Antonio and Jul'ka is 'a great and terrible world' ('terrible' in its original sense of 'awe-inspiring'), which comes from the novel *Kim*, by Rudyard Kipling, one of Gramsci's favourite authors. This phrase provides the subtitle for the present volume.

SCHOOL IN SARDINIA (CHAPTER ONE)

From the age of seven Antonio was brought up mainly in Ghilarza, home village of his mother Giuseppina (familiarly called 'Peppina'), in western central Sardinia, but he was born in Ales, about fifty kilometres to the south, on 22 January 1891. The child was registered five days later at the municipal office as Antonio Francesco and, two days after that, was baptised Antonio Sebastiano Francesco, Sebastiano being the name of the officiating Vicar General. Only the name Antonio (often familiarly abbreviated to Nino) was ever actually used, the exception being on his marriage certificate (see the section on the Schucht family in this introduction) which, Russian-style, gives Frančeskovič as his patronymic.

Some of the letters Gramsci wrote home as a school student in Sardinia – from his middle school in Santulussurgiu, not far from Ghilarza, or from the 'liceo' (lycée or high school), much farther away in Cagliari on the southern coast, have now been redated as compared with Gramsci (1992). The new dates take account of what was studied in each year, of Gramsci's teachers in the various years at school, and, naturally, of the internal evidence of the letters themselves. For example, the very first letter, from Santulussurgiu, was written in 1908 and not, as stated in the 1992 volume, 6 February 1909, a date added in another hand at some later time.[3]

The letters from this period show a family, which certainly existed above the extreme poverty of the peasantry and shepherds on whom much of the island's life and economy depended, but was still one of very modest means, trying to give their most academically gifted child the possibility of a higher education. They read as a constant plea for money, interspersed with occasional thanks for clothing or foodstuffs sent according to season and availability; to avoid repetition, a number of these letters repeatedly asking for money, especially from Cagliari, have been omitted. At this point Antonio seems often not to have fully appreciated the notable sacrifices being made for him. His father was struggling to provide for his family while by all accounts having no head for finance – one of the consequences of which was that he had frittered away all the money that his wife had brought into the marriage.[4]

Political themes begin little by little to come into the letters during the time at high school. First of all this aspect is implicit, as for example when mention is made of Massimo Stara, one of the teachers at the Santulussurgiu school (see p62), who later emerged as a key figure in the Sardinian socialist and trade union movement. It is through such people that Gramsci began to be exposed to the relatively new ideas of socialism, moving on from the Sardinian nationalism, even in its progressive aspect, to which he had earlier been attracted. Then, while at the Dettori Lycée in Cagliari, he had an eye-opening school excursion to the mining area of Gùspini in the west, where he encountered not the peasant and shepherd environment he was used to, but that of an important section of industrial proletariat (see p72). Just afterwards, he was invited to be correspondent from Aidomaggiore, near Ghilarza, for the progressive newspaper *L'Unione Sarda*, a collaboration which was limited to one isolated article (25 July 1910), on the basis of which he received his journalist's card. During this period, his brother Gennaro (Nannaro) was elected secretary of the Chamber of Labour (Trades Council) that united the various trade union branches in Cagliari; this led to a certain amount of alarm in the family, for which see Antonio's letter to their mother of January 1911 (p74).

On finishing school, Gramsci sat an entrance examination in autumn 1911 for the University of Turin. Despite fainting two or three times, he was placed ninth out of the 39 winners of the study grants that were offered to students from financially needy families in the former Kingdom of Sardinia (Piedmont and Sardinia).[5] Backed by a promise of financial support from his family he registered for a degree in modern philology. Palmiro Togliatti, later to become his successor at the head of the Italian Communist Party, but as yet unknown to him, was placed second in the examination, though he enrolled in another faculty. The modern philology course was the nearest thing at that time to a degree in linguistics, a subject to which Gramsci was to return time and time again. Given the renewed interest from the beginning of the 1990s in Gramsci's views on language and on the translatability of language and experience, as well as a conjecture about his indirect influence on the linguistic philosopher Ludwig Wittgenstein through their mutual friend Piero Sraffa, this current selection of letters has been careful to pay attention to this aspect of Gramsci's interests.[6]

THE UNIVERSITY STUDENT: LINGUISTICS AND THE SARDINIAN LANGUAGE (CHAPTER 2)

After some initial payment problems because of not producing the right certificates on time (see p82), the university registration fee was paid and Antonio was able to begin his university studies. From two other letters, not included here (15 and 18 November), one sees his exasperation with his father who, according to him, had done nothing to get all the necessary certificates sent on; even some time later (letter of 3 January 1912, p84) Antonio felt he had yet again to return to the subject. Moreover – typical of the Italian bureaucracy – a mistake was made which meant that, although he was entitled to exemption for half his fees, the full amount was asked for, with the remainder only being finally reimbursed in the following year.[7] Gennaro now played a hand in helping Antonio financially, perhaps unbeknown to the rest of the family. He sent 20 lire to his brother in January 1912, with a promise to do so again on a regular basis, although whether and for how long he was able to do so is not known. Confirmation of this help is however alluded to in a letter from Antonio to his father of May 1912 (not included here), in which he states his intention of taking two exams over the summer and another in the autumn. In fact he sat all three in the autumn 1912 session, getting top marks with distinction in the glottology examination (comparative historical linguistics) with Matteo Bartoli, and achieving both exemption from his fees for that academic year and the renewal of his grant (Zucàro, p1099).

Life continued to be difficult, both for Antonio and for his family who were trying desperately to support him, and it was certainly not the case that Gramsci wasted money. A waiter in a milk bar, interviewed some twenty years after his death, recalled him normally consuming a solitary 'very frugal' meal (Zucàro, p1094), while a fellow student on his course later testified to the 'extremely modest' nature of his lodgings, 'having no heating and being poorly furnished'. This student also commented on the strong personality that already characterised Gramsci, which was well illustrated by an incident involving the Latin Literature professor. The latter, as was his wont, introduced some rather vulgar remarks when commenting on sexually ambiguous phrases that occurred in the love poetry of Catullus, even though there were novice nuns present. Despite the authoritarian nature of the university of the time, and of this teacher in particular, Gramsci publicly took him to task for this; after a period of dead silence the professor continued the class, but now reading from the official course notes and leaving out any potentially embarrassing comments.[8]

The harshness of living conditions in Turin aggravated the health problems that dogged Gramsci throughout his life. In a letter of late November 1913, written to his father once again in 'anger and desperation', Gramsci expressed the fear that all was lost as regards his student career, and begged his father to ask for a loan from the public notary. 'Don Ciccillo' – as Francesco Gramsci was known – replied to his son in an understanding and affectionate tone, telling him that some money had already been sent while the rest, which was needed for paying the university fees, had been telegraphed to him.

In the following autumn (1914) Antonio obtained a good result

(27/30) in one of his examinations, but was not able, yet again for health reasons, to take a further three, meaning that his grant was suspended. In the winter of 1914-15, however, after an introduction by Bartoli to the philosophy lecturer Annibale Pastore, he followed Pastore's official course and also took private lessons with him – course and lessons both being based on a critical interpretation of Marxism. After managing to pay an instalment of his tuition fees, Gramsci was then able to sit and pass one of the previous year's three outstanding examinations, Italian Literature, in April 1915 (as was the rule, his grant was suspended until he caught up with the examination schedule). But this was to be his last examination, and in the end he never actually finished his university degree (Zucàro, p1110).

In the letters from Turin we see the development of what Bartoli hoped would be a lasting collaboration between himself and Antonio, 'the archangel destined to put to definitive rout the neo-grammarians'.[9] The esteem in which Bartoli held Gramsci was shown when he gave him the task of transcribing his course for use by the other students.[10] As later recounted by Alfonso Leonetti, Gramsci's comrade in Turin and later in Rome, Gramsci was a 'precious collaborator' for Bartoli in tracing information on the dialects of the Sardinian language. This can be seen in Bartoli's request to his Italian-Sardinian bilingual student for information on the pronunciation of a number of words in the dialect of the village of Fonni, whose geographical isolation had led to a linguistic 'fossilisation' that was important for establishing more clearly certain aspects of Latin pronunciation.[11] Later that year (24 November 1912) Nino asked his favourite sister, Teresa, for the meanings of various words in the two main dialect divisions of Sardinian, including the terms used in important work processes.[12] The details of his request suggested that work was being done on some sort of dictionary, but it is only recently that it has been established that the fruits of this research were included in the authoritative *Romanisches etymologisches Worterbuch* (1911-1920), edited by Bartoli's own thesis supervisor Wilhelm Meyer-Lübke (and not in Bartoli's planned but unfinished *Linguistic Atlas* of Italy). The words about which Gramsci was enquiring were published in the *Worterbuch* in 1914, just over a year after the exchange of letters with Teresa.[13]

More aspects of Gramsci's language interests are shown elsewhere in this Turin period, including indirectly in a postcard (see p97) to Ezio Bartalini, a friend called up to the military front with whom

Gramsci worked on 'philological projects'.[14] Confirmation of his wish to continue his studies comes in a letter to his sister Grazietta, datable no more precisely than to 1916, while later there is a side-swipe at artificial languages such as Esperanto or Volapük as being unable to convey the richness of real life (see p99). And even as late as 1918, he still intended to complete his degree, with Bartoli supervising his thesis, which in Gramsci's words would study the 'history of language ['linguaggio'], seeking to apply even to this research the critical methods of historical materialism to language'.[15]

Had Gramsci wanted it, a brilliant academic and scientific career awaited him. However other events intervened, especially in the wake of the Russian revolution, and these dashed the hopes that Bartoli had placed in his student. Gramsci's other ruling interests led him to give up formal academic work. Having said this, the reputation of being a linguist followed him for years, so that, for example, an article published in the British *Sunday Worker* just before his trial describes him as a 'former M.P., professor and well-known etymologist'.[16] And by no means the least important instance of Gramsci's work on language questions can be seen in the very last Prison Notebook of all, which has very important remarks on grammar – and of a sociolinguistic nature – fully three decades before sociolinguistics took off as a separate discipline.[17] As Italy's senior linguist, Tullio De Mauro, remarked, with his tongue firmly in his cheek, when 'orthodox' political Gramscians take no notice of the linguistic side to Gramsci, linguists feel compelled to protest in response that 'Gramsci wasn't a Marxist at all. Gramsci was nothing like a politician. Gramsci was a linguist, Gramsci was a follower of Ascoli who just by chance became Secretary of the Communist Party'.[18]

THE BEGINNING OF FULL-TIME POLITICAL INVOLVEMENT (CHAPTER THREE)

In the initial period in Turin Gramsci was attracted by the workers' movement and was committed to a left outlook, but it seems that it was only some time later that he became a socialist in a strict sense. One part in this was played by friends he had made, such as Angelo Tasca, who later emerged as one of the key figures in the Turin movement and in the infant Communist Party. Indeed Tasca was 'cultivating' Gramsci as early as 1912, as can be deduced, for example, from a couple of postcards that he sent Gramsci that summer from a holiday in the mountains. According to Battista Santhià, a prominent Turinese communist worker, it was during or immediately after the victorious three-month strike of 6500 Turin automobile workers early in 1913 that Gramsci asked to join the Socialist Party (PSI), sponsored by Tasca, although the long administrative process delayed his formal membership until the end of the year.[19]

Two years later, at the end of 1915, he was offered a remunerative post as head of a school in what is now the ski resort of Sauze d'Oulx, about 65 kilometres west of Turin. But he turned this down in order to accept a more politically and culturally rewarding position (though much less so financially) as a journalist on the Turin edition of the official Socialist Party daily *Avanti!*, a post offered to him by the paper's editor, prestigious political leader and journalist Giacinto Menotti Serrati. It was during the first months of his work on the paper that he wrote the letter to his oldest sister, Grazietta, that perhaps constitutes his most striking and moving testament of the existential crisis he was experiencing and – despite all the goodwill and sacrifices made by his family – of the hardships that were still afflicting him.[20] As this letter also shows, he was finding it ever more difficult to reconcile the conflicting demands made on him by his linguistic studies and his political involvement. He was rapidly attracting attention for his political comments in *Avanti!,* his regular column *Sotto la Mole* ('Under the Spire' – the 'Mole Antonielliana' that towers over Turin) and for his regular theatre criticism, a small selection of which is available in English in Gramsci (1985). As he was to write shortly after his arrest, he was the first to have 'discovered and contributed to the popularity of Pirandello's theatre'; his writings on Pirandello, from 1915 to 1920, 'were original and without precedent', 'enough to put together a book of 200 pages'.[21]

Gaps in the letters notwithstanding, Gramsci's correspondence during this period gives some insight into his political-cum-journalistic activity, finishing with a mention of the newly founded review, *L'Ordine Nuovo,* with which his name is intimately linked. The first series of this came out, normally on a weekly basis, from May 1919 to the end of 1920. According to Vladimir Degot', a Russian revolutionary then passing through Italy, the orientation that Gramsci gave the paper was 'very important', despite the fact that both Serrati, and 'a Russian comrade known under the pseudonym Niccolini', were 'extremely dissatisfied' with Gramsci. Degot' goes on to say that despite the criticism of *L'Ordine Nuovo* – sometimes in public – by both Serrati and Niccolini (real name Ljubarskij), 'they did not succeed in suffocating the journal'. In fact, as he added, 'in a very short time this small publication went on to become the central organ of the Italian Communist Party'. Elsewhere in his book he notes that 'Gramsci understands the situation in much more profound way than the other comrades. He has understood the Russian Revolution much more clearly'.[22] And certainly Gramsci's assessment – of Russia and also of developments in Italy – was indeed different from that of Serrati, who would later become one of his main targets in his criticisms of the Italian left of the early 1920s.

Apart from a letter of a few lines at the beginning of January 1921, the period from late winter 1920 through to the beginning of his stay in Moscow (June 1922) is again not documented through any letters that have come to light; the documentary evidence we have for this period is from his articles, mainly in *L'Ordine Nuovo,* from occasional comments about him by others, and from press reports. Covering this gap, we include as an appendix to Chapter Three, the very rarely reproduced report of Gramsci's speech at the conference of the Communist fraction of the Socialist Party in Imola on 28-29 November 1920.[23] The speech shows his frame of mind, his assessment of the situation, and his hostile attitude towards Serrati and the centrists within the PSI. Two months after the Imola meeting, on 21 January 1921 Gramsci was one of the intransigent delegates who walked out of the PSI's Livorno Congress and, in a nearby theatre, founded the Communist Party of Italy (the PCd'I or, more simply, the PCI).

MOSCOW: PCI REPRESENTATIVE AND COMINTERN LEADER (CHAPTER FOUR)

On 16 May 1922 Gramsci together with Amadeo Bordiga (the same Bordiga criticised in Lenin's *Left Wing Communism: an Infantile Disorder* but at that time the acknowledged leader of the PCI), and Antonio Graziadei (an economist on the right wing of the young party), left Italy to attend the Second Enlarged Executive (often called 'Plenum') of the Third International in Moscow, arriving there at the start of June. Gramsci then stayed on in Moscow as one of the PCI representatives at the Comintern until the end of November 1923. From the first two months in Moscow, three important letters are known, all included here. One was written to the Italian Party jointly with Grigorij Zinov'ev, President of the Comintern Executive, another was written to Zinov'ev on the question of fusion between the PCI and the left socialists, and a third was addressed to Karl Radek on the subject of a manifesto to the Italian socialists.

On his arrival in Moscow, at the meeting of the Enlarged Executive (13 June 1922), Gramsci was elected to the Comintern Presidium. The International nominated him to defend Lidija Konopleva, a young member of a group of Social Revolutionaries who had been involved in terrorist activities against the State; she along with one or two others had however dissociated herself from the group, or had perhaps been an undercover Bolshevik agent in the group.[24] But by the time the trial opened, Gramsci had suffered a collapse in health and been admitted to a sanatorium at Serebrjanyj Bor (Silver Wood), then outside Moscow but now a city suburb. The German communist Hugo Eberlein was given the responsibility of 'providing comrade Gramsci with a doctor, necessary treatment and proper nutrition'.[25] It was here that he met and quickly got to know Evgenija Schucht, a Bolshevik who spoke fluent Italian; and in late summer 1922, Evgenija introduced him to her younger sister, Jul'ka.[26]

News of Gramsci's health problems had earlier begun to trickle out, and after Bordiga's return to Italy he wrote to enquire whether or not it was true that Gramsci was ill.[27] Initially, a high temperature gave rise to suspicions that Gramsci had malaria, but it soon became obvious that he was suffering from what Ersilio Ambrogi (who was then the other main PCI representative in Moscow) described as a nervous breakdown.[28] However, there were temporary periods of respite. He was able to attend the Comintern Presidium meeting on 6 August and, as two researchers, Alessandro Carlucci and Caterina Balistreri, have very recently discovered, the following day he made a speech, as one of six fraternal Comintern delegates, all with a consultative vote, at the Twelfth Conference of the Russian Communist Party. An oral translation summary of this speech by the French communist Charles Rappoport, published in *Pravda*, in which Gramsci draws parallels between the Social Revolutionaries' terrorist attacks against the Bolsheviks and rising Italian fascist activity, is included as Appendix 1 to Chapter 4.[29]

Only a few days after this speech, however, on 11 August, Gramsci was said by Ambrogi not to be 'here', meaning not at the Comintern in the centre of Moscow, but presumably back in the sanatorium.[30] Throughout August and September, Gramsci's health had ups and downs and this continued at least into the start of the next year.[31] He was sometimes able and sometimes not able to attend Presidium meetings, and Ambrogi deputised for him when he was ill. In October, however, he was well enough to speak at a factory meeting at Ivanovo-Voznesensk, about 250 kilometres from Moscow, with his new acquaintance Jul'ka Schucht acting as interpreter.[32] All told, from what emerges from this skeleton reconstruction, based on various documents and on the letters themselves, there were periods in his first few months in Moscow when Gramsci was able to make important political contributions, directly or through consultations held with him in the sanatorium. His own description of his state of health in this period perhaps contains some slight self-justificatory exaggeration, but there is no doubting the seriousness of his breakdown and its aftermath.[33]

In the months in the sanatorium, he co-signed letters that were almost certainly drafted mainly by Ambrogi; and apart from one whose text Ambrogi merely says was 'approved' by Gramsci whom he had consulted in the sanatorium, these letters are included here.[34] Then, in a letter dated 8 September, he was able to respond to a note from Trotsky, like Gramsci a person with a strong literary bent, on his views on the Italian artistic movement known as futurism (see p121).[35] Gramsci's response does not have the usual linguistic refinements of a piece intended for publication and is rather jerky in style, due either to the translation into Russian or perhaps to his state of health.[36]

In Moscow, Gramsci found himself in a milieu that it is now hard to imagine. Reading through the documents of these early years of the Comintern, including Gramsci's letters from Moscow, Vienna and Rome, one is struck by their freshness, and the strong sense of urgency that was felt by the leading participants, who believed that the time was ripe for a radical upheaval that would dispossess the ruling and exploiting classes. This atmosphere goes a long way towards explaining the PCI's political hostility to groups and sectors that might, in other circumstances, have been considered as part of the left.

One cause of such hostility was the signature in August 1921, of a non-aggression pact with fascism by a group of reformist PSI leaders and CGL trade union confederation leaders (the PSI was divided at that time into two main groups, known as the 'maximalists' and 'reformists'). In fact, as it turned out, the pact was repudiated by the fascists later that autumn. Gramsci was even more critical of the Unitary Socialist Party (PSU), which was formed a year later, in October 1922, when a group of reformist socialists broke away from the PSI. The PSU was led by people who occasionally appear in these letters including the veteran leader Filippo Turati; Ludovico D'Aragona, who was head of the CGL from 1918 onwards; Giuseppe Emanuele Modigliani, brother of the painter; and Giacomo Matteotti, who became PSU secretary. Mistrust was further heightened when, after the fascists became the governing party at the end of October 1922, albeit still within an ostensibly parliamentary regime, a seat in Mussolini's first cabinet was offered to Gino Baldesi, who was a national leader of the PSU, and of the CGL engineering workers. (The offer however came to nothing.[37]) The fear of the young PCd'I was that the PSU, together with the right wing, and perhaps even the centre, of the Socialist Party, would put a stop to any substantial leftward shift. The result of such an alliance would have been an Italian-style version of what was later to emerge in Britain as Ramsay MacDonald's 'Lib-Lab' government, and any such alliance would have been regarded as an abject compromise with sectors of the bourgeoisie.[38]

All this helps to explain the different evaluations within the PCI, as to whether the reformists were merely the right wing of the workers' movement or were the left of the bourgeoisie, and therefore at the very least allied to the class enemy. The general view in Comintern circles was that the majority in the Italian PCI leadership at this time was adopting a sectarian approach towards the Socialists; the Comintern leadership, and Zinov'ev in particular, believed that the Socialist Party's left (the pro-Comintern 'terzinternazionalisti' or 'Third Internationalists'), and perhaps also its centre, led by Serrati, had to be brought over to membership of the International as soon as was feasible. The 'terzinternazionalisti', usually called the 'terzini', led by Fabrizio Maffi, Ezio Riboldi and others who figure in the letters, were in favour of membership of the Third International, but wanted in the mean time to stay within the PSI in order to shift its revolutionary socialists into Comintern membership. The wavering centre group in the PSI under Serrati had initially declared unconditionally for the International, and Serrati had indeed briefly edited an early Comintern journal. But Serrati continued to believe that, whatever the positions of its individual members, the Socialist Party in its entirety remained a revolutionary Party – a view that was at odds with those of both the PCI and the terzini.[39]

Relations between the PCI and the left and centre currents of the Socialist Party formed part of a private discussion between Gramsci and Lenin on 24 October 1922, but its contents remained unknown until the partial publication in 2008 of a letter written by Camilla Ravera (who was on the spot at the time as a PCI representative) to Gramsci's younger son, Giuliano.[40] The two men discussed the overall situation in Italy, including the assessment to be made of fascism, and were in agreement that Bordiga's position – bourgeois State against proletarian State, with little or no account taken of the specific nature of fascism – was a schematic contraposition and was far too rigid. Gramsci paid tribute to Bordiga's work in constructing and holding together the young Party, but distanced himself from the latter's intransigent position towards the maximalist socialists, fusion with whom represented a particular reference point for Lenin. According to Ravera, Gramsci 'assured Lenin' that he 'approved the policy of the International towards Serrati', i.e. winning him over. Assuming Ravera's memory of what Gramsci told her is accurate, this represents a shift in his position as compared with his letter to Radek, referred to above, of July 1922 (see p111). During the conversation, or as a result of it, Lenin possibly suggested that Gramsci should move back closer to Italy to facilitate his leadership role in the Italian Party.[41] But immediately after this talk events in Italy led to the king's nomination of the first fascist government and any immediate return to Italy was ruled out by a warrant for Gramsci's arrest there that was issued in early January 1923.

THE FOURTH CONGRESS OF THE INTERNATIONAL AND DIFFERENT CURRENTS IN THE PCI (CHAPTER FOUR)

Just a fortnight after Gramsci's talk with Lenin, on the fifth anniversary of the Russian revolution the Fourth Congress of the Communist International opened in Moscow. Gramsci did not speak in the plenary sessions; the designated chief speakers for the Italian delegation were Scoccimarro and Bordiga who, as Party leaders coming over directly from Italy, had their fingers on the pulse of the situation. Archive material in Rome and Moscow shows however that Gramsci took an active part in the meetings of the Italian delegation and also in the negotiations with leading Russian members of the Comintern, in particular on the question of who could be won over from among over the maximalist Socialists and how to do it.

The latent divisions in the PCd'I began to come out into the open at the Congress. From its beginning the Party had been fundamentally composed of three groupings: the left, sometimes called the 'abstentionists', under Bordiga, a man of enormous talent and energy; the *Ordine Nuovo* group of Turin, named after the famous journal, whose main leader became Gramsci himself, and which, even until some time after the Fourth Congress of the International, was still allied to Bordiga's left group; and a right minority led by Tasca, also of the Turin group. (It should be noted here that, when Gramsci is writing of Party affairs and uses the term 'minority', unless the context makes it clear otherwise, he is almost always referring to the group headed by Tasca.) And it was the right minority at this time which, more than the other groupings, had the ear of the Comintern leadership, mainly in the figure of Zinov'ev, whose strategy was to win over the entire maximalist Socialist Party, minus the right wing of Arturo Vella and Pietro Nenni.[42]

The PCI currents each had their own separate view on the fusion issue, especially on the thorny question of attitudes towards the centre grouping of the PSI. According to the unpublished minutes of the Italian delegation at the Fourth Congress, it was on this occasion, and on the issue of fusion, that for the first time within the PCI majority – still composed of Bordiga's abstentionists and the bulk of the *Ordine Nuovo* grouping – differences of opinion and emphasis began to appear openly, and Gramsci's divergences from Bordiga began to emerge. Gramsci's growing view, reinforced by the exchange of opinion with Lenin, was that the Party had to re-orient its policies, to adapt, as he was doing, to the line of the International. Indeed, in a letter of 24 November (Appendix 2 to Chapter 4), signed by five of the Russian Party's 'big guns' – its five Comintern Executive members Bukharin, Lenin, Radek, Trotsky and Zinov'ev, here writing as members of the Russian Central Committee – the Italian Party leaders were advised in no uncertain manner that the PCI should modify its position. Gramsci was detailed by the PCI to inform Zinov'ev, in a letter written the next day, of the points that the Party regarded as essential if fusion with the terzini was to take place.[43]

It was the centrist 'maximalist' grouping, rather than the terzini, that continued to cause the PCI headaches in relation to the fusion. Serrati, as leader of this current, had been the target of some of Gramsci's harshest polemics after the formation of the PCI: apart from the above-mentioned letter to Radek of July 1922 Gramsci had also claimed a month later in a letter to Zinov'ev (see p119) that 'Serrati is continuing to play a most perfidious double game'. Radek for his part had been equally harsh from the other side, arguing that the Italian Party's willingness to apply the united front in the trade-union field, while failing to 'estimate it at its true value in the political field', demonstrated 'the political dangers which follow from theoretical mistakes'. 'The old bitter struggle against Serrati', he went on, had been 'the source of the theoretical and practical mistakes'.[44]

One of the decisions taken at the Fourth Congress was that, as the main Italian Party representative in Moscow, Gramsci should be one of the PCI members of the commission on fusion. In the months that followed, this commission met partly in Moscow and partly in Italy, with some of the Moscow minutes bearing Gramsci's double signature as a representative of the PCI, as well as candidate member of the Presidium.[45] While there were differences between the PCI and the terzini, procedures for unification between the two went ahead, despite misgivings within the 'centre group' (still in formation) of what was still the formally undivided majority in the PCI leadership, and opposition from Bordiga's left group within the majority. But, as Gramsci explained, 'fusionism and anti-fusionism have constituted the "polemical terminology" of the discussion' between centre and left, 'not its essence'.[46] This latter consisted, rather, in whether or not the guidelines that the PCI was giving the masses were convincing for the crucially important national and international political questions. In his time in Moscow, as noted, Gramsci's position underwent a modification: in walking a tightrope between the PCI majority position and loyalty to the International and its line and, within the Italian Party, between increasing opposition to Bordiga and continuing firm opposition to the right, he began to realise the need to avoid a head-on conflict with the centralised world Party.

During the whole first period of the PCI's life, the right minority in the PCI had found support from revolutionaries of Russian origin or from connections who simply happened to be living Italy during the first world war and had frequently returned there, such as Carlo Niccolini, alias Ljubarskij (see above), and Chaim Haller, or Heller, alias Antonio Chiarini (see below), or other Comintern representatives who were sent there subsequently, including the Hungarian Mátyás Rákosi. Different advice to the Comintern, however, came at times from, among others, the Bulgarians Vasil Kolarov and Christo Kabakčiev, the Swiss communist Jules Humbert-Droz, and Dmitro (often seen as Dmitri) Manuil'skij whose advice at this time, whether he was in Moscow or Italy, was of great value.

Of these representatives, Rákosi in particular was the subject of strong opposition from the PCI majority, expressed as early as August 1922 by Ambrogi, who was at that time on the Comintern Executive and working in tandem with Gramsci in Moscow.[47] This opposition to Rákosi developed into outright hostility at meetings of the Italian Party Central Committee, where Rákosi was present as the Comintern representative, as was customary practice. Part way through 1923, the Italian leaders then in Moscow protested vigorously about Rákosi's behaviour and reports to Moscow; and their jointly-signed letter of 24 May 1923 is published here for the first time (see p163).[48]

PARTY ORGANISATION ABROAD AND DISCIPLINARY QUESTIONS (CHAPTER FOUR)

The Moscow letters are not merely political in the narrow sense; they also provide an insight into the all-round work of a representative of a foreign Party in Russia. Letters (not all included in this selection but described here for the sake of completeness) show that such work entailed, for example, making sure that people were paid, ensuring that comrades had their correct official credentials and had access to a communal mess, etc, or smoothing the way towards legal concessions for Russian agricultural cooperatives to be leased and worked by Italians.[49] Negotiations with the Comintern Budget Commission, which was headed by Pjatnickij, were frequent as for example in the last letter we currently have from Gramsci's Moscow period. This letter contains his explanation to the PCI Executive in Rome of the tight rein on which Pjatnickij kept Third International finances, which meant that funding for the new paper *L'Unità* would have to be found by reallocating already available PCI funds.[50]

A key problem for the Italian Party was how to manage the mass of Italians who had been forced into exile for political or economic reasons, whose numbers by the middle of the first world war Gramsci and Egidio Gennari put at six million, three quarters of them in the Americas.[51] Later on, in a letter to Terracini of 23 December 1923, not included here, Gramsci says that one political task of the anti-fascist emigration was to 'sabotage the finances of the fascist State by sending, out of their savings, what is strictly necessary for the upkeep of their families and not investing the surplus either in government bonds or in savings banks'.[52] A far from negligible number of the economic emigrants and political émigrés were in Russia and Gramsci writes that 'thousands of comrades' were then living outside Italy, a huge proportion of the total Party membership.[53] One issue that arose was whether the politicised Italian community in Russia, which was distributed across various cities, should be organised in a section of their own – and if so in what form – or whether it should be incorporated into the Russian Party. This is the substance of a letter of 10 April 1923 to the Central Committee of the Russian Party, and the letter later the same month to the Central Committee and also to Stalin, the person in the Russian Party in charge of organisational questions. The letters are written in a rather imprecise Russian, either by Gramsci (now making progress in learning Russian), or by his co-signatory Armando Cocchi, who was secretary of the Italian Communists in Russia, or possibly by the two of them jointly.[54] At the end of the second letter, they make known their dissatisfaction with the way in which the issue had been treated by Stalin, who had ignored protocol by not consulting with Gramsci, 'the sole person authorised as such' to speak in the name of the Italian Communist exiles. This letter is published here, soon after its first publication in Italian in Volume IV of the *National Edition* of Gramsci (Gramsci 2012).

Internal Party questions also included disciplinary matters, some of which arose during the time Gramsci spent in Moscow, as for example in the letter of 6 September 1923 on Ernani Civalleri, and in one on Gino De Marchi (omitted from this selection[55]). Russia during the following decade would not be as conciliatory towards suspects – real or invented – as the PCI was in this period, and some of the people who come into the letters were later shot, to be rehabilitated only in the post-Stalin era.[56] One example of Gramsci taking a 'hard line' on disciplinary matters was a 1925 case concerning the activity of the Party Left's Liaison Committee. Ugo Girone, a journalist on *L'Unità*, was initially expelled from the Party for having gone beyond the bounds of acceptable political behaviour (telegram of Gramsci, transmitted to Zinov'ev on 25 June 1925). Zinov'ev however urged caution on possible expulsions, and Girone was rapidly reinstated in the Party by the Comintern (Spriano 1967, p479).[57] There was a further negative judgement by Gramsci in the case of the early Comintern functionary in Italy, Chiarini (Heller), who was considered untrustworthy and thought possibly to be an undercover agent.[58] The presence of agents is not in doubt – probably at very high levels – but in Chiarini's case the suspicions (outlined for example in Gramsci's letter to Terracini of 23 December 1923) proved groundless. As representative of the Comintern, Chiarini was instead acting on behalf of the right wing of the PCI and the terzini, despite (as mentioned in Gramsci's letter to Togliatti and Scoccimarro of 1 March 1924, p236), often being found in Bordiga's entourage.

THE FORMATION OF THE NEW LEADERSHIP GROUP OF THE PCI (CHAPTER FIVE)

After eighteen months in Moscow, Gramsci arrived in Vienna on 4 December 1923, to open a long-planned office that was intended to act as the PCI's Foreign Bureau; from here, even without precise duties being initially assigned to him, he could be closer to events in Italy and thus be more able to help direct Party activity. One of his main undertakings was the start of a new series of *L'Ordine Nuovo* as a review. Additionally, at a meeting of the Presidium of the International in late summer 1923, it had been decided that a daily newspaper should be published by the Italian Party. The matter was first broached in a letter from Gramsci written in Moscow (12 September 1923, see p169), and the new newspaper eventually came out on 12 February 1924. In a reference to the need to unite the developed North and less industrialised South, the paper bore the title *L'Unità*.

In the Vienna period one begins to see explicitly Gramsci's reconsideration of his political position and the outcome of his realisation, based on his Moscow experience, that there was an international majority that had to be respected. The right in the Italian Party had to be opposed, but in Gramsci's view, their leaders could be won over. As he wrote of this group, it would 'not be difficult for us to demonstrate that the minority's orthodoxy vis-à-vis the tactics of the Comintern is just a smokescreen to have leadership of the Party in its hands' (letter to Terracini, 13 January 1924, p200). On the left flank, Gramsci's differences with Bordiga, which had been growing in the wake of the Fourth Congress, now began to come to a head. He had kept quiet on these differences since the Second Congress of the PCI and – of the letters we have – first explained the reasons for his silence in a letter to Togliatti of 18 May 1923 (p157). Subsequently, in the first months of 1924, the various differences – and Gramsci's wish to make them explicit – came out into the open in his exchange of letters with members of the Party leadership. This period marks the real beginning of his campaign to form a new majority, first on the PCI Central Committee and then in the Party as a whole; a campaign that came to fruition later that year, and was consolidated in the following year, beginning with the Fifth Enlarged Executive of the International in spring 1925.

One indication of the differences with the Party Left was Gramsci's suppression (with some difficulty) at the Party's Second Congress of two theses that stated the impossibility 'for a fascist or military dictatorship to come to power' (see p157). Here he was – at least in the direction in which he was travelling –in line with the International's criticism that the Italian Party had 'not yet overcome its "Left Communist" errors' which were rejected by the Third Congress of the Comintern.[59] It is instructive on this point to quote in full the motion of the Comintern Executive, adopted when Gramsci was present, regarding the February 1922 Congress of the PCI:

> The Executive Committee of the Communist International takes cognizance of the explanation of the majority of the Italian Communist Party according to which the 'tactical thesis discussed in the Rome Congress of the Italian Communist Party was not a decision on the party action, but merely to take in course of preparation for the Party Congress to portray its view'. This view must be brought into harmony with the decisions of the Communist International. The Italian Communist Party is informed that the Executive Committee of the Communist International finds this thesis incorrect. The Executive desires

> that the Italian Communist Party in its next congress make decisions that will be in accord with the tactical line of the Communist International.[60]

That the theses on tactics were purely consultative in nature is taken up by Gramsci in his letters to Scoccimarro (5 January 1924, p196), and to Umberto Terracini, the person who, it seems, had explained to the Comintern the nature of the PCI's Congress motion.[61] After the Congress the theses on tactics were eventually set aside, given that it was accepted by everyone that in the case of a difference of opinion, the International, as the higher body, had the final word. Indeed Trotsky, in relaying the views of Italian comrades, said that, 'with the sole exception of Gramsci', the Communist Party 'wouldn't even allow the possibility of the Fascists' seizing power'.[62]

As part of his battle, Bordiga circulated a 'Manifesto of the Party Left' that he had drafted in prison, and asked for signatures in support of it.[63] In Gramsci's judgement, however, the manifesto was in opposition to the line of the Comintern from the Third Congress onwards.[64] One of its main features was a refusal to countenance a fusion with the terzini, a policy that, however, was backed by the International with the explicit support of the Russian Party's five Comintern Executive members. Despite this, and despite finding himself in a minority on this issue within the Italian delegation at the Fourth Congress of the International – and true to his politically upright but also rigid character – Bordiga continued to insist, even after the Congress, that the terzini could come over to the PCI only as individuals and that, at the organisational level, the forming of a wider Communist Party that incorporated their fraction (then still working inside the Socialist Party) was unacceptable.

Bordiga's divergence with the International was widening, in part because, as he said, 'the International had modified and was continuing to modify its directives apparently regarding tactics, but now even as regards its programme and basic organisational norms'.[65] To a large extent the disagreements concerned the notion of the united front, which in turn involved the whole issue of the theory and practice of the Party's relations with the masses – the workers and peasants – and with their organisations. A major issue here was what was meant by 'workers' government', which for the International was sometimes a shorthand for a transitional phase, which *might* mean a government of workers' organisations in a potentially pre-revolutionary period. For Bordiga, on the other hand, a workers' government was an institution that could only be formed 'after the overthrow of the bourgeois regime'.[66] In his view, the Comintern had drifted rightward since sometimes the phrase was used as a 'pseudonym for proletarian dictatorship' while later on it sometimes seemed merely to mean 'parliamentary and governmental participation'.[67] Gramsci's answer to these and other positions of Bordiga's is partly contained in sections of his letter to Togliatti, Terracini and others of February 1924 (see p217), while some of it is in his letter to Terracini of January 1924 (see p200), as well as in the letters, mentioned above, to Terracini (see p217) and Scoccimarro (see p196).

The 'legalitarian' general strike at the beginning of August 1922 (baptised as such by the reformist leader Turati) highlighted many of the issues concerning relations with other forces that arose during the early part of the PCI's existence. The strike was called for by a broad-based Labour Alliance ('Alleanza del lavoro'), ranging from reformists through to the socialists and communists, and to libertarians and the anarcho-syndicalists of the railway workers' union. From the information Gramsci received from his vantage point in Moscow, the action appeared to confirm the effectiveness of the PCI's year-long campaign for it, and demonstrated the 'revolutionary capacity of the masses who, far above any expectation, have responded with enthusiasm and fighting spirit', and had drawn political conclusions from their experience (see letter to Zinov'ev of 28 August 1922, p118). At the same time, however, Gramsci argued, the strike also showed up the vacillations and weaknesses – or worse – of the other Parties supporting it. In this he was still near to Bordiga, for whom the strike action had unmasked the maximalists in the PSI, whom he was to define in his 1923 Manifesto as traitors who had deceived the workers 'thanks to the fact that Moscow was inviting them to join [the Comintern], thus perpetuating the old and fatal ambiguity' of whether or not they would become part of the International.[68] The difference between Bordiga and Gramsci here was that Bordiga saw no positive side in united action 'from above', a lesson that was over time absorbed by Gramsci during his stay in Moscow. It must however be added that, eighteen months after the strike, Gramsci was to revise his view drastically. In an article headed 'The Elections', in the first issue of the new series of *L'Ordine Nuovo* as a periodical (1 March

1924), his considered assessment was that 'the August 1922 "legalitarian" strike had as its sole result that of driving the industrialists and the Crown towards fascism and having the Hon. Mussolini decide on a coup d'état'.[69] (Mussolini had staged his so-called 'March on Rome' three months after the strike.)

On the surface Bordiga may therefore seem to have been nearer the truth in his attitude towards the strike, but as so often with him, it was an abstract 'correctness', which apparently involved waiting in expectation for the masses to come over to his (and the PCI's) position. Gramsci and the Turin group on the other hand had been trying to broaden the base for action, not merely to 'expose' the shortcomings of other organisations.[70] As Togliatti put it, the question was whether the Party was to base itself, as in Bordiga's view, 'on foreseeing a future moment when it will be called upon to lead the working class in the final assault for the conquest of power', or whether, as he and Gramsci maintained, it should accompany the class 'in all the intermediate positions that it goes through'.[71]

Bordiga's adamancy represented, in Gramsci's view, an attempt to negate the decisions of the Third Congress of the International and to throw into question the whole line that had been elaborated of a united front of proletarian elements, a line that was subsequently followed after that Congress and confirmed at the all-important Fourth Congress. Additionally, Bordiga was making the mistake of posing himself as representative 'of an international minority' whereas it was more important to adopt 'the standpoint of a national majority' – and not yield leadership of the Party to a 'national minority' (the right wing of Tasca, whose alignment with the International in Gramsci's view was only apparent – see letter of 9 February 1924, p217).[72] But in the section on Bordiga in a letter written less than two months later to Togliatti and others (27 March), Gramsci expressed his optimism that the new majority being formed in the leadership group could absorb the Tasca minority 'as a mass', since 'in general' there were no 'questions of principle' dividing them; and this absorption did indeed later come about.

Bordiga's temperament precluded compromise and mediation; and, it may be further added, in Gramsci's view, Bordiga's position stemmed from a conviction that the International's tactics at the time were predominantly affected by the Russian, not the international, situation. Against this, Gramsci expressed the opinion that 'the political conception of the Russian Communists was formed on an international, and not on a national, terrain'.[73] Here it is not without relevance to add that, in the Italian Commission at the Fifth Congress of the Comintern (17 June-8 July 1924), Bordiga was invited by the head of the Commission, Manuil'skij, to become Vice-President of the Comintern Executive, alongside Bukharin who would counterbalance him on the right.[74] As well as exploiting his enormous capacity for work, it was hoped that having to deal with international, and not solely national, problems would lead to a change in Bordiga's perspective, similar to the change in Gramsci's during his period in Moscow. True to type Bordiga turned down the offer. Notwithstanding this, he was elected to the Comintern Executive, although he refused to take part in important discussions, including those on Trotsky, being criticised for this in Gramsci's report to the PCI Central Committee.[75]

It was in the middle of all the events in Vienna here outlined that, apparently unexpectedly to Gramsci, the news arrived of Jul'ka's first pregnancy. Despite earlier references he had made to tiredness on her part (see pp207 and 235), he had apparently not realised – or perhaps he had been too nervous to ask – that this might have been due to a pregnancy; it was only in the letter of 6 March, probably in response to a letter from Jul'ka that had just arrived, that it is evident that Gramsci had come to know that she was expecting a child. At the personal level, his letter bubbles over with joy and excitement (a 'rush of blood' in his words), as do others of the period. As he said, they had 'been together too little', in time stolen from destiny – enjoyed 'in a mysterious hut in the forest': they had been more like lovers on honeymoon than an established husband-and-wife partnership (letter of 16 April 1924, p279). True to the nature of their relationship, the political aspect is never, however, forgotten, and in his letters he asks, for example, about progress on their joint project to translate Rjazanov's 'Introduction' to the *Communist Manifesto*, meanwhile keeping her informed of political developments such as Bordiga's retreat into a private, left, 'Aventine secession' of his own (p325) or his own election to Parliament (p325).[76]

Before moving on from the Vienna period and dealing with events after Gramsci's return to Italy, it is worth commenting on the last letter (24 April 1924) we have that was written from Vienna, regarding the situation in Yugoslavia, at that time officially the 'Kingdom of Serbs, Croats and Slovenes', and the more general question of the peasantry as the natural allies of the urban workers. The Balkans had historically been important for Italy, including for some of the statelets that had later come together to form Italy, and Gramsci himself was well-informed on the Balkans from various sources, including the Comintern Balkan conference he had attended in November 1923. In his letter, he deals among other things with the peasant question and with Stjepan Radić, the leader of the Croat peasant party. At this time, in the quest to create workers' and peasants' governments, the Comintern was making strenuous attempts to set up a sister peasant International, the 'Krestintern' ('Krest' coming from the root of the Russian word for peasant), and independent peasant organisations and parties, like that of Radić, were being wooed. Radić was however probably attracted more by the Comintern's policies on nationalities than by its radical policies on the peasantry and was to prove an unreliable ally; he left the Krestintern in 1925, less than a year after joining it. (Three years later, in 1928, Radić was to die as a result of gunshot wounds sustained in a Serbian nationalist attack in the Belgrade Parliament.) Another peasant leader mentioned in the letter is Aleksandăr Stambolijski, prime minister of Bulgaria, who had been assassinated by rightist forces in June 1923. Gramsci urges the PCI to adopt a more understanding approach to Stambolijski's Party, since it had been 'working with the Communists'; the situation seems however to have been more complicated than this would imply, since it is likely that only one faction of the Bulgarian communists had been fully in favour of the collaboration.

The influence of Bolshevik policies in Russia towards the poor peasants in particular comes out markedly in the Vienna letters and becomes a hallmark of Gramsci's policies, and then of the PCI's, as seen in his letter from Moscow of 12 September 1923 (p168), when he proposes a 'Federal Republic of the Workers and Peasants'. This watchword, taking account of the Italian South and islands, was Gramsci's adaptation to Italy of the Bolshevik programme for the countryside at the time, aimed at winning over key strata of the peasantry; it was also essentially the classic Turin-*L'Ordine Nuovo* model of workers' councils, now extended to the peasantry as class ally. And, though this did not always come out explicitly, the precise terms of an alliance with the peasantry and rural forces in general formed one of the differences between Gramsci's centre group and the Party Left. This is borne out by the summary, given to the PCI Central Committee in late May 1925 by Ruggero Grieco, since mid-1924 head of the PCI's agrarian section, of his own report to the Krestintern Conference (Comintern Archives 513-1-296/61-4), which was held simultaneously with the Fifth Enlarged Executive of the Comintern, attended by Gramsci.[77] Grieco – who until the Fifth Congress in mid-1924 had been closely allied to Bordiga – was fully in favour of an alliance with genuinely left, though non-communist, figures such as Guido Miglioli, who was leader of the left of the catholic Popular Party (Partito Popolare Italiano, or PPI) and of the catholic, or 'white', peasant unions. And he also was appreciative of the moves that had been made by the Krestintern in relation to Radić. Later on, confirmation of collaboration with Miglioli is contained in a joint telegram of Grieco and Gramsci to the Comintern Executive (25 September 1925), here reproduced from the Russian translation made at the time in Moscow.

THE RETURN TO ITALY: THE SITUATION IN THE COUNTRY AND IN THE PARTY (CHAPTER SIX)

By the time of the 6 April 1924 parliamentary election in Italy – after the decisions taken on fusion at the Fourth Congress, and the work on fusion in the first part of 1923 by commissions in both Moscow and Italy – the road to unity between the PCI and the terzini had become relatively smooth. Gramsci's position had undergone a radical shift: from a near-complete rejection of the entire maximalist Socialist Party, including the terzini, as seen in his July 1922 letter to Radek (see p111), to a stipulation of fourteen points for agreement on how to reach fusion with the terzini (letter to Zinov'ev, p126), to – despite misgivings – full acceptance of them in the unified Party.[78] The PCI and the terzini ran on a joint list (*Unità proletaria*) in the elections and – to Gramsci's relief, and in confirmation of the political position for which he had been fighting since the Fourth Congress – the preference votes gave the PCI thirteen seats to the terzini's five. (The relative numbers of deputies elected for the terzini and the PCI were in fact in proportion to the numbers of candidates fielded by each group (48 to 108).) In addition to these eighteen, an ex-maximalist and officially independent candidate, Guido Picelli, then passed over to the PCI.[79] Gramsci's assessment was that the Party had come out 'with immensely increased prestige' (letter to Terracini, p276) and these electoral successes facilitated the long-awaited fusion. This finally took place over a period of a couple of months beginning in earnest a few days before the PCI Central Committee meeting of mid-August 1924, thanks among other things to skilful diplomatic mediation by Manuil'skij in the Italian Commission at the Fifth Congress of the Comintern a few weeks earlier. In the newly united Party, according to Tommaso Detti's political biography of Serrati (who was now at long last back in the International, and was the member of the Central Committee in charge of trade union affairs), the terzini helped fill a gap in the PCd'I organisation through their cadre strength in various country areas, and in particular in the South, where the *Unità Proletaria* list actually obtained almost half as much again in 1924 as the PCd'I had received in the 1921 election.[80] And this was naturally of no small consequence for Gramsci's conception of a 'Federal Republic of the Workers and Peasants'. Gramsci himself was elected to parliament as one of the two deputies for the *Unità proletaria* list in the Venetian inter-regional constituency and now that he had parliamentary immunity against his arrest warrant he was able to return to Italy.[81] (It was suspension of immunity under the fascist dictatorship that later led to his arrest in November 1926 and subsequent trial and imprisonment.)

On his return to Italy on12 May Gramsci was ostensibly in a politically weak position, as may be seen from the results of the illegal Party conference, that was held only days later, near the Northern Italian city of Como.[82] At the conference, which was attended by the Party's national leaders and middle-level inter-regional, regional and federation secretaries, the line of the centre grouping was supported by only a small, even tiny, minority and could count on just one out of the five members of the Executive, although it did have a wafer-thin majority in the larger, 15-strong, Party Central Committee. Three counterposed motions had been published on 15 May in the Party organ *Stato Operaio*; of these (with a couple of dozen absentees, including three members of the Central Committee who supported Gramsci's new line) 41 delegates voted for Bordiga's left, ten for Tasca's right and only eight for the Gramsci-Togliatti centre group, with two abstentions, as seen in Gramsci's letter to Jul'ka of 17 July 1924.[83] The weakness of the centre group was, however, more apparent than real, as may be evinced from the same letter to Jul'ka. For example, *L'Unità,* which began to carry the new line out to the masses of readers, more than doubled its normal circulation to over 50,000, sometimes reaching 60,000 – and each copy had a multiple readership, being customarily read out to supporters who were not fully literate. Gramsci's interpretation was that the rank-and-file of the Party, and the workers outside the Party, were swinging over to the policy that he and the centre grouping were now forging.

With support from the ordinary members – bypassing as it were the middle-level leadership – and with the prestige of the International which had first encouraged, and then at its Fifth Congress sanctioned, the new line, Gramsci became General Secretary of the Party. His name was put forward by the new PCI Executive Committee (five-strong like the old one) in mid-August 1924 at the meeting at which the old Central Committee tendered its resignation and the new one took over. According to an agreement reached at the Comintern Congress the Central Committee included representatives of Bordiga's left and Tasca's right, as well as Maffi of the terzini and, after wavering for so long, Serrati; while flanking Gramsci in the new majority centre grouping were prestigious comrades such as Camilla Ravera, Scoccimarro, Terracini and Togliatti. For security reasons the Central Committee decision to nominate Gramsci as General Secretary was not committed to paper in any minute that we know of (either of the Central Committee or of the Executive Committee), and the only directly published evidence for his election was until now in Gramsci's correspondence with his wife.[84] However in the course of background work for the present volume, there resurfaced an unpublished report in French, sent by Togliatti to Moscow.[85] The report, dated 25 August 1924, summarises the proceedings of the mid-August 1924 meeting, stating that, among the decisions taken at the first sessions of the new Executive Committee, 'le camarade Masci a été nommé Secrétaire général du Parti' ('Comrade Masci [i.e. Gramsci] was nominated General Secretary of the Party').[86] The lack of any written evidence that the police could lay their hands on – as a highly confidential document, Togliatti's report would have been taken to Moscow either by courier or in the Soviet diplomatic bag – probably saved Gramsci from an even heavier prison sentence than he actually received at his trial in 1928; for, despite all the documents seized and produced, the prosecution was unable to prove that he was anything other than 'a leader' and not 'the leader' of the Party.

Events in Italy in these first few months after Gramsci's return were tumultuous. In a speech in the Chamber of Deputies on 30 May, a week after the opening of the new Parliament, the Unitary Socialist Party secretary, Giacomo Matteotti, denounced fascist ballot rigging and electoral fraud; a few days later, on 10 June, he was kidnapped and murdered by fascists, his body being found only in mid-August. In a hypocritical speech to Parliament three days after the kidnapping, Mussolini stated that Matteotti's disappearance indicated a 'crime that, if committed, could not but give rise to the disdain and emotion of the Government and of Parliament'. The next day the anti- and non-fascist opposition Parties, from the catholic Popular Party across to the Communists, withdrew from the Chamber and formed an opposition committee, formalised two weeks later as the so-called 'Aventine secession', with the intention of re-entering the Chamber only when full light was shed on the 'Matteotti affair'.[87] Public opinion was shocked and for a time the fascists were isolated. But the non-communist members of the Aventine secession, together with the reformist leaders of the CGL Union Confederation, put their trust in purely constitutional channels, renouncing any possibility of mass opposition through strike action. The PCd'I then withdrew from the opposition committee; and, in Gramsci's view, by the second half of the month the most acute phase of the crisis had passed (see letter of 22 June to Jul'ka, p308), due partly to a face-saving operation by which the most heavily compromised fascists were removed from office. In this same letter, as in another of the same day to Vincenzo Bianco, Gramsci was still thinking he could go to Moscow for the latter stages of the Fifth Congress, but said that, because of the disappearance of Matteotti, he was 'living through very serious days that will perhaps be decisive for our movement'. He was of the opinion that fascism had been abandoned by its 'class base' and would have to come to terms with the conservative non-Aventine opposition of the old school (Salandra, Giolitti, Orlando etc). In a letter to Jul'ka of 30 June (p311), he wrote that he would leave for Moscow perhaps a week later, although in a letter to Bianco of the same day he wrote that the situation was such that his presence in Italy was 'indispensable'.[88] The discrepancy is probably only apparent since other leaders were in the process of returning from the Congress;[89] and Gramsci would still have been able to make a useful personal report to the Comintern leadership if he had arrived later.

The situation was on a knife edge and despite his reference to a 'stabilisation' of the situation, in his letter to Bianco of 30 June Gramsci really did believe that the government could be toppled, and that fascism was 'in its death agonies', an opinion repeated in different words in his letter to Jul'ka of 4 August (p317). In between these two letters, there is one to Jul'ka of 21 July (p314) that contains a particularly graphic description of events on a typically hot Roman evening, when the streets of the area where he was living were flooded with workers sporting red carnations in their buttonholes, in a spontaneous demonstration of their opposition to the regime. According to this letter, some sections of the troops, if not actually fraternising with the people, at least showed some signs of hostility to the fascists, or their extreme fringes (cf letter to Jul'ka of 22 June). But, as Gramsci wrote a few weeks later, the Aventine secession's hopes with regard to the armed forces were pinned not on attempting to win over the lower ranks, but on 'detach[ing] the king, in other words the army and the carabinieri, from fascism' (letter to Bianco of September 1924, p325); even more piously, they hoped to introduce some 'moralisation' into the regime.[90] The more resolute of the opposition forces were however 'organising a military movement and are arming ... our comrades' (p325).

Notwithstanding all this, by September the PCI was – to many intents and purposes – illegal (cf same letter to Bianco). As against this, there were also positive signs for the Party: membership had risen from 12,000 to 20,000 in a few months, reaching 25,000 by the early autumn and then 30,000, not counting political and economic emigrants.[91] Despite harassment and the worsening conditions of semi-legality, Gramsci told Bianco in his November letter that there had never before been a Party Executive that could make comrades work like the one operative from the Fifth Congress.[92] This assessment indicates a great improvement in the internal Party situation as described during the summer to Jul'ka, when Gramsci was taking on the general secretaryship, and the Party was weak and overall 'working very badly' (p250).

The situation during the autumn was, as seen here, contradictory. On Gramsci's return in early November from a visit to his native Sardinia, he was still speaking of a headlong rush of events, whose outcome was unpredictable. Despite two years of fascist rule, even in the isolated areas of Sardinia the common people were avid for news of what was happening in Russia and how society was being organised there.[93] In a letter to Bianco written towards the end of November, he draws attention to the contrast between, on the one hand, growing support for the Party (expanded on the next day in a letter to Jul'ka), and increasing respect from its adversaries, and, on the other, a malfunctioning of the middle levels of the Party, whose cadres wanted to work but were unprepared for taking the initiative, and were too often waiting for orders from above.

The letters from the latter part of 1924 are not explicit about any turn of events for the worse, and Gramsci's assessments, as we now know, were over-optimistic. In contrast with the relatively rosy picture he gives of the PCI, other evidence shows a far weaker situation in relation to the Aventine opposition parties and other forces in society. A resolute stance that included a policy of political alliance between the socialists and the Popular Party would have been of great importance but, even at the trade union level, an attempt at action through a joint committee – formed in August 1924 between the 'white' trade union confederation (the CIL) and the predominantly reformist CGL – foundered. The Aventine parties continued in their 'indecision and passivity' – to quote the description of Don Luigi Sturzo, founder and main leader of the centre left of the Popular Party – while the Populars themselves did not go beyond a 'cautious opposition'.[94] In addition, the influential Jesuit review *Civiltà Cattolica* and the catholic hierarchy, through the Vatican's Cardinal-Secretary of State, Pietro Gasparri, intervened with a particularly heavy hand to prevent any unity of action between catholics and the moderate left, which was judged not to have shed its anti-clericalism. Don Sturzo, who had been forced out of the secretaryship of his Party in Summer 1923 – though at first he still remained an influential figure – was in October of the next year 'invited to leave Italy by a highly placed Vatican personality' and sent packing into exile, first in England then in the United States.[95] And three months later, in January 1925, Guido Miglioli (see above) was expelled from the PPI. Despite these negative signs, Gramsci judged events in autumn 1924 to be still finely balanced and he told Jul'ka that, to defend its interests, the bourgeoisie was having to 'cling on desperately to fascism' (letter of 26 November, see p333).

The situation took a serious change for the worse at the start of the new year when parliament reopened after the Christmas recess. In his 3 January 1925 speech to the Chamber, Mussolini arrogantly accepted responsibility for all the crimes and aggressions committed by fascism, including the murder of Matteotti, while the secretary of the Fascist Party, Farinacci, pressed for repressive measures against all opposition forces. Liberty was reduced to a minimum and the dictatorship can be dated from what was, to all events and purposes, this coup d'état, the point when the 'liberal State finally ceased to exist'.[96] There followed measures that gave free rein to the subsequent frequent seizures of, and fines on, newspapers and a law – ostensibly aimed at outlawing secret associations – that was a prelude to suppressing non-fascist organisations outside the catholic sphere, meaning most of all the PCI. This law was the subject of Gramsci's only speech in parliament on 16 May 1925.[97]

Nevertheless, Gramsci's optimism continued into the start of 1925. In his view, the situation created by Mussolini's speech could 'not last for long', and support for this position came when the arrest of a handful of communist journalists turned out to be only temporary.[98] However, there were also negative aspects, as emerges from Gramsci's report to the Central Committee in February 1925, in which he admitted that the Party's aim of creating workers' and peasants' committees had not taken root, though he did not think that it should be abandoned.[99] The hope was that – as the had happened before with the factory council movement during the great strikes in Turin in 1919-20 – the workers and peasants would reject the barriers erected against the Communists by the CGL's reformist leadership, and the situation would become more favourable to the formation of such committees as the embryonic form of a new State.[100] Gramsci had to admit, however, that the government was making life difficult. Over the summer, the communist press became the particular object of repression and, wherever they went, Gramsci and other Party leaders were subject to continual police harassment, including – as ever – house searches and arrests.[101] In this period of spring and summer, he saw society polarising between the left, represented by the Communist Party, and the fascists.[102]

It was during these events, that there exploded the question of the Liaison Committee formed by the Party Left. The committee numbered prestigious comrades among its founders, including the parliamentary deputies Onorato Damen, Bruno Fortichiari, and Luigi Repossi, and for a short time another deputy, Fausto Gullo.[103] A letter of the Liaison Committee was published on 7 June 1925 in

L'Unità, with a polemical reply from Gramsci, who argued that the fractionalism represented by the formation of the committee was typical of social-democratic rather than communist practice. Gramsci's interpretation of the international 'Bolshevisation' of the Communist Parties was that, given especially the situation of the Party's near-illegality, the political line fixed at congresses had to be elaborated at leadership level collectively by all, irrespective of initial positions, and subsequently carried out. In this he had the support of Grieco, who in a document written in French at or immediately after the Krestintern Conference and Fifth Plenum of the Comintern, 'having taken cognisance of the text of the resolution of the Italian Commission', accepted the 'need for all currents in the Party to work in the central executive organs'.[104] While Grieco was not yet fully aligned with the centre grouping, this stance did give Gramsci further important top-level, albeit partial, support within the Party. But this concept of Party leadership went against the temperament of Bordiga, who, especially when he felt he would be in a minority, tended to turn down the offers of membership of leading Party bodies delegated with executing, rather than formulating, policy.

The Liaison Committee question was pursued by Gramsci in a telegram that is reproduced here, received by Zinov'ev on 25 June. Gramsci's position was not so much that free discussion that should not be allowed in what was then a pre-Congress period – given that there was no ban on this – but rather that it should be carried out within the limits of the general approach defined by the Congresses and Enlarged Executives of the International, as interpreted by the normal Comintern Executive, the 'Ispolkom'. Zinov'ev replied on the same date advising that discussion should take place not in the daily press but in the Party's more specialist reviews.[105] In the light of the Party's delicately balanced legal status, and the first moves to outlaw it, fractionalism – such as the PCI Central Committee judged the Liaison Committee's activity to be – was not to be allowed.[106] Taking account of its conditions of semi-legality, the Party had also to think of how to organise in the trade union field; the possibilities included the setting up of a national factories committee, somewhat along the lines of the British experience of the National Minority Movement, or the adoption of some variant of the United States Industrial Workers of the World, as suggested by Piero Sraffa the previous year.[107] Repression intensified in autumn 1925, and important bourgeois newspapers such as *La Stampa* and the *Corriere della Sera,* the mainstays of the Aventine opposition, had their editors forcibly changed, while *La Stampa* was also banned for a time. Finally, in November, after an absence of fourteen months, the Aventine secessionists decided to re-enter the Chamber; but the reformist Unitary Socialist Party was then banned after the arrest of one of its members for having plotted the assassination of Mussolini.

An important part of Gramsci's work in these months was given over to preparing the Party's long-delayed Third Congress, held illegally in the French city of Lyon on 23-26 January 1926, four years after the previous one. He himself drafted some of the congress theses, and advised on sections of other important ones, as well as taking part in the local congresses that discussed them and elected the delegates. The work of the centre group in the Party leadership now bore its fruit and, with the incorporation of Tasca's right, the new majority had the support of 90 per cent of the delegates. Bordiga, having the support of the remaining delegates, did however accept election to the new Central Committee.[108]

THE LAST MONTHS OF FREEDOM (CHAPTER SEVEN)

After the letter to Jul'ka of 3 September 1925, there is a gap of around ten months, partly explained by the fact that Jul'ka herself came to Italy for several months, with the couple's son Delio and her sister Evgenija. The decision has therefore been taken to divide the Rome letters into two chapters, with the last chapter beginning in mid-1926 during Gramsci's last few months of freedom.

The final chapter opens with an important letter to the Sardinian parliamentary deputy, Emilio Lussu (12 July 1926). Here Gramsci again shows his desire to form alliances with other forces, in this case the popular masses of Sardinia represented by the left wing of the regionalist Sardinian Action Party, and he pointedly asks Lussu which groups were seen by these – especially rural – masses as the allies who could further their social demands.

The letters in the whole of this volume demonstrate Gramsci's independence of mind in his judgement of all the post-Lenin Bolshevik leaders, bar none. This comes out explicitly in a number of places, including his critical comments on how he understood Stalin to be handling the beginning of the rift with Trotsky and his request for information about the matter.[109] In a letter to the Russian Central

Committee three months earlier, Trotsky had criticised bureaucratic methods of work in the Party, criticisms backed up in part by forty-six leading Bolsheviks and endorsed, rather guardedly and partially, at the top level in the Party.[110] Trotsky then wrote his famous article *The New Course*, published first in *Pravda* and then as a pamphlet; this prompted Gramsci to ask Terracini, then the main PCI representative in Moscow, to send him a copy.[111] In the mean time the internal evidence in Gramsci's letter to leading Italian Party members of 9 February 1924 shows that he had received news of events in the Russian Party, possibly from Jul'ka; and in the section of the letter headed 'The internal situation of the International' he sketches out his understanding of the positions of the top Russian leaders immediately after the death of Lenin.

But it was in autumn 1926 that Gramsci's independence of judgement was seen most forcefully, when the splits in the Soviet Party between the majority of the Central Committee and what Gramsci calls the 'bloc of the opposition groupings' (the 'joint opposition' as it is usually known in English) emerged into the light of day.[112] At the international level this resulted, at the Comintern Executive meeting of 25 October 1926, in Zinov'ev's replacement as Comintern President by Bukharin, the decision being that the leader of an opposition group within the Russian Party could not legitimately head the International. The consternation at what was happening in the Russian Party is expressed in very clear terms in Gramsci's celebrated letter of 14 October 1926, written – seemingly with the previous collaboration of Grieco – on behalf of the Political Bureau of the Italian Party to the Central Committee of the Soviet (All-Union) Party.[113] The letter was handwritten by Gramsci in the Soviet embassy in Rome and, as was usual for top-level important and sensitive questions, sent to Moscow in the diplomatic bag. The letter was immediately translated into French, for ease of understanding at the Comintern, and then shown to Humbert-Droz, Kuusinen, Manuil'skij and Bukharin, who between them were representative of both leaders of the International and the main advisers on Italy. It is surmised that Bukharin showed it to Stalin, who since his nomination as Party general secretary had also had at least a watching brief on Comintern afffairs. Togliatti took the decision not to transmit the letter officially to the Russian Central Committee, explaining this decision in his reply to Gramsci of 18 October (reproduced in the appendix to chapter seven, p383). On the basis of his knowledge of events in Moscow, Togliatti also sent a telegram in French to Scoccimarro in Rome (16 October), in which he said that the opposition was isolated, 'in full retreat', 'in negotiations with the Polburo regarding its capitulation', and that 'proletarian dictatorship and Party unity' were not in danger.[114] Negotiations over the next few days between the PCd'I leaders in Rome and Togliatti, Manuil'skij, and possibly others in Moscow, resulted not in withdrawal of the letter by the Italian Political Bureau but in the authorisation it gave Togliatti not to transmit the letter to the All-Union Party Central Committee.[115]

Gramsci together with the majority of the Italian Party (especially when what emerged as the centre had still been in alliance with the left) had often been in conflict with the Comintern Executive, under Zinov'ev's leadership. Differences had, however, always been a matter for debate within and between Parties, with opposing points of view respected. So it is that, while Gramsci's letter largely contains a criticism of the position and tactics of the opposition groups rather than the political position of the majority of the Russian Party, at the end of his letter, although accepting that the opposition leaders (Zinov'ev, Trotsky, Kamenev) were the people most responsible for the current situation, he also acknowledges their earlier role in educating the Italian Party 'for the revolution': 'sometimes they have corrected us very forcefully and severely, they have been among our teachers'. Gramsci and the PCI Political Bureau feared the possibility that some in the majority group of the Russian Party leadership wanted to gain a victory that would lead to the exclusion from any meaningful role of comrades holding opposition and minority opinions. (Later on, in prison, Gramsci expressed his criticism of the lack of collective leadership in the International after the Seventh Plenum, held only weeks after his arrest.)

The position outlined in this letter, written literally less than a month before Gramsci's arrest, is fully consonant with the positions he had adopted in the Italian Party. His interpretation of Bolshevisation did not mean not that the leadership should be composed solely of a majority tendency, but rather that it should be composed of representatives of all views within the Party, in order that a collective line should emerge through – when these occurred – direct clashes of opinion. And such indeed was the practice normally followed in the early years of the Comintern, as anyone who reads the documents and publications of the period can verify for themselves. Of course the question of how much such practice was then observed in the subsequent history of the International and of the various Communist Parties – and how much it was followed in the breach rather than the observance – is a matter of further analysis and opinion.

THE SCHUCHT FAMILY

A special mention is needed in this introduction of the Schucht family and Gramsci's relations with two of the three sisters who appear in these letters. The sisters' father, Apollon, a friend of Lenin and long linked to the Bolshevik tendency in the RSDLP, was of partly German descent, the surname probably originally being Schacht. On the other side of the family, through their grandmother, Ottilija, there was a strong artistic influence, coming in part at least from Ottilija's father Franz Xaver Winterhalter, who had painted portraits of royalty throughout Europe, including members of Tsar Aleksandr II's family.

The first of the Schucht sisters that Gramsci met was Evgenija, who often appears in the letters in the diminutive form of 'Genia' ('Ženja' in the standard transliteration system used here). Evgenija was a patient in the Serebrjanyj Bor sanatorium, a few kilometres from the centre of Moscow, where Gramsci worked and where, when not a patient in the sanatorium himself, he had a room in the famous Hotel 'Ljuks' (or 'Lux'), which was home to the main foreign Comintern representatives. Gramsci's collapse in health in June 1922 only weeks after his arrival in Moscow led to his admission to the sanatorium; Evgenija was already there because of a nervously induced semi-paralysis of the legs that had confined her to bed from the end of 1919, and she would remain there until at least spring 1923,[116] around which time she gradually got back the use of her legs. It was Evgenija who introduced Gramsci to her sister, Julija (Jul'ka), seven years her junior and six years younger than Antonio.[117] Both sisters were members of the Bolshevik Party, Jul'ka having joined in September 1917 while Ženja's membership, sponsored by Lenin, dated to January 1919.[118] Like Ženja, Jul'ka spoke fluent Italian. She had spent some time in Italy during the family's exile, and had graduated from Rome's Santa Cecilia Conservatory – one of her teachers there was mentioned in Antonio's letter to her of 16 April 1924; indeed, after going to live in Russia for the first time, she had won warm reviews from *Izvestija* for a 1918 violin recital in Moscow before 8000 people.[119] From prison, Antonio recalled to Tat'jana (Tanja) – his main link there with the outside world – that he and Jul'ka had first met in September 1922 and that Ženja later remembered him saying, after Jul'ka had gone, 'What a magnificent face your sister has; there's something of the Byzantine about it, isn't there?'.[120] On the occasion of the first meeting between Antonio and Jul'ka, he had been somewhat overawed.[121] The following month, when his health was partially back to normal, as mentioned earlier, Jul'ka was his interpreter for his speeches, as foreign delegate to the forthcoming Fourth Congress of the International, to factory workers in Ivanovo-Voznesensk, the textile city and centre of left Social Revolutionary influence where she was then working. By this time, Jul'ka seems to have been very much taken with Antonio, as seen in the care she took in writing five separate drafts of a letter to him, presumably after the factory meetings. The final version of this letter has unfortunately not come to light, but one sees from the drafts that, beneath the surface level of her ironic and witty comments, there is an obvious desire to follow up the relationship. Rather surprisingly, perhaps, she calls him 'Professor':

> Professor, today I have 'found the sun'. Since I have come back to Ivanovo, there has been bad weather, with grey skies [...] And yet I'm sure I've seen the sun. [...] I have also been to the communist youth congress (young people, in Ivanovo!). [...] You must have been working ... At the Comintern on an article ... Or at Serebrjanyj Bor on a wheel? I will be happy to see how, through the steady heroism of the knife and of comrade Gramsci, the wheels, with spokes unique of their kind since the world began and the bourgeois States fell, are now creaking along.[122]

A consensus has now emerged, through work at the Gramsci Institute, that some of Gramsci's letters, that up to now were thought to have been to Jul'ka, must instead be considered as having been written to Ženja.[123] Most obviously, and the starting point for the reasoning that follows, in one of two letters dated 13 February 1923 Gramsci speaks of the ability of the recipient 'to jump across the streams' – found for example in the grounds of the sanatorium. Since at this time Jul'ka was physically perfectly healthy, while Ženja was just beginning recover the use of her legs, this can mean only that the letter was to Ženja. Additionally, in this letter Gramsci writes that the person to whom he is writing is *not* 'a Byzantine madonna' whereas, as seen above, Jul'ka's face did 'have something of the Byzantine about it'. The conclusion can only be that this letter, with its expressions not only of affection, but love, is to Ženja. The other letter of the same date is explicitly to Jul'ka, since here Gramsci says that 'comrade Ženja [...] has learned to walk and keep her balance'. In two other letters that had the character of love letters, Gramsci refers to a 'horrid letter' ('lettera cattiva') he had received; and in one of them he also wrote of the letter that it was 'so good and at the same time ... so horrid'. It is unlikely that he had received 'horrid letters' from the two sisters simultaneously; and, since these two letters both contain mentions of the same subject (his difficult childhood), they are presumably to the same person. In what appears to be the earlier of these two letters (18 January 1923, or possibly a day or two afterwards) he speaks of being blocked in Moscow 'for some days yet', with the implication that he wanted to go and to visit the sister in question; and in the second of these letters, probably dating to later on that month, he speaks of coming to see her 'in a few days' time'. The implication is that the journey would be relatively easy – which was indeed the case when travelling from the centre of Moscow to the outlying district of Serebrjanyj Bor, but not for a journey from Moscow to Ivanovo-Voznesensk, which was 250 kilometres away: Jul'ka had to make special trips when she wanted to see her sister (and Gramsci). It ought to be added that the tone and content of the letters of this period to each sister also differ. Those to Jul'ka are more in the nature of rather impersonal 'business letters', while the other letters have a far different tone, much more personal and loving – in contrast to his letters to Ju'lka, in these letters Gramsci does not feel the need to add a phrase to round them off, except for the closing line 'and you mean a lot to me' in the letter about jumping across streams.

The conclusion to be drawn is that before Gramsci and Jul'ka began their relationship, he had been paying court to, and had been – or had convinced himself that he was – in love with Ženja. She however may have rebuffed him. This is one reading of the lines about 'obtaining the external manifestations of love' in the letter of late January 1923, and his asking in the letter of 13 February 1923 'Why do you say "It's too soon?". Why do you say my love is something foreign to you, that doesn't concern you?'. It may be that Ženja suppressed any feelings of love for him, or their outward signs, and he may shortly afterwards in some way have rejected her. Certainly, by some time later in 1923, the focus of his affections had definitely switched to Jul'ka, the younger and – for what it matters – more beautiful sister who, as we have seen, had shown considerable interest in Gramsci from the first few weeks of their acquaintanceship. It may be that Jul'ka had to be convinced of Gramsci's having switched from Ženja to her, for, as Gramsci wrote to her from Vienna (21 March 1924), 'maybe I was wrong to tell you one particular evening that it was really, indeed, you that I loved passionately'.[124]

All this adds an important aspect to Gramsci's biography, since in all three letters, here reattributed to Ženja as recipient, Gramsci expresses his love for the sister in question, not actually using the word 'love' itself, but often using a 'catch-all' expression in Italian 'le voglio bene', which can mean everything from 'you mean a lot to me' up to 'I love you' – and here translated in various ways in the letter to Ženja of 13 February 1923 to try and give an indication of the spectrum of meanings.

Even as late as August 1923, in a letter now redated from August 1922, Jul'ka and Antonio were still using the formal mode of address for each other – 'lei', and not the familiar form 'tu' – though this was normal practice for the times, and indeed is also found in Gramsci's Rome letters to Piero Sraffa.[125] The commonly accepted view is that the following month, on 23 September 1923, Antonio and Jul'ka were married, and a note to this effect was added in the 1990s in the margin of the parish registry at Ales. The surviving certificate attesting to the marriage and its date is however back-dated from 12 January 1926, and the couple's younger son Giuliano in later life expressed doubt as to whether his parents were actually married in a strictly legal sense.[126] A comment by Antonio himself on whether he had formally to recognise the child (letter to Jul'ka of 4 August 1924) might also be indicative of the absence of an 'official marriage'. But, against this, Soviet marriage laws were very elastic in the early and mid-1920s, and it was often enough for a man and woman to be living together for them to be considered married; in addition Gramsci may not have known exactly the legal niceties regarding surnames.[127] As regards Italy, it may be recalled that, while Gramsci was in detention awaiting trial, he wrote to Tanja on 4 April 1927 to say that juridically he was still considered as single, since his marriage had not yet been registered there.[128] Whatever the case, around two months after the real or supposed date of the wedding, in November, just before Gramsci's departure for Vienna, Jul'ka became pregnant with their first child, Delio, who was born in August 1924.[129]

Later on, when Jul'ka and Ženja, together with Delio, came to Italy, Ženja continued to play an active role, indeed a domineering one in the view of Nilde Perilli, a Roman friend who had known Jul'ka since her time at Santa Cecilia. Despite the fact that Tat'jana – whom Gramsci had finally met in early 1925 – had found rooms for everyone (see Antonio's letter to Jul'ka of 15 August 1925), Ženja decided that Antonio should have different lodgings from the three sisters and Delio, ostensibly for security reasons. Indeed, on one occasion, Ženja caused a great scene when she found out that Antonio had spent the night in the Schucht sisters' flat; but rather than security, a certain jealousy or similar feeling may have played its part. Ženja was very attached to Delio, as demonstrated by the fact that in their lodgings in Rome his cot was right next to her bed, while Jul'ka's bed was on the other side of the room, the justification this time being that Jul'ka needed more rest since she was working at the Russian embassy.[130] Given that the other two sisters were both working, Ženja minded the child, and often it seems – again according to Perilli – behaved with her friends in Rome as if the child was actually hers. Then, when Delio was just beginning to speak, he was in the habit of calling both Ženja and Jul'ka 'mama', as if both of them were his biological mother, something accepted by Ženja but causing suffering to Jul'ka and giving rise to consternation and disapproval on the part of Apollon Schucht in particular.[131] In all this Antonio put up little resistance. Jul'ka, for her part, could be fragile psychologically, but also, on other occasions, according to a letter of Ženja's, 'spiritually strong'; later on, when Gramsci was in prison, Jul'ka was prey to other ills, including what was probably epilepsy, which was kept hidden from her husband. Despite Ženja's authoritarian nature, she could also be supportive of Jul'ka, even sometimes while being simultaneously hostile towards Antonio, attitudes that are by no means in contrast.[132] At this point, further detail regarding the relations between Antonio, Ženja and Jul'ka is either a matter of speculation or, if contained in family papers, still awaits publication.

In all their periods apart, Gramsci wrote as regularly as possible to Jul'ka, often on a regular weekly basis, the letters sometimes being sent with the official Party correspondence that was taken to Russia by Comintern or Russian embassy couriers. And, it should be noted here in passing, another personal way he kept in contact, though examples are not included in this volume, was through picture postcards, which included such items as photographs of Brahms and other composers as well as one of the Isola Tiberina, the island in the Tiber as it passes through Rome. In conclusion, what can be seen from their joint correspondence is both their personal relationship – affection, love, and later the joys and tasks of parenthood – and their political comradeship, illustrated by their joint translation of Rjazanov's commentary and the frequent exchanges of information on political events in their respective countries.

THE LETTERS IN CONTEXT

There is a general tendency to see Gramsci as the author of concepts that emerge, full-blown, from the pages of his *Prison Notebooks* and *Prison Letters*; insufficient attention is paid both to the genesis that lends them their substance or to their non-static, ongoing and evolutionary nature. What the current selection shows, among other things, is the emergence of these concepts through dialogue, always essential for his mode of thought – a dialogue which for him took place both within and outside the confines of the family (both his family in Sardinia and, more especially, the one he formed with Jul'ka) and of the revolutionary movement of the time.[133] The reality of the events that took place before his arrest forms the basis of the prototype concepts that he began to develop as a leader of the PCI and of the International, and these in their turn, through his reflection in prison on past and contemporary events, led to the forging of the conceptual tools he developed that have by now passed into general circulation.

Many of the themes that characterise Gramsci's overall approach are here seen in their initial form. The nature of the superstructures of society – a notion taken over from Marx's mere handful of references to them and then elaborated theoretically in the *Notebooks* – is, for example, introduced by Gramsci in the letter to Togliatti and others of 9 February 1924 and occurs again in his letter to Togliatti of 26

October 1926 in the course of the polemic on his letter to the Central Committee of the All-Union (Bolshevik) Party. Other key Gramscian themes also seen here are centralism and Party organisation (cf the letters of 2 March 1924 to Terracini , and to Bianco and Jul'ka of 25 and 26 November 1926);[134] 'high' and 'popular' culture; passive revolution (without the term itself necessarily being used – as for example, the claim, in a letter to Vincenzo Bianco of September 1924, that the constitutional opposition wanted to 'overthrow fascism without popular intervention'); the Southern question; the subaltern groups (here especially, but not only, the peasantry); and social and political alliances. The latter question, for example, starts to be posed in earnest towards the end of Gramsci's stay in Moscow and is further developed in Vienna and on his return to Italy. Gramsci was, naturally, a child of his times – those of the Russian revolution – and consequently an alliance between parties does not come into his conceptual framework, except as a short-term measure or within the context of a Constituent Assembly charged with finding an adequate transitional form for a post-fascist State.[135] From what emerges from these writings, Gramsci was firmly convinced that a communist State in the foreseeable future would be characterised by a single Party that was able to represent the interests of the 'working masses, stratified politically in a contradictory way, but tending in their entirety towards unity', whatever the situation might be in a more distant future.[136] Pluralism enters his schema, instead, by way of autonomous organisations, including those of class allies, notably the peasantry, and his never-forgotten experience of the factory councils as the basic cell of the new State. And in these recognitions of autonomy, there is of course the notion, taken over and developed from Hegel, of civil society. The term is nowhere found explicitly in these letters but its presence is felt in Gramsci's sense of a mode of existence of a society, which he recognised as being more articulated in western European countries such as Italy, partly through their greater stratification, even among the proletariat – for example in the existence of a 'working-class aristocracy'; such stratification then produces attendant problems such as corporativism, reformism and bureaucracy within the organisations of the working class.[137]

Closely associated to notions of social and political alliance, social stratification, and civil society, is that of 'hegemony' which, starting from its various uses in these letters, goes on to be developed in detail throughout the *Prison Notebooks* as it is applied to specific situations.[138] It was during his stay in Vienna, immediately after his exposure to the debates and policies taking shape in the young soviet State, that the term itself first appears explicitly. But it is at first still used in a fairly standard way for the period, reference being made for example to 'bourgeois parliamentary hegemony', to the *de facto* hegemony of the Russian Party in the International, and to 'Piedmontese-Northern hegemony' in Italy – this latter mirrored by the 'military and administrative hegemony of the Serbs' within what was the Yugoslav Kingdom.[139] The worker-peasant alliance came to the fore as a result of Gramsci's experiences in Russia and became a recurrent theme, but the explicit connection between alliances and hegemonic praxis remains still a matter for development in the *Prison Notebooks*. In the current selection of letters, however, there are to be seen the first signs of hegemony as an economic and cultural phenomenon – in references to the New Economic Policy in the 14 October 1926 letter to the Central Committee of the All-Union Communist Party. And yet another aspect of hegemony, namely education, emerges as all-important, beginning with the 'Club for Moral Life' (letter to Giuseppe Lombardo-Radice of March 1918), and continuing through the experiences of the review *L'Ordine Nuovo* and other publications (mooted or actually launched), as well as in the Party schools – all questions dealt with in letters from Vienna. Gramsci here grasps what he later goes on to theorise – in his prison notes on education and the intellectuals – as the fundamentally hegemonic nature of the pedagogical relationship, read in the context of words from Marx's *Third Thesis on Feuerbach*: 'the educator must himself be educated'.

NOTES

1. For the Prison Letters see Gramsci 1994a in the Select Bibliography at the end of this volume. For biographies see Fiori 1965 (English edition 1970) and Davidson (1977).
2. New material has recently been published in Italian in the *National Edition* or, in the case of a number of letters from Vienna, by Francesco Giasi (Giasi et al, 2009).
3. A full explanation of the revised dating is contained in Gramsci (2009).
4. Cf the statement of Gramsci's sister Teresa (Teresina), now in the anthology edited by her daughter, Mimma Paulesu Quercioli (1977), pp11-21, especially pp17-19.

5. See Gramsci 1994a, Vol. 2, p139.
6. See Ives and Lacorte (eds) (2010) for a selection of essays on language and translation questions in Gramsci; and for the possible Wittgenstein connection see the seminal essay by Sraffa's Nobel prize-winning pupil Amartya Sen, 'Sraffa, Wittgenstein, and Gramsci', *Journal of Economic Literature*, XLI, December 2003, pp1240-55.
7. See Zucàro (1957), p1093.
8. Alfonso Leonetti (1978), reporting the words of Azelia Arici, later a highly-regarded translator of Latin authors.
9. See letter of Gramsci to his sister-in-law Tat'jana: Gramsci 1994a, Vol. 1, p84. The neo-grammarians' were the academic opponents of Bartoli – the 'neo-linguist'.
10. Links between Bartoli's course and Gramsci's later work are discussed in Derek Boothman, 'Gramsci's interest in language: the influence of Bartoli's *Dispense di glottologia* (1912-13) on the *Prison Notebooks*', *Journal of Romance Studies* (2012), Vol. 12 (3), pp10-23.
11. See Antonio's letter to his father of 3 January 1912.
12. Gramsci asks his sister Teresina for information through the letter to his father of 3 January 1912, and asks her directly in the postcard of 12 November 1912 and the letters of 13 January 1913 and 26 March 1913.
13. Schirru 2011, especially pp953-63.
14. Franco Lo Piparo, 'Gramsci and Wittgenstein: an intriguing connection' in *Perspectives on Language Use and Pragmatics* (2010), Alessandro Capone (ed), Lincom GmbH: Munich, pp285-319.
15. Letter of Gramsci, then a journalist on *Avanti!*, to the paper's editor, G.M. Serrati, published 29 January 1918 under the signature of 'The anti-esperantist editorial staff member from Turin', a description of Gramsci used in an article three days earlier by Serrati, who had also defined him as a 'distinguished glottology expert': see Gramsci (1982), pp612-3.
16. *Sunday Worker*, 3 June 1928. See Derek Boothman, 'The British Press on Gramsci's Trial' in *Counter-Hegemony*, University of Reading, No. 8, 2003, pp52-66.
17. See Gramsci 1985, pp179-88.
18. Tullio De Mauro, 'Some notes on Gramsci the linguist', English translation in Ives and Lacorte, op cit, pp255-66; this quotation, in a slightly different wording, is on p258. G.I. Ascoli was Italy's leading nineteenth-century linguist.
19. Letter (18 June 1964) from Santhià to Alfonso Leonetti; Togliatti, who joined in 1914, like Santhià relying on memory, in another letter to Leonetti (1 April 1964) wrote that Gramsci became a member earlier, probably in 1912. See Alfonso Leonetti, *Note su Gramsci*, Argalìa: Urbino (1970), pp165-6 and 169-70 respectively.
20. No letter of Gramsci's has yet come to light for the period between an

anti-Mussolini postcard, published by *L'Avanti!*, that he sent in October 1914 to Teresina (with the sole word 'greetings' and his signature), and his letter to Grazietta of 1916. Then, between that letter and the next ones at the end of 1917, when he was already a journalist on *Avanti!*, we have only a jointly-signed postcard of November 1916 and a hitherto unpublished telegram, in possession of the Paulesu family, consisting of Antonio's Easter greetings (8 April 1917) to his mother: 'Most fervent wishes Stop Well Antonio Gramsci'.

21. Letter to Tat'jana of 19 March 1927: Gramsci 1994a, Vol. 1, p84.
22. V. Degot': *V 'svobodom' podpolye* (*Underground in 'freedom'. Reminiscences of underground work abroad 1919-21*) State Publishers: Moscow-Petrograd, 1923, pp30 and 50 respectively. Degot' refers to the role, not of Gramsci's famous review *L'Ordine Nuovo*, whose first series ended three weeks before the PCI was founded, but, possibly with some exaggeration, to that of the daily paper published under the same name from January 1921 through to 1922.
23. Report in the 5 December 1920 number of the communist fraction's weekly paper *Il Comunista,* edited by Amadeo Bordiga.
24. *Inprecorr*, Vol. 2, nos 47 & 49, 12 and 16 June 1922.
25. Comintern Presidium minutes for 18 July 1922, Comintern Archives 495-2-12/158.
26. Gramsci dates their first meeting to September 1922 (see the section later in the Introduction on the Schucht family), while his grandson in one place refers to it as having taken place in August (Antonio Gramsci jr, 2010, p56).
27. See letters to Gramsci and Ersilio Ambrogi, then the other main PCI representative in Moscow: APC 513-1-157/1 and 513-1-091/6).
28. See letter of 4 August 1922, APC 513-1-091/9-10, signed by both Gramsci and Ambrogi; and letter of Ambrogi to the PCI Executive of 4 September 1922: APC 513-1-091/14-15).
29. There is also a stenographic record of Rappoport's oral summary of Gramsci's speech (Comintern Archives 49-1-3/332-34), but the conference stenographic records contain glaring errors, complained about by Zinov'ev; further background information, including the choices made to establish a reliable text, is in Carlucci and Balistreri (2011).
30. Ambrogi, unsigned letter to the PCI Executive: Comintern Archives 513-1-092/4.
31. Cf the letter to Jul'ka of 13 February 1923, p133.
32. The subject was at least in part working-class education and culture, according to a local paper, *Rabočij Kraj* ('*Working-class Region*'), quoted by Antonio Gramsci jr (2010), pp56-7.
33. See letter of 1 March 1924 to Togliatti and Mauro Scoccimarro.
34. For the letter omitted, 3 September 1922, see APC 513-1-091/55-62.
35. On 30 August 1922 Trotsky wrote to Gramsci: 'Dear comrade, Could you

perhaps tell me what the political role of futurism is in Italy? What was the position of Marinetti and his school during the war? What is their position now? Does the Marinetti group still exist? What is its relationship with futurism? What is D'Annunzio's relation with futurism? I thank you in advance for your reply.' The note is included in D. A. Volkogonov's biography of Trotsky in Russian (p118), but not in its partial English translation. See *Trotsky: The Eternal Revolutionary*, Free Press: New York 1996.

36. Gramsci's letter, whose original, if it has survived, has not yet come to light, is included in the Russian editions of Trotsky's *Literature and Revolution*, as well as in a German translation of the book undertaken at the time (see the endnotes to the letter in Chapter 4), but not in the book's English editions.
37. Baldesi had previously come out in favour of breaking the link between the trade unions and the Socialist Party at the formers' congress in March 1921; and in a misguided and vain attempt to save the unions from the onslaught of fascism, the link was officially broken in autumn 1922.
38. See letter of 1 March 1924 to Scoccimarro and Togliatti.
39. See the section entitled 'The Manifesto's Conception' in Gramsci's letter of 9 February 1924.
40. Information about the meeting, confirmed by Lenin's diary of engagements, is in Ravera's letter of 1972 to Giuliano (Antonio jr's father), now published in full in Antonio Gramsci jr (2010), pp180-84.
41. Ravera suggests this (Antonio Gramsci jr, 2008, p54, and 2010, p183) without being definite. A plan to send Gramsci to Berlin was turned down, partly on the advice of Terracini who, in a letter from Moscow of 8 September 1923, stated that the work in Berlin would be too heavy for Gramsci's still precarious state of health.
42. For Vella and Nenni see Gramsci's letter of 25 November 1922 to Zinov'ev, written during the Congress, and his letters to Togliatti of 18 May 1923 and to various leading PCI comrades of 21 March 1924.
43. An additional point was added almost immediately afterwards (cf Gramsci's letter of 29 March 1923 to the PCI Executive, p147).
44. See Radek's article 'The Results of the Session of the Enlarged Executive Committee' (i.e. the first Plenum), in *Inprecorr*, Vol. 2 no. 49, 16 June 1922, p360, also cited in Chapter 4.
45. See APC 513-1-160/1-4. Possibly for health reasons, and possibly because of what was thought to be his imminent transfer to Vienna, the Fourth Congress replaced him as full member of the Presidium with Egidio Gennari.
46. Letter fragment of August 1923 to Togliatti, see p168.
47. Giovanni Somai (1979) is very illuminating on these relations and was instrumental in shedding much light on Gramsci's activity in both Moscow and Vienna.
48. The protest about Rákosi lies on the borderline between a Party 'docu-

ment' and 'letter', but is certainly not an official Party 'report', since it refers to a report on the same subject to be sent to the Comintern Executive. Although not included in Gramsci (2012), it has here been considered a letter and therefore included in the present volume.

49. On the issue of pay see letter in German not written, but signed, by Gramsci, to Osip Pjatnickij of 23 January 1923. For Italians working in agriculture see letter of 20 March 1923, p140.
50. Letter of 15 November 1923, omitted here but published in Gramsci 2009; the only version we have is one in the Italian State Archives, decoded by the Italian police.
51. Letter of 20 March 1923 to the PCI Executive.
52. Another letter to Terracini of the same date is instead included here. The letter not included, on fairly organisational questions, is in the AAG and the Italian Central State Archives (Interior Ministry's documents seized from the PCI 1922-25, folder 3, fascicule 34, sheet 91).
53. Letter to the PCI Executive of 14 January 1924, see p208.
54. We do not know how quickly Gramsci progressed with Russian. Towards the end of 1923 it was certainly good enough to allow him, together with Jul'ka to correct him, to begin a draft translation of Rjazanov, referred to later in this Introduction.
55. For this letter, of 12 July 1923, see Comintern Archive 495-221-1331/1.
56. Among the Italians mentioned in the letters who were shot during the late 1930s, but rehabilitated a generation later, were Civalleri, De Marchi and the polyglot *Inprecorr* correspondent Edmondo Peluso; leading Bolsheviks and Russian comrades also figuring in the letters who met this fate include the early Comintern representative in Italy Ljubarskij (Niccolini), Sedler (cf Gramsci's personal letter to Terracini of 23 December 1923) and Elanskij (letter to Jul'ka of 26 November 1924).
57. The uncoded Russian original of the coded telegram he sent Gramsci on 25 June is in the AAG.
58. See the letter to Terracini of 27 March 1924.
59. Radek, op cit, p360.
60. *Inprecorr*, Vol. 2, No. 58, 14 July 1922, p438. The text here is a word-for-word transcription, and its awkwardnesses probably arise from the pressure under which translators worked.
61. Letter to Terracini of 10 February 1924, not included here.
62. Frank Rosengarten (1984-5), p75, quotes this comment by Trotsky, taken from his *What Next? Vital Questions for the German Proletariat* (trans. Joseph Vanzler), Pioneer Publishers: New York (1932), p86.
63. The entire text of the manifesto was later published by Stefano Merli (1964, pp515-21) – based on the draft version that was seized when Togliatti was arrested in September 1923.
64. Cf the letters to Terracini of 24 December 1923 and to Scoccimarro of 5 January 1924.

65. See Merli 1964, p517.
66. Spriano (1967), p217, quoting minutes of the PCd'I Central Committee held on 29 June 1922, just after Bordiga's return from the Enlarged Executive of the Comintern earlier that month.
67. See Merli 1964, pp517-8.
68. Ibid, p518.
69. Gramsci 1978a, p164.
70. See Spriano, p204, and its note 2; and also pages 213-14.
71. Cf Gramsci's letter to Vincenzo Bianco of 25 November 1924, p331; and Togliatti, 'La nostra ideologia', in *L'Unità*, 23 September 1925, quoted in Spriano (1967), pp482-3.
72. Gramsci's analysis in his letter of 9 February 1924 of the relationship between the different tendencies is very complex, For an interpretation of a particularly difficult passage in this letter see p217.
73. Also in letter of 9 February 1924.
74. Letter from Terracini to Gramsci and Togliatti of 25 April 1924, reproduced in part in Togliatti (1962), pp331-2; see also Spriano (1967), pp353-4 and Hajek (1969), pp107-8 (note).
75. For Bordiga's election to Comintern Executive, see Degras 1960, p572. For Gramsci's report to the PCI Central Committee see transcript dated 17 July 1925: Comintern Archive 513-1-296/11-12.
76. For the Aventine secession see below, p325.
77. Grieco's formal nomination as head of the section is included in Togliatti's report to Moscow on the August 1924 PCI Central Committee meeting, which also confirmed Gramsci's nomination as general secretary (APC 513-1-241/20-22).
78. This question is dealt with in the report of 20 October 1924 by the Comintern representative in Italy, Jules Humbert-Droz, to the Comintern Presidium (Comintern Archives 513-1-226/91-97 for the original in French and 513-1-226/113-124 for its English translation).
79. Picelli had led a heroic and successful three-day pitched battle against the fascists in Parma at the time of the 'legalitarian' strike; he was later killed in defence of the Republic in Spain.
80. Notwithstanding Gramsci's polemics against Serrati, as also against Bordiga, his personal relations always remained friendly with both and, after Serrati's untimely death by heart attack in May 1926, Gramsci's obituary of him (Gramsci 1978a, pp109-13) was a moving and dignified tribute to a man who personified the travails experienced by many in the Italian left in those years. For terzini strength in the rural areas see pp449-502 in Detti, especially p474.
81. See the letters to Terracini of 13 April and to Jul'ka of 13 and 16 April 1924.
82. Gramsci refers to this conference, without naming it, in his letter to Jul'ka of 21 July 1924.

83. APC 513-1-241/19; see also Spriano, 1967, pp349-59.
84. See letter to Jul'ka of 18 August 1924.
85. APC 513-1-241/20-22.
86. A fleeting reference to Gramsci's appointment as General Secretary is in Spriano (1967), p401. News of his position did circulate within restricted Comintern circles, and is confirmed in a newly-found fragment of a letter in German of 6 September 1924 to Bela Kun, leader of the short-lived Hungarian 'Republic of Councils' (Comintern Archives 513-1-244/2) and in Humbert-Droz's report, cited above, of 20 October 1924.
87. The original Aventine secession was undertaken in the mid-fifth century BCE, by the Roman plebs in their struggle against the patricians. For more on the secession of 1924-5 see Chapter 6.
88. Gramsci wrote that he wanted to go to Moscow to give a detailed report on the situation, but in the end, he and Scoccimarro stayed behind to direct party action in Italy. Gramsci's substitute was Togliatti, who went to Moscow for the first time.
89. Cf a telegram signed 'Marco' (i.e. Scoccimarro) of 18 July to the Comintern Secretariat, Comintern Archive 513-1-243/116.
90. See Spriano 1967, p382.
91. See Spriano 1967, p414; and letters to Bianco of 25 November 1924 and to Jul'ka of 18 September.
92. For repressive measures see letter to the Party Executive of 14 January 1924.
93. Letter to Jul'ka, 10 November 1924, p329.
94. Luigi Sturzo, *Italy and Fascismo* (trans. Barbara Barclay Carter), Faber and Faber: London 1926, p214; for an authoritative reconstruction of events, including especially the activity of the catholic hierarchy see Giorgio Candeloro, *Il movimento cattolico in Italia*, Editori Riuniti: Rome 1961, pp474-84.
95. Stefano Jacini jr, *Storia del P.P.I,* Garzanti: Milan 1951, p189, cited in Candeloro, op cit, p483.
96. Giuliano Procacci, *History of the Italian People* (trans. Anthony Paul), Penguin: Harmondsworth, 1968, p422. See also Spriano 1967, p425.
97. Mentioned in the letter to Jul'ka of 25 May 1925, p341. See Gramsci 1978a, pp75-85, for the transcript.
98. See letter of 5 January 1925 to Scoccimarro, who had taken over in November as Party representative in Moscow.
99. Spriano 1967, p433.
100. See the letter to Humbert-Droz of 25 April 1925 (p340) – written on Gramsci's return from Moscow, where he had attended the Fifth Enlarged Executive of the Comintern (21 March-14 April) – which mentions important Communist victories at FIAT.
101. See letter to Zinov'ev, 18 July 1925 (p346); and to Jul'ka on 15 August (p349).

102. Letter to Jul'ka of 1 June, p342.
103. Bordiga himself thought it prudent not to figure among the founding members. Gullo, as Minister of Agriculture in the short-lived governments of national unity after the fall of fascism, was to promulgate important agrarian law reforms.
104. 'Déclaration écrite du camarade Grieco' (Comintern Archives 513-1-285/61).
105. AAG: telegram in Russian not reproduced here.
106. See Gramsci's letter to Bordiga of 18 August 1925, p351.
107. For both suggestions cf letter of 21 March 1924 'to Togliatti, Scoccimarro, Leonetti etc', p252.
108. A recourse by Bordiga to the International claiming that the Congress was invalid was turned down; see Chiara Daniele (ed.) (1999), pp215-9, citing Togliatti's letter to the PCI Secretariat (APC 513-1-364/1-5).
109. See letter to Jul'ka of 13 January 1924.
110. See Carr (1954), pp367-73 for the platform of the forty-six, and the various riders added by the signatories; the resolution on the subject, passed by the XIII Conference of the RCP in January 1924 and confirmed by the XIII Party Congress (May 1924), is in *Inprecorr*, Vol. IV (1924), No 64, pp691-3.
111. In a letter of 9 March 1924, not included here. See Carr (1954), pp292-341. Other background information is in R.V. Daniels (1960), pp220-3 and his *Rise and Fall of Communism in Russia*, Yale University Press: New Haven and London (2007), pp181-3.
112. Trotsky, on one side, and the Kamenev-Zinov'ev bloc on the other, had announced their opposition to the majority position of the Central Committee; the PCI leadership was informed of this by Togliatti, then representing the party in Moscow.
113. During meetings held much later in Moscow that reorganised the PCd'I leadership, Grieco confirmed his role in advising on the letter's contents: see APC 495-19-8/1 for the statement of 29 June 1940, signed by him as 'Garlandi'. This whole episode is reconstructed in Giuseppe Vacca (2012), p26.
114. APC 513-1-410/20. Manuil'skij also replied to Gramsci (letter in French of 21 October, not included here), stating that 'never has the power of the Soviets and the dictatorship of the proletariat been as strong as now' and 'never had the opposition undergone such a lamentable check as that of the last few months': APC 513-1-410/27, reproduced in Chiara Daniele, op cit, pp426-7.
115. Communication of 26 October, signed by 'Micheli', i.e. Camilla Ravera: APC 513-1-420/42. Some of the background here, including Grieco's role, relies on Michele Pistillo's article 'Grieco corresponsabile della lettera di Gramsci al Pcr del 1926' in *Critica Marxista*, 2001, no. 1, pp44-50; Chiara Daniele, op cit, pp434 and 440, reproduces Camilla

Ravera's communication and a further reply by Togliatti to Rome of 1 November 1926.

116. Confirmed by the address on a postcard, here included, that she received from Gramsci and her brother Viktor, dated 24 April 1923.
117. Gramsci uses 'Giulia', the strict Italian equivalent of her name, only once in the present selection, when for the first time he tells his mother about her (letter of 7 June 1924).
118. For Julka and Ženja's membership see Antonio Gramsci, jr (2010), p54 and pp108-113 (specifically pp110-11).
119. Cf Antonio Gramsci jr, 2010, pp54-5.
120. Letter of 24 August 1931: Gramsci 1994a, Vol. 2, p59. See also Paulesu Quercioli (1987), p33.
121. Cf the letter to her of 30 June 1924, p311.
122. The drafts, all in Jul'ka's Italian, were first published in *L'Unita*, 18 October 2007; Antonio Gramsci, jr (2010), pp56-7, gives the draft quoted from here, confirmed by him to be written in October 1922.
123. Among those contributing to this interpretation are Leonardo Pompeo D'Alessandro, Francesco Giasi, Eleonora Lattanzi and Luisa Righi of the Institute, with inputs from the author of this introduction, from Jeni Nicholson and from Anita Weston. This interpretation now also has the backing of Antonio Gramsci jr (2014, pp126-30).
124. The new attributions made here, published for the first time by Luisa Righi of the Gramsci Institute (Righi 2012), are corroborated by circumstantial evidence from a hitherto unconsulted source. There are two folders, 519-1-095 and 519-1-104, in the Comintern Archives containing typewritten transcriptions of Gramsci's letters to Jul'ka, with handwritten corrections for accuracy where necessary; many top copies bear Evgenija's signature, presumably as confirmation that the transcription is a faithful and accurate copy. There are only three letters written after February 1923 – two of them unambiguously to Jul'ka (13 January 1924 and 16 April 1924) and one other, probably written in March 1923 – that are not in these folders, possibly because they had not surfaced or were otherwise unavailable when the transcriptions were made. (All three of these letters are included in the present selection.) And if the third of these letters was indeed written in March, it must also be to Jul'ka, since Ženja was still confined to the sanatorium and therefore could not 'come back and wait' in Gramsci's room. But there are another three letters – written before the end of February 1923, that are not in the folders – exactly those three which here are suggested to be to Ženja.
125. By the time of Gramsci's arrest, two years later, they had passed to the 'tu' form: see Gramsci's letter and postcard to Sraffa of December 1926, sent from his detention on the island of Ustica (Gramsci 1994a, Vol. 1, pp44-5).

126. A photographic reproduction of the certificate is in Antonio Gramsci jr (2010), p140.
127. Their elder son bore the surnames of both his parents, but until after World War II their younger child bore only his mother's; however, after legal recourse she then managed to have Gramsci accepted as his surname too.
128. Gramsci 1994a, Vol. 1, p93. Subsequently the marriage must have been recognised in Italy, allowing Tanja, as his legal sister-in-law, to visit him.
129. See Gramsci's letters to Jul'ka of 18 August and to his mother of 5 September 1924.
130. What must be Ženja's plan, in Russian, of the sleeping arrangements, showing Delio's cot next to what she labels 'my bed', with 'Jul'ka's bed' on the other side of the room, is reproduced in Antonio Gramsci jr (2010), p141. On p67 of the same book Antonio jr quotes a letter extract included in Adele Cambrìa's *Amore come rivoluzione* (*Love as Revoulution*), SugarCo: Milan, 1976, p91, in which Nilde Perilli says that it was Tanja and Ženja who slept in the room with Delio; either Perilli's memory was at fault, many years afterwards, or at some point Tanja and Jul'ka switched rooms. The point remains however that Ženja had Delio next to her.
131. Cf Tanja's letter to Antonio of 4 May 1930 and his letter to her of 13 January 1931, now in Antonio Gramsci-Tania Schucht, *Lettere*, Einaudi: Turin 1997, pp511 and 648 respectively; the latter is in English in Gramsci 1994a, Vol. 2, p2.
132. See Antonio Gramsci jr (2010), especially pp68, 70 and 115-17, quoting family letters from Ženja to Tanja from the time when Antonio was in prison; and also, again, Nilde Perilli's views on Ženja.
133. In a letter from prison to Tat'jana (15 December 1930: see Gramsci 1994a, Vol. 1, p369), Gramsci commented that 'ordinarily', he had 'to set out from a dialogical or dialectical standpoint'.
134. On the question of centralism see Gramsci (1971), pp185-90; and (1996) p164. Thanks go to Angelo Rossi for pointing out that the latter of these two notes, on centralised command and independent initiative or lack of it in the Battle of Jütland, is also a metaphor for the same factors in politics, confirmed by its inclusion, in a slightly more elaborate form, in Gramsci's Notebook 13 on Machiavelli.
135. Letter to Togliatti and others of 21 March 1924. Gramsci favoured this approach in talks held towards the end of 1930 with fellow prisoners. For a summary of his position, relayed to the PCI leadership in 1933 by Athos Lisa, a fellow communist prisoner, see *Rinascita*, 12 December 1964, and Lisa's *Memorie*, Feltrinelli: Milan (1973), pp82-90.
136. Letter to Togliatti of 26 October 1926, see p378.
137. Cf the letters of 9 February and 1 March 1924, pp217, 236.

138. For the question of the ongoing evolution of Gramsci's concepts, including 'hegemony', see two volumes originating from Rome's Gramsci Seminar: Frosini and Liguori (eds) (2004, reprinted 2011) and Liguori and Voza (eds) (2009), the latter being an exhaustive Gramscian dictionary with contributions from over sixty Gramscian specialists worldwide.
139. For these explicit uses, see the letters, all of 1924: 5 January to Scoccimarro, 9 February to Togliatti and others, 1 March to Togliatti and Scoccimarro, and 19 April to the Italian Party Central Committee.

1. School and home in Sardinia

To Francesco Gramsci

[SANTULUSSURGIU, JUNE 1908][1]

Dearest father,

If you can do so in time, do not send the money order by telegraph but send the money by post, and send it on Tuesday; if not, it doesn't matter. However the Director at Oristano has written again to say that we have to pay 120 lire, not just 100. Professor Stara has told us to pay now, so as not to get into an argument before the examination, out of some huffiness, and then try to claim the money back if possible;[2] send me 120, then, or get the receipt at Ghilarza. The birth cert[ificate] I have here is on plain paper, and for the exam it has to be on revenue-stamped paper. Given that, you ought to have sent the money order to the municipal authority in Ales, and not through the mayor; a lot of trouble for nothing, so hurry up, then, and make completely sure it's on revenue-stamped paper. If you have sent the money order, send a telegram to let me know. In the meantime, I'm sending the other documents, asking the Director to put my name on the official exam list anyway. You can write to uncle at Oristano, since it may be that I will go off on the 21st or 22nd and go directly to Oristano, if not I'm going to make a fool of myself at Ghilarza; certainly, I'm absolutely not going to pass the exam at the first attempt because in six months we've only just dipped into the coursework, without doing anything of any consequence. Everything is up to chance; I can pass in everything or they can fail me in everything just like that; so no certainty whatever; and I don't want you then to come out with useless reproaches; I'm warning you beforehand; I want them to pass me at the 2nd exam session. Pay attention, then; 120 lire, birth cert[ificate] on revenue-stamped paper, otherwise no exam: there's no getting away from it, and pay attention that for exam purposes, the birth cert[ificate] is needed on official revenue-stamped paper. Only for other things on plain paper, but now with the revenue stamp. Hurry up, then, if you don't, it's good-bye to everything. If you don't pay at Ghilarza, send me the money order or the insured registered letter tomorrow so that I can send it to Oristano. Kisses to everyone and good luck.

Your most aff[ection]ate,

Nino

Source: Archivio Antonio Gramsci (AAG)

To Francesco Gramsci

[CAGLIARI, NOVEMBER-DECEMBER 1908]

Dearest father,

With the money order you sent me you promised to write, but I don't know why you thought I had moved and it was just a matter of luck that the order arrived together with a postcard at the right address, so it did arrive but I don't know what's happened to the letter. If you have in fact sent it, let me know at once because I'm going to try and track it down.

You did well to send me on another five lire because I've had to pay 1 lira 20 for the official school result sheet, and 60 centesimi to make the official request to be exempted from gymnastics, and you can imagine the rest!

I'd appreciate it if you would let the agent know that he should send me the money that is owed me[3] because, if I don't get it within a week, I'll write to him myself, because I really need it since I have to buy some instalments of the Petrocchi dictionary, given that you obviously don't want to bother about it, and all this so that I don't lose what I've spent up to now.

See to the middle school leaving certificate as soon as possible because if I can't hand it in within a week, I'll be suspended from lessons, as the head teacher has already made absolutely clear.

Send this month's *Secolo XX* ['*Twentieth Century*'] to me too, because I need it, together with the other things that have arrived for me, as well as the *Tribuna Illustrata*, as my mother had promised.

Send on the Greek books that I wrote to you about, because they're of very great use to me for the revision for this term's work.[4]

I hope you'll remember me at Christmas. I'll send you some music magazines for Grazietta and Emma, and for Teresina too.[5]

A big kiss for mother, Grazietta, Emma, Teresina, Mario, Carlo and you.

Lots of kisses from your very aff[ection]ate

Nino

Source: AAG

To Francesco Gramsci

CAGLIARI, 14 JANUARY 1909

Dearest father,

Unfortunately yet again I'm having to write to you to ask you for money. That's plain to see! You sent a message with Chicchino saying you'd be sending the rest shortly, but there's still no sign of it. Well, I'm waiting! It seems clear now that I don't write except when I have to ask for something; I'm always afraid you're not going to send the money on time and that I'll have to beg the landlady to wait for the rent. In the meantime, you've sent me 30 lire, I have to pay the rent, we're already at the fifteenth of the month, I've nothing left and I don't know how I'm going to manage. Well, all right. In the meantime, no one is sending me the money for books, and I can truly say this year has gone splendidly. I've never had a coin in my pocket, because with 45 lire there's nothing to spare at all; indeed if I weren't with Nannaro there just wouldn't be enough to live on.[6] During the holidays I've had to make sacrifices, whereas with my constitution it would have done me good to relax and enjoy myself, and now I'm having to stay sacrificed just the same. But it's clear that patience is the one thing that isn't lacking. By now I'm tired of repeating myself over and over again, you turn a deaf ear, and I can't do anything about it. At least when I'm grown up I'm going to remember that I've never had a happy moment in my life. Always with the nightmare of tomorrow hanging over me. At least you could have told me first: spend your money because I can't see to everything. Then I'd have been able to manage some way and wouldn't have found myself so much off keel. Just think well on all this and you'll see that I'm right. A kiss to everyone, from Nannaro as well. Lots of kisses.

Nino

Source: AAG

To Francesco Gramsci (AAG)

[CAGLIARI, JANUARY 1909]

Dearest father,

I've finally been told my average marks for the term. Certainly they ought to have been different, but that's not my fault, because as Nannaro has perhaps written to tell you, I was off school suspended for three days for not having brought my middle school leaving certificate, right during the days of the end-of-term exams. This meant I didn't get a mark for Natural History, while in History I only got 5. The teacher even gave me a good telling off, but it wasn't my fault at all, because I was always writing to you for it: send me the diploma, but you turned a deaf ear. Despite all that I got through reasonably well, because for Natural History the two marks in the 2nd and 3rd terms are sufficient, and in History it would indeed be strange if I didn't come back up to scratch. These are the marks:

Italian	written	6	oral	8
Latin	idem	6/7	idem	7
Greek		6		7
Philosophy				6
Mathematics				6
Chemistry				8

As you see, my results are reasonably good, and you have to remember that this is the first term, and I didn't come from Santulussurgiu with the best preparation, especially in Latin, Greek and mathematics.

Please do send me my monthly allowance straight away, which I hope will be 50 lire because I'm finding myself up against it, since the forwarding agent didn't send the money on and here am I with a subscription to a newspaper, so I had to borrow money from Piredda and I've now got to pay him back. I hope you'll speak to the forwarding agent, because this is called really making a fool of people;[7] if you don't then I'll write and let him have a piece of my mind and then we'll see what's what. As regards the Dictionary, let me know by letter, otherwise I'm going to sell everything and that'll be that. Tell Teresina to write to me, tell her I'll always send the magazine on to her and that I'll send her the stamps, too, so she can send me on the *Tribuna Illustrata*. Write back immediately because I'm waiting. Lots of kisses to mother, and to all three of you. Yours aff[ectionately]

Nino

And all best wishes from Gigina Badalotti and the Piellucci family

Source: AAG

To Francesco Gramsci and to Giuseppina Marcias

[CAGLIARI, 18 MARCH 1909]

Dearest father,

I wouldn't have disturbed you for all the gold in the world because I understand all the sacrifices you're making, and with what I'm able to do I'm trying to play my part, but absolute and extreme necessity have given me the courage of a lion. I can already imagine your face after reading these introduction: it's money, that's predictable enough. And on that you're right. It seems to me that up to now I've had enough to keep me happy, and moreover I'm not expecting you to fork out, just to give me an advance to take care of what his Lordship the forwarding agent should have already sent me five months ago. Believe you me that if it hadn't been because of you, because of your position as regards the agency, I would have really made my voice heard and gone right to the manager.

How can I tell you about all my odysseys in Cagliari where, totally inexperienced, I found myself unexpectedly without any money. Then, to cap matters, a school friend went off back to his village taking with him my last 5 lire. I don't believe your father's heart won't be moved, even more because you will then get the money back from the agent: but I beg and pray of you to send the money on without delay today, because

Piredda hasn't any and neither has Putzolu, the landlady won't lend any and I'm at my wit's end, in a foul mood and you know my easily excitable temperament. And then there are the end-of-term exams, just to put me in a good mood! and I have to stay at home with this injured foot of mine, with the sun shining outside, and with the constant thought in my head that we're still only at the 18th of the month: there's enough to make stronger heads than mine go into a spin. For all these reasons, I beg of you, if I'm still a presence in your thoughts, let yourself be moved, do a good deed, something that will cost you nothing and which I certainly will know how to repay. I'll see, if not it's certainly going to be an unhappy Easter for me this year. Once again, kisses

to everyone and a special prayer to you

yours, Nino

Dearest mother

Although I have no great propensity for the saints in general, still, following the usual practices I'm sending you greetings for your saint's day tomorrow, greetings that are no less ardent for not being accompanied by high-sounding phrases. Certainly I would much have liked to see you together with the others (I've never been away from home for so long before), but a series of events do not allow me to come back, with what anguish you can imagine. Assure Grazietta that for Easter I'll send on to her 'La Montanina' with Putzolu as well as some other publications, but if it is not to their liking, don't put the blame on me, since I don't understand these things, and my school friends play the piano rather than the rustic mandolin.[8] Enjoy yourself during the festivities, singing and dancing; I'll amuse myself looking at the bare walls of my room because, just like last year, all the skin has rubbed off my foot, I can put my shoes on only to go to school, and even then only by ignoring the pain. Kiss everyone and to you, again with my greetings,

lots of kisses from your most aff[ection]ate

Nino

Source: AAG

To Francesco Gramsci

CAGLIARI, 5 NOVEMBER [1909][9]

Dearest father,

Yesterday was the first day at school; not all the staff is there as yet, but lessons have started all the same and we've been told at least part of the books that we have to buy.

Chicchino hasn't found lodgings yet and I've taken a room on a daily basis where I have my meals with Nannaro, but we'll now have to rent a room for at least a month.

You'll have to tell Putzolu that the head teacher hasn't yet got here, and that the teacher who is here doesn't want to hand anything over to us until the head arrives.

There's also a message from Mario for Raffaele Corrias to say that I've been to Ghera who told me I have to pay 50 centesimi for secretarial fees, and another 1 lira 20 centesimi for having a copy made of the leaving certificate from the Middle High School; he should write to me saying what should be done on this.

Nannaro has said that you should use what was left from the money for the partridges to have a shirt made for him, which you can send with Coghe.[10] Please also send with him lots of chestnuts, mushrooms and eggs; if not with him, you could send them by special delivery, letting me know beforehand.

You should let me have the following books straight away:

The two volumes of mathematics
Monti's translation of the *Iliad*
The *Bellezze* of the *Iliad*, the *Odyssey* and the *Aeneid*.[11]

Please send these to me as soon as possible and, in addition, my monthly allowance, because I have to pay the rent for the lodgings and have nothing left to pay it with.

Here is the book list:

Corbino – *Physics*	2 lire 50 for 1 lira 45
Rinaudo's *History* – Vol. II	2 lire 50
Marchesini – *Logic*	2 lire for 1 lira 20
Ghisleri – *High School Atlas*	3 lire
Tacitus – *Germany*	60 centesimi

Cicero – *Brutus*	80 centesimi
Mercalli – *Mineralogy*	1 lira 40
Poli and Tanfani – *Plant Structure and Function*	2 lire 50
Socrates – *Panegyric*	60 centesimi
Catullus – *Selected Poems* (Pestalozza)	1 lira 50
	15 lire 55[12]

For now the books are these listed, but there should not be many more. Meanwhile send me the money as soon as you can because I have to buy all the books new. Send letters to me care of the Marzullo ice plant so that Nannaro can give me them, and the same as regards the newspapers.

Give my best wishes to Zizzu Coghe, Filomena and the young heir, together with those of Nannaro, who can't wait to congratulate Filomena.

Greetings and kisses to everyone

Nino

Written by the two of us[13]

Source: partial copy in AAG; rest as in Gramsci (2009) and in previous publications)

To Francesco Gramsci

[CAGLIARI, JANUARY 1910][14]

Dearest father,

At last I can write to you. Up to the first few days of January I felt rather poorly and wasn't able to write; on top of that I was having at the same time to think about the end-of-term exams, which left me drained of energy. I've waited in vain for you to make a move and send me the money – I still haven't seen any of it. Indeed last month you sent me just 40 lire; just think whether it's humanly possible to live on 40 lire in Cagliari, but it's obvious that you don't give the matter a thought. Give my thanks to Grazietta who sent 5 lire to me; I'd decided to buy a hat because the one I have is a disgrace, with its entire brim falling to pieces, but I had to hand over the 5 lire to the landlord. So I'm now waiting for you to send 5 lire to me (the 5 that you didn't send me last month) so I can buy the hat. Besides this, please do send without delay the money order for this month because I've had to get credit from the landlord, and that has been exceptionally hard on me, having then to put up with all his insinuations. Write straight away with news about how everyone is. I went to the Port Authority about Mario; there's a new call-up in February, but one mustn't have turned 18 by April. I don't know if Mario satisfies these conditions; in case he does let me know. Once again, I beg you, hurry up and send me the money, including the 5 lire, and specify that the money is for the hat. Otherwise, if Nannaro sees that there's nothing written, I'll have to hand it over to the landlord and I'll have to keep on with this dreadful hat. As regards the end-of-term exams, I still don't know anything. As soon as I know the marks I'll let you know. A big kiss to everyone and write to me with their news.

Nannaro will send his photo on to you.

Kisses

Nino

I'm waiting

Source: AAG

To Francesco Gramsci

31 JANUARY [1910][15]

Dearest father,

Yesterday the headmaster gave us the marks for the term. Here they are as follows:

Italian: no mark because there was no teacher

Latin:	7-8	Greek culture	8
Greek	8-8[16]	History	8
Physics	6	Natural history	6
Philosophy	6		

As you can see I've obtained good marks, and this term hope to improve them, because the marks of 6 were due to mishaps.

I beg of you to send me the money immediately, because I need it urgently. Tomorrow, 1 February, send it on as soon as you receive this letter. Further, I have to buy two new books

Foscolo: *Poetry*	1.50
G. Setti: *Greek Literature*	2.50

The first is for the Italian that we've now started, and the second will be starting in a few days' time.

Further, remember that still ... But it's useless to take up the old refrain once again; by now you understand and you won't fall down on this. Just remember that I have to study if I have to prepare for the leaving certificate, so I mustn't have too many worries.

The headmaster has raised a number of difficulties for giving me the leaving certificate. First of all, I have to present a certificate to say I am able to do military service. I most certainly cannot produce this, and neither can the others, since being 19 years old and not having had the medical examination, I cannot present any document. So maybe this demand is going to disappear; it's possible that I may not be able to do the exam, and on this you just have to be patient.

Yet again I beg of you, don't make me wait. I'll send the elastic to Carlo very shortly when I have the money, so tell him that his 2.90 lire were like manna from above. I'll send it to him with Toriggia's mother, who is setting off soon. Kisses to everyone and for you

lots of kisses from Nannaro too

Nino

Source: AAG

To Francesco Gramsci

CAGLIARI, 10 FEBRUARY 1910

Dearest father,

I have received the money order, but not your letter, so I've waited a couple of days to reply.

You should know that I still haven't received the money from the Agency; at the Office they just had me write a letter of complaint and that was it. Who knows how long I'll have to wait. Meanwhile, I haven't had the suit made up, and this time it really is your fault, because when I told you I'd have it made up and charged it to you, you didn't want to know. And so now it's me who has to shoulder the burden. On 26 February the second and third year students of the lycée are going on a trip to Gúspini to study the mines at Montevecchio since we're studying mineralogy, so I'll have to go too, but I'm nowhere near decent enough to go anywhere, with this two-year-old jacket that is threadbare and shiny, so send me a letter for some tailor's so they can make me up a suit at your expense, and on top of that think about getting the Agency to pay back the money, because they don't pay any attention to what I say. And please don't put it off because this month I'm really at my wit's end. Today I didn't go to school because I had to have my shoes soled, and 3 lire went on that, then I had to buy the Foscolo book, and 2 lire went on that. Now I don't know where to turn next; this Carnival time I've been sulking in the house all the time, crouched up in a corner, and not been out for an instant, so much so that Nannaro thought I was ill. Remember that you still have to send me 10 lire for the first list of books, for which up to now you've sent me just 5 lire. And remember that I'm counting on 10 lire for the trip.

This month make sure that you do things in the way I've said and that you see to sending me what I ask for, because I don't know how I'm going to manage. And I'm expecting this as soon as possible.

Lots of kisses to everyone, from Nannaro as well, and lots of kisses to you too

Nino

I'll send the thing on to Carlo as soon as possible.

Source: AAG

To Francesco Gramsci

[CAGLIARI, 24 MAY 1910]

Dearest father,

It's already the 24th and we still haven't seen anything from you. Not only that but you don't even reply to all the letters that Nannaro and I have sent, or if you do it's a couple of lines to promise that without fail you're going to send the money within a couple of days, meanwhile we never see a thing. Up to a certain time I excused you, but now, knowing what you're like, I'm beginning to have the suspicion that it's more just neglect that's behind things. That a father shouldn't think about his son when the son is in the city and has no means other than what comes from the family, to my way of thinking is a bit too much. I'm not in a village where you know enough people so that you can go on for a bit without having to pay straight away; here you're forced to pay on the nail, if not you don't survive even for a day. Great heavens, there are some things that have to be thought about! Nannaro has sacrificed himself enough, he's had money paid him in advance, but now he doesn't know how he can go on. I can see that he's getting more and more serious with each day that passes, to the extent that today he was ready to send me back to Ghilarza because he didn't know what to do any more, and it was costing him quite enough to think just about himself. It was only my beseeching that convinced him that, if I wrote tonight, we'd be able to straighten things out. So I now find myself in this bed of roses. I don't know what to think of you, because you, in some way or other, would get by, while, if you don't send the money immediately – that is as soon as you get this letter – I will have to come to Ghilarza, and that'll be the end for me because the end-of-term exams start within days and I'll have to miss them, which means I'll lose the whole year. I'm between the frying pan and the fire, lots of them. The head teacher has warned me that I have to pay the second instalment of the school fees, which should have been paid by April 1st, and he's even wanted to suspend me from school until I pay. It's just as well that we've got 5 days' holiday for the King's visit, so I didn't need to go to school anyway. But this holiday is going to come to an end, then what? I'm dreading the moment when they send me away in the sight of my classmates because I haven't paid the fees. But in the meantime, think about everything that has to be done and send the monthly allowance by return courier without fail. It seems that one way or another my student career is about to come to an end, because as far as I can see you don't give two hoots. It's just 'let whoever wants see to it'. You've put the whole weight on Nannaro's shoulders so that it's crushing him. Yet Nannaro had already done enough because certainly without his support I wouldn't have been able to exist on a miserable 45 lire a month. But you just don't think about these things. Well, I'll see about that. We're now talking about my future and certainly I'm not saying that Nannaro is wrong in his decision. I'll see what you do; we'll see what all your promises are really worth. Kisses to everyone

Nino

Source: AAG

To Giuseppina Marcias

[CAGLIARI, LATE JANUARY 1911]

Dearest mother,

I'm replying by return post to stop this mad idea of father's of coming here. Have you really got scared because the police are seeking information on one of us? There's no reason at all to get so worked up. What on earth is running through your mind at this moment – that Nannaro is under lock and key or has got 4 carabinieri on him? Rest assured that nothing of this kind is going to happen.

Nannaro has taken on some responsibilities for the Trades Council, so his name, which up to then was quite unknown, has now come to the eyes of the police, who have wanted to know who this revolutionary is, this new scourge of the constabulary who's coming to the fore, so they've asked for some information.

Put your mind at rest. As you can see, there's nothing untoward, and the whole thing is over and done with. Since there has been a strike, and since Nannaro is treasurer of the Trades Council, the police wanted to know his address, so as to impound the funds and bring the strike to an end. But the strike in any case stopped on its own account and the funds stay where they are. But since the name Gennaro Gramsci came up unexpectedly, the police wanted to know who he was; now their curiosity is satisfied and that's the end of the matter.

I was about to write over the last few days; I didn't send a letter with Adele because I only got to know the evening before that she was leaving the next morning at seven. The same as regards Nessi. I received the present you sent on for St Anthony's day and thank you for it.[17] Another time when you get know of these things, stay calm, just laugh in the face of the lieutenant and the whole flock of carabinieri, as has been my habit for some time. Poor fellows, basically you've got to sympathise with them, having to deal with socialists and anarchists leaves them no time to think about thieves and ne'er-do-wells, and then they're afraid someone's going to come along and steal their lanterns.

The other night they took note of me up in the gods, because I made some comment out loud on the fine moustache of a policeman, telling him he should shave it off if he didn't want comments. And so what? Because of my splendid mane, which even the slightest breeze ruffles, they took me for a girl, and were then amazed that a woman should make such a commotion in the theatre. This was because they could only see my head with my fingers to my mouth blowing a raspberry. I didn't take it badly, I even thanked them for the attention they were paying me. Nothing wrong with that. As long as they don't bring out the handcuffs they can ask as much as they like. A kiss to everyone there at home for me, dry the tears from everyone's face, and don't worry. Kisses from Nannaro too, who's developed a big appetite after all this.

Nino

I've got to know the following marks:

Latin – written 7 oral 8
physics 6 – Greek culture 8

no others as yet, but at least as good if not better.

Source: AAG

To the Carlo Alberto Royal College, Turin

CARLO ALBERTO R[OYAL] COLLEGE
TURIN

The undersigned Antonio Gramsci, son of Francesco Gramsci, having obtained the lycée diploma from the R[oyal] Lycée of Cagliari, hereby requests to be included in the list of those competing for the study grants offered by the above Institution for the degree course in Letters, and requests permission to take the written examinations in

Cagliari.[18] He declares that he has no other study grant, and that he resides with his family in Ghilarza, in the province of Cagliari.

Ghilarza, 28 June 1911

Antonio Gramsci

Source: University of Turin Archives, XI F 7, p1, students requesting admission to the entrance examination; as printed in Gramsci (2009)

NOTES

1. Santucci, in Gramsci (1992), gives the place as Cagliari and date as 6 February 1909, but that date was added in another hand; reassessing the internal evidence gives the place and date indicated here.
2. Teachers from middle school onwards are called 'Professor'; the 'director', with an office at Oristano, thirty kilometres from Santulussurgiu, was the administrator in charge of Gramsci's group of schools. Any direct influence on Gramsci by Massimo Stara, then a leading Sardinian socialist, is still a matter of speculation.
3. Gramsci was owed money for work done during the summer vacation at the Land Registry in Ghilarza: cf his letter of 3 October 1932 to Tanja Schucht (Gramsci 1994a, Vol 2, p215).
4. The manuscript here reads 'inoltra' ('send on') not 'inoltre' ('furthermore') as mistakenly understood in both Gramsci (1992) and Gramsci (2009).
5. In a letter of December 1908, not included here, Gramsci complains he has not received the *Secolo XX* magazine, so in retaliation, if his sister is not spending 10 centesimi on the post, he is not sending her the music magazines. Further, despite having written four or five times about the result sheet, he had not received it, and could not therefore register officially at the high school, so that a term's work risked not being recognised.
6. These words have been rendered 'if I weren't with Nannaro', but the person of the verb used seems to indicate that Gramsci had in mind 'if it were not for Nannaro', the resulting phrase in Italian being an amalgam of the two.
7. See the letter here dated November-December 1908.
8. 'La Montanina' was a composition by Ermenegildo Carosio for guitar and mandolin, instruments played by Gramsci's sisters.
9. The list of books in the letter corresponds to what was studied in the school year 1909-10, so the letter (dated simply 5 November) must have been written in 1909, not 1908 as said in Gramsci (1992).
10. Gennaro added a note on the reverse side of the last page saying that he needed the shirt and to send it with Coghe.

11. The *Bellezze* was a frequently reprinted anthology that included translations of some of the best-known passages from the three epic poems.
12. Gramsci's handwriting sometimes leaves doubt as to whether a figure is '5' or '9'. The best interpretation is that the Poli and Tanfani volume cost 2.50, not 2.90, and the Catullus 1.50, not 1.90, both prices here corrected as compared with Gramsci (1992); the total then comes to 15 lire 55, as in Gramsci (2009).
13. The phrase 'Greetings and kisses to everyone' is in rather shaky handwriting, indicating it was both Antonio and Nannaro together who were holding the pen.
14. Originally dated 1909.
15. Gramsci wrote '1909' but since in the letter he says he is 19, this means that the year was in fact 1910.
16. A double mark means that one was for the written and one for the oral part of the exam.
17. This is St Anthony Abbot whose feast day, 17 January, falls very near Gramsci's birthday (22 January), and so is Gramsci's name day. The 'Adele' mentioned by Gramsci is probably Adele Villassanta, the wife of Francesco ('Chicchino') Oppo.
18. A prerequisite for the grant was that there should be no mark of less than 8 out of 10 in the final school examination (6 being the pass mark). Gramsci's average exonerated him from the lycée finals since, in the final year course work, he obtained an exceptional 9 (written) and 8 (oral) for Italian, and the high mark of 8 for all the others.

2. University student in Turin

To Francesco Gramsci

[Turin, 20 October 1911]

My dearest father,

I've just got back from the University where I went to see what mark I'd got for the Italian examination; I've passed, which is just as well. Unfortunately though, that's not at all reassuring because, of the seventy or so who took it, only five didn't get through, which means that everyone had prepared well for it and that the exam was much more serious than might be thought. The journey here was quite reasonable, and even the part by sea didn't bother me at all. I stayed overnight in Pisa where I said hello to Uncle Zaccaria who was setting off for Tripoli, and then I spent the evening with Uncle Serafino, Uncle Achille and my aunts. At the station in Turin I met Oppo and his wife and they told me straightaway about a house but unfortunately I had to pay three lire a day for the rent and the same or more for meals. Today, however, when I went along to the College to get reimbursed and told the secretary about my odyssey, he was kind enough to find another room for me at 1 lira 50 a day. I haven't seen Oppo again; he lives about 5 or 6 kilometres away, if not further, out of my normal way and outside the city boundary, and I haven't ventured out as far as his place because I shudder at the thought of having to go on foot after having risked getting knocked down by I don't know how many cars and trams. I've found myself in trouble about the journey; the cashier asked me if I'd travelled by second class and when I said yes, he asked me for the railway booklet, which costs 10 lire 25, and gives you the right to a discount for the return trip too. You can just imagine how I felt when I couldn't do anything but admit I'd given up everything at the exit from the station; they advised me to go back to the stationmaster and ask him to have someone look for it. That's the current state of affairs and unfortunately I don't know how to go on.[1] I can see I'll be playing the role of the simpleton or worse. Don't write or send anything to me by post until I get some exact information, because I'll still have to stay on about 5 days for the written examinations, after which I may well be on my way home; in any case I'll send a telegram straight away. I was the only candidate from Sardinia in the examination since the other one didn't turn up; then there are about thirty young ladies from Turin; almost everyone has taken the exam before, so they're much better prepared than I am, and in consequence my hopes have gone down quite a lot. Tomorrow (Saturday) I have the history exam, then Monday, Tuesday and Wednesday those of Latin, Greek and philosophy. On Thursday, then, I'll know the outcome of the written exams.

Kisses to everyone.

Nino

Source: AAG

To Francesco Gramsci

[2 NOVEMBER 1911]

My dearest father,

I wanted to write to you immediately I found out the result of the examination as I said in the telegram, but then I thought it best to put it off until I had finally fixed up my lodgings situation, so I could then send you the exact address. Meanwhile let me say that however many times I've been to the post office I've never found anything, although a number of people have promised to write and send me newspapers. So let me say once and for all that you have to write surname and name very clearly because if, by oversight, a package is put in the wrong pigeonhole instead of the 'G' one then it just waits there to be thrown away. I still haven't found any possible lodgings and I don't know when I will be able to. Everybody asks me for a rent I just can't afford and in the meantime I'm forced to eat in a milk bar, but even this has brought me down to my last reserves. I wanted to be able to go on by my own means but I can see that's not possible; with the 70 lire grant from the college I would just be able to eat without having anywhere to stay and hardly even that. So, if you want me to keep on, it'll be necessary for you to promise to help by at least, take note of this, sending me at least 20 lire a month so I can just get by, since apart unfortunately from the lodging, there's also the laundry, the ironing, and the tram for getting to school, because with this cold and a fair mass of water and mud I can't manage half an hour on foot. But not only that: I have to think about stationery, about buying lecture notes, about buying the most essential books. I don't believe you would want to neglect me completely and I think you'll understand; I've done as much as possible to get the grant which, modest though it is, is still a great help, and moreover the secretary has given me hope that it will go up in the years to come. For the moment then it's up to you. I don't think it's really too great a sacrifice for you and, after all, you have made promises on a number of occasions that now it's up to you to keep. Don't waste any time in replying, so that I can go to find lodgings straightaway, because with every day that passes I have to make a great sacrifice.

In the meantime would you be good enough to contact the Head of the Lycée, giving him enough money to send my high school leaving certificate, either directly to me or to the Carlo Alberto college at the University, so that I can then obtain the diploma that I have to hand over to the University for regular registration. In addition, get all the documents prepared that are necessary for registration and for exemption from tuition fees, then forward them as soon as possible, otherwise I'll miss the closing date for handing them over. In any case write by return because here at the college I've left in suspension the question of giving up the ticket for an immediate return until I know what you've decided. According to how you're writing, I come back immediately, because I don't want to be left here stranded in the middle of the street, so get a move on. Further, get my mother to send me the things she has to, and let me have them straightaway, because otherwise I haven't a change of clothes. In any case don't waste any time so that by the fifth of this month I know something definite. Here's a list of what I need you to send me by fast courier so that they are brought to me at the door, otherwise it'll cost me a fortune:

All the Latin and Greek books that are on the last section of the bookshelf;
The atlases and the Petrocchi dictionary;
The volumes entitled 'Cultura dell'anima' ['Culture of the Soul'];

The volume 'Maine de Biran';[2]
Flamini's Italian literature.

All these books are not just on the bookshelf but on the last part of it, so don't send me everything, as I'd asked Teresina to do, but only these books I've listed; the others can be left where they are.

Then don't forget the shoes, which I need greatly, the collars and so on. Mother should take note of the shirt size in case she has to have others made for me. Remember that the collars are size 14 and don't send me any others that aren't mine, like they have done, given that I've found two collars in the drawer that didn't belong to me, so I've had to buy replacements.

Everything to be sent to the following address: corso Firenze, 57. If I'm not there any more they will forward them to me; likewise for the correspondence, so no longer to a post office box where I never find anything. I'm waiting for a reply from you immediately and then I can then let you have definite news.

If you don't believe that at the college they give me only 70 lire I'll send you a statement from the secretary or the treasurer, so I don't waste time in idle discussion. So I'm expecting your reply. A kiss to everyone at home and best wishes to my friends. I'm now having to go out to carry on my pilgrimage in search of lodgings.

Nino

Turin, 2.XI.911 *Corso Firenze 57*

In particular don't forget the documents that I've told you about, but send a money order to the headmaster without wasting time talking like you usually do.

Nino

Amongst the books, there is also the pack of exercise books that I've got ready.

At the station in Abbasanta make sure they tell you the lowest cost for sending packages to Turin, with all the reductions for the Exhibition, since the question isn't ended yet, and write to me immediately.[3]

Source: AAG; the letter bears the date at the end

To Francesco Gramsci

TURIN, 6. XI. 911

Dearest father,

I'm writing again to urge you to send on the documents and the tuition fees and everything I've written to you about together with a list of the various documents so that if there's something you've overlooked you can see to it without wasting time.

For the exemption of half the fees:[4]

I) Family status / name, age, profession, place of birth, previous places of domicile, and permanent dwelling place of each member of the family, the property and wealth of whatever nature of the individual members, including earnings from their professions etc, both in their Municipality and elsewhere.

II) Certificate from the Tax Authority responsible for all the places mentioned above. These certificates must name all members of the family, and in the certificate there have to be included the taxable income both for their work and for their professional income.[5]

III) The father's declaration that no member of the family possesses any more than is stated in the documentation produced, this former declaration to be franked by the mayor.

For the registration:

1. Birth certificate / legally authenticated.
2. Receipts of payment of registration and admission.
3. 10 lire deposit.
4. 2 recent photographs, without backing.

I'm also sending two forms that you will have to have filled in at the Municipal office. Please do not delay on any account, because I don't know what to do any longer. Without the registration they are not going to hand over to me the 70 lire and I'm broke. I just hope you've sent me the 30 lire, as I asked. Once again I beg of you not to delay, but to send on at once the documents that you have because, if they are the most essential ones, I can register all the same. Best wishes to everyone. Kisses.

Nino

Remember that registration closes on the 15th.

Source: AAG

To Francesco Gramsci

TURIN, 20 XII. 911

Dearest father,

The other day I received the parcel you sent me; my most heartfelt thanks to my mother for the beautiful idea. I think you'll already have received the letter I posted to you before I got Grazietta's, in which I included a list of the books that I wanted; when you can please send them to me. I have to beg you to send me without fail and before the end of the month the 20 lire you'd promised me. This month I've only received 62 lire from the college, out of which I've given 40 to the landlady as an advance on the rent and now by the end of the month I have to hand over another 40 to complete the payment, and I've no idea where the money will come from if you don't send me the 20 lire I need. So I can only beg of you not to forget because if I saw myself thrown out on the street at this time of year I wouldn't know where to turn. I'm already going to have a wretched Christmas and I don't want to make it even grimmer with the vision of walking the streets of Turin in search of some miserable hole with the icy cold up here. I thought this month I might have been able to get myself the overcoat made up because Nannaro sent me 10 lire, but because the college held back the 8 lire I can't do anything and will have to wait until I don't know when. And just think how fine it feels to leave the house and go across the city, shivering like mad, and on returning find the house freezing, and then not be able to warm myself so I stay there a couple of hours, still shivering. If I'd have been able to, believe you me, I wouldn't at any price have chosen to live in this icebox. And the worst is that worry about the cold stops me studying because either I pace up and down the room trying to get my feet warm or I have to wrap myself up like a cocoon, absolutely still because I can't manage to hold a frozen pen.

I hope you won't want to forget about me and that you'll send me what I've asked for straightaway, since otherwise I'm going to find myself in an even grimmer position than now. I hope that all of you have a happy Christmas, not disturbed by the danger of being turned out of your house or having to stamp up and down the rooms trying to get your feet warm

Write immediately. Kisses to all

Nino

Source: AAG

To Francesco Gramsci

TURIN, 3.1 [1912]

Dearest father,

The day before yesterday I received the money order for 15 lire that you telegraphed me and I really am very grateful since, believe me, I really was in deep waters and, after having received your postcard of the 26th, I gave up all hope of receiving the money. I hope that from now on you won't find yourself in financial difficulty because you must believe that, even by making the hardest sacrifices, without your 20 lire I wouldn't be able to go on. I haven't as yet received the certificates of poverty that I asked you for from Sorgono, Ales and your home town.[6] I can't understand why you haven't bothered your head about this and I further don't know if we are still in time, because there was a limit for the documents to be handed in at the Land Registry Office and we're now past that date. I wouldn't like to have to pay 75 lire in March and lose the 35 that have already been paid. Put some pressure on, then, and if we're outside the limit, try through some contact to get them accepted all the same, but do it before the Academic Council meets because after there's no point. I hope your Christmas went well; mine was neither bad nor good.

If you haven't already sent the books off, don't do so any longer because I wouldn't now know what to do with them. I'm sending a list of words:[7] could one of you take on the job of finding the equivalents in Sardinian, but in the Fonni dialect (get the information from someone who knows precisely the pronunciation) and include a clear indication of whether the 's' {ʃ} is voiced {*dolce* ['soft']} as in *rosa* in Italian or voiceless {*sordo*} as in 'sordo' ['deaf'] itself in Italian.[8] Please don't make any mistake, since the task was given me by a professor whose exam I have to do this year, and I don't want to fall down over some silly mistake. As soon as you've written the list down send it on to me straightaway since the professor needs it for a work he's doing in linguistics.[9] Give my thanks to Teresina and Carlo who sent me a card at Christmas; I'll bring Carlo a collection of stamps when I come back in July. Keep me in touch with everybody's news. Kisses

Nino

Remember:

> *s* {ʃ} – when this is pronounced voiced {soft} in the Fonni dialect, as in *rosa* in Italian [as in 'rose' in English – trans. note]
> s – when it's voiceless {hard} as in *sole* in Italian [as in 'sun' in English – trans. note]

Source: AAG

To Teresina Gramsci

[24 NOVEMBER 1912][10]

Dearest Teresina,

Could you please ask someone to answer the following questions and reply by return with the courier service:

1st Whether there exists in the Logudoro[11] dialect the word *pamentile* and whether it means 'pavimento' ['floor'].
2nd Whether there exists the phrase *omine de pore*, which would mean 'uomo di autorità' ['man of authority'].
3rd Whether there exists the word *su pirone* as part of a weighing scale, and if so which part.
4th Whether there exists as the word corresponding to the Italian 'pietraia' ['quarry']: *pedrarza* or whether it is pronounced in some other way.

5th Whether there exists the word *accupintu* meaning 'ricamato' ['embroidered']
6th Whether there exists the word *ispinghinare* = 'sgrassare' ['take off the fat']
7th Whether there exists " " *pinnula*
8th " " " " " *pisu* = 'piano' (of a house etc.) ['storey of a house']
9th Whether in the Campidano dialect[12] one says *piscadrici* for 'pescatrice' ['anglerfish'] or whether this is the name of some sea bird.

I would be very grateful to you if you could reply straightaway. Ask Marcello, too, to ask someone (Father Licheri or some other person who knows about these things and is from the Capo di Sopra).[13]

Kisses

Nino[14]

Source: AAG; postcard

To Giuseppina Marcias

TURIN 13. I. 1913

Dearest mother,

Finally I can write to you after a short period when you heard nothing from me, and I don't wonder that you were worried. If I had to tell you all the things that have happened to me over the last month I would have to write fifty pages which, after all, you wouldn't find all that interesting. What I can say is that on December 22nd I went to bed with the onset of bronchitis, which I finally got over only the day before yesterday, and only now will I be able to go out for the first time in three weeks to post this letter. As you can imagine, the Christmas festivities passed me by without me even noticing them, and it's only now that I can eat the sweets and the cheese that arrived from home a couple of days ago. In the meantime, as you can see, I've not much to rejoice over, because from now on I'll have to be very careful not to go out in the evening, or during the day if there's a lot of fog, so that I don't catch anything else, and this does not take into account that

I fled (exactly that – fled) from the house where I was before because life had got unbearable for me there, and now, without realising it, I've fallen into another house where I'm not much better off and which I'd leave quite willingly if I could find some secure lodgings. But in order to be more or less alright, I'd have to pay a lot more and that's just not possible. In the meantime, please, please talk with father to get him to send me the 10 lire 60 centesimi that I've had to spend on the books for Carlo, because I just can't do without that money. If possible, get him to send me the money at once, as soon as you receive this letter, because I need it really urgently. Believe me that between tuition fees, books and illness, I am not in a good condition at all and I have to find all sorts of supports so as just to carry on. I think that by now Carlo will have returned to Oristano; I'm amazed that he says I haven't written to him, when on the contrary I sent him a letter at the start of December with a stamp enclosed for the reply, a letter to which he has thought fit not to reply for reasons of high-level politics. Today, too, I'm sending you a Latin grammar for Teresina. Tell her that she should let me know what books she has and what she has done up to now. When I know what she needs, I'll try and see to it. I haven't received the wedding invitation from Chicchino Deriu, to whom all the same I send my best wishes and congratulations, with the intention of writing him a long letter on some matter within a few days. From Marcello I've now received a number of very old newspapers; I don't know if he's left for Bologna so I can't reply to him. Send me some family news from Ghilarza and tell Emma that I will quite willingly send her the flower seeds, but I think that we're now past the time for planting them. Please ask Teresina to put together a list for me of all the terms she can think of for bread-making, from when the wheat is taken to the miller's to when the bread is eaten (and if she can she should also include the names of all the parts of the 'mola' [millstone]) and then a list of the words referring to *weaving*; if she wants, she should send me her drawing of a Sardinian loom, done as well as she can, just so as to have an idea, and the name of the part next to the part itself; the list that I wrote down during the vacation is very incomplete; she should do this as thoroughly as she possibly can, then I'll see if there's something missing and write to her. She should also ask for the words for everything about spinning linen, beginning right from when the flax is harvested. I'll be very grateful for this and try to do something for her in return for the trouble I've put her to.

Greetings to everyone who shows some interest in me; kisses to those in the family, and to you, dear mother, lots of kisses

Nino

Try seriously to have the 10 lire 60 sent to me; you must believe that I really do need the money urgently. Maybe one day I'll write to you or tell you in person how it was that Nino Gramsci found himself not being able to do without 10 lire four months after having left his native village with his bundle of belongings.[15]

Nino

Source: AAG

To Teresina Gramsci

TURIN, 26. III. [1913][16]

Dearest Teresina

I think this time you'll have received the 'Italian Grammar' that I've sent you; last time I must have lost it on my way to going to post it, because then I didn't remember whether I actually had posted it or what I did with it, but this time I'm certain that I've sent it and hope it will have arrived.

Please write back as soon as possible when you've obtained the following information:

> whether there exists in Logudorese the word '*pus*' (but *pus* not '*pust*' or '*pustis*') meaning '*poi*' ['then'] in the sense of '*dopo*' ['after']; just simply *pus*, have you got that? Then the same for '*puschena*', and what the meaning is for everything; *portigale* (perhaps meaning 'porticato' ['colonnade']?), *poiu* and *poiolu*. I don't think it will be difficult for you to find out and you can reply by return courier post.[17]

Kisses to everyone

Nino

Let me know something about how your studies are coming along. The same for Carlo, since I haven't heard anything more about him.

Source: AAG

To Attilio Deffenu

GHILARZA, 28 SEPTEMBER [1913]

Dear Deffenu,

I have already sent you … quite some time ago at that, a money order for 2.00 lire as membership fee for the Sardinian Anti-Protectionist League;[18] but up to now, I have heard nothing. If you have not received it, do me the favour of letting me know so that I can complain to the post office.

Best wishes to Alfredo, too.

Antonio Gramsci

Source: Bruno Maiorca (ed.) (2007), Gramsci sardo, antologia e bibliografia. 1903-2006. *Tema: Cagliari, p60.*

To Francesco Gramsci

[LATE NOVEMBER 1913][19]

My dearest father,

I'm writing to you with anger and desperation in my heart. Today has been one of those days that will remain in my mind for ages and unfortunately it's not over yet. It's useless, I've been working as hard as possible for a month and really furiously over the last few days, but now after a crisis that's torn me apart I've come to a decision: I don't want to make my condition any worse, and I don't want to lose completely what I can still hold on to. I am not going to sit the exams because I'm half-mad, or half-stupid, or completely stupid, I don't know which yet, I'm not going to sit the exams so as not to lose the College grant, so as not to be totally ruined, because, dear father, in a month during which I've been studying and working as hard as I can I've done nothing except get spells of dizziness, and get agonising headaches again, on top of a form of cerebral anaemia which makes me lose my memory, which is devastating my brain, and which hour after hour is driving me mad, without my being able to find any relief either by walking up and down or by lying down on the bed or by lying on the ground and in certain moments writhing in fury. Yesterday I (or rather the landlady, frightened out of her wits) had to call the doctor, who gave me a sedative injection; I'm now taking morphine, yes even that, but as well as the trembling that I still have, there's the idea that's tormenting me of the inescapable ruin there in front of me. A companion has persuaded me: I'll see if I can manage to get something by presenting a medical certificate, in the hope that perhaps the professorial commission may decide to let me keep the grant and allow me to take the exams in the March session.[20] In the meantime I have to pay the tuition fees and as such, as best I can – given these circumstances – I've written to you. Have a word immediately with the notary and tell him what the situation is; I had hoped it wouldn't be necessary to go back to him since I already had the promise of doing some private lessons that would have brought me in about fifty lire a month. However it's now quite different since, if I don't pay the tuition fees by the end of November, I'll miss out on the whole year, I'll lose everything, and I'll be forced to come back home, with no alternative, because what else can I do?

Tell the notary all this: he will understand that it's not a trifling light-weight matter; in this case I think even my grandmother would have given her whole-hearted consent. And what I'm begging of you is to do all this just as soon as you humanly can, since every day that goes by in this appalling torture is a day in hell for me: think well on this, father, because it really is a serious state of affairs, it's a question of sending me forward or cutting the ground from under me, and not just as regards studies. And bear in mind that I don't have even the smallest coin in my pocket, that the 15 centesimi it costs to send this letter are the last I have and that the landlady will show me the door at the end of the month; try to do something in some way, then, because I'm no longer master of myself and I don't know what to think or what I can manage to do. If you have already sent me the 45 lire I asked for, have the notary send the 120 lire for the fees;[21] if not, add that sum on, but I hope you won't have waited until now.

Father, I don't know what else to add. I hope that this time you won't neglect things and you'll get down to doing what is necessary. I would like to instil into you the anxiety that I am feeling and something of the desperation that is torturing me; and, let me say again, do things just as soon as is possible, in the hope that it's not too late and the damage has not already been done. To struggle, and not to see that there is a hope of better times, at the same time as all the difficulties of money, health and life in general, and then on top of this the neglect of one's own relatives, believe me this is not something that can be put up with indefinitely.

Kisses

Nino

Source: AAG

To the Administrative Council of the Royal Carlo Alberto College

To the Administrative Council of the R[oyal] Carlo Alberto College
Turin

The undersigned, pupil of the royal foundation of the Carlo Alberto College, having been seriously ill, was not able to sit the examinations for the year 1913 relative to the second [year] course in Letters, and, having notified the Secretary, Adv[ocate] L. Aceto of this fact, requests to be exonerated from all responsibility

Turin, 4 December 1913

Antonio Gramsci

Source: State Archives, University of Turin, Royal Carlo Alberto College, Competitors' fascicule, XI F 7, p1

To Grazietta Gramsci

[MID-1914][22]

Dear Grazietta,

I hope these lines find you still at Oristano. You say you've written to me on a number of occasions. I give you my word that, when I replied to you, it was the first time that I'd received any news directly from you. You have to believe, my god, that I'm less indifferent and less lazy than it might appear to some people; I am not enormously expansive and often it takes a lot to write an affectionate word, but this will not come as any great surprise either to you or the others at home. Lots of kisses for Uncle Serafino's little daughter and my greetings to all the uncles and the cohorts of aunts, and tell them they should write to me some time and that I will reply; writing to everyone is however impossible, and it isn't polite to choose between so many.[23] So, if it really matters to someone that I'm alive and kicking, I'm waiting expectantly to know who, but I don't believe it a great deal. Innumerable kisses to you

Nino

(Source: AAG; Picture postcard from an art exhibition in Venice)

NOTES

1. At this point there about 20 words regarding the ticket are crossed out.
2. Giovanni Amendola had given a series of lectures in 1911 on the French philosopher Maine de Biran, which were then collected together in book form; *Cultura dell'anima* was a series of philosophically-oriented books edited by Giovanni Papini.
3. Special rail discounts were being offered for passengers and goods going to Turin for its National Exhibition celebrating the fiftieth anniversary of Italian unification; Abbasanta was the mainline station serving the Gramsci family's nearby village of Ghilarza.
4. In a letter a couple of days previously Gramsci told his family he was exempt only from half of the tuition fees, and not the whole as had been thought.
5. The Italian here is very unclear. Gramsci (1992) contains an unacknowledged editorial addition of the word (shown in italics below), thereby giving the meaning that the members of the family must be included 'both for work ('industrie') and for professional income *and* taxable income'. The version here follows the manuscript by omitting this word, thereby making 'taxable income for both work and professional income' the subject of a plural verb, ungrammatical especially in Italian.
6. Gramsci's father was born in Gaeta, on the coast between Rome and Naples, but spent most of his adult life in Ghilarza.
7. This list has not survived.
8. Fonni was an isolated shepherd village, just north of the highest parts of the central Sardinian Gennargentu mountains, and about 30 kilometres east of Ghilarza. The village's isolation meant that its dialect was a 'living fossil' of great interest to linguistic historians.
9. This is the first reference to Gramsci's linguistics work and to his pro-

fessor, Matteo Bartoli. The examples in brace brackets [{] respect the words and sounds intended in the original; the literal translations ('hard' and 'soft') of the sound of the 's' are not, however, those used by phonologists in English.

10. The date is that on the postcard.
11. The Logudoro district, stretching in a belt from the west to the east coast, starting just below the northern city of Sassari, was one of the four historic parts of medieval Sardinia and is where the Sardinian language shows the greatest influence of Latin.
12. The Campidanese dialects – distinct from Logudorese – cover the whole south of the main island of Sardinia, from about the Gulf of Oristano in the west to Lanusei in the east; there are also other less important dialect regions.
13. Fr Michele Licheri was the author of a book on the civil and ecclesiastical history of Ghilarza; the 'Capo di Sopra' ['Upper Cape'] refers to the province of Sassari.
14. Teresina's reply has not survived. Gramsci was trying to study but, in a letter now in the Turin University archives, written just four days after the postcard to Teresina, he asked to delay the examinations because of a nervous breakdown involving 'crises of weakness and of memory'; see below, endnote 20.
15. The 10 lire 60 mentioned, which came from his tuition of a high school student during the 1912 summer vacation (Fiori, 1970, p80), was duly sent to Gramsci, together with other much-welcome money.
16. The card is franked with the date 31. III.1913, and arrived at Ghilarza two days later.
17. Teresina's reply of 3 April is now in a typewritten transcription in the AAG: '*Pus* – does not exist – in Logudorese it is "poi"; *Poiu* – means stagnant water in small quantities and for a quantity of non-flowing water is called *pischina*. *Puschena* – does not exist. *Portigale* – means "porticato" but is not used in Logudorese'.
18. Gramsci's membership of the Anti-Protectionist League is confirmed in the membership list published in *La Voce*, Vol V, No 41, 9 October 1913, p1175.
19. Date deduced from internal evidence.
20. The College executive council minutes for 19 February 1914 state that Gramsci had been unable to take any examination due to what a medical certificate described as a 'grave form of neurosis', but that he wished to catch up with his examination schedule in the special March session. The College had temporarily to withdraw his grant 'to be restored to him in its entirety' on passing the previous sessions' examinations in Greek, Modern History and 'one other examination of his choice', which he did by passing Modern History (27/30), Moral Philosophy (25/30) and Greek culture (24/30), the latter delayed from March to a few days after

the 14 April Executive meeting that restored his grant. See Zucàro (1957), pp1100-1102.

21. Francesco Gramsci, replying to his son in an understanding and affectionate tone (letter of 28 November 1913, now in the AAG), told him that 25 lire had already been sent on the 24th of the month and the 120 lire had been sent by telegraph on 27 November, the day before he wrote.
22. The postcard, without a stamp or date, was probably in an envelope. The exhibition where it was bought ran from spring to autumn 1914, indicating mid-year as the probable time of writing.
23. Gramsci (1992) has this as 'costs me a lot' ('mi è costoso') but actually it is 'is not polite' ('non è cortese').

3. Revolutionary Journalist: *Avanti!* and *L'Ordine Nuovo*

To Grazietta Gramsci

[1916]

My dearest Grazietta,

I have just now received your letter. And I feel deeply saddened since I feel that you at home have lost confidence in me and think that I may be dishonouring myself in some way. I never thought that such a doubt could enter the minds of my brothers and sisters and my parents.[1] I thought you knew and understood me better than that. But let that be. The fault is mine, I feel that, and I ought to have behaved differently. I should not have shut myself off from life in the way that I did. For two years I have lived outside this world, in something of a dream. One by one, I have let all the threads that bound me to life and to people be severed. I have lived everything for the mind and nothing for the heart. Perhaps this has been because my mind has suffered, because my head has been racked with pain the whole time, and I have ended up by being able to think only of this. And not for what regards you, only, but for the whole of my life. (For two years I have lived an entirely self-centred existence, for my own self-centred suffering.) Inside and out, I have become more like a bear than a man. It has been for me as if other people did not exist and I was a wolf in its lair. But I have worked. I have worked, maybe too much, more than my physical strength allowed. I have worked to live, while to live I should have rested, should have enjoyed myself. Perhaps in two years I have never laughed, just as I have never wept either. I have sought to overcome physical weakness by working, and I have weakened myself even further. For at least three years I have not lived a single day without a headache, without my head spinning, without a dizzy spell. But I have harmed no-one, except myself. I have never done anything for which I can reproach myself. And, in my conditions, I do not know how many other people might say that.

I would like to know this acquaintance of yours who didn't want to introduce himself. He must really be very silly, not to say a complete fool. I'd like to know who it is just to know one more fool, to see someone who really must be a complete and utter fool. Maybe it would be me who didn't want to introduce myself to him, so as not to soil my own conscience and soul. I'm sorry for your suffering on account of words and stupid idle chatter. And I'm holding you to it to tell me who this man is; I'm making this a question of esteem and affection. But let that be.

I have to say that my life is miserable only as regards my conscience, in the feeling I have about not being able to conquer my weakness and produce as much work as is necessary for me to live and be free to work for myself and my future, instead of living a hand-to-mouth existence. I can tell you that if I always felt well I would have the possibility of earning as much as 500 lire a month. What hurts is being alone, always having to trust others, having to live in the trattoria, spending a lot just to live badly. If I were sure of my health and of steady work and earnings, I could have one of you come to Turin and I would be better all round. But can I take on the responsibility of possibly making other people suffer? This thought has always stopped me from speaking to you of the possibility of one of you coming to Turin.

But I feel that perhaps the time has now come for taking a decision, I can't stay as I am for much longer without making up my mind. I'll write to Mario to see what he wants to do. I would not need much, and it would be just for a time. What I need is to have a little free time that I can devote more seriously to studies, while at the moment it is only my spare time that I can give over to them. I'll write to Mario myself to see if something definite can be arrived at. I fear however that you are getting frightened by gossip and letting yourself be influenced too much by other people's idle chatter.

I'll write again in a few days' time. I can't add anything more now because I have to work and because I'm tired. Kisses to everyone, for you especially, dear Grazietta, and for mother.

Nino

Source: AAG; handwritten on headed notepaper of Avanti!

Gramsci and others to Ezio Bartalini

[TURIN, 5 NOVEMBER 1916]

Private Ezio Bartalini[2]
1st Garrison Company, 9th Battalion
Fosse di S. Anna d'Alfaedo, to be forwarded to him
Verona

Believe us, we're sorry about the eyebrows, but the thought of the beard makes us hate any sign of hairiness on your part. And when are you making the supreme sacrifice? Waiting for your reply, we salute you and wish you all possible good.

A. Gramsci
G. Emanuel
Andrea Viglongo

And up with the beard!
Bucci Bruno

Source: AAG

To Angelo Corsi

TURIN, 22 OCTOBER [1917]

Dear Comrade Corsi[3]

Comrade Sotgia of Iglesias often talks to me of your cordiality and your love for the treatment of the concrete problems that form part of our party's programme, and so I've resolved to write to you. I already knew you a little by name – I've read one of your articles in *Avanti!* and one in Prezzolini's *Voce* some years ago and I've followed through *Sardegna Socialista* your assiduous work as mayor and provincial councillor. Given that the Turin party branch has temporarily given me the responsibility of editing the *Grido del Popolo*, I would be very pleased to be able to publish an article by you.[4] I am sending to you separately the issue of the *Grido* devoted to the tariff question. Would you be able to write something on this for us? I would be very grateful to you for this, and our readers equally so. Could you personally also write something on the political-economic movement of the Sardinian proletariat? Or if not, would you be so good as to ask someone else who is capable to take this on? I believe it would be of great use to have the new Sardinia known in the North of Italy, and I think we are also duty-bound to do this, so as to better strengthen the united consciousness of the Italian proletariat.

I await your reply. Comrade Sotgia sends his greetings

Yours sincerely

Antonio Gramsci

Corso Siccardi 12, Turin

Source: photographic reproduction in Angelo Corsi (L'azione socialista tra i minatori della Sardegna 1898-1922, *Edizioni della Comunità: Milan, pp176-7; Handwritten on headed notepaper of the Turin edition of Avanti!*

To Oddino Morgari

TURIN, 29 DECEMBER 1917

Dear Morgari[5]

Our last plenary branch meeting voted unanimously to express to you its congratulations and its solidarity on the occasion of the speech you recently made in the Chamber of Deputies and the attacks and insults you were subject to.

In particular there are to be added to the vote of the branch meeting those of its executive committee and of the Turin editorial staff of *Avanti!*

Please accept out warmest greetings

Antonio Gramsci

Source: Central State Archives, Morgari papers, Sc. 12, F. 7, SF. 10, ins. 29, as reproduced in the Rivista storica del socialismo, Vol.10, no. 32, 1967, p187

To Leo Galetto

[TURIN, FEBRUARY 1918]

My dear Galetto,

I am enclosing the manuscript. There's no need to ask how you are. You're obviously bursting with health since you're in such good spirits: mens sana in corpore sano.[6] Pastore and I are managing fairly well as you can see from the Turin page; we're working hard. Are you getting the *Grido*? Write and give me your opinion and Serrati's about the form I'm trying to give it. You should of course take into consideration the intermittent and at the same time oppressive nature of our work, given the restrictions in the use of electricity and, as a consequence, both discontinuity and haste in typesetting. See if you can get hold of some numbers of *Verité* for me, together with *Vague* and *Europe nouvelle*, as well as the newspaper *Sardegna*.

Best wishes

A. Gramsci

Down with Esperanto! Tell Serrati that he was wrong to call me a 'Purist'. Purism is a rigidified and mechanical linguistic form and therefore the mentality of the purist is similar to that of the Esperantist. I am a revolutionary, a *historicist*, and therefore claim that the only forms of social (linguistic, economic, political) activity that are *useful* and rational are those which arise spontaneously and reach fruition through the action of free social energies. So I say … down with Esperanto, just as I say down with all privileges, all mechanistic approaches, all rigidified and sclerotic life forms, corpses that attack and infect life as it is developing.

All best wishes to Serrati

Gramsci
Panta rei!
        Heraclitus
Everything moves[7]
        (Trans.) Gramsci

Source: AAG; handwritten on plain paper

To Giuseppe Lombardo-Radice

[TURIN, MARCH 1918][8]

Dear sir,

I have pleasure in sending to you an article that my colleague, Andrea Viglongo, has written for the *Grido del Popolo* on your booklet *Il concetto dell'educazione* [*The Concept of Education*]. Viglongo is a self-taught young man and this will explain to you why there are certain contradictions and a lack of precision in his article. I know and admire the work that you have been undertaking for the spiritual rebirth of Italian youth and it is on this account that I am now writing to you, wishing to inform you of the work, limited though it may be, that we socialists are attempting to do here in Turin, a city dismissed in Italy as the kingdom of proletarian and defeatist bestiality and stupidity. I think your goodness and kindness have kept you free of the current epidemic-scale contagion of degeneration. To have a different conception of the task that the socialist proletariat must fulfil during the war cannot be allowed to cancel mutual respect.

We in Turin believe that simply preaching about the principles and moral precepts that will of necessity come to fruition in the coming of a socialist civilisation is insufficient. We have instead sought to give life to this preaching through what (for Italy) are new examples of organisational forms, and thus a *Club for Moral Life* has recently come into being. Our aim is to get young people who become involved in the socialist economic and political movement to become used to the objective, unbiased discussion of social and ethical questions. We want to get them used to research, to disciplined and methodical reading, to the simple and calm exposition of their convictions. The work proceeds as follows: as founder of the association, I have had to accept the duties of sentinel, and it is up to me to assign a *task* to each of the young people, be it your short book on education, or a chapter of Benedetto Croce's *Culture and Modern Life*, or Salvemini's *Educational and Social Problems*, or again Salvemini's *French Revolution* or *Culture and Laicity*, the *Communist Manifesto*, or a 'Postilla' ['Commentary'] of Croce's from *La Critica* or some other publication which however shows some influence of the present-day idealist movement.[9] The young person reads, sketches out formally what to say and then, before his fellow members, expounds the results of his research and reflections on the topic. One of those present, who has read up the subject matter, or I myself, give the other side of the case and put forward different solutions, and broaden out the field with some concept or line of reasoning. Thus a discussion opens up and we try not to close it until *everyone* present has been able to understand and adopt the most important results of our joint labours. In addition to this, the *Club* has among its aims that the members should mutually exercise a check over the activity of everyone, in the family, in the workplace, in their daily routine. We would like to reach a situation such that everyone should have sufficient moral fibre and courage to *confess* publicly, accepting that their friends should advise and exercise some control over them; we want to create mutual trust, the intellectual and moral communion of everyone.[10]

Viglongo's article is the result of one of our sessions; he is a seventeen-year-old clerical worker in the private sector who has not gone beyond the level of junior middle technical school. In the *Grido* there have so far appeared one article on Croce's *Faith and programmes*, and Croce's own *Sensual nationalism*. Viglongo is now preparing another on the *Southern question,* basing himself on Salvemini's writings.[11]

I should be very grateful if you, who follow with interest all the new educational experiments, would have the goodness to write and give us your judgement on our attempt, which certainly is not establishing itself and developing without some difficulty. The youngsters are all workers, and indeed the socialism of Turin is near-exclusively working-class, with the few university students far away on military duty. Although the Club members are intelligent and willing, we have to begin with the simplest and most elementary things: with language itself. Would it be possible for you to help by giving me some advice, suggesting an approach that would flesh out and complete my proposals, and showing me some of the errors into which I may fall? I would be very grateful indeed, and my young friends would gain new force from your words in order to continue and strengthen their will.[12]

Your most obedient servant

Antonio Gramsci

Corso Siccardi 12 – Turin

Source: Rinascita, *7 March 1964; the letter is not in the Lombardo-Radice archives, while the photocopy in the Gramsci Institute is no longer legible.*

To Carlo Gramsci

19. 11. 1918

My dearest Carlo,

My best wishes on your promotion. Remember that this imposes duties and responsibilities on you. Every single thing that we take on in life we must try to carry out in the most perfect way possible. Your obligations have increased, not decreased; you will have to study and, through good will and work, make up for the inexperience due to your youth and the interruption of your studies. You will have to feel these duties even more keenly in so far as they involve the safety and life of others entrusted to your capacities and competence.

Very affectionate kisses

Nino

Source: AAG; handwritten postcard

To Giacinto Menotti Serrati

TURIN, 21 FEBRUARY [1920]

My dearest Serrati,

I have to beg your pardon a thousand times for being so late in replying. I've been punished automatically for this by the publication of the 'Scampolo' ['Polemic'], which was then republished in '*Battaglie Sindacali*' ['*Trade Union Battles*'].

I am not the editor of *L'Ordine Nuovo*; the question of editorship has been put off until May Day 1920, and was posed to try and remove any power I had to consign to the waste paper basket articles by that group of comrades who have been collaborating from the start. Our good Leonetti is greatly exaggerating in *Compagni* ['*Comrades*'] when he says that the *O[rdine] N[uovo]* group has managed to put together a 'guild' of experts. Your letter is coming out in the current number of *L'O[rdine] N[uovo]* accompanied by a note of Terracini's; the next number will be dedicated to the general tactics of the Party and the Unions. I have a note all ready to justify your position: 'If the bourgeoisie offer us 10, we must demand 100', in other words to whatever offer made by the bourgeoisie we must counterpose our revolutionary programme. By a cheap hackneyed formula Terracini has impoverished a tactical thesis that will be of exceptional use up to the moment of the revolutionary act and probably afterwards, too, that is to say right up to the real expulsion of the capitalists from the process of production and exchange; in the note Terracini will not receive kid-glove treatment.[13]

The situation in Turin is becoming clearer. We of *L'O[rdine] N[uovo]* have had to assume a clear position on the elections for the E[xecutive] Com[mission] of the party branch. There is a twofold division in our ranks, with Togliatti and myself on one side and Terracini and Tasca on the other. My support, together with that of Togliatti and Matta, for the abstentionist line does not however mean that we favour abstentionism as a matter of principle. We carried out an immense amount of propaganda work to stem the propaganda in favour of a split, and had succeeded in convincing the majority of the abstentionist fraction; the electoral Committee had accepted a programmatic agreement, and then, suddenly, in order to favour the manoeuvres of certain people, the agreement was broken, the programme was changed, and the list for the E[xecutive] C[ommittee] was drawn up, with some very wily right-wing elements included, together with a majority of maximalists, good comrades but lacking the necessary will and with no critical spirit.[14] Bordiga was in Turin to bring back into the fold the sheep led astray by *L'O[rdine] N[uovo]*; we – Togliatti, Matta and myself – took on the responsibility of demonstrating the possibility of an agreement on the basis of concrete and positive work.[15]

For your 'Scampolo' column, I would ask you to note that neither I nor others have given interviews to any bourgeois newspaper.[16] *La Stampa* and the *Corriere* have published articles based on cuttings from *O[rdine] N[uovo]*, something that we could certainly not prevent. As regards our collaboration, neither Togliatti nor I have ever wanted to misuse our position on the editorial staff to include signed articles and acquire the reputation of 'initiators' and 'promoters'. Our work has been directed towards persuading the Socialist Party branch and the C[hamber] of L[abour] [Trades Council] to take on the task of initiating and guiding the movement of the [factory] Councils and in this we have succeeded. We want neither 'credit' nor 'responsibility' for a movement of this type, which has value only in so far as it is the expression of the broad masses. The only 'responsibility' that we can assume is an intellectual responsibility regarding those who challenge us and a political responsibility within the party. Were we wrong in not having written in *Avanti!*? If you think that articles of ours may be of use, let us know and Togliatti and I will write them. I am preparing the article for *Comunismo* and, in so far as I am able, I would like to do it well.[17]

My dear Serrati, if I have offended you in some way, do not hesitate to tell me openly and to 'preach me a sermon': I have a lot, even too much, to learn (and I do not say this out of modesty, because I don't give two hoots about modesty!) and your advice and counsel as a loyal and open-minded comrade can only be of value to me. If you think fit, publish a short correction regarding the business of the interviews, which I want in no way to have on my conscience.

Cordially yours

Gramsci

Source: AAG; handwritten on headed notepaper of the Piedmontese edition of Avanti!

To Jules Humbert-Droz

TURIN, 3 JANUARY 1921[18]

Dear citizen Humbert-Droz,

For a communist review whose first number will appear on 15 January, the day of our national congress in Livorno, we would ask you to send us a report on the last Congress of the Swiss Social Democratic Party and its consequences for the movement in Switzerland.

With communist greetings,

Antonio Gramsci

Source: Humbert-Droz archives (in French)

APPENDIX TO CHAPTER 3

Report of Gramsci's speech (29 November 1920) at the Conference in Imola of the communist fraction of the Italian Socialist Party

Gramsci observed that we have come to this conference with the psychology of those taking part in the constitution of a party. This is our state of mind. Furthermore, the Unitarians too are tending towards being a party – but one similar to the social revolutionaries in Russia. Perhaps it is not by chance that Serrati, at the start of the Russian Revolution, saw its personification in Černov, the petty bourgeois opportunist adversary of Lenin.[19]

Gramsci expressed the opinion, as did Bordiga, that the discussion should not have the aim of being a polemic with the other fractions. We must insist on propaganda in the work to be carried out in order to arrive at the communist party in Italy.

He did not share the idea of a social democratic phase in Italy; we are, he said, much nearer the phase of the conquest of power by the proletariat.

The speaker came out in favour of the name 'Communist' for the party. He answered some of the objections made by Caroti, who also said that we should not worry about bringing the intermediate fractions over to our side.[20] The Unitarians are in actual fact counter-revolutionaries. It is a useful tactic to push them to the right in order to be better able to unmask them (*great applause*).

Source: communist fraction's weekly publication, Il Comunista, 6 December 1920

NOTES

1. Probably to underline the significance of these lines, someone else, possibly a family member, added square brackets from 'and think that I may be dishonouring myself' to 'my parents', as well as putting a double vertical bar ('||') at the start and end of the first paragraph.
2. Bartalini was a fellow-socialist and a fellow-student of Gramsci's, and tells how, when Gramsci was still 'more a philologist than a revolutionary', they sometimes worked together in his 'poor student's room': see Gramsci (1976), p180.
3. Corsi became secretary of the Anti-Protectionist League, and contributed to the Florentine periodical *La Voce*; on returning to Sardinia he became a union organiser, mayor of the mining town of Iglesias and, seven years later, in 1921, parliamentary deputy.

4. The paper's editor, Maria Giudice, a primary school teacher and mother of eight, had been arrested, so Gramsci, as assistant editor, took over from her, paying much attention to the growing revolutionary situation in Russia: see Fiori (1970), pp101 and 114.
5. Later on Morgari was to write officially from the Italian Socialist Party, when it was still (at least in its words) unanimous in wishing to join the Comintern (declaration of 18 March 1919), expressing 'to Bolshevism [the Party's] enthusiastic, grateful and unqualified sympathy, which is fully shared by all thinking members of the Italian proletariat' (letter of 3 March 1919: see the Comintern review *The Communist International* for that year, p29).
6. 'A healthy mind in a healthy body'.
7. Often translated as 'all is in flux'. This and other comments of Heraclitus on the world as a process ('you cannot step into the same river twice') rather than a static object are quoted favourably in Marx's doctoral thesis.
8. Date added later by hand.
9. Idealist here is used in its philosophical sense; it should be remembered that Marx's philosophically materialist stance was still not yet clearly understood in the workers' movement, and that a main struggle of would-be revolutionaries in Italy was at that time against positivism; and that aspects of Croce's idealism seemed for a time to represent a way out of the impasse.
10. This is perhaps the earliest explicit reference we have to the famous 'intellectual and moral reform' motif, a key concept of the *Prison Notebooks*.
11. The article 'Sensual nationalism' had only just been published in the first months of 1918 in Croce's review *La Critica*; it is now in his book *Pagine sulla guerra* (*Pages on the war*). The other article 'Faith and programmes' dates to 1911 and is in his *Cultura e vita morale* (*Culture and moral life*). Gaetano Salvemini's *Problemi educativi e sociali dell'Italia di oggi* (*Educational and social problems of present-day Italy*) was published in 1914.
12. Gramsci was given short shrift by Lombardo-Radice, in a post-card from the military front in which he criticised the 'bad faith' and 'abstractness' of the socialist officers, claiming that Mazzinian-type action was needed against Germany 'for the Fatherland and for the Fatherlands'.
13. *L'Ordine Nuovo* of 21 February 1920 (see *L'Ordine Nuovo*, 1976) published a letter from Serrati denying that he had ever said that one had to 'demand 100 lire to get 10 lire from the bourgeoisie', as well as Terracini's rejoinder claiming that this was certainly the spirit of Serrati's position. Gramsci's intended note, critical of Terracini, never apparently saw the light of day.

14. No substantial difference is made in this letter between 'Executive Committee' and 'Executive Commission'; unlike in other letters, there is no indication here as to which form is actually being used.
15. On the suggestion of Gramsci's *Ordine Nuovo* group, the new Executive of the Turin branch of the Socialist Party approved near-unanimously an alliance with Bordiga's abstentionists, against the reformists representing the trade union bureaucracy. Angelo Tasca, of the right of the *Ordine Nuovo* group, attempted to make an alliance with the reformists, but this failed when an improvised list of eight abstentionists and three '*Ordinovisti*' (Togliatti, Matta and Gramsci) won. The Executive thus elected, as Gramsci notes, then 'had the honour of leading the April 1920 strike': see Gramsci (1978a), pp187-90, especially p188.
16. The editorial of *L'Ordine Nuovo* of 21 February 1920 replied to this charge by Serrati, explaining that no interview had ever been given to bourgeois press organs.
17. The promised article for this review of Serrati's was never published, and presumably was not sent in.
18. At the moment this is the only letter of Gramsci's of 1921 that is known.
19. Serrati was one of the leaders of the 'unitarians', who were later known as the 'maximalists'.
20. Caroti had said there were 'considerable rural masses in the [Socialist] Party, whom we have to try to attract to our side; what will we say to them about our programme regarding the land question, a matter of direct concern to them? We cannot ignore this'.

4. Comintern leader in Moscow

Gramsci and Zinov'ev to the Executive Committee of the PCI

3 JUNE 1922

The Presidium of the Executive Committee of the Communist International has become convinced that, precisely in relation to the most recent events within the Italian Socialist Party, the present moment is the most favourable one for launching among the masses the slogan of the 'workers' government' as it also is for taking the strongest possible initiative in the fight against fascism, through a call to the workers of all parties.[1] We ask you to do this as soon as possible. We await your reply.

Zinov'ev

Gramsci

Source: APC 513-1-081/88, and copy in 513-1-080/82; typewritten in French, with handwritten signatures and the stamp of the Comintern)

Gramsci and Ambrogi to Zinov'ev

MOSCOW, 10 JULY 1922

To Comrade Zinov'ev, President of the Comintern

We have sent a telegram to the Executive of the PCI to inform the Party of the decisions taken by the Presidium regarding comrade Maffi's journey to Moscow and in general to have instructions on the method it is thought most suitable to adopt regarding the relations between the Comintern and the Maffi-Lazzari-Riboldi fraction.[2]

The Italian Executive has replied to us confirming its point of view, namely the one already outlined by comrade Gramsci in the meeting of the Presidium and then repeated in the personal talks that the

Italian delegation had with you. In our view, the news that comrade Maffi will not be coming to Moscow does not change the general situation.

Any step taken by the International independently of the PCI may create difficulties for the latter in attaining the goals that the International has set. The Party has by now demonstrated its firm willingness to carry out the undertakings agreed to by comrade Bordiga at the session of the Enlarged Executive Committee.[3] Further to this, the manifesto published by the Maffi fraction in the lead-up to the Rome Congress, a manifesto that was directed in particular against Serrati's maximalists, shows that the present communist fraction of the PSI has been forced to assume the same precise attitude that had previously been assumed by the Imola fraction before the Livorno Congress.[4]

Through the current development of the crisis in the P.S.I., the comrades of the Maffi fraction, too, have understood that the Serrati fraction absolutely does not want to split off from the reformists, and that all its attempts to give rise to the idea that it might instead want a split in the reformists have one sole scope: that of hindering the growth of a strong communist fraction within the P.S.I. and thus reducing to the minimum the inevitable leftward split.

Essentially, the Maffi fraction has already broken off relations with that of Serrati. At the national council of the CGL, the Maffi fraction voted along with the PCI, even though Serrati's maximalists were there at the Council with their own group, and put forward a motion aimed at putting the reformists in a minority.

We believe that the Comintern's relations with the Maffi fraction must pass solely through the agency of the PCI, or in any case by means of prior agreement with it, among other things for organisational and political reasons in general.

The organisational forces of the Maffi fraction are very thin on the ground and the fraction has very little spirit of initiative. It has a sizeable following in only four out of seventy provinces in Italy. In the other provinces it has just single individual followers or very small groups which can be organised only if the fraction is linked to an organisation that already exists at the national level as the PCI does. Only a systematic plan of action agreed between the Maffi fraction and the CP before the Congress in Rome will be able to organise a split within the socialists in such a way as to be politically useful for the Comintern.

The disintegration of the S[ocialist] P[arty] that began at the Livorno Congress then continued after the Milan Congress, without the proletarian and revolutionary elements who left the SP becoming organically assimilated by the communist movement.[5] From the Milan Congress up to today, the SP has lost 50% of its members (from 120 thousand members it has dropped to less than 60 thousand) and of these just two or three thousand have spontaneously gone over to the CP.

And it is not that the CP's tactics can be held responsible for this, since, although the Party did not want to assume direct responsibility for organising a fraction, neither did it adopt a hostile attitude to any such organisation, and its press did not fail to suggest any proposal that could serve to make such a fraction useful to the communist movement.

During the Milan Congress the communist journals published an open letter to comrade Lazzari expressing the delight that all sincere revolutionaries felt in seeing the old fighter for the Italian Revolution lining up with the Communist International.

Com. Lazzari replied privately insulting the CP and stating that never would he join its ranks.[6] Obviously the fraction had been constituted at Milan by the Comintern representative without any precise directive and without any overall plan of action.[7] Only over the last few months, through the insistence of the communist newspapers, has the Maffi fraction decided to organise work of its own in the trade unions in agreement with the CP. This work too, which is of very great use, and must be aimed at avoiding the split in the unions wanted by the reformists, must and can be extended on a large scale only in so far as direct relations are established between the Maffi fraction and the PCI, under the control and following the lines of the International.

We are convinced that you will want to take this argument of ours into account and will want to aid our party in its effort to broaden its sphere of influence among the Italian proletariat.

The Italian delegation to the Comintern

A. Gramsci

E. Ambrogi

Source: APC 513-1-166/18-20; typewritten, with the words 'The Italian delegation to the Comintern' and the signatures handwritten

To Karl Radek

MOSCOW 22 JULY 1922

Dear Comrade Radek,

I have read the manifesto to the Italian workers. I approve it in its general lines. I cannot approve the part that deals personally with Serrati. Instead of obtaining a split in the SP, with this part included it will bring about a split in the communist movement. Serrati does not have one single worker of the masses behind him, just his own party fraction, which itself is not even made up of workers, but of trade union officials and local councillors.

Serrati cannot speak in public; he is hooted down by all the workers, not just by the communists. The part regarding Serrati can be modified by having it refer to the 'maximalists' in general.[8]

I would ask you to accept these points, which for me are of fundamental importance and without which I cannot agree to the manifesto.

Communist greetings

signed: Antonio Gramsci

Source: APC 513-1-091/1; typewritten with copies on following pages and also in APC 513-1-166/22

Gramsci and Ambrogi to the Executive of the PCI

MOSCOW, 4 AUGUST 1922[9]

To the Executive of the Italian Communist Party – Rome

We here propose to explain to you in detail the work we have been doing and the resolution of the various cases of dissent with the E[xecutive] as regards the Maffi fraction and in general the crisis of the P.S.I.

We think it is useful here to send you a copy of the translation of a letter written by Chiarini, from which it is clear that he was doing things behind the back of the Italian Party, in the full knowledge that this work was absolutely contrary to our Party's tactical plan.

The discussion that opened began first with the decision to invite Maffi to Moscow to negotiate directly with the C[ommunist] I[nternational]. We argued that it was better not to take Maffi away from the work of preparing the Congress and insisted above all that no step should be taken without the knowledge and agreement of the Italian Party. Gramsci maintained this stance in private conversation with com. Zinov'ev and afterwards at the meeting of the Presidium; despite the fact that Gramsci was convinced that he had reached an agreement with Zinov'ev, the Presidium unhesitatingly resolved to invite Maffi. Gramsci then spoke immediately with Ambrogi and the two were in total agreement that a new approach should be made to Zinov'ev, with this time Ambrogi going to see him. Com. Zinov'ev, however, raised the objection that a decision had already been taken by the Presidium, which Gramsci had not opposed (which is not exact as may be seen from the letter – copy included – that we then wrote to Zinov'ev), and that the question could eventually be raised at the E[xecutive]. This latter suggestion we thought was completely useless, because a way would be found of making dissent appear in the Delegation where no such dissent existed.

All that we could obtain agreement to was that the Italian Party would be *informed* of the steps taken by the I[nternational] vis-à-vis the Maffi fraction. Before the session of the E[xecutive] we again spoke with com. Zinov'ev, but to no avail.[10] We therefore sent you a telegram and following your reply we wrote the above-mentioned letter.

After much wavering between yes and no, Maffi reached Berlin and from there was sent back to Italy. Only just now have we received news from Berlin, which we shall send on to you as soon as we can.

In the meantime news reached us of the position Serrati has taken in regard to the reformists, decidedly in favour of a split. The question then hinged on the attitude that the Maffi fraction should then assume; whether, in other words, it should not hesitate to split off or whether it should remain with the party, shorn of the reformists. We, with just half a Czechoslovak vote (Ilič) in our favour, supported the first thesis.[11]

It was therefore decided that the fraction should not split off, and that immediately after the Congress it should send a Delegation to Moscow to decide what should be done; and it was also decided to publish a manifesto to be drawn up by Gramsci and Radek. But

Gramsci's conditions of health (he had developed a fever due to malaria) meant he had to go into convalescence outside Moscow and did not allow him to complete the draft, as had been agreed. The manifesto was thus written by Radek and the text communicated as a matter of urgency the same day that it was to be sent. Ambrogi went to see Gramsci immediately to go over the manifesto together and, since it contained a reference to Serrati, we decided to oppose it. Gramsci himself wrote a letter to Radek, a copy of which is included, and Ambrogi was delegated to confer with Radek.[12] But Radek was out of Moscow, and the manifesto was sent off just as it was; a telegram followed saying it was not to be published before new confirmation. Two days later Ambrogi was able to confer with Radek. It was agreed that, by telegram, the manifesto should be modified in the sense that where Serrati or his followers were called on to act, that invitation should instead be directed to the maximalists, while leaving unaltered all the part that constituted an attack on Serrati. Radek, however, did not hide the fact that this was a way of drawing a veil over affairs, the real plan being to draw Serrati into the International, since behind him there were in fact revolutionary workers.[13]

We are not going to repeat here the discussion that took place, since Radek stated he was expressing his own personal point of view, and the discussion was taken up again by Ambrogi at the last meeting of the Presidium. In any case A[mbrogi] went off immediately to confer with Gramsci, and it was understood that the situation could get worse, with unpleasant surprises in store, and so we thought it necessary to be prepared to be ready to take extreme measures. The letter in code here enclosed, which now – at least for the moment – may no longer have any value, may have its value in principle as evidence of the attitude we had adopted. We also already have an explanatory letter ready for all the members of the E[xecutive]. However, following on the letter that arrived from Berlin (copy here enclosed) and following on the return from Berlin of Lozovskij, who had met com. Repossi there, the Presidium had an unscheduled meeting and there was not even time to send for Gramsci.[14] Radek spoke of the disagreement that had arisen regarding the manifesto, of Gramsci's letter, and of the talk with Ambrogi. Lozovskij then stated that he had been informed by Repossi that Serrati's group had contacted the communists with a view to reaching an agreement in the trade union against the D'Aragona clique. Ambrogi then made the Italian point of view clear: it is not true that we have any prejudice against the socialist masses, indeed we maintain that extremely good revolutionary elements may be found alongside Serrati, but this does not authorise us to take steps towards Serrati, just as it does not authorise us to take steps towards D'Aragona, behind whom there may also be found part of the revolutionary proletariat. We consider Serrati and the heads of his fraction to be enemies of the CP, as we do D'Aragona and his comrades. If Serrati decides to break with the reformists, this is not because he has taken some step to the left, but because the reformists have quite openly taken quite a number of steps to the right. In the course of his activity up to now, Serrati has in point of fact shifted to the right. To take steps towards Serrati means making the International march to the right, disowning all the work that the PCI has done up to now. The situation has changed for the masses, but we maintain that Serrati has not changed, since if he were once and for all to line up with the Third International, he would do so out of personal interest, finding within it his own 'refuge for sinners'. In our estimation the fact that the masses either are coming to us because they are oriented towards our Party, or that they are coming to us because Serrati is leading them there, are two quite different things. In any case, we recognise that the situation is such that the masses, including those with Serrati, are looking in our direction. We acknowledge the need to isolate the reformists, and we do not wish to discuss what has already been decided, namely that the Maffi fraction should not break immediately with the Serrati fraction if he splits off from the reformists, and we are making concrete proposals: I. Separate agreements must be made with the Maffi fraction in order that, in the new independent party, it should continue to exist as a fraction. II. This fraction must establish immediate contact with the PCI as the direct representative of the Third Internat[ional] and, with control by the PCI, must give itself a discipline such as to make fusion possible in the near future. We shall of course be very happy if this discipline can be enforced on the whole party. In any case, the I[nternational] must put a stop to its direct relations with the Maffi fraction, and no step must be taken without the agreement of the Italian Party. After a short discussion, this order of ideas was accepted and we have already checked in the minutes themselves that this time full agreement with the PCI was recorded.

With the question posed in these terms, it seems to us that the question of Serrati and the other leaders is somewhat secondary, and in any case may be disposed of in the way the Italian Party best thinks fit. In the same session of the Presidium it was decided that on the occasion of the Socialist Congress, the delegates of the International will be coms. Frossard, Vaillant-Couturier, and Böttcher.[15] They will have to make immediate contact with and act in agreement with the PCI and will intervene only after the split off at the Congress sessions of the independents (Third Internationalists and maximalists). Ambrogi, while insisting only on the point of agreement with the PCI, also observed, to no avail, that it was not appropriate to choose as delegates, who would be listened to by the communist masses, elements who were well-known to be on the right, thereby maintaining a thesis that, among our masses, creates the impression of a rightist orientation, at a time when among the masses there is a widespread opinion that the Internat[ional] itself has shifted too far to the right.

Immediately after the session A[mbrogi] went to inform Gramsci and gained his full agreement. Both had occasion to confer with com. Rákosi, with whom they again insisted that what has already been stated above should clearly be explained in the mandate to the delegates.

We are of the opinion that this conclusion has improved the situation a lot and we think we have interpreted in the best possible way the needs of our Party along with those of the International itself. In any case we await your further instructions at the same time as informing you that we still have not received your promised report on the crisis in the SP.

From the last, difficult-to-interpret, telegram of yours, and from the latest Russian papers we see that the situation is developing headlong in our favour and we are anxious to have new news and your forecast of developments.

A. Gramsci

E. Ambrogi

Comrades Zinov'ev and Lozovskij were entrusted with writing to you and to the delegates of the International.

Source: APC 513-1-091/9-10 with copies on pages 64-65 and 71-2; typewritten, but the signatures of Gramsci and Ambrogi and the note at the end are handwritten

Gramsci and Ambrogi to the Executive of the Italian Communist Party

MOSCOW, 4 AUGUST 22

To the Executive of the Italian Communist Party – Rome

ITALIAN GROUP

Some of the members are out of Moscow for reasons of work.

We have written a letter to the Russian Party, and for information, to the Secretariat of the Comintern and to the OMS, in order to have information on all the communists, real or self-styled, currently in Russia, bearing in mind that there is an opportunity to ask the delegation's opinion before Italians are taken on, in whatever capacity, within the party or Soviet organisations.[16] We have not as yet had any reply.

ITALIAN SECTION OFFICE

A few days after Bordiga's departure, the rooms we were using were unexpectedly taken away from us and assigned to another office. We have now finally been able to have other office space, even better, and can make a start on our work.[17]

We have received a pack of back numbers of newspapers that, with a few exceptions, date from March onwards. We have also received two copies of each of the publications of the Library of the Communist International up to no. 10, with the exception of number 2, which was not published, and then also up to no. 10 and number 15 of the Little Communist Library. Of the Library of the Communist Party we have the volumes of Bordiga on the *Agrarian Question* and *From the Capitalist Economy to Communism*, as well as the booklet on Neapolitan Socialism.[18] Of the Little Library of Communist Culture, we have two copies of volumes 1, 2 and 3 and just one copy of volume 4. Of the Library of the ICG we have two copies of the 2nd volume.[19] Furthermore, we have two copies of the *Theses* of the first congress of the Red Trade Unions – Lozovskij, Action Programme – Statute of the Red International of Trade Unions – Lozovskij's *Moscow against Amsterdam* – the *E[xecutive] C[ommittee] of the C[ommunist] I[nternational] in Favour of the United*

Front – the *Communist Almanac* (two copies) – the *Congresso dei Morti* (two copies) – *The Capitalist World* – *Rosa Luxemburg* by Radek – numbers 1-3 of the IG – numbers 16 and 17 of the review *C[ommunist] I[nternational]*, everything in two copies – number 15 of the *C[ommunist] I[nternational]* and the main report from Livorno and, in four copies, the C[entral] C[ommittee] Report to the Second National Congress.[20]

INFORMATION ON VERDARO

Comrade Stragiotti was left with the task of doing this but since com. Kollontaj has been out of Moscow, it has not yet been possible to do anything.

INFORMATION ON THE HUNGARIAN QUESTION

Comrades Landler for one fraction and Santos for the other have promised a brief report, which up to now has however not been delivered.

MATTERS RELATING TO FOBERT (Bogdanova)

We have written to the Soviet Office of the Kiev Oblast' asking it to provide a passport for Bogdanova and at the same time we have written to her asking her to inform us on how the procedure is progressing. Up to this moment we have not received a reply.

MATTERS RELATING TO MISIANO

Because of the difficulties in understanding your telegram (for reasons you know from other sources), following on Münzenberg's request by telegram, Misiano left with our agreement and without further delay.[21]

We have to inform you that, before his departure, procedures were set in motion to have him nominated Secretary of the Latin Section. This position, because of the French question, involves a certain political responsibility, so much so that while the Presidency of the Section was left to Leiciague, the secretary's position was assigned (debatably, Ambrogi's comment) to Gramsci.[22] These procedures were overseen directly with us by Souvarine and with Misiano by Brandler, both with Zinov'ev's support. We stated that the Party had assigned him to other responsibilities and that they should not insist.

Misiano left, with his departure paid for by the Aid Committee. Since Jung has been absent for some time, on his return we will give you more exact information regarding the final sum of money that he was paid.

THE SPANISH ADDRESSES

We are including the list for you so you can send the newspapers and our publications.

REFUGEE QUESTION

This is a difficult problem that has to be resolved. We will bring it to the attention of the E[xecutive]. But meanwhile we cannot, through inertia, continue taxing the Italians who live here. We really need to have a small fund at our disposal. Gabiati is in hospital and we must help him, among other things for the needs of the new economy.[23] Lucchesi too is in hospital because of an accident at work which led to a double fracture of his right arm. It seems that with a rather longer period of cure, he will make a good recovery.

In closing this brief parenthesis of discontent and gossip, the spirits of our small community are now in excellent health.

A. Gramsci

E. Ambrogi

Rudas is asking you to send him a copy of his volume, which has just been published.

Source: APC 513-1-091/5 and copy in 513-1-091/81; both copies are typewritten with signatures, date and the note regarding Rudas handwritten

---

Gramsci and Ambrogi to Zinov'ev

MOSCOW, 28 AUGUST 1922

To comrade Zinov'ev, President of the C[ommunist] I[international]

The recent events have modified the situation in Italy radically. The general strike has had an enormous effect.[24] It demonstrates the following:

I. The effectiveness of the campaign for a general strike, conducted for over a year by the PCI, thanks to which the strike has now been imposed, against the pacific campaign of the coalition of all the other self-styled revolutionary parties.

II. The lack of organisational and revolutionary capacity of the current leaders of the masses, who, given that the strike was being imposed on them, passively accepted it, without any precise instructions, without any adequate preparation, without adequate organisation, without bothering to choose the most appropriate moment declaring it.

III. The betrayal by many socialists, who intended to exploit the strike – a peaceful and legalitarian strike – as a suitable weapon to exert pressure for a solution to the ministerial crisis.

IV. The revolutionary organisational capacity of the PCI, the only party that, by word and action, has given the movement overall direction and shown itself up to the task.

V. The lack of any direction at all on the part of 'Serratian maximalism', its complete absenteeism when faced with its responsibilities.

VI. The revolutionary capacity of the masses who, far above any expectation, have responded with enthusiasm and fighting spirit, despite the treachery of the leaders, despite the lack of technical and spiritual preparation that they had been left with by these leaders.

VII. As a logical consequence of all this, the crisis has now sharpened to an extreme within the SP, while the masses are ever more favourably oriented towards the PCI.

Serrati is continuing to play a most perfidious double game. Attracted yet again by the hope of a possible agreement with the reformists, the socialist congress has been put back, and meanwhile the polemic with the reformists has been softened and there is no longer any talk of a split. Except that, faced with such cowardly uncertainty, the reformists are hoisting their standards with increasing bare-faced cheek. Baldesi is writing of the need to remove the trade unions from any influence on the part of the SP, and meanwhile the parliamentary group is demanding that a congress be convened. *Avanti!*, for its part, is praising a speech of Treves, ultra-pacific to the point of cowardice with new calls for the need for unity. It has however had its shoulders put firmly against the wall by a letter from Maffi, occasioned by the letter from comrade Zinov'ev, and has had to confirm that 'the right wing have taken it upon themselves to burn all bridges and have done this so well, thanks to the sincerity of their secretary, Baldesi, that any understanding would be insincere and ridiculous'; but they are not replying even indirectly to the question of defining their position in regard to the Communist International.

The SP is launching a vacuous manifesto, critical of how the strike was called and carried out, without indicating any line, without in any way committing itself to any programme. Meanwhile, in this crisis, in this ambiguity, the working-class revolutionary forces within the SP are continuing to melt away, as has happened from the Milan congress onward. Nor has the Maffi fraction an organisational capacity or an authority such as to be able to halt this dispersal of forces. We, on the other hand, must not waste the opportunity offered us: any delay is harmful. As a result of their recent experiences the masses are moving towards us, and we have to meet them half-way. The Italian Party has to come out with a manifesto inviting them to line up beneath our banner. The Maffi fraction could adopt the manifesto, and echo it by demanding the early convening of a SP congress, and committing itself to convening one in the immediate future should the statutory organs not do so. It is then no longer necessary to pay heed to the Serrati fraction. It may be that the moment of its final liquidation has arrived. The Maffi fraction's exit, with its acceptance of the manifesto launched by the CP, may give it sufficient authority to halt or at least reduce the dispersal of revolutionary energies. But we have to speed things up, both so as not to lose the favourable moment, and because the pressure of events poses the CP with the ever greater necessity of assuming ever more serious responsibilities if it wants to avoid abandoning the proletariat and the consequent disintegration of this latter, a class which has now given the most commendable proof of its revolutionary capacity.

The situation is very serious and full of unknowns. On the one hand there are paeans of praise for D'Annunzio as putative first president of the Italian Republic.[25] While denying *for the moment* any fascist military march on Rome, Mussolini is letting it be known through an interview he has given that he has at his disposal all the technical means to this end. The fascist manifesto speaks of a forthcoming great definitive act, and both in the Chamber of Deputies itself and in the Senate there are repercussions in favour of a dictatorship, and certainly not a proletarian one.

We are perhaps on the eve of events of an unpredictable significance. In these conditions, to give credit to hypothetical forces means contributing to the betrayal of the proletariat by favouring the possibility of its lining up under the banners of the false revolutionaries. And on the other hand, on pain of losing its own credit, the CP cannot give up the responsibility it has at this moment. One clear word must be spoken: that only one revolutionary force in the country has the capability of leading the proletariat, and that is the CP, and without avoiding the question, without delay, the proletariat must be invited to line up with us, abandoning reformism and abandoning those who, through their indecision, even more than the reformists themselves, have up to now been responsible for its routs.

We are asking for the Presidium to be convened immediately to discuss this, our proposal.

Italian delegation

Gramsci

Ambrogi

Source: APC 513-1-166/23-4 and 513-1-080/179-80; typewritten, the former copy having both signatures and the latter copy just that of Gramsci

---

To Trotsky

MOSCOW, 8 SEPTEMBER 1922

Here are the replies to the questions that you put to me on the Italian futurist movement.

The post-war futurist movement in Italy has completely lost its defining characteristics. Marinetti is paying very little attention to the movement. He is now married and is devoting all his energies to his wife. Currently there are monarchists, communists, republicans and fascists all taking part in the movement. Recently a political weekly has been founded in Milan with the name *Il Principe* [*The Prince*], which is upholding or seeking to uphold the same theories that

Machiavelli was preaching for Italy in the sixteenth century, in other words that the state of combat among the local parties, which is leading the nation into chaos, can be eliminated by an absolute monarch, by a new Cesare Borgia, who will slice the heads off the leaders of all the parties in combat.[26] The review is edited by two futurists, Bruno Corra and Enrico Settimelli.[27] And Marinetti, who in 1920 was even arrested for quite a strong speech against the king at a patriotic demonstration in Rome, is collaborating with this selfsame weekly.[28]

The most important members of the futurism of the pre-war period have now become transformed into fascists, with the exception of Giovanni Papini, who has become a catholic and written a Life of Christ. During the war the futurists were the most vocal supporters of 'war right up to the final victory' and of imperialism. Only one fascist, Aldo Palazzeschi, was against the war. He has broken with the movement and, while he used to be among the writers of greatest interest, as a literary figure he has finished up in silence. Marinetti, who always went out of his way to praise the war, has published a manifesto by means of which he wants to demonstrate that war is the only means of cleansing the world. He took part in the war as a captain in an armoured car unit, and his latest book, *L'alcova d'acciaio* [*The steel alcove*] is an enthusiastic hymn to the armoured car in war. Marinetti has written a pamphlet *Al di là del comunismo* [*Beyond Communism*], outlining his political doctrines, if the sometimes sharp-witted and always strange products of this person's fantasies can be called doctrines. Before I left, the Turin section of the Proletkul't invited Marinetti to a futurist art exhibition so that, at its inauguration, he could explain its significance to the working-class members of the organisation. Marinetti accepted the invitation very enthusiastically and, after having visited the exhibition together with the workers, expressed his satisfaction that he had succeeded in convincing himself that the workers understood far more of the topics of futurist art than the bourgeoisie. Before the war, futurism enjoyed great popularity among the workers. The review *Lacerba* had a print run of 20,000 copies, four fifths of them being distributed among workers.[29] During the numerous manifestations of futurist art in the theatres of the main Italian cities, the workers took on the defence of the futurists against the semi-aristocratic and bourgeois youth who were coming to blows with the futurists.

Marinetti's futurist group no longer exists. His old review *Poesia* [*Poetry*] is now being edited by a certain Mario Dessy, a man of no intellectual or organisational significance. In Southern Italy, most of all in Sicily, there are lots of small futurist magazines that Marinetti sends articles to, but these reviews are published by amateurish students, who mistake ignorance of Italian grammar for futurism. The strongest cell among the futurists is that of the painters. In Rome there is a permanent gallery of futurist painters organised by a failed photographer, a certain Anton Giulio Bragaglia, a cinema impresario and agent for theatre actors. The best-known among the futurist artists is Giacomo Balla.[30] D'Annunzio has never taken up any position on futurism in public. It must be borne in mind that, at its birth, futurism had a marked anti-Dannunzian slant, and indeed one of Marinetti's first books bore the title *Les dieux s'en vont, et D'Annunzio reste* [*The gods go off, and D'Annunzio remains*]. Although Marinetti's and D'Annunzio's political programmes coincided on everything during the war, the futurists have remained on their anti-Dannunzian position. They did not show any interest in the Fiume adventure, although then they took part in the demonstrations.

It may be said that, after the signing of the peace agreement, the futurist movement completely lost its characteristic image, and fragmented into various currents, created and formed as a result of the landslip effect of the war era. The young intelligentsia became reactionaries in their near-entirety. The workers, who saw in futurism the elements of a fight against the outmoded academic culture of Italy, fossilised and distant from the masses of the people, now have to fight for their freedom, weapons in hand, and are little interested in old disputes. In the big industrial centres, the Proletkul't programme, which aimed at reawakening the creative spirit of the workers in the artistic and literary fields, is absorbing the energy of those who still have the will and the time to become involved in these problems.

Source: 'A Letter from Comrade Gramsci on Italian Futurism', published in Trotsky's Literatura i revoljucija [Literature and Revolution], *Krasnaja Nov': Moscow, 1923, repr. 1991, pp116-8.*[31]

Gramsci and Ambrogi to Bordiga

11.10. 1922

Urgent Bordiga Rome

We propose not implementing decision on Ersilio[32] until your arrival in Moscow due to his main duties here if [his] presence in Berlin not linked to extreme urgent necessity Stop Advisable to make preparations for departure We await telegraphic reply with explanation of end of your telegram.

Gramsci

Ambrogi

Source: 513-1-091/30; telegram of 11 October 1922, translated from the Russian transliteration of the sole copy that has come to light

---

Gramsci, Jul'ka and a third person to Evgenija

Com[rade] E.A. Schucht
Post Office no. 22
Krasnaja Presnja,
Serebrjanyj Bor Sanatorium, Moscow

Dearest comrade and also sister,

We are met together in room no. 5 – in *Soviet numbers* – it's one o'clock in the morning, we are thinking about the cart and are full of envy that you can play while we are forced to make speeches in congresses of the činovniki [bureaucrats], to translate them and review them for the papers.[33] Have you started making the oxen? Can you still find a few minutes to eat the flesh of the unknown one? Since it's late and we're tired we'll just send our greetings with the song

'Long live the cart
Long live the wheel
Long life to the spokes
Long life to Pan!'

Written this 16th day of October 1922 with the fountain pen that leaks on your fingers.

A. Gramsci
Юлька [Jul'ka]
[and third, illegible, signature]

Source: AAG; postcard, date-stamped 16 October 1922, with drawing and words in Gramsci's hand

JUL'KA'S CROSS

(Runaway bed): Everyone carries a cross around here

(Jul'ka): Get him, get him, he's a counter-revolutionary

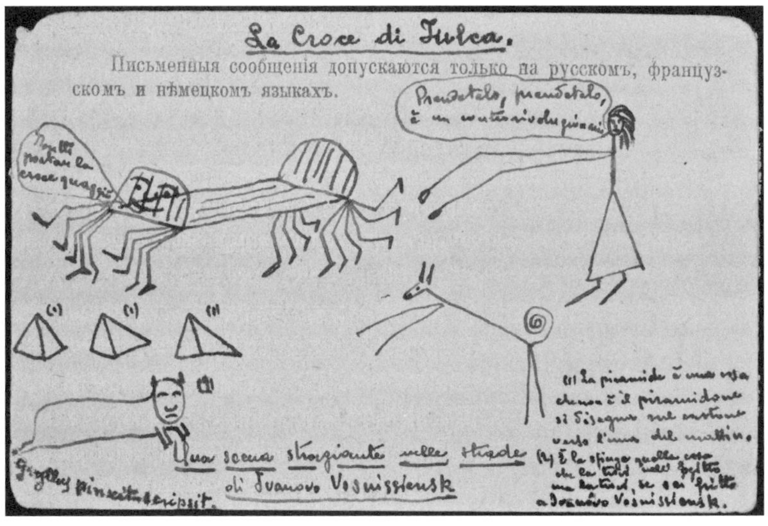

Gryllus pinxit-scripsit[34] A heartrending scene in the streets of Ivanovo Voznesensk

(1) the pyramid here – the great one is not/what's been drawn on this card/by our artist and bard/at one in the morning in our nightspot

(2) the sphinx is that thing that/you find in Egypt; and you,/dog-tired, will find it too/in Ivanovo Voznesensk

To Zinov'ev

To the President of the Commission on the Italian question

Regarding the fusion with the PSI, the delegation of the Italian Communist Party proposes the following conditions:

1. Before proceeding with fusion, the PSI must exclude the Vella fraction from its ranks.
2. With a view to their exclusion, the Central Committee of the PCI reserves the right to present to the Executive of the Comintern a list of members of the Socialist Party who, for lack of personal probity, cannot be members of any proletarian party.
3. All those who have been members of the Italian Communist Party and who, following resignation or expulsion, have rejoined the Socialist Party cannot be admitted to membership of the Communist Party.
4. All the *non-working-class* elements who have entered the P.S.I. after the Livorno split are in the same position as new members and follow the dispositions of the PCI rules.
5. The maximalist trade union committee must make an immediate clear pronouncement on the question of Moscow or Amsterdam for publication in the whole of the proletarian press, adopting a very clear attitude on this question in the trade union movement.[35]
6. The reorganisation of the cooperative movement after the fusion of the two parties will be carried out following the principles of organisation and dispositions already fixed in this sphere by the PCI.
7. The maximalist parliamentary fraction as well as the municipal and provincial councillors will be subject to review, following which the PCI, in agreement with the International Executive, will have the power to withdraw its mandate from all those it thinks fit.
8. The Central Committee of the united party will be composed on the following basis: 2/3 to the communists and 1/3 to the socialists.
9. The CP, in agreement with the Executive of the C.I., will have the right to veto entry into the leading organs of all those it thinks fit.

10. The principle of homogeneity must be respected in the constitution of the executive bureaus of the Party.
11. Fusion between the federations and branches of the two Parties will be carried out on the same bases as for the central organs.
12. The Central Committee of the united Party will have the right to promulgate particular dispositions for special local situations.
13. The personnel of the editorial staff of the Party journals will be composed of communists for the local press; all weekly and periodical publications of the P.S.I. will be absorbed into the corresponding organs of the PCI. Where there is only a socialist organ, this will become a communist organ, its title being modified if necessary.

For the Italian delegation

A. Gramsci

25/XI. 1922

To the President of the Italian Commission[36]

Among the conditions presented by the Italian Delegation regarding the fusion of the PCI with the PSI, due to an oversight the following condition was omitted:

> The organisational order procedure for fusion must begin after the Congress of the PCI.

for the delegation

Source: APC 513-1-157/7-825 November 1922; typewritten with handwritten signature but no date; other copies, dated but with no signature are at 513-1-073/23-4 and 26-7. The additional fourteenth point at the end, located at 513-1-073/25 and 513-1-069/93, is unsigned and dated 26 November. All is in French.

To Jul'ka

[DECEMBER 1922]

Dear comrade,

I learnt yesterday from your mother that you will arrive in Moscow on Saturday morning on your way to Serebrjanyj Bor. Would you like to come and see me as soon as you get here? I will try to have a car ready at three o'clock on Saturday afternoon to take us together to the sanatorium. In any case I would like to come with you to spend New Year with you and comrade Evgenija. Would you like that? Are you pleased?

Write to me immediately and let me know what I have to buy because, as regards these things, I have no spirit of initiative. For Serebrjanyj Bor, I've thought of something grand to do: baptise the cart! You will be godmother, Evgenija will have the spirit of motion descend upon it, while, more modestly, I will be content to play the role of the stable boy. Can you too suggest something?

I await. Affectionately

Gramsci

Source: AAG

To Jul'ka

MOSCOW, 10 JANUARY 23

Dearest comrade

I'm leaving Moscow for Italy in a few days' time, together with the commission entrusted with the fusion between communists and socialists.[37] At first the ECCI, in agreement, as it seemed, with the Italian Commission and therefore with Serrati too, had nominated me as an editor of *Avanti!* with equal powers to Serrati himself, and it was therefore decided that I should leave immediately to take on this post, one that is unfortunately not to my liking and full of difficulty. Yesterday evening something absolutely unheard-of happened. Serrati said he had understood that I would become joint editor of *Avanti!* after the fusion Congress and not as from now, and he argued that keeping to the decision would have meant losing the majority of the Socialist Party, losing *Avanti!* and so on and so forth. The news that Serrati has received from Italy on the state of mind in his party must be really serious if it has led him to act so ridiculously as to claim that, because of comrade Bukharin's bad French, he had approved such delicate and important deliberations without having realised what they meant in practice! The reasons for my departure, whatever the outcome of this strange and somewhat bizarre incident, still hold, and have maybe become more compelling; I am certainly happy to be able to take up revolutionary work again in what is such a difficult and tragic moment for the proletariat, and so totally new tactically as regards the relationships among the various currents in the working class and among single individuals. When can I see you again? Before leaving I'll go to Serebrjanyj Bor to spend a day together with comrade Evgenija. It is my great hope that we'll be able to see each other again in Italy. Comrade Evgenija is going to get better and you will be able to come with her to Italy: we'll work together. Or will all this be just a little dream, built artificially, during an interlude of enforced rest, just like one builds a cart ... without its oxen? Who knows. The world is great and terrible: will we meet again perhaps in Peking, in Lhasa, in New York, in Sydney?

I'd like to write a whole heap of things to you but I can't; maybe some of them you will be able to guess. Saying them would be easier; I'll say them to comrade Evgenija who will pass them on to you.

I'm going to leave a pack of Italian books for you. Write and let me know where I should leave it.[38] Maybe it would be best with that woman poet friend of yours who we went to see before that dreadful walk we took in the snow?[39] You can remind me of the name and exact address.

And your translation? Please send it me if it's ready: I'll have it published in Italy. Write to me at length, about all sorts of things. It will seem as if I'm once again in your company. Could you send me a photograph of comrade Evgenija? You'd do me a great favour; I can't foresee when it will be possible to see each other again so I'll keep it as a small, precious memory of all the days we've spent together. I thought I was totally barren and desiccated but I've discovered inside myself a tiny (very, very tiny ...) source of melancholy and of moonlight fringed with blue.

A warm handshake.

Gramsci

Source: AAG

To Evgenija

[18 JANUARY 1923, OR IMMEDIATELY AFTERWARDS][40]

Dearest comrade,

I am going to be blocked in Moscow for some days yet. The C[entral] C[ommittee] of the CP has sent a telegram to say that there's a warrant out for my arrest in Italy and that for the moment it's impossible to cross the frontier illegally. As soon as the telegram arrived, on Wednesday morning, since I was not at the Hotel Ljux and since none of the Italians knew where I'd gone, there was an incredible brouhaha. They went off in a car searching the whole of Moscow to see where I had got to, and even the ГПУ [GPU] was notified that I'd gone missing.[41] I came back in at 7 in the morning to be greeted like someone back from the dead. The Presidium, which met that evening, then decided I had to stay here until further notice.

That letter of yours – so horrid – was given me late on Wednesday evening. I did you wrong, too brutally. I am a brute, really. There's still a lot in me to be destroyed. You will help me, won't you? Because there are also some scars that are still hurting and maybe also wounds still bleeding from when I was a child.

Gramsci

Source: AAG

To Osip Pjatnickij

MOSCOW, 23 JANUARY 1923[42]

To Comrade Pjatnickij
Secretary of the Comintern

Given that comrade Mario Stragiotti has worked for the Comintern since June, I would like the Secretariat to regularise his position for this month.

Comrade Stragiotti is now leaving for Italy to carry on his work there.

Thank you and fraternal greetings

Antonio Gramsci

Source: AAG and Comintern Archive 513-2-16/65; on headed notepaper of the Comintern Executive with Gramsci's handwritten signature, but the rest, in German, is in another hand

To Evgenija

[LATE JANUARY 1923]

Dearest comrade,

In a few days' time I'll come and see you. But why did you write me a letter that was so good and at the same time … so horrid?[43] Nothing can come between us unless we want it to, and I certainly don't want it. It's been no small thing for me to tell you what I feel for you. I've told you so many stories about my childhood, the colourful ones, those that bring back pleasure, but I've never even hinted at the other side of the coin. My life has always been a spent flame, a desert. How was I able to tell what you mean to me? I thought about it often, during the period of silence; I laughed at myself, at you, at everyone, awful things came into my mind, the sewer of my past brought things back up that for some time left me poisoned. But all this had to happen. I came back to you, still troubled, because everything seemed to me to be completely changed, completely different; I too must have changed, become another person. Maybe my nervous breakdown was even more serious than I could have imagined and could have had far more dangerous psychological consequences than anything I might have feared. But now my will is categorical, absolute. In this intervening period I have thought, I have sought to convince myself that I'd been putting on a pretence with you, just as I had on other occasions (because other times I really had done this), when I declared myself, convinced that I could not be loved (do you remember our discussion of a certain line from Dante?), convinced of obtaining for myself the outward signs of love in order to succeed, to dominate, to be the strongest, with all means available, through ruses, and even through deception.[44] I thought, I sought to convince myself, I carried out the game yet again to see whether I was able, whether I had not lost my energy, I did wrong, I know, but I don't regret it at all, and now I want, with all my being, I absolutely want you to continue to feel for me, because for you I will still break anyone to pieces (I remember a phrase: I would hate it if I knew that a woman loved her comrade and companion) and all these things I have taken very seriously, very much to heart. I want it and you too must want it. We'll take this up again in a few days.

Gramsci

Source: AAG

To Evgenija

13/2 – 923

Dearest,

I am still not sure whether I'll be able to come to see you on Sunday. They're convening us every single moment, at the most improbable times, and I wouldn't at all like to miss a meeting and send apologies for absence without good reason.[45] I want very much to come. I would like to tell you lots of things. But will I be able to? I often ask myself this and rehearse long speeches. But when I'm near you I forget everything. And yet it ought to be so straightforward, straightforward like us, or at least like me. But you are mistaken in finding so many complications and so many meanings in what I say. No, no, the words are a faithful reflection of calm and peaceful states of mind. You mean a lot to me and I am certain that you share these feelings towards me. For many, many years I have truly been used to thinking of the absolute impossibility, almost a decree of fate, that I might be loved by someone. This conviction has served for too long as a defence against myself, so as not to return to self-inflicted wounds or go into black depression. From the age of 10 I began to think along these lines as regards my parents. I was forced to make so many sacrifices, and my health was so fragile that I was convinced I was a burden that had intruded into my family. These are things that one does not easily forget, things that leave much deeper marks than can be imagined. All my feelings have been poisoned to some degree by this deep-rooted habit. But today there has been such a big change in me that I hardly recognise myself and so, to me, it seems strange that you should notice and give importance to nervous tics and little starts which are outside my control and perhaps have a purely physical basis. I feel very close to you. Why do you say 'It's too soon?' Why do you say my love is something foreign to you, that doesn't concern you? What exactly are these entanglements, these deceptions? I am not a mystic and neither are you a Byzantine madonna.[46] I advise you to count up to 10,000 when your mental processes are forcing you into shooting off a hail of abracadabras of this type.

We are strong and feel for one another. And we are straightforward, everything is natural in us. And most of all we want to be strong and don't want to drown in Matilde Serao-like sloppy psychological intrigues.[47] We want to be strong spiritually, and straightforward and healthy and be close to one another as we do, because we do cherish one another and this is the finest and biggest and strongest reason in the world.

Will you be able to come and meet me when I arrive? Have you been sensible and good? I measure your will to cherish me by your efforts to make yourself fit enough to jump across the streams ... And you mean a lot to me.

Gr.

Source: AAG

To Jul'ka

13/2. 23

Dear comrade,

Rooted to the ground, I awaited the terrible Degot'.[48] I was lucky enough not to see him. Last Sunday I went to Serebrjanyj Bor. Comrade Ženja was a little nervous and depressed, but in general I think she is better: she ... has learned to walk and keep her balance. I think this is the most critical phase of her convalescence, the one in which the desires and wishes that spring from the rush of nascent forces urge and drive one beyond one's real capacities.

And you, when is it that you come back to Moscow? Meanwhile, write and tell me of your work, of your new experiences, which are of the greatest interest for me. I am waiting and am still able to work only with difficulty, irregularly. And your translation? How is it that you haven't sent it on to me? I was told you had it with you. As regards the Italian party (socialist), there is just one collection of material from the III Congress, which I have two copies of and which will probably be of use to you.[49]

Affectionate greetings

Gramsci

Source: AAG

To Jul'ka

[MARCH (?) 1923][50]

Dearest comrade,

I have had to go to a Commission, which however I hope will not go on too long. By two o'clock I should certainly be back at home. If you like, come back and wait in my room, where there is an Italian comrade,

Greetings,

Gramsci

Source: AAG

Gramsci and Gennari to the Executive Committee of the PCd'I

15 MARCH 1923

Dear comrades,

Despite the storm that has buffeted our Party and despite the impossibility of using A[madeo], which represents the most serious loss we have suffered, we are sure it will be able to resist and rebuild its cadre force which, albeit weakened, will resist until the arrival of better days so that proletarian action may commence once more.[51]

We understand the responsibility you have to shoulder and how many difficulties you now have to overcome, but we have full confidence in your spirit of sacrifice and in the results of your defence and rebuilding work.

IMPRESSIONS REGARDING THE EVENTS IN ITALY

We must first of all inform you of the repercussions on the comrades here of the most recent events in Italy. The impression produced on the members of the Executive, as on the Russian comrades, has been by no means good.[52] This we understand from what is being said openly and, much more, from the allusions and smirks when the illegal activity of our party is mentioned. The whole of our illegal apparatus was spoken of as something solid and secure, and we ourselves on more than one occasion have cited it as an example for other parties (most recently for example at the Prague Congress).

Now, even and especially on the part of those parties who have attempted nothing or have succeeded in nothing in this field, the occasion is being taken to believe that what we always said, and which really did represent the result of a whole two years of patient labour, was merely a bluff or, at least, contained a good amount of exaggeration.

We shall naturally do our best to re-establish the truth as regards our Party, but it is necessary that, on your part too, you should do as much as possible in this direction. We advise you among other things to be very careful in your reports. For example, the one that attributes the discovery of the illegal bureau simply to bad luck made an extremely bad impression. It is also said that you were offered the possibility of keeping what was seized in a safe place, but that you refused, and that again has been chalked up very negatively to your account.

All this has led to a slump in the International's assessment of our Party.

We must all of us increase [our efforts], so that with renewed work and good tactics the Party will regain all the confidence that it enjoyed among the other communist parties. Otherwise we run a very grave danger that the left of the S[ocialist] Party will gain credit and become the centre of all the hopes and cares of the C[ommunist] I[nternational]. That would naturally lead in good time to much greater disappointments than those we have caused it, but this would represent only small comfort indeed for us, and, in any case, would represent great damage for our movement and for the future of the Italian proletariat.

THE WORK OF THE COMMISSION

We know that Giacomo is no longer with you. Finally here it has been realised that it is preferable for him not to return. It will instead be arranged for Beruzzi to extend his visit and for someone else to take the place of Giacomo.[53] Better late than never ...

Yesterday the secretariat also discussed (in our presence) the tasks of the Commission, and Giacomo's request by telegram for support for his thesis of abandoning work on fusion, and instead limiting ourselves to the constitution of a simple proletarian front. But it was, however, acknowledged, as we argued, that it would be disastrous to label as a failure something that has already been decided by a World Congress, and that, therefore, we must continue the fusion work, while at the same time extending the schedule so as to give time for the fusionist fraction within the SP to carry out a more effective work of preparation and organisation.

The Commission ought therefore to insist that the SP Congress should be delayed, that the leadership of the SP should be more active and forceful, that the organisational work of the fusionist fraction should be carried on with all speed and that it should oversee all activity of the SP organs, most of all *Avanti*.

This is the view we maintained and this, it seems, was acknowledged useful.

We think it necessary for you to entrust Scocci[marro] with sending, not only the personal information we receive, but also the official reports (as secretary of the Commission) to the Comintern to be translated and distributed to the members of the Executive. In the meantime it would be of use for him to prepare and send on a detailed report on all the work done in Italy up to this moment by the Commission, mentioning briefly the decisions taken here before his departure. That would give a complete picture of the activity of the Commission and will be of great use in putting all members of the Executive in a position to have all the elements of judgement necessary for examining and deciding as to the problem of fusion.

Just to give you an idea of the necessity of what we are suggesting, we are letting you know that the discussion on the tasks and activity of the Commission sprang from the question that some were asking on whether it was useful or not to continue going on with it.

REPORT ON PARTY ACTIVITY

It is also necessary to send more complete reports here on Party activity. For example, we have no precise news on what is happening in important centres such as Turin or Milan. On this subject, we believe that it is useful, in the main regions, to give nominated people the task, every fortnight, of sending reports that should be as exact and complete as possible on the movement involving the Party. These will make it possible for you to have a sure basis for sending summary reports with information regarding our movement in general.

INTERNATIONAL CONFERENCE OF 17 MARCH

We have no news here whether the Party and the Trade Union Committee will be represented and by whom at the 17 March conference on the Ruhr and on fascism.[54] On being asked, we advised that a telegram be sent to A[mbrogi] in Berlin to see if he knew anything of your arrangements. Then, speeding things up, we wrote to the same comrade, saying that if you had not had the possibility of seeing to the matter, then he, who is your representative in Berlin, should represent you at this conference too. This was done to ensure we should not miss having a representative of our Party at the conference.

We here briefly outline what A[mbrogi] mentioned in a letter addressed to you about a preliminary meeting held in Berlin. I (Gennari) and Bombacci received an invitation for both of us to go to a meeting that took place a few hours later, without the subject of the meeting being specified. We went to it, given that A[mbrogi] was confined to bed, ill, and we stayed there. *I alone spoke*, and the same evening informed A[mbrogi], handing over to him the short report that he has sent to you. I am explaining this to avoid even the slightest risk of there seeming to be a conflict, which would be totally out of place and ridiculous.

To this we still have to add something. It is also necessary to coordinate the entire action to be deployed abroad against international fascism and against specifically Italian fascism. You know the deliberations of the Executive on the subject. Radek has concretised such action in a letter whose precise tenor we still however do not know.

One of us (Gennari) wrote an organisational plan to be presented from us as rank-and-file comrades, and as material to be developed, awaiting your judgement and your concrete proposals. This plan was worked out in Berlin after an exchange of ideas with comrades who were there and because an initiative had already been taken in this sense by Š[aš] (who is one of the signatories to the proposal you have received). We did not know that part of this action had already been discussed and decided on by the Executive. From a telegram of Beruzzi's it then appears that he too recognises the need for this action in the sense that we are proposing. But this is still not sufficient. We are also insisting that organisation of propaganda be provided for, that funds be collected, aid distributed and political emigration be subject to regulation.

The activity of comrades abroad should thus be deployed along the following three lines:

In the sense contained in the letter for the creation of the bureau;[55]
Action against fascism;
Collection of funds, aid and use of refugees.

For the second of these aims, the most convenient site for a headquarters has already been chosen by the Executive. For the third of them (for which ROTE HILFE already has some funds at its disposal), we think it best to choose the same place as the Bureau.[56]

THE BOMBACCI CASE ETC

We think it useful to outline our thought for this case, too, especially from the standpoint of the possible repercussions that a conflict might have in Italy and here at this moment.

Given that as a primary question, discipline must especially in these times be stricter than ever, and that, not the single individuals involved, but the relevant Party organs should determine the activity of each member, the Executive must in our view examine the opportunity at this moment in time of avoiding, as far as possible, any not strictly indispensable act that might give the impression of any disorientation and disintegration of our Party. We are saying this for a number of reasons; for example even in the event of an eventual disavowal by the *other* members of the Communist parliamentary group.

Today, more than ever, we have to judge each act of ours not only from the disciplinary point of view but also, primarily, from the political one, and to always ask ourselves what effect these acts will have among the masses and within the International.

Once we have established, therefore, that the Executive must be able to determine what all its members do, and therefore what Bombacci too has to do (Terracini's letter, which would allow any member to re-examine his own capacity for sacrifice and discipline, therefore seems to us inappropriate), the Executive itself must reflect on how a measure that can be avoided would be exploited in Italy, a measure that in the International and in the foreign parties would give the impression of personal squabbles and struggles between tendencies.

We are therefore of the opinion that *all that can be avoided must be avoided and, indeed, it was avoided in calmer times that were less fraught with danger*. It is instead preferable to try to use all comrades as they are and for what they are able to offer. Faced with certain necessities, while maintaining its prestige and the principle of discipline, the Executive should see whether, for example, it may not be better to use B[ombacci], temporarily as may be, for propaganda work and for collecting funds abroad.

MARABINI-SILVA

Marabini has finished the work that was assigned to him and we are sending his report to you. He is waiting for you to let him know how you now intend to use him. He would be very useful in the bureau that we intend to set up, just as he would be useful here. Examine the question and let us know your decision.

Up to now Silva has remained here, completely unused. Procedures are underway to complete what Bruno wanted and what had been asked for here by Amadeo.[57] But up to now nothing has been concluded, which will come as no surprise to you. Do you think he might possibly be used elsewhere (for example with Gennari) in a technical capacity? Look at this possibility together with Bruno and let us know what you think.

And ... – that's enough for today. We know too well the amount of work weighing you down and the situation in which you are having to carry on and fight at this time, and do not wish to toss in your direction yet more typewritten pages, while at the same time knowing you have no lack of strength and courage.

In spite of everything, keep on, and ... warmest greetings.

Heartiest greetings to A[madeo]

PARTY ACTIVITY ABROAD

We sent you last time the letter from the E[xecutive] about the constitution and tasks of a bureau abroad.

Gramsci

Gennari

Source: AAG; unsigned copy. Signed copy in the Comintern Archives: 513-1-187/5-10

Gramsci and Gennari to the Executive Committee of the PCI

To the E[xecutive] C[ommittee] of the PCI
Moscow 20 March 1923

Dear comrades

The Executive of the C[ommunist] I[nternational] has decided to set up a central bureau in Berlin for the fight against fascism and one in Vienna, for which comrade Gennari is earmarked, to help the Executive Committee of the PCI in the organisation of illegal work etc.

But at this moment the CP of Italy must in our view take on another task among Italian refugees and émigrés abroad. Funds have to be collected to help the victims of fascism and to aid the fight against fascism. This collection of funds must be carried out in agreement with and coordinated by Rote Hilfe. But above all since we can find a broad consensus among the émigrés who have already been living abroad, many for long, long years, a special Italian committee must be set up which, if thought desirable, might be an Italian section of Rote Hilfe. This Aid Committee should then take on the task of distributing aid, regulating the flow of refugees and seeking to provide for their placement.

Moreover, since the work may be carried out simultaneously and in parallel with that of the collection of funds, in deciding its deployment the committee may also, in agreement with the parties of each single country, provide for propaganda and trade union and political organisation among Italian refugees and émigrés.

To make ourselves clear we shall call this committee simply the Aid Committee, and it must work in close relation with the Party Executive and the other two committees.

Given that for the reasons we have already seen, the other two committees have been agreed on, one in B[erlin] and the other in V[ienna], we are of the opinion that V[ienna] should also host this third one, both since it is close to it in work and has an overlap with that of the V[ienna] bureau, and since we can use in part the personnel and apparatus of this latter, and, finally, because of the closer and speedier contact that it can have with the Party executive.

Through A[mbrogi], Gennari has already sent you concrete proposals regarding this activity from B[erlin], proposals with which the other comrades resident in B[erlin] are in agreement. But since, in the meantime, the E[xecutive] of the C[ommunist] I[nternational] in Moscow, through the creation of the committee in B[erlin] and the bureau in V[ienna], was taking measures to carry out part of the work we have indicated, in order that you can take the relevant decision we think it is useful to have your judgement on what should be done to complement what has already been decided. What we will try to explain in the most concrete way possible, so as to expedite your work and speed up its being put into practice, is for us of the utmost urgency.

In view of this urgency we think it appropriate, before Gennari leaves, to mention this work project to the secretariat, to the Rote Hilfe and to the Arbeiter Hilfe.

However all this is naturally just by way of an exchange of views and is in the nature of preliminary agreements, with no definitive binding commitments before your decision.

In our view it is of the greatest urgency to begin aid and propaganda work since we are convinced that there is much to be done at this time, because there are Parties – for example the American Party – which are coming to us and asking for our people for propaganda among the émigrés, because we are receiving many letters from refugees urging us to action and because intense work on our part at this time would increase our party's cadre force, bringing good revolutionary workers over to us from among the refugees who are disgusted by the inaction and cowardice of the other proletarian parties and are putting their hopes and expectations only in us.

To waste further time would have the result of their losing confidence in us too and they would be lost to the proletarian cause.

TASKS OF THE AID COMMITTEE

The tasks of this committee are propaganda and trade union and political organisation among Italian refugees and émigrés, regulation of the outflow of refugees and directing them towards where there are more chances of placing them, utilisation of refugees for the work of political and trade union organisation, collection of aid items and their distribution.

For a more detailed explanation of this work, it is best to divide it into various parts:

a) *Propaganda and organisation among refugees abroad and émigrés*

Fascism has forced thousands of revolutionary Italian workers and militants to take refuge abroad. Taking account of past experience, it is to be feared that if the Italian émigrés abroad are left to themselves, they will be lost for trade union and political organisation.

Until now, when abroad the Italian labourer has always lost contact with the organisations of his own country and has not established any (or only to a minimal extent in a negligible number of cases) with the organisations of the country he has emigrated to.

It is thus indispensable to organise a whole work of propaganda and organisation among Italian workers abroad in order to make use of their forces, in order to coordinate them with those of the Parties and organisations of the countries where they have found refuge, and in order to constitute and maintain intact those cadres who will be able once more to operate in Italy at the side of what it has been possible to maintain there, just as soon as the in Italy political situation allows it.

This work must be carried out not only among political refugees who have fled from the fascist terror, but also among the Italian working-class masses who have emigrated from Italy in the past or have emigrated for reasons of work. There are enormous numbers of these especially in the Americas (Argentina, United States etc).

It is enough to bear in mind that it was calculated that in 1916 there were 6 million Italian foreign emigrants, over 4,693,000 of them in the Americas alone.

For this reason we must send Italian propaganda workers who, through talks, visual projections, etc, have the task of carrying out propaganda against fascism, who initiate and take charge of the collection of aid and at the same time of trade union and political organisation among the masses. All this must be taken charge of by the Aid Committee abroad, in agreement with the Executive of the PCI and with the Communist Parties and trade union organisations in the various countries.

The need for this propaganda is also much felt and requested by several Parties outside Italy. For example the United States are now asking the PCI for two Italian organisational comrades. The same request was made quite some time ago by the Argentinian CP. We are also receiving many letters urging in this direction from lots of workers who have taken refuge abroad.

We have to bear in mind that many socialist workers, or those who simply belong to trade union class organisations, are disillusioned and disgusted by their leaders' lack of interest and could become good militants, fighting alongside us, if the CP took the initiative without delay and started work on this organisational work.

For this work to be effective it is necessary for it to be coordinated and continuous. From this stems the need for an appropriate body, such as the one we are proposing.

b) *Regulation and placement of refugees*

The Communist Party of Italy has up to now sought to send abroad only those comrades who, after receiving heavy sentences or having very serious accusations pending, could absolutely not remain in Italy.[58] We have held to the general principle that, right up to the extreme limits possible, the comrades must carry out their activity in their own country without deserting the field of struggle.

But various workers, given they have found themselves in such pitiful conditions that they have had to choose between dying of hunger and submitting to the fascist yoke, have made their own decision to emigrate, wandering aimlessly without any guide, and with their revolutionary spirit totally downcast.

We must therefore keep a closer eye on the flow of emigrants abroad and their life there, check their identity as refugees, know where to send them, and where work can more easily be found for them; who and how they can be used for propaganda and Party work, and who should go back to Italy etc.[59]

c) *Collection and distribution of funds*

We shall have to deal with the collection of funds for aid to refugees and to the victims of political persecution who have stayed in Italy, for the political, trade union and cooperative organisations and for the fight against fascism.

This collection must be made in agreement with the Rote Hilfe and with the Parties of the individual countries. Particular attention must be paid to the foreign Italian emigrants, especially in the Americas.

In the most important countries, sub-committees can be set up or trustworthy people be chosen, who then work in agreement with the Parties and class organisations on the spot. These sub-committees must however be attached to and led by the central Aid Committee in V[ienna].

The expenses for the running of the Aid Committee will of course come out of the fund collected.

This work will be carried out in parallel to that of propaganda and organisation.

The Rote Hilfe has already collected some funds that it has allotted to the victims of Italian fascism.

With that, we have, then, the initial fund for the start of the work.

d) *Placement of refugees*

Sure information on the possibility of placing refugees in the various countries can be obtained through the help of the Parties and sub-committees. This is connected to the possibility of sending groups of workers and agricultural labourers to Russia, obtaining some small land concessions there.

As regards concessions of factories, the question is more complicated and must be studied before making any concrete proposal. The question may instead be resolved more easily as regards agricultural concessions.

On the subject of the initiative of the Italian Cooperatives, which the Executive gave comrade Marabini the task of dealing with and reporting back to the Party, the change in the political situation in Italy and the consequent crisis of the Cooperatives there makes it impossible to put the project into operation in the initial wide-ranging way that was envisaged. It could instead be reduced to more modest proportions as suggested in comrade Marabini's report and in the summary of that report, here attached.[60]

In order to know whether any initiative on the subject may possibly be undertaken by our Party I have already spoken, for information purposes only, with comrade Eiduk, who is head of the Arbeiter Hilfe.[61]

The project, which naturally must be subject to study, could be made concrete in the following terms. Under the auspices of the Arbeiter Hilfe, subscriptions (or shares) might be launched (maybe very few in Italy, but many in the Americas) to collect the capital necessary for the concessions in Russia for Italian agricultural labourers (or workers) who have been driven out by the fascist terror. These concessions should be given to those labourers who are already skilled in the use of modern means of cultivation and provided with the necessary machinery.

We ought to emphasise and insist on the fact that, by subscribing, a double goal is reached, that of helping the Italian refugees and that of contributing to economic reconstruction and the development of agriculture in Russia.

Given the mentality of the Italian émigrés, we could obtain much more than has been achieved up to now through the generic action of Arbeiter Hilfe. Once we have put together a fund with this precise aim in view (comrade Eiduk is speaking of 12,000 dollars) we could buy some small concession, such as for example some Soviet undertaking that could be managed with no great capital expenditure and could be given over to a first Italian colony. Eiduk says that with this sum we could take over and manage about 500 *desjatiny* and give employment to about 100 peasants.[62] An agricultural cooperative could be set up under the leadership and with the responsibility of the Arbeiter Hilfe.

It would be dangerous and perhaps an illusion to think straight away of vast undertakings like this. Neither is it even advisable, at least for now, to foster large-scale emigration that, from a revolutionary viewpoint, impoverishes our masses to an excessive degree.

But keeping the thing to modest proportions, at least for the moment and given the current situation, there would be a reasonable degree of certainty about its success. The affair must be looked at above all from the political point of view, which is what this part of the activity of our Party through the Aid Committee also advises us to propose to you.

CONSTITUTION AND FINANCING OF THE AID COMMITTEE

The Central Aid Committee can justify and give legal status to the residence and the work of the comrades entrusted with the running of the V[ienna] Bureau.

However it must be subordinated to this latter and therefore to the Party Executive.

With the Aid Committee carrying out a task that in part coincides with and integrates that of the Bureau, use can in part be made of the same people. As well as Gennari, comrade Marabini is highly to be recommended.

Marabini is a member of the C[entral] C[ommittee] and a parliamentary deputy. In dealings with the Austrian Government, this latter role of his may facilitate the residence and activity of the Aid Committee, which would also serve as a cover for the activity of the Bureau.

Furthermore, Marabini was a member of the Aid Committee for the children of Vienna, and in 1920 went to the city to bring back the Viennese children who had been put up by the proletariat of the Romagna region. This fact too can be put to good use if the government in V[ienna] should pose possible obstacles.

It may be added that, both because of all his activity for the Party over a long number of years and because he has involved himself directly in these affairs in Rome, he has wide contacts and is very well known among the masses among whom political emigration has been the highest (for example Emilia).[63]

Finally, for the bureau too, both as collaborator and above all for the administrative part (which will become very big indeed when the publication of newspapers and pamphlets begins), he is one of the most appropriate people because of his seriousness, known to all, and because he also gives the widest guarantees vis-à-vis the International.

We do not believe that at this time he can be put to better use in Italy. The Chamber does not meet before 16 May and probably will not remain open more than a few days. In any case, if on that occasion his involvement is required in Italy, he is always able to go immediately (given the short distance) and start his work again in V[ienna].

As for the technical apparatus necessary, this can be dealt with when the Party Executive agrees to set up the committee and when it is seen what the needs are and what elements will eventually be used on the spot, making use of the other apparatuses present there.

As regards financing, when we know what sum will be put at our disposal by the Rote Hilfe, we shall be able to see what and who can top it up in order to have a first initial fund.

A. Gramsci

E. Gennari

Source: Central State Archive, Ministry of the Interior General Public Security Headquarters, A.g.e.r. [General and reserved matters]. PCI documents seized by the Milan Police Authorities (1920-1925), b. 1, f. 10; typescript with handwritten signatures

Gramsci and Gennari to the Executive Committee of the PCI

MOSCOW 29-3-1923[64]

To the E[xecutive] C[ommittee] of the PCI

Dear comrades,

Yesterday we received two documents that we had been expecting since the first day that the fascist government unleashed the offensive against our Party; these documents are Grieco's report and the reply by Fortichiari to the commission on illegal work. Here we were living on impressions and judging the Party's position on the basis of the catastrophic news in the papers. We have been absolutely without any concrete news. The only Italian paper giving full information has been *Avanti!*. What Terracini has written has been more journalistic articles than reports, no factual data but just generic judgements and polemical comments that in the Presidium provided the cue for bitter attacks against our Party, which was depicted as a kindergarten of irresponsible children who don't understand the first thing about the situation, who don't even know what is happening in their own Party (the absence of information was becoming proof of the Party's complete disintegration), and who are taking on the International with toy swords. Some meetings of the Pres[idium] have been disastrous for us and utterly demoralizing. The arrival of two of Scocci[marro]'s personal letters to Gramsci has allowed us to redress the situation a little. We have argued that the responsibility for the situation created in the SP lies with the Penguin and have succeeded in stopping him being sent back to Italy, as Bukharin proposed;[65] not only that, but, in the resolution passed, we managed to have a statement approved that the systems operated in Italy by the Penguin to have the views of the INT[ernational] triumph were both wrong and damaging.

ILLEGAL APPARATUS

We are giving you a brief 'historical' sketch of the opinion that has here become current regarding the Party's capability of organising an illegal apparatus, and about the effectiveness of the apparatus already in existence. At the Congress, as you will recall, an extremely good impression was created on the arrival of the *Comunista* and *L'Ordine Nuovo*, printed semi-illegally at the time of the fascist coup d'état.[66] After the congress, in a closed meeting of the Presidium, com. Eberlein reported on the talks held with the representatives of the various parties on the subject of illegal work. For Italy he said that the impression had been formed, from the words of com. Bordiga, that a real and proper illegal apparatus did not exist, and that he had not received the necessary details to be able to say what really did exist.

The news that arrived at the moment of Bordiga's arrest confirmed this judgement, giving rise to a sinister impression of us. Terracini's ingenuousness, in insisting in every letter of his on the 'unfortunate incident' that had caused the arrest of the head of the party and the seizure of its funds, threatened to introduce an element of farce into the proceedings. It will be difficult to get rid of this impression. Everyone agrees in maintaining that the question is not an organisational but an essentially political one; a party of doctrinaires that does not want to become a mass party, which is not doing anything to win the sympathy of the great masses, cannot organise a solid and secure illegal apparatus: this is the reasoning that is being put forward.

In the last report of the sessions of the Central Committee it was stated that Repossi was opposed to the formation of factory groups, without it being stated what approach was established on the subject. This is a question of principle. After the third Congress, all Communist Parties ought to be organised on a factory basis, combined with a territorial basis, so as to include elements who because of unemployment or other reasons do not work in the factories. The Central Committee should take a clear and precise decision on the question and make sure that this organisational measure has been carried out.

THE FUSION QUESTION

The arrival of Beruzzi's report has notably modified the impressions on this subject given rise to by Giacomo's reports and Terracini's polemical points. We have to persuade ourselves that the policy of the International will always be based on winning over the Socialist Party, in order to have *Avanti!*, which over the last few months, through its circulation and the subscriptions collected from readers, has shown itself to be the journal closest to the hearts of the Italian masses. This means that the International will change tactic every time that it deems it necessary in order to avoid losing the majority of the Socialist Party and being thus reduced to the previous situation. On the point that the fusionist minority should remain in the Socialist Party, we were in agreement, and thus could not but be in agreement as regards the formation of the proletarian bloc, which ought to be a real fusion with a distinction being maintained in the central bodies.

To be more precise, we may recall that when, in the last meeting of the Presidium, before the Commission had begun its work, a decision was taken that the fusionists would leave the Socialist Party even if they were in a minority, this was done solely to commit Serrati to fight with all his might for the fusionists to triumph at the congress; but, from that moment on, it was thought it would be politically more useful to give the Comintern representative the faculty of advising the opposite approach at the appropriate moment. This was also known by Scoccimarro, who will be able to give you more detailed information.

Now, at the Presidium meeting, all are agreed that the fusionist minority should remain within the Party; we supported this thesis and managed to ensure that no hasty decision should be taken, and that a waiting stance should be adopted, with the fusionist fraction being urged to work actively and forcefully to improve the position.[67]

For this reason, as regards the proletarian bloc, we were opposed (albeit in splendid isolation) to what, according to Giacomo's proposal, would have meant a surrender and would have been a substitute for fusion.

The problem must be studied carefully by our Central Committee. The question is whether we can develop a great strategic action that, given the general situation, given the greater homogeneity of the communists, and given the support of the International, will allow us to absorb the socialists completely. We here quote the wording of the resolution of the Presidium of 16 March: 'The Presidium reconfirms its resolution of 20 February on putting back the date of the Socialist Party congress and on the formation of the proletarian bloc. This means: joint local groups, joint actions, joint journals, joint action in the trade unions, joint struggle against fascism. The Presidium charges com. B[eruzzi] with carrying out these decisions without delay and has him note that the procedures adopted up to now for carrying out the decision were wrong and damaging.[68] The decisions of the fourth Congress (14 points) remain, of course, valid and all members of the Communist International are duty bound to carry out in practice propaganda in favour of these decisions.[69] But the immediate execution of the 14 points has been set aside, given the unfavourable political conditions. Propaganda in favour of fusion must therefore be continued.'

In short, we are dealing with an operation of undercover work in the grand style, undertaken according to circumstances allowing it, with the aim of conquering *Avanti!*, that is to say the organ that in reality today exercises a predominant influence over the majority of the revolutionary working class.[70] It presupposes, of course, that there exist groups of communists who are homogeneous and highly in tune with one another, and an Executive able to make the most of all opportunities to demonstrate that it is on the right road in the effective struggle against fascism. We too believe this is the only way and the only possible tactic at the present time. The latest events are demonstrating that fascism is in effect entering its phase of decomposition. It wants make up for lost time and in a headlong dash arrive at its final results, namely the disappearance of all bourgeois and petty bourgeois parties, and the concentration, including at the organisational level, of all suitable elements of the bourgeoisie in its ranks. But since fascism has had to begin concrete activity in the economic field, it has had to choose between the various capitalist groups, and naturally the choice has fallen on that of steel, which represents the essential base for an imperialist policy, for a fresh development of the armaments industry, for a programme that in essence is founded on the perspective of a coming war on the side of France. A symptom of this grave situation is the attitude adopted by the *Corriere della Sera* and *La Stampa*, representatives of the engineering and textile export industries, whose interest is in conflict with the steel industry, and who cannot look favourably on a military link with France.[71] We believe that, in this situation too, new life will be breathed in Italy into the tendency towards the autonomy of entire regions (Sardinia, Sicily and Southern Italy), which will offer a very wide base for the fight against fascism and for the dissolution of the bourgeois State.

Of course all these perspectives make it necessary to unify the revolutionary proletariat, make it necessary that there should be one sole party of the communist masses.[72]

Since we cannot use the same coercive and terrorist systems as the fascists to obtain an end that is similar for the two classes, the only tactic possible becomes that advocated by the International. The Central Committee should carry out a detailed discussion of these problems and set out a brief set of theses on the perspectives for the situation in Italy, to be transmitted to Moscow for discussion in the Executive Committee.

PRACTICAL PROPOSALS

We should like to put forward two proposals for you to study in the light of the situation and its possibilities.

First, we think it useful to create a Party economic research bureau that will bring together all the necessary elements for the struggle it undertakes and for its intellectual training. The bureau could operate legally and be managed by persons under Party control while not necessarily being Party members. It could propose the following aims: a monthly or fortnightly bulletin on the national and international situation of the working classes (unemployment, wages, trade union struggles, organisation) as compared with capitalist organisation. On a small scale it ought to do what the British Labour Party's Department for Research on Labour does.[73] The bulletin could be available on subscription and could offer a paid service for information requested by unions of all hues and shades. One might also think of publishing a fortnightly of political culture, of the English *Common Sense* type, dealing with all the national and international problems of the working class from a substantially communist viewpoint, but in an objective form, offering dispassionate information and discussion.[74] The name *Senso comune* [*Common Sense*] could be the title and this could be … a programme in itself. It would not be difficult here to organise a network of good correspondents from all countries and an information and correspondence service from Russia. We can give you the names of two people for this work.[75] One is Piero Sraffa, known to Togliatti, who has worked on labour problems in England for the Labour Research Bureau of the Labour Party and who is a specialist in banking questions. Gramsci could write to him about this. Sraffa had already spoken with Gramsci some time ago about a project of this type and was favourable to it. He is a person who has worked indirectly at Turin, and who has given *L'Ordine Nuovo* a lot of material on confidential questions, making use of the dossier of his father, a big name in freemasonry circles and in the Banca Commerciale; outside a restricted circle the son is not known for his communist opinions. Another name could be Molinari, the same person who was already working alongside Niccolini in 1920 and who, until a short while ago, was employed in the municipal labour office in Milan. Although of anarchist origins, he was a communist sympathiser and, in [19]21??, had already begun to send material to *L'Ordine Nuovo*.

Second proposal: at the national level you could organise a complete service of party reports on the general situation in the country in its various aspects. There should be someone in each branch to provide information. The subject matters should be organised according to broad municipal area, to wider administrative area or to provinces, and worked up gradually so as to give a monthly series of zonal reports divided according to subject matter which would go to the Executive and on which the Executive should make detailed reports for Moscow.[76]

Sending us material We are completely cut off from Italy. We can read only AVANTI, the LAVORATORE, and the CORRIERE. We do not have direct information on the Italian Party and on the confederations, we do not have information on fascism, on its journalistic and trade-union manifestations.[77]

With every courier you ought to send us a series either of press cuttings or other material on the most important happenings and discussions.

Send us Mortara's 'Prospettive Economiche' ['Economic Outlook'] for [19]23; the numbers of Einaudi's RIFORMA SOCIALE (including the back numbers – if possible, from July 1922), the numbers of PROBLEMI ITALIANI and whatever you think is useful for our information.

Greetings

Source: incomplete version in AAG, part typed and part handwritten; the up-to-now missing end of the letter is in the Comintern Archives at the location 513-1-187/47, with a typescript of most but not all the rest at 513-1-187/14-17

Gramsci and Armando Cocchi to the Central Committee of the Russian Communist Party

[10 APRIL 1923][78]

To the C[entral] C[ommittee] of the R[ussian] C[ommunist] P[arty] (B[olshevik])

It had been decided between the Executive Committee of the Comintern and the Central Committee of the Communist Party of Italy to unite all our emigrants in sections that, under the control and with the help of their Party, would be grouped together for the work of reorganisation of the Italian movement.

With this goal, the Italian Party has already organised a Central Bureau.

It is necessary for all our sections abroad to be our reserves as regards people and forces.

Our section, side by side with the Russian party, has great tasks within the Italian movement, for the freedom in which it may realise its work, for the example and the teachings of the great revolution and of its men, which with your help it can receive.

But in order to carry out our organisational work now, many things are necessary which we here permit ourselves to ask of you.

1) A member of the Russian Communist Party or a collaborator of the C[entral] C[ommittee] who knows Italian or even French, to whom we could turn each time that big or small problems arise. We should be able to know where to find this comrade each time that there was need.

2) We need to know the rules of the Russian Communist Party, and therefore we are asking for four copies in Russian, which we will attempt to translate with the forces we have.
3) We have been told that some small premises will be given us for our meetings.
4) We are presenting our Party questionnaire forms. There are Italian comrades who are not in Moscow, but in far-off cities such as Per'm, Gomel', Odessa etc, we must also know what the form of relationships is that we have to tell them for communication with the local sections and with us.

There are also in Russia Italian comrades whom we do not know; we have been told of Italians in Petrograd and of a section of Italian communists in Kiev. We need to have news of them that we can receive only by means of the Russian Communist Party.

With communist greetings

Source: Comintern Archives 508-1-099/1, typewritten in Russian

---

Gramsci and Armando Cocchi to the Central Committee, RCP, to J.V. Stalin, copy to O. A. Pjatnickij

[APRIL 1923]

To the C[entral] C[ommittee] R[ussian] C[ommunist] P[arty], to Com. STALIN

Copy to com. PJATNICKIJ

We have received a positive reply from you regarding the negotiations between com. Cocchi and com. Ivanov and regarding our letter of 10 April of the current year (copy attached), the purpose of which is the creation of a section of Italian emigrants under the R[ussian] C[ommunist] P[arty].

This corresponds to the decision already taken by the Comintern on the activity of the Italian movement abroad.

Perhaps we have misunderstood something thanks to our poor knowledge of the Russian language, but in the last 24 hours, when we should have received our membership cards from com. Smirnova, we have received the impression that the situation before our eyes has altered.

The basic form of the Russian communist movement is the cell at the work place and each of us will go into our cell with due discipline and enthusiasm because we know that there we will find much of what we need to learn from you, we will learn the values and defects that go hand in hand with the experience of day-to-day work; [we will go into the cells] in order to take an active part in the work together with the Russian comrades.

But, as a group of emigrants, by force of necessity dispersed all over Russia, [a situation] to which our Italian communist party has been compelled, we also have other tasks, other parallel obligations: those regarding culture and also information ones, exerting a control over ourselves and other Italian emigrants who are not communists yet, keeping in constant correspondence with our movement, with our centres, from which we need to receive direction, and need to carry out their orders in an organic centralised form.

So, in order to keep our forces steady, in order to direct and centralise our spirit, *we need an Italian section.*[79] And for that, in order that the section, and its executive committee, may develop the necessary work of discipline and control, it needs to be officially recognised by the Russian Communist Party, and needs to have its own definite hierarchical and juridical status within the Party itself. You will define its confines and limits: for example, we understand clearly that no special rights will be given us to intervene in your political activity and so on. We think that you will recognise the need for this section and we also ask you to define which exactly of the organs of your party we should turn to for the work in common when this is needed. Together with the Ital[ian] Communist Party you will be in control of the work and activity of our section.

This decision is necessary: thousands of Italian emigrants, pursued by hatred and famine, are looking to Russia as their sole refuge, and several hundred of them, despite the difficulties, will come to you. But is it perhaps not our section that should be the best equipped body for control over and support of them, for the education and support of their fighting spirit? Is it not our section that should bring them into the Russian communist movement as disciplined and reliable members?

Conversely, drawing them in and dispersing them within the Russian communist movement would mean suffocating one of the means (the Italian section in Russia) of support for the Italian communist uprising. Other parties might follow our example (not permitting the formation of an Italian section) and by doing so nullify every action of our Central Bureau on activity abroad.

One more question arises: length of party membership is determined as equal for all of us from 1921. In our party questionnaire forms we have described in detail our work in the Italian party.

b) For this reason we ask that in our party membership cards the following should be indicated:

Transferred from the Italian Communist Party to the
R[ussian] C[ommunist] P[arty]_________________ April 1923
Entered the Italian Soc[ialist] Y[outh] Feder[ation] ______ (date)
Transferred to the Soc[ialist] P[arty] of Italy ___________ (date)
Transferred to the Italian Communist Party____________ (date)
(or to the Young Communists, depending on the circumstances).

Then everything will be clear.

We especially insist that it must appear clear on our membership cards that we are not being admitted [to membership] but are transferring to the R[ussian] C[ommunist] P[arty] on the basis of the international statute.

c) And you, comrades, we wish to have you note yet one more circumstance: the official representative of the Italian Communist Party in Russia is com. GRAMSCI Antonio who is the sole person authorised as such by the Italian Communist Party to speak in the name of the PCI when there is need for such and, speaking frankly, we have to tell you that we were very surprised to know that he was not invited to give his explanations regarding our admittance.

We are putting these questions to you because we maintain that it is better to clear up all these problems immediately so as to avoid any misunderstandings.

With communist greetings

Representative of the It[alian] C[ommunist] P[arty] at the Comintern
Antonio Gramsci (ГРАМШИ)
Secretary of the Italian section
Cocchi Armando (КОККИ)

Source: Comintern Archive 508-1-099/2-4; typewritten, including the names Gramsci and Cocchi in Cyrillic, after their handwritten signatures in the Latin alphabet[80]

To Evgenija

24/4/23

Greetings. Gramsci

See you again soon in the meadows of red, red poppies under the Crimean sun[81]

Vittorio

Source: AAG; picture postcard of Čičerin, People's Commissar for Foreign Affairs, signed 'Vittorio' i.e. Viktor, Evgenija's brother, and – almost hidden under the postmark – 'Gramsci'.

To Togliatti

18 MAY 23

Dear Palmiro

I'll reply at length to your letter and explain my current opinion on the situation in the party and the perspectives to be worked on for its future development and for the approach of the groups constituting it. In general I'll say straight away that you're too optimistic: the situation is much more complex than appears from your letter. During the Fourth Congress I had a number of talks with Amadeo that have led me to think that we must have an open, once-and-for-all discussion between us regarding certain questions which now seem, or may seem, intellectual quarrels, which I consider, should there be a revolutionary development in the Italian situation, such as to become the motive for a crisis and for an internal disintegration of the Party. The basic question today is this, the one which you yourself have posed: we have to create within the Party a nucleus of comrades, who will not be a fraction, who will have a maximum of ideological homogeneity and who therefore can succeed in endowing practical action with the greatest possible singleness of leadership. We, the old leading group from Turin, have made lots of mistakes in this field. We have avoided taking to its extreme conclusions the dissent over ideas and practice that sprang up with regard to Angelo [Tasca], we did not clarify the situation, and now we find ourselves at the point that a small group of comrades is exploiting for its own ends the tradition and forces that we developed and brought into play, and so Turin has become a document to be used against us.

In the general field, because of the repulsion we felt in 1919-20 against creating a fraction, we remained simple, isolated individuals or nearly so, while in the other, abstentionist group the tradition of organising as a fraction and working together has left deep traces that even today have quite considerable implications for the life of the party regarding ideas and practice. But on this I will write to you at length and in detail. I want further to write you a more general letter for the comrades of our old group, like Leonetti, Montagnana and so on, in which for their benefit too I will explain my attitude as from the Fourth Congress, which reproduces the self-same situation I had in Turin in 1920. If they recall, I did not then want to go into the Communist electionist fraction but instead maintained that it was necessary to have a closer relationship with the abstentionists.

I think that today, up here, given the general conditions of the movement in Europe, it is easier, at least in substance, to resolve in our favour the questions that are being posed. At the formal level, we have committed gross errors which have damaged us enormously, and which have made us seem lightweight, childish and prone to introduce disorganisation. But the situation is now in our favour all along the line. As regards Italy I am optimistic, given – it goes without saying – that we know how to work and to remain united. In my view we must look at the question of the PSI more realistically, and think, as a reflection on this, of the period after the taking of power. Three years' experience has taught us, not only in Italy, how deeply rooted the traditions of social democracy are and how difficult it is to destroy the residues of the past through simple ideological polemics. We have to carry out vast, far-reaching political activity that, day after day, takes to pieces both this tradition and the organism that incarnates it. The tactic of the International is up to the task. In Russia, out of 350,000 CP members, only 50,000 are Old Bolsheviks, the other 300,000 being ex-Mensheviks and Social-Revolutionaries who came over to us through the political action of the original nucleus. This nucleus has not however been overwhelmed by this element, but has continued to lead the party and even to become stronger as regards Congress delegates and within the general movement of the leadership stratum.

In the German Party the same thing has happened: the 50,000 Spartacists have completely taken over the 300,000 Independents, and of the 20 delegates to the Fourth Congress only 3 were former Independents. And take note that the delegates were to a great extent chosen by the local bodies. I think that, on our part, there are too many worries, and, if I look at what their psychological root is, I can find only one explanation. That is, we are aware of being weak and of running the risk of getting swamped. Note that this has enormously important practical consequences. In Italy we have cultivated, as if it were in greenhouse conditions, an opposition that is starved of any ideals and any clear vision. What is the situation that has thus been created? The mass of the party and its sympathisers form their opinion on the basis of the public documents which contain the line of the International, and, as a reflection of this, that of the opposition. We detach ourselves from the masses; between us and the masses a cloud is formed, full of incomprehension and misunderstanding, of complicated wrangling. We will at a certain point appear to be people who want at all costs to remain in our places – that is, the role that corresponds precisely to that of the opposition will be overturned, to our damage. I believe that we, that our group, must remain at the head of the Party, because we really are in the line of historical development, because, despite all our mistakes, the work we have carried out has been positive and we have created something. The others have not done anything and now want to liquidate Communism in Italy, in order to lead our young movement back to the traditional path. But if we continue to assume the formalistic attitudes we have adopted up to now (and note that they are formalistic for me, for you, for Bruno, and for Umberto, but not for Amadeo) we will reach exactly the opposite result to what we want: the opposition will to all effect become the Party's representative and we will remain cut out, will be subject to a total and perhaps irremediable defeat in practice, and this will inevitably mark the beginning of our disintegration as a group and of our rout as regards ideas and politics. Having said that, we must not worry overmuch about our leading role, we must press on, carry on our political action, without looking too much into the mirror. We are in line with the current of history and we shall win because we are *rowing* well and have the rudder firmly in our hands. If we know how to work effectively we shall absorb the Socialist Party and resolve the first and fundamental problem of the revolution, that of unifying the proletarian vanguard and destroying the demagogic and popularistic tradition. From this point of view I did not find the comments you made at the Socialist Congress satisfactory. You appear there as the communist who is looking in the mirror. Instead of disintegrating the Soc[ialist] Party, all your comment did was to strengthen it by placing the entire socialist movement in an insuperable antithesis to us. For the leaders, for Nenni, for Vella, and so on, this is undoubtedly true, but is it true for the mass of the members, and what counts more, for the area under the influence of the proletariat? Certainly not, and we are firmly convinced that the overwhelming majority of the proletarian vanguard will be attracted to and assimilated by us. What is it then that we have to do?

1. We must not insist on antitheses *en bloc* but distinguish between leaders and the mass.
2. We must seek out all the elements of dissent between the leaders and the mass and deepen them, widen them, generalise them politically.
3. We must carry on a discussion of the current political situation and not an examination of general historical phenomena.
4. We must make practical proposals and show the mass practical directions for action and organisation.

For your better understanding I will give an example of this and widen the question to include the Congress of the Popular Party, which has not been politically exploited by us, even though, together with the Action Party of Sardinia, it offered us the opportunity to make essential statements about the problem of the relations between the proletariat and the classes in the countryside.

The socialist problem was this: we had to show up the strident contrast between the words and deeds of the socialist leaders. When the International advised us to adopt as our own the watchword of the right-wing socialists of the bloc between the two parties, it did so because it was easy to see that, given the general situation, fusion had become impossible and it was necessary to fence Vella and Nenni in, in the sure knowledge that their attitude was demagogic and that their line diverged from ours. The truth of this was seen in the response to our proposal. In the comment on the Congress we ought to have noted that the ban on the fusionists organising autonomously, and the fact that they were excluded from the Central leadership and their youth federation dissolved, were political elements of the first order, that should have been exploited. The socialist masses should have been confronted with this precise fact: leaving aside the confusion of the polemics and verbiage, it was essential that we should have worked towards tracing out for these masses the concrete overall directions to be taken, and explained them clearly and understandably.

The same holds for the Popular Party Congress. In my opinion, given the ties linking this organisation and the Vatican, every movement of the Popular Party is of special importance for us. In my view the Congress of the Populars means that there exists widespread discontent among the masses of the peasantry against the policy of the Party, a discontent caused especially by the new taxes on working farmers. This state of mind is extending from the countryside to the city, among wide strata of the petty bourgeoisie. The composition of the P[opular] P[arty] is a reactionary and fascist right, based on the clerical aristocracy, a left based on the countryside, and a centre constituted by urban intellectual elements and priests. The campaigns of the *Corriere* and *La Stampa* are bringing grist to the mill of the centre of the Popular Centre. The elements that are being detached from fascism by this subtle campaign are of necessity going in the direction of the Popular Party, the only organisation in existence that offers some hope, due to its flexible and opportunistic tactics, of being able to counterbalance fascism and to reintroduce some governmental competition in the parliamentary field, that is to say liberty as understood by the liberals. The fascist tactic towards the Populars is very dangerous and will of necessity push the party to the left and bring about split-offs towards the left. The Populars are being faced with the same situation as the one during the war, except that it is now enormously more difficult and dangerous. During the war the catholics were neutralist in the parishes and the villages, while the newspapers and the higher church circles were vociferous in their support of the war. At that time the government did not force the centre to oppose the outlying areas or to assume the same position everywhere. The fascists do not want to behave in this manner. They want to have open consent and want declarations of co-responsibility, especially before the masses, in the base-level cells of the mass parties. This is impossible to obtain from the P[opular] P[arty] without implicitly asking for its death. It is evident that we must accentuate and widen the crisis within the Populars, by obtaining declarations from left elements, among other places in our newspapers, just as we once did in Turin with the case of Giuseppe Speranzini.

This letter has turned out to be longer and more complex than I thought. Since there are some of these questions I want to deal with more amply, for the moment I'll stop.

Warm greetings to the comrades you see

and for you a fraternal embrace

Antonio

Source: APC 513-1-189/1-12 in the paper fascicule 189; handwritten[82]

Gramsci, Scoccimarro, Fortichiari and Terracini, probably to a leading organ of the Comintern

24.5.23[83]

OBSERVATIONS ON THE REPORT BY COM. RÁKOSI

One can well explain the reason for the many mistakes to be found in Com Rákosi's report to the 18 May E[xecutive] of the C[ommunist] I[nternational] since, in carrying out his mandate, the Comintern delegate to Italy was almost always obliged to work in the Socialist Party milieu, meeting up on only a few occasions (no more than 4 or 5 times), each time for half an hour, with the leading members in charge within the Communist Party, without taking any part at all in their desperate attempt to defend and recover the position lost.

We wish here in a few words to rectify first of all the above mentioned false allegations:[84]

In Section II on 'The Communist Party'

No one had foreseen the victory of fascism on 27 October 1922, many did not believe in any victory at all of fascism and in its seizure of power; our Party was expecting this later, but it was indeed expecting it. And, in effect, a week before the coup d'état our E[xecutive]

C[ommittee] launched an appeal with concrete instructions to its members and to the mass of the working class for the possibility of an open struggle between fascism and the democratic government (see *Inprecorr* – series of articles in November 22).

It is absolutely untrue that at the moment of victory of fascism the majority of the party's leaders were in Moscow;[85] just one of the 5 members of the E[xecutive] C[ommittee] was there, namely comrade Bordiga, there for the Fourth Congress, while Repossi, Grieco, Fortichiari and Terracini were in Italy, in their place;[86] and only 4 of the 15 members of the C[entral] C[ommittee] were in Moscow (Gennari, Gramsci, Azzario, Marabini), while all the others were in Italy.

It is absolutely untrue that the party remained in this situation, without leadership and prey to panic. Com. Rákosi at that time was in Moscow and must therefore have known of the reports sent to the Comintern, which were relayed to the Fourth Congress and which clearly demonstrated that the Communist Party suffered no harm during the October government crisis.[87] Quite the contrary, it continued to carry out its functions in a normal way; at that time and with no hesitation *Il Comunista* and *L'Ordine Nuovo*, which had been suppressed through government violence, began to be distributed illegally. The Party contested the administrative elections in Milan in mid-November, 15 days after the coup d'état. It obtained a brilliant victory against the fascists and the reformists in the elections at the beginning of December for the engineers' Unemployment Fund in Turin etc. On the return of the delegates from the Fourth Congress, there was therefore no special increase in activity by the Party, which was already well advanced, still more given that only comrade Bordiga amongst them had a post of responsibility and work in the Party organisation. Three of the four members of the C[entral] C[ommittee] who were abroad (Gennari, Gramsci, Marabini) did not come back to Italy and, for needs of the Party, are still abroad.

It is absolutely untrue that the Communist Parliamentary Group refused to read the declaration decided by the E[xecutive] C[ommittee] of the Party. This declaration was read at the session of the Chamber of Deputies by comrade Rabezzana, and printed both by the legal and illegal Italian Communist press, as well as by *L'Humanité*, and by *Inprecorr*.

It is absolutely untrue that at the time of the arrests in February many members of the E[xecutive] C[ommittee] were imprisoned.

Only comrade Bordiga was arrested. The arrest of comrade Grieco followed two months later.

It is untrue that, during the searches carried out in February, the police found a considerable number of documents; in actual fact 98% of the [comrades] arrested at that time were freed, no evidence being offered against them. Even those who had positions within the Party, as for example all the journalists of *Il Lavoratore* who had been accused of being at the centre of the conspiracy, were freed at that time.

It is untrue that, in the course of the arrests, the police discovered the Party's Central Illegal Bureau. This Bureau was in Milan, while the office discovered was in Rome. Moreover, the office discovered was only comrade Bordiga's work office. The real Central Bureau of the Party was subdivided among 4 other places where all the documents of the Party were being kept. These 4 Offices have never been found by the police.

It is untrue that up to now a great number of illegal local institutions have been discovered. The PCI possesses no special illegal local institutions. All the normal local sections are organised on an illegal basis. Consequently, the mass arrest of some thousand militants suffices to destroy (not, however, discover) a great number of sections.

We reject in the most absolute terms the assertion that at that time panic possessed everyone, the Executive included. When one makes such assertions one has the duty of proving them with facts, which are completely absent in comrade Rákosi's report. It is, on the contrary, true that in the very days of the mass arrests the E[xecutive] C[ommittee] of the Party, with the effective aid of all the members, and with the recommencement of general organisational work, ensured the regular and continuous publication of *Il Lavoratore*, all of whose journalists and administrative staff had been arrested by the police; it sent its delegates to the International Congresses (Leipzig, Frankfurt); it put the problem of the Italian communist émigrés etc, on concrete foundations. All this is sufficiently proven and documented in the report that we are about to present to the Comintern E[xecutive].

The events in Italy from October 1922 to May 1923, characterised by the alliance of all the reactionary forces against the CP, demonstrate to a high degree the force of the organisation which, from time to time damaged by stronger pressure, has always once again regained its integrity.

The reproach of having based the reorganisation of the Party solely on its established cadres, and not having tried to attract the working masses is, once more, only a generic criticism and not based at all on fact. Certainly it is not in the periods of the most frightening reaction, such as the one that is currently underway in Italy, that the Communist Parties have the best chance of attracting into their ranks the working masses or new individual elements. In these periods the Party's problem is not that of increasing its membership but that of losing the least possible number. This problem has been well resolved by the PCI, whose ranks number about 6000 members. The extraordinary delegate of the C[ommunist] I[nternational], who worked closely with us in March and April, estimated a membership of no more than 3000.[88]

It is untrue that the Party Secretary (we have a Secretariat composed of 5 members – the E[xecutive] C[ommittee]) gave the Party membership at 200 to 300 in February. Up to two months after the mass imprisonment the Party E[xecutive] C[ommittee]) did not think it possible to publish figures regarding the reorganisational work. In any case it was impossible to do so, at the actual time of the arrests, since communications had to a great extent been interrupted.

As for the action of the PCI regarding fusion with the PSI, we refer you to the report of the Secretary of the COMMISSION ON FUSION nominated at the Fourth Congress, and to the reports sent from Italy by the extraordinary delegate of the C[ommunist] I[nternational].

Section IV – Proletarian tendencies in fascism[89]

On the proletarian forces in fascism comrade Rákosi cannot refrain from an exaggeration which may lead to very dangerous errors when going on to decide the future tactics of the PCI

Within fascism there is no proletarian tendency in the sense of currents favourable to the proletariat and to the methods being shown in its class action, even if this action is reduced to mean nothing more than legal action in the defence of the legal corporative interests of the working people.[90] Through violence and terror, fascism has created its own trade unions, and the following two orders of phenomena have been developed on the objective basis of these organisations.

On the one hand, the formation of a layer of trade union officials who want, as is quite natural, to be sure of maintaining their position, and who, in consequence, from time to time, adopt a demagogic attitude, without through that developing any continuity of action and systematic conception.

On the other hand, as a consequence of the ever increasing opposition within fascism coming from numerous, particularly industrial, bourgeois groups, the fascists are making use of trade union organisation as a threat and a continual ransom.[91]

It is totally absurd to assert that fascism has given rise among the working masses to illusions similar to those which socialism had in its time given birth to. There is nothing that can demonstrate this assertion.

Fascism was to a certain extent demagogic only in the period between March 1919 and June 1920. From that moment on it had to resolve the formidable problem of absorbing the 30 to 40 thousand reactionary officers who had had given it their support. And it resolved this problem through rejecting its compromising past and bringing about a separation between its movement and De Ambris's Italian Union of Labour.[92] It was at this moment that the strongest conflict came about between fascism and D'Annunzio and his legionnaires who were under the influence of De Ambris.

The E[xecutive] of the Comintern must judge in the best way possible all the phenomena that will be produced by fascism relating to the existence of the fascist trade unions, which cannot escape the consequences of their objective composition, if one wants to seek their origin in violence and terror, and not in the consent given to the programme of fascism by one part of the working masses.

But the E[xecutive] of the Comintern must steer clear of all these amateurish exaggerations, which lead to erroneous assessments and incorrect predictions regarding the development of the Italian situation.[93]

Moscow, 24 May 23.

Negri, Martini, Urbani, Gramsci

Source: French version APC 513-1-166/6-11; German version Comintern Archive 513-1-167/4-8; the date is handwritten at the top in the French version and typed at the end of both French and German versions).

To Zinov'ev

MID-JUNE 1923

At the session of the Italian Commission yesterday evening, I did not wish to speak and correct your allegations about my duplicity and insincerity on the question of fusion between the Socialist Party and the Communist Party. There and then I should have denied this, and [in so doing] I would have made the position of the Italian delegation even worse with a personal diatribe against the President of the International, who ought not to make such serious allegations against a member of the Executive, when these allegations of his cannot be backed up even by a glimmer of proof.[94]

Source: APC, 513-1-112/45, handwritten fragment[95]

To Jul'ka

[MOSCOW, AUGUST 1923]

Dear comrade,

Did you come to Moscow on August 5th as you had told me previously? I waited for you for three days. I didn't move from my room for fear that something could happen like last time. I was waiting for you because I felt and still do feel rather tired and demoralised in the stressful wait before I set off, and I would have been (and still would be) very happy to see you once again. But you didn't come to Moscow, did you? You would certainly have come to see me even if only for a moment. I wanted to write to you straight away, then I waited for you to let me know something. You will come soon, won't you? I'll see you again I hope? I'm right in remembering, aren't I, that you have a month's leave in September? I will wait ... maybe I'll still be in Moscow for a week, maybe a fortnight, maybe a month, perhaps we can again talk together for an hour or two and perhaps even go on some long walks together. Please write to me. All your words do me a world of good and make me feel stronger (you see? I'm less strong than I thought and had others think).

Affectionately

Gramsci

Did you know that I've almost learnt the *Одеяло-Убежало* [*Odejalo-Ubežalo* or *The Runaway Blanket*] book by heart?[96]

Source: AAG[97]

To Togliatti and other PCI leaders

To comrade Paolo Palmi (and, for information, to comrades Silvestri, Leonetti, Montagnana, Bruno, Platone, Urbani, Silvia, Edmondo)[98]

[MOSCOW, AUGUST 1923]

Dear comrade,

I am replying to your letter, giving you my point of view on the situation that has been created in our Party following on the decision of the Enlarged Executive. I am putting forward for your consideration a suggestion for a general plan of action; by putting it into practice, in my opinion, the situation itself can find a real and concrete solution. I am absolutely convinced that, today, all discussion on our part that is limited to the organisational and juridical aspects of the Italian situation can have no useful result, but, rather, could just make things worse and make our task more difficult and dangerous. We must instead get down to concrete work and demonstrate, through the Party's entire activity and a practical political engagement that measures up to the Italian situation, that we are what we claim to be, rather than going on in the attitude adopted up to now of being 'misunderstood geniuses'.

1st point. You now think that the discussion here in Moscow has hinged round fusionism and anti-fusionism. This is only apparently the case. Fusionism and anti-fusionism have constituted the 'polemical terminology' of the discussion, not its essence. The discussion was this: whether the PCI has understood the general situation in Italy, and whether it has been able to lead the proletariat; whether the PCI is able to develop a vast political campaign, in other words whether it is ideologically and organisationally equipped for decisive action; whether the leading group of the PCI has assimilated the political doctrine of the Communist International, which is Marxism as developed in Leninism, in other words in an organic and systematic body of organisational principles and tactical stances [...][99]

Source: APC 513-1-112/1-2; handwritten fragment

To unknown recipients, possibly the Central Committee of the Russian Communist Party

Conclusions for the Civalleri affair[100]

On the Civalleri affair, the C[entral] C[ommittee] of the Communist Party of Italy requests:

1. That Civalleri be kept in segregation until the end of the work that citizen Ferruccio Virgili is engaged in, an end that may be fixed approximately for the month of May 1924;
2. That Civalleri should be put in such a position that he cannot communicate with any outside body, for whatever reason and in whatever way. If for whatever reason Civalleri is put in the position of having the right or necessity to communicate with an outside body, that must only take place with the consent and under the direct control of the representative of the PCI in Moscow;
3. As regards his inner-Party relations, Civalleri will undergo the procedure that is operative within the Russian Communist Party.

Moscow, 6 September 1923

Antonio Gramsci

Member of the C[entral] C[ommittee] of the PCI

Source: Comintern Archives, 513-2-017/14, handwritten signed original; also APC 513-2-017/1

To the E[xecutive] C[ommittee] of the PCI

12 SEPTEMBER 1923

Dear comrades,

In its last session the Pres[idium] decided that in Italy a working-class daily paper should be published under the general guide of the E[xecutive] C[ommittee], and open to the political collaboration of the Third Internationalists excluded from the SP.[101] I want to give you my impressions and opinions on the question.

Given the current situation in Italy, in my view there is a great need and use for the paper to come out in such a form as will ensure its legal existence for the longest time possible. Not only therefore must the paper not bear any indication of a Party nature, but its appearance must be such that its actual dependence on our Party does not emerge too explicitly. It must be a newspaper of the left, of the working-class left, that has kept faith with the programme and tactics of the class struggle, that will publish our Party's actions and discussions, as it possibly will for those of the anarchists, republicans and syndicalists, and will give its judgement dispassionately, as if it had a position above the struggle and were adopting a 'scientific' stance. I am aware that it is not very easy to fix all this in a written programme, but the important thing is not to establish a written programme, but rather to ensure for the Party itself, which historically has a dominant position within the left currents of the working class, a legal tribune that will allow it continuously and systematically to reach the widest sections of the masses.

The Communists and Serrati's supporters will collaborate with the paper openly, i.e. having their prominent members sign articles under their own name, following a political project that month by month, and even, I would say, week by week, takes account of the country's general situation, and of the relations that develop among the social forces operating in Italy. We shall have to be careful of Serrati's followers, who will tend to transform the paper into a fractional organ in the struggle against the SP leadership. We shall have to be very strict on this and avoid any type of degeneration. Polemics are necessary, but the spirit in which they are carried out must be political, not that of a sect, and always contained within given limits. We shall have to be on our guard against the attempts to create an 'economic' situation for Serrati, who is unemployed and who will, in all probability, be proposed by his comrades as an ordinary member of the editorial staff. Serrati will collaborate with signed and unsigned articles; his signed articles will however be within a limit to be fixed, and the unsigned ones will have to be accepted by our E[xecutive] C[ommittee]. In order to avoid falling back into the chaotic situation of 1920, it will be necessary to carry out polemics on principles with the Socialists – or rather with the socialist spirit of Serrati, Maffi, etc – that will be useful to strengthen the communist consciousness of the masses and prepare the Party unity and homogeneity that will be necessary after fusion.

As a title I propose *L'Unità* pure and simple, which will be significant for the workers and have a more general significance. I am proposing this because I think that after the decision of the En[larged] E[xecutive] on the Workers' and Peasants' Government, we must give importance especially to the southern question, that is, to the question in which the problem of the relations between workers and peasants is posed not only as a problem of class relations, but also and especially as a territorial problem, that is to say as one of the aspects of the national question. Personally, I believe that the watchword 'Workers' and Peasants' Government' has to be adapted in Italy to the 'Federal Republic of the Workers and Peasants'. I do not know if the present moment is favourable to this, but I do believe that the situation that fascism is creating, and the corporative and protectionist policy of the trade union confederations, will lead our party to this watchword. On this subject, I am preparing a report for you to discuss and examine. If useful, after a few issues of the paper we can open up a polemic, under pseudonyms, and see what repercussions it gives rise to in the country and in the left strata of the Popular Party and the Democrats, who represent the real tendencies of the peasant class, and who have always had the slogan of local autonomy and decentralisation in their programme. If you accept the proposal of the name *L'Unità*, you will leave the field open for the solution of these problems, and the name will be a guarantee against autonomistic degenerations and against reactionary attempts to give tendentious and authoritarian interpretations to the campaigns that may be foreseen. I believe, moreover, that the regime of the Soviets, with the political centralisation given it by the Communist Party, its administrative decentralisation, and its recognition of the status of the local popular forces, finds an optimal ideological preparation in the watchword 'Federal Republic of the Workers and Peasants'.

Communist greetings

Gramsci

*(*Rivista storica del socialismo, *Vol. 7, No 18, January-April 1963, pp115-6)*[102]

APPENDIX 1 TO CHAPTER 4

Report of Gramsci's speech at the XII Conference of the Russian Communist Party

Rappoport: Comrades, I ask Comrade Gramsci's forgiveness if I do not translate every single word. I will limit myself to the basic concepts. Comrade Gramsci spoke first of all of the condition that was created after the most recent events, saying that, morally, the bourgeoisie may be considered to have disappeared. At this moment of time in Italy there is no government – neither bourgeois, nor socialist nor anarchist – there is just no government. There exist a number of cliques, each independent of the others, who are in control of the country. He then went on to speak of the actions of the fascists. They have killed over five thousand workers, wounded more than thirty thousand, destroyed five hundred cooperatives, devastated fifteen hundred municipal administrations. The tragic conditions of the proletariat are there for you all to see.

As regards the Socialist Party, it too is going through a period of complete disintegration. It believed in different reformisms, and in the fact that it could peacefully overcome the bandit movement of the fascist black hundreds. However, as demonstrated by experience, the Socialist Party is mistaken, and in Italy only the Communist Party remains to carry on the battle.

Comrade Gramsci proposed an interesting parallel between the SRs (Socialist Revolutionaries) and the fascists, even though on a first impression this may sound strange. However, knowing the members, it may be claimed that fascism has sprung up on the basis of that same psychology that the SRs came from. They too, ex-anarchists and terrorists, are now hand-in-hand with the bourgeoisie. Their head is the renegade Mussolini, and in their ranks are to be found a mass of socialists and renegade anarchists. The fascists are only more open than the SRs, and they have straight away dropped their masks. So it is that the bourgeoisie, totally disoriented when faced with the terrorist attacks of the fascists, not knowing what to do, are turning to the Church in search of help, are giving it enormous sums of money and have recently given it two billion lire. And when abroad we speak of two billion, it is not two billion rubles. The deficit is enormous. The bourgeoisie is refusing to make any form of financial sacrifice.

These facts undoubtedly constitute conditions that are ripe for revolution. There is no Party capable of representing a serious centre of opposition to the elements of the old system, now in decay, except the Communist Party.

Serrati's reformist Party has now split, and it is the Communist Party that is ever more grouping around itself all the really vital revolutionary elements. And the Italian proletariat, which has given you so much hope and which on other occasions has disappointed you, the Italian proletariat, led by the Communist Party, the sole revolutionary Party, will ever more gather the forces around it, bring in a sovietist regime and, in close union with sovietist Russia, will contribute to the triumph of the world revolution.

(Translated from Charles Rappoport's oral summary as printed in Pravda, 9 August 1922)

APPENDIX 2 TO CHAPTER 4

From Lenin, Zinov'ev, Trotsky, Radek, Bukharin to the Italian Delegation to the Fourth Congress of the Communist International

24 NOVEMBER 1922

TO THE DELEGATION OF THE PCI

Dear friends,

The situation of the Italian question at the Congress is such that, as good comrades, we believe it our duty to say the following to you explicitly:

The 'full commission' of the Congress has declared itself unanimously in favour in principle of the fusion of the PCI with the PSI. There is no doubt that the Congress will approve this decision unanimously. This is a fact of which you cannot but take heed. Your various opposition opinions have been listened to. But the Congress will decide – and this is totally clear – differently.

Now, the whole question consists in this: *how* is this question going to pass in the Congress Plenary session, if on your part errors are not admitted such as could weaken the position of the Italian communists towards the vacillating elements of the maximalists.

If even in the Plenary sessions the speakers for your majority want obstinately to oppose fusion, this will only reinforce the position of those maximalists whom least of all we want to strengthen. Such a spectacle will be undesirable in the extreme.

At the E[xecutive] C[ommittee] of the C[ommunist] I[nternational] it will be difficult to support the PCI during and after the fusion process. The PCI will be wholly isolated. The political damage will be enormous. The error will be irreparable. Our advice is: you can make a brief statement at Congress, saying that the majority of your delegation was against fusion and has already adduced the reasons for this, but, at the same time, you have to say that, since the Commission has decided otherwise, you accept the decision and will carry it out conscientiously. If you do this, you give us the possibility of turning the whole polemic against the earlier position of the PSI and the perspective will not be undermined.

Our duty is to warn you against a huge political error.

We await your prompt reply

On behalf of the C[entral] C[ommittee] of the Russian Communist Party

LENIN
ZINOV'EV
TROTSKY
RADEK
BUKHARIN[103]

Source: APC 513-1-086/1-3; typewritten in Italian on headed notepaper of the All-Union Communist Party (Bolsheviks)

NOTES

1. From 'as it also is' to 'all parties' was added as an emendation between the text of the letter and the signatures.
2. What appears here in the Italian as the 'Centrale' of the Party usually in this period meant the Party Executive (cf Spriano 1967, p175), and as such translated here; later on it was known as the 'Political Bureau' (*Ufficio Politico*); just on occasion the term may refer to the wider 'Central Committee'. The Maffi-Lazzari-Riboldi fraction was the Third Internationalist fraction of the Socialist Party, often known as 'Terzini' (see the Introduction). Zinov'ev then wrote 'An Open Letter to Lazzari, Maffi and Riboldi', whose English version is in *Inprecorr*, Vol. 2, no. 68,

12 August 1922. The letter took the maximalists (for more on the maximalist/reformist split in the PSI see Introduction, p21) to task for their manifesto published in *Avanti!* (9 July), and claimed that, in supporting the Terzini 'we do not doubt that thousands of workers who stand behind the Maximalists have honestly recognised that the Comintern was right', before going on to demand that 'the Maximalists agree to break with the reformists once and for all'.

3. See Karl Radek's article 'The Results of the Session of the Enlarged Executive Committee' in *Inprecorr*, Vol. 2 no. 49, 16 June 1922, p360.
4. As noted in the Introduction, Imola was the place where the communist fraction of the PSI had held a conference prior to the formation of the PCI.
5. The Milan Congress of the Socialist Party (October 1921) was without the communists, who had split off at Livorno nine months earlier; as indicated in this letter, however, varying degrees of pro-Comintern views were present within the socialist ranks.
6. Lazzari's position was different from that of Maffi and Riboldi (cf. Spriano, 1967, p111) and, while favouring collaboration with the Comintern, he was probably never really convinced of going over to it.
7. Of the two Comintern delegates at the Congress, Clara Zetkin and the Polish communist Henryk Walecki (Maksymilian Horowitz), it is the latter, not liked or respected by the Italian communists, who is referred to here.
8. The draft of the Manifesto, signed by the 'Executive of the Communist International' and containing many handwritten amendments (not in Gramsci's hand), is in the Comintern Archives, 513-1-072/2-13. Serrati is still criticised, but one amendment in particular reads 'If the maximalists have recognised their errors …', replacing a crossed-out reference to Serrati; like Gramsci's letter the Manifesto is dated 22 July 1922, and it was published on 30 July in the daily newspaper that bore the same name – *L'Ordine Nuovo* – as Gramsci's review.
9. The copy on pp64-5 of the Gramsci Institute digital version seems to bear very faintly the date of 4 August. A date of 24 August, sometimes reported, is in fact the date the letter was received.
10. See next letter in this selection.
11. There were two Czechoslovak delegates, Bohumil Jílek and Bohumír Šmeral. Ilic was Jílek, the non-voting candidate member (hence the ironic 'half a Czechoslovak vote'), who favoured the delegation's position, having a similar position to the Italian Party majority, to the left of the official Comintern line.
12. This is the letter to Radek, 22 July (p111).
13. This opinion was however contested by Gramsci in his 22 July letter.
14. The words in brackets were added by hand in the margin by Ambrogi.
15. By mistake Gramsci and Ambrogi here write Becher, i.e. Johannes

Becher, already a communist militant in the early 1920s, and later East German Minister of Culture. It was however Böttcher who followed events in Italy; the three people named were known collectively as the 'fenicotteri' ('flamingoes').

16. The OMS (Otdel Meždunarodnykh Svjazej) was the Comintern's International Liaison Section, founded in 1921 and headed for much of its life by the Old Bolshevik Osip Pjatnickij.
17. Both before and after this letter, Bordiga had complained bitterly from Rome of what appeared to him to be inactivity on the part of the Italian delegation in Moscow.
18. In 1921 the PCI publishers (the 'Libreria editrice del Partito Comunista d'Italia') brought out Bordiga's *La questione agraria. Elementi marxisti del problema*, *Dall'economia capitalistica al comunismo* (by a slip transcribed by Gramsci and Ambrogi as '*Dall'economia politica al comunismo*') and *Il socialismo napoletano e le sue morbose degenerazioni*. Titles in Gramsci and Ambrogi's list have been translated except for the novel by Zini (see below).
19. The ICG (*Internazionale Comunista Giovanile*) was the Young Communist International. It is referred just afterwards in this letter as the 'IG' (*Internazionale Giovanile*, or 'Youth International').
20. *Moscow against Amsterdam* was a pamphlet in favour of the Comintern-backed Red International of Labour Unions. *Il Congresso dei Morti* (*The Congress of the Dead*) was an anti-war novel by Zino Zini, first published in instalments in *L'Ordine Nuovo*, available again today in a 1996 reprint. *The Capitalist World* was the manifesto issued by the Second Congress of the Comintern. Karl Radek's *Rosa Luxemburg. Karl Liebknecht. Leo Jogiches* was published in translation by the Italian Party (as was Rudas's booklet on the 'split' – between communists and socialists – that is mentioned in a note at the end of this letter). Re the issues of IG: '1-3', given here, is correct, as in Gramsci (1992); '13', as given in Gramsci (2009), is incorrect.
21. A brilliant propagandist, Willi Münzenberg, a German communist, was at first head of the Young Communist International and then helped to found the Comintern's worker's aid and propaganda sections.
22. The French communist Lucie Leiciague was one of the few women occupying a leading position in the Comintern.
23. I.e. the New Economic Policy, initiated the year before.
24. See the Introduction for the background to the Alleanza del Lavoro strike. There had already been disillusion after a failed strike ten days earlier in the industrialised North and North-West, and the August strike ended in waves of fascist thuggery (see Spriano 1967, pp.192-215).
25. Gabriele D'Annunzio, a linguistically highly inventive poet of an extreme nationalist bent, led a raid in 1919 on the Croatian port of

Rijeka (in Italian 'Fiume', both names meaning 'river'), installing a republic there in the hope of reclaiming for Italy both the city and the Italian-speaking part of the coastal zone of Yugoslavia. A year later the Italian government cleared the city after the post-war treaty signed at Rapallo. (For the 'Fiume adventure' see also the letter to Trotsky, p121.)

26. A Russian verb with an ambiguous meaning has led to discrepancies in previous translations. Did Cesare Borgia ('Duke Valentino') 'put himself at the head of' the leaders of the factions in struggle, as in a German translation of 1924 (and also in two Italian translations), or did he 'slice their heads off', i.e. 'decapitate them'? Vittorio Strada, one of the most authoritative Italian writers on Russian literature, gives the latter interpretation, which indeed does correspond to the actions of Borgia as narrated in Chapter VII of Machiavelli's *Prince*, a key reference point for Gramsci. For this reason we here follow Strada's interpretation.
27. It was actually founded by Mario Carli and Emilio (not 'Enrico') Settimelli only weeks before Gramsci left for Moscow, so the confusion is understandable, especially since Corra and Enrico Settimelli had collaborated on other futurist initiatives.
28. Here Gramsci misremembers and confuses two events, both in 1919, not 1920. One was Marinetti's interruption of a parliamentary debate, and the other, just before the 1919 elections, his arrest in Milan with Mussolini for alleged illegal possession of firearms.
29. The Russian version has a mistaken transliteration, giving the name of the review *Lacerba* as *L'acerbo*, basically meaning something unripe, and explains that this means a stubborn or headstrong person.
30. Mistakenly in the letter called 'Giorgio', the Russian typographer compounding the error by omitting the 'r'.
31. The letter on futurism is not in the English translation of Trotsky's *Literatura i revoljucija*, but is in the German one of 1924 (see introduction).
32. There were various communications (letters, messages by radio link, and telegrams), largely from Bordiga, requesting Ambrogi's (Ersilio's) transfer to Berlin to take up again his 'first mission', and criticising his 'moral conduct' in Moscow. These include an 'absolutely secret' coded one from Bordiga to Gramsci of 16 October instructing him to set in motion 'immediately' the procedure for Ambrogi's departure (APC 513-1-081/63, now in Gramsci 2009, p271).
33. Room No 5 was probably Gramsci's room in the Hotel Ljuks. Gramsci underlines here his transliteration into the Latin alphabet of the words as they appear in Russian.
34. Gramsci's postcard is a private 'in-joke'. Ivanovo-Voznesensk's city museum had various Egyptian relics, including mummies, hence the reference to pyramids. He adds 'Gryllus pinxit-scripsit' as author of the drawing and words (with an oblique reference to a turn-of-the-century

magazine). His signature 'Gryllus' (pig) refers among other things to 'St Anthony of the Pig', his name-day saint (see the letter to his mother of January 1911). 'Everyone carries a cross around here' refers to his parody, now in his private papers (UA3, document 1), of a piece of religious doggerel containing this line.

35. For 'Moscow versus Amsterdam' see note 20.
36. This is the fourteenth point referred to in the letter of 29 March 1923, above.
37. Gramsci however remained in Moscow until the end of November 1923. At least one document in 513-1-157 relating to the Moscow meetings of the Commission on fusion bears Gramsci's double signature for both the Commission and the Comintern Presidium.
38. Gramsci was not quite himself when writing this letter; the handwriting is uncharacteristically irregular and at this point he writes *dopo* ('after') instead of *dove* ('where').
39. Most probably Anna Aleksandrovna Barkova, a native of Ivanovo-Voznesensk, who in 1922 went to work in the People's Commissariat for Education in Moscow.
40. Bordiga sent a telegram on 11 January warning that a warrant had been issued for Gramsci's arrest and that he should not come back to Italy; Gramsci was informed almost immediately. The Comintern Presidium met on 17 January, so this letter was written on the day or days immediately afterwards.
41. The state security police, given here in Cyrillic by Gramsci.
42. By error, the original has the year 1922 instead of 1923.
43. The 'horrid letter' is likely to mean the one mentioned in the letter of 18 January, or immediately after, as having just arrived. Assuming there was only one 'horrid letter', this would put the date of the present letter as probably the last ten days or so of January, and probably to the same sister.
44. This was previously surmised to be the line from Dante's *Inferno* 'Love, that exempts no one beloved from loving', quoted explicitly in the letter from Rome of 6 October 1924; that letter was however to Jul'ka, not Evgenija, the most probable recipient of the present letter, and so the supposition is now in doubt.
45. This interpretation is more convincing than the one given in the excellent English translation of Giuseppe Fiori (1970, p161), which has Gramsci offering apologies for absence from meetings with the recipient of the letter.
46. See the section on the Schucht family in the introduction.
47. Matilde Serao (1856-1927) was a journalist and novelist of the naturalist tendency.
48. For Degot', see the Introduction; at the time of this letter he was the Bolshevik textile-worker organiser in Ivanovo-Voznesensk (cf. Giuseppe Berti, 'Il compagno V. Degott', *Rinascita* Vol. 24, n. 6, pp26-7).

49. This was *La questione italiana al terzo congresso della Internazionale Comunista*, reprinted, with an introduction by Paolo Spriano, as the supplement to *Rinascita*, Vol. 37, n. 48, 1980. Gramsci adds the word 'socialist' above the line to avoid ambiguity about which Italian party he means.
50. The 'Commission', probably that on fusion between the PCI and the terzini, held meetings in Moscow in early 1923. Since Evgenija was still in the sanatorium (see the postcard to her of 24 April) and, according to a letter of Jul'ka's (cf. Antonio Gramsci jr, 2010, p111), not really able to walk, this means that, despite its absence from the collections of letters to Jul'ka in the Comintern Archives, the letter must be to her.
51. A quarter of the Party's militants had been arrested, including 'its head, comrade Bordiga': letter (13 February) from Terracini in Rome published in *Alba nuova* (*New Dawn*), organ of the Italian section of the Workers' Party of America, cited in Spriano 1967, p260.
52. Executive here means the Comintern Executive.
53. Manuil'skij and Rákosi respectively.
54. Only two months beforethis letter French and Belgian troops had occupied the industrial valley of the Ruhr. The German government limited itself to calling for passive resistance but working-class protest led to a wave of strikes there and the formation of 'proletarian hundreds' as a defence against the rise of German fascism; cf. Hajek (1969), pp65-9.
55. See Gramsci and Gennari's letter of 20 March.
56. Rote Hilfe is the German for the organisation known in Italian as 'Soccorso Rosso'; the name also appears as MOPR, the Russian initials signifying the *International Union for Aid to Revolutionaries*. In English it was 'International Red Aid', which then became 'International Class War Prisoners Aid' in Britain and 'International Labor Defense' in the USA. Arbeiter Hilfe ('Workers' Aid'), a sister organisation also mentioned (see the letter of 20 March 1923), dealt among other things with aid to the USSR.
57. Bruno is Fortichiari.
58. Meaning sentenced in their absence, when they were already underground fugitives.
59. In Gramsci (1992) the words 'they can be used for propaganda and Party work' were omitted by an oversight, while Gramsci and Gennari's 'vigilare maggiormente' (here 'keep a closer eye on') was read as 'vagliare maggiormente' (metaphorically 'sieve' or 'select' more carefully).
60. Marabini's report on the land concessions to Italian agricultural workers had been transmitted to the Italian Party Executive the previous month; detailed maps of the land are in the Comintern files.
61. A.V. Eiduk was chairman of the USSR's Commission on Agricultural and Industrial Immigration.
62. A *desjatina* (plural *desjatiny*) was an area equal to 2.7 acres or nearly 1.1 hectares.

63. Emilia-Romagna now forms a single administrative region; Emilia stretches west from Bologna, while the Romagna, mentioned just above in the letter, stretches east from outside Bologna to the Adriatic.
64. By a slip the partial copy in the Archives in Rome is dated 29-5-1923 rather than 29-3-1923; however the incoming protocol date is 16-4-1923, and the copy in the Comintern Archives is unequivocally 29-3-1923.
65. The 'Penguin' is Rákosi.
66. The reference is to the fascist march on Rome. 28 October 1922, and the Fourth Congress of the International; *Il Comunista* was the official organ of the PCd'I Central Committee in the earliest period of its life and *L'Ordine Nuovo* here is not Gramsci's review but its continuation as a PCI daily.
67. The words 'for fusion' were added here and then crossed out.
68. 'Comrade B.' is Beruzzi (Manuil'skij), given that Bordiga had been arrested the previous month.
69. The typescript here has the singular 'point' rather than 'points', but any ambiguity about whether '14 points' or '14th point' is cleared up a few lines later on by the use of '14 points', for which see Gramsci's letter to Zinov'ev of 25 November 1922 and its follow-up with the addition of the fourteenth point.
70. 'Undercover work' is a translation of the French word 'noyautage', which in the original was mis-written by Gramsci or his secretary as 'noyotage'.
71. The same points were taken up again by Gramsci a year later in his article 'The Mezzogiorno and Fascism' in *L'Ordine Nuovo*, 15 March 1924, now in English in Gramsci (1994b), pp260-4.
72. The first letter or two at the beginning of the lines here are missing in the Rome Party Archives. The Moscow Archive copy confirms that the expression is 'communist masses' not the 'communist class' printed in Gramsci (1992).
73. This is a literal retranslation of what Gramsci writes. However here, as a few lines later in the letter, he misunderstood Sraffa, who had worked not at the Labour Party but at the Labour Research Department (LRD), founded as the Fabian Society Research Department. Any documentation regarding Sraffa's work there was almost certainly destroyed in World War II bombing raids (oral information from the former secretary of the LRD, Roger Simon). Around the time of the Comintern's Fifth Enlarged Executive, the leading British communist, Tom Bell, had to clarify that a statement imputed to him 'that the Labour Research Department is under party control' was 'inaccurate and misleading. No such statement was made' (*Inprecorr* 1925, Vol. 5, No. 45, p596).
74. The word 'English' is an addition by hand in the Moscow archive version (513-1-187/17), which also quite unambiguously states 'political culture', not 'political content' as transcribed in Gramsci (1992).

75. The letter breaks off here at page 17 of 513-1-187 in the Comintern Archives; the last part of the letter, with a gap in the text, is on page 47 of the same fascicule.
76. At this point the letter in the Rome Archive, published in Gramsci (1992), breaks off. The letter continues on a torn-off sheet – see previous endnote – in the Comintern Archives.
77. The words 'direct' and 'on the Italian party and on the confederations, we do not have information' are a handwritten addition, presumably by Gramsci's secretary.
78. Dated from the reference to this letter in the following one.
79. A request for premises for what was simply called the 'Italian group', without further specification, was decided at a meeting of Gramsci, Bordiga and Gennari on the previous 15 December (1922): see Comintern Archives 513-1-85/24.
80. Given the elementary nature of the Russian of the letter it is probable that it was written directly in that language by one or both of Gramsci and Cocchi.
81. The date is that franked on the postcard, one of a series published by the International Workers Aid, with proceeds going to aid famine relief in Soviet Russia. The card is addressed in Russian to 'Tov. E. A. Schucht' at the sanatorium (as on the postcard of 16 October 1922). The phrase rendered here as 'See you again soon' is in a rather approximate Italian, meaning that the words were actually written by Viktor [Vittorio], rather than by Gramsci.
82. Not to be confused with the digitalised fascicule 513-1-189 containing the first letter from Vienna (6 December 1923).
83. One version of this letter, contained in the Rome Party Archives, is written in what at times is a rather inaccurate French, with some words invented and not corresponding to current usage; although the letter is co-signed by Gramsci, this French version was evidently not written materially by him. Fortunately the Comintern Archives contain a version in a rather Italianised German, possibly written by Umberto Terracini (signing himself here, as elsewhere, as 'Urbani'). Any Italian original, if such existed as a basis for the French and German versions, has however not yet been found. The German version seems more authoritative, at times containing additional detail not in the French one, and it is therefore the German letter that has here been relied on as the main guide, and used as a means of removing ambiguities from the French version.
84. The words 'the above mentioned unjustified allegations' appears in the German version but not the French, whereas 'on "The Communist Party"' is in the French version but not the German.
85. The adjective 'untrue', chosen to fit all the circumstances here, appears time after time, in the French version as 'non vrai' and in the German as 'unrichtig'.

86. The phrase 'there for the Fourth Congress' is in the German but not the French version.
87. While the German has 'government crisis' the French has 'crisis of regime'.
88. Presumably the ECCI delegate is Beruzzi (Manuil'skij): cf the letters of 15 and 29 March 1923.
89. The French version has this in the singular.
90. 'Corporative', found in the French version, is preferred to the 'cooperative' of the German, given that left cooperatives hardly existed after armed action by fascist squads in 1921 (Spriano, 1967, esp. pp123 and 131 and also Appendix 1 to the present chapter); the adjective 'legal', not found in the French version, is maintained from the German one.
91. The German here is unclear but the French fortunately is unambiguous.
92. Alceste De Ambris was a revolutionary syndicalist and, after 1919, the leader of the 'Unione Italiana del Lavoro' referred to here.
93. The German has 'Übertreibungen' ('exaggerations'); the French version has the archaic 'amplistions' whose meaning makes no sense here.
94. Some of the wording is quoted almost to the letter in *Stato Operaio*, 24 April 1924, in one of two issues which, a year after the Third Enlarged Executive of the Comintern, gave an extensive summary of the sessions held between 14 and 19 June 1923 on the fusion question. This note to Zinov'ev, as in the case of the jointly signed letter of 24 May that immediately precedes it, is published here for the first time.
95. Here three lines are crossed out; in the legible parts Gramsci denies having written a private letter that Zinov'ev was attributing to him.
96. This is not a phrase book for beginners in Russian, as said in publications of this letter up to Gramsci (2011), but a humorous children's poem by the well-known translator and author Kornej Čukovskij, published in book form in 1923. The title refers to a boy who was so dirty that even his blanket ran away from him.
97. All the internal evidence in this letter – the date of the couple's first meeting (September 1922), Gramsci's improving state of health in envisaging going outside Moscow, his growing knowledge of Russian indicated in the postscript (before the first meeting with Jul'ka he had to ask Ženja if Jul'ka was a man's or a woman's name: cf. Paulesu Quercioli 1987, p33) – points to August 1923, not 1922 as in Gramsci (1992).
98. Scoccimarro, Leonetti, Montagnana, Fortichiari, Platone, Terracini, Camilla Ravera and Peluso respectively.
99. In Togliatti (1962, pp100-102), followed by the translation in Gramsci (1978b, pp159-60), this incomplete letter has two other fragments appended to it; examination of the Communist Party archive copies indicates these were later notes, not part of a letter, and as such are not included here.
100. Ernani Civalleri, working at the time with Virgili, was arrested on

charges of theft from workmates. A PCd'I Central Committee resolution of 18 September 1923, signed 'Antonio Gramsci', asked the Central Committee of the Russian Party for Civalleri to be kept isolated until the end of his work at the Virgili factory, for him to be expelled from the RCP, and for his case to be brought to the attention of the security police (APC 513-2-017/1; in Russian, with date and signature in Gramsci's hand). In March 1924, Terracini suggested to Gramsci that Civalleri could be moved from where he was (without using the word 'prison') to a place where conditions were less severe.

101. Among those excluded were Serrati, Buffoni, Maffi and Riboldi, all of them on the editorial board of the review *Pagine Rosse* (*Red Pages*), and all of whom were then to become important within the Communist Party. After their exclusion, the Comintern wanted to find a counterbalance to the inevitable rightward shift in *Avanti!*, one of the reasons behind the newspaper which began publication as *L'Unità* on 12 February 1924.

102. This letter is translated from the version published by Stefano Merli as 'Lettera inedita per la fondazione de *L'Unità*' ('Unpublished letter on the founding of *L'Unità*') in the journal indicated. The abbreviations used in Merli's publication are typical of how Gramsci wrote, and a near-guarantee that he was working from the original, now lost or stolen.

103. While the five of them here signed as members of the Russian Party, they had the extra, and institutional, weight stemming from their nomination at the Third Congress of the International as the Russian Party's five representatives on the Comintern Presidium.

5. Vienna: towards the new PCI leadership

To the Executive Committee, PCd'I

VIENNA, 6/12/1923

Dear comrades of the E[xecutive] C[ommittee],

I arrived without any problem in Vienna on the fourth of this month. I was late in leaving due to the prolongation of the sessions of the Balkan conference and the fact that we were waiting for the departure of a comrade who could accompany me on the journey.

From the correspondence that was waiting for me on my arrival I still do not understand exactly the precise nature of my tasks. I would therefore appreciate it if you would give me a precise mandate for my range of action.

Regarding the publication of *L'Ordine Nuovo* I would like you to note that, if its publication in Italy meets with total approval, there will still however be a number of difficulties to be faced immediately. We shall have to define the relationship between myself, the comrade in charge of make-up and composition, and the Executive. It is obvious that the relationships that we establish should be direct, both between myself and the Executive and between myself and the comrade working on the paper. With no exception, all editorial material must pass through my hands. Unsigned articles will be published only when I say they can go to press. If in dealing with the various questions some comrade wishes to express opinions at variance with those of the editorial group and open a polemic, such articles must be signed and the editorial reply will be unsigned or bear my signature. I am fully aware that this may lead to delays but I believe: 1) that *L'Ordine Nuovo* cannot aspire to immediacy in its coverage; as in the first series, it will be up-to-date insofar as it is close to the most urgent and vital problems of the

Italian working class. 2) that we must avoid the trap of appearing to be an anthology and encyclopaedia and must ensure a precise and unswerving ideological unity even at the cost of delays in reporting current events.

It would be good to start the campaign for subscriptions and fund donations immediately in all party organs. The paper's watchword for this campaign will be what it was in '19-20, which read more or less as follows: '*L'Ordine Nuovo* proposes to develop a vanguard from within the working class and the peasant masses that is capable of bringing into being the workers' and peasants' State and creating the conditions for the advent of a communist society'.[1] I do not consider it useful to set out a programme for the new series. The first article will be dedicated to an examination of the current situation and the immediate problems facing the working class and thus implicitly contain the programme. I do not yet know what official form the review will take. I think it will be useful for it to maintain a form that does not strictly depend on the Party: '*L'Ordine Nuovo*: review of working-class politics and culture'. In this way we shall be able to get a distribution even in intellectual circles.

I think that in the negotiations with the printers you will have kept our traditional format and, for typesetting, the same typeface.

Get hold of a run or two of the old *L'Ordine Nuovo*. Com. Tasca once mentioned that he had a couple surplus to requirements. It will not be difficult to have them sent here. Urbani's brother should still have in his hands the manuscript of a study of Niccolini's on the agrarian question in Italy. Niccolini has given me permission to take the manuscript and make use of use it when appropriate. Ask Urbani's brother to give you the manuscript.

As soon as possible try to get hold of the catalogues of the main publishers in Italy, and a list, or better still a copy, of the main publications on fascism.

I can't understand the last paragraph in Negri's letter of 17/11. I told you in advance of Monti's arrival in Vienna two months ago. There should therefore not be any surprise or upset of plans. In any case let me know the nature and scope of the work that Zamis should be doing, who the comrade is that you are thinking of sending over to me, and what you had in mind in doing this.[2] In general I think it is necessary for my work to have someone working alongside me whom

I can trust implicitly and whom it is up to me to choose, bearing in mind the methods of work I intend to pursue and the concrete goals to reach, I would therefore ask you for a reply as soon as possible on all these points and also, indeed, some indication by coded information sent by post.[3]

Greetings,

Source: APC 513-1-189/1-2; typed except for the handwritten addition 'of the E.C.' at the start; unsigned but signed copy in the Italian Central State Archives

---

To Jul'ka

16. XII. 923

Dearest one,

What are you doing now? What are you thinking about? How are you working? It's now more than a fortnight since I left and I still have no news from you. In the impossibility of my writing to you since I arrived, I've waited to hear from you, but without success.

I arrived safe and sound after an uneventful journey. They didn't even open up my baggage or search my person in the whole trip. Here I haven't yet however been able to put my legal position in order and I don't know what could happen to me. Things go slowly and the wheels of organisations grind exceeding slow. We have to shift from one place to another in seemingly never ending tram rides (the city stretches everywhere), we lose the whole day … and start the whole thing again the day after. Here too the world is great and terrible and, what's more, it's in the hands of the bourgeoisie. You know, you get a dreadful feeling passing out of proletarian territory into bourgeois territory. To give this feeling a more direct and lasting impact I immediately ran into a general strike of the clerical staff in the state post, telegraph and telephone sector. Then another thing – I've taken lodgings in the house of a 'comrade' who's a card-carrying member of the Comintern, since she's the wife of a prominent member of the local Party.[4] She bitterly misses her dear old emperor, she's Jewish converted to catholicism, but gave up this second religion to marry a communist, only then to go back to being a practising catholic again. She's forever cursing the Party for forcing her to have in her house boring and troublesome people like me, who could give her problems with the police, but she keeps up her card because otherwise the Party fraction headed by her husband in this highly unfortunate party would lose one whole per cent of its followers. This 'phenomenon' too has brought me sharply face to face with past knowledge that, at a distance of a year and a half, I had almost forgotten.

I'm very isolated where I live and, for quite some time, there will be no change in this. I miss you, and feel a great void all around me. I now understand better than yesterday, and better than before then, how much I love you, and how with every day that passes this love can grow. When will it be possible for you to come and work alongside me? Maybe that day will come soon. The fascist government has suppressed all our legal journals. The need to have a fully efficient press centre abroad is ever more pressing.

Write to me often and at length, even though I may not always be able to reply as often as I would wish. Let me have an address to which I can send letters directly through the post. The 1923 communist Yearbook has unfortunately left out the address of the Rajkom where you work.[5] Send me news about life in Russia; write me the conversations we had in Moscow. I'm reading short reports in the papers, but I don't know how to interpret them. I read that on the 5th of December there was a Party Conference that was very important from the organisational point of view.[6] Let me know your impressions and tell me about the discussions and the most important articles. Remember the booklet by Keržencev on questions of organisation. Has there been anything of interest published on the Rabkor Conference?[7] If you want to send me anything (newspaper cuttings, publications) hand them on to comrade Terracini (room 9, Hotel Ljux) and do the same for your letters, which I await eagerly.

Dorogaja, milaja, ljubimaja Юлька [Dear, sweet, darling Jul'ka]

Gr

Source: AAG

To Terracini

U.9. VIENNA 23/12/23

(Personal)

Vienna 23/12/1923

Dear Urbani,

I am replying to the more strictly confidential part of your last [letter by] courier. I think we have an understanding that letters of this nature must not be protocolled and they should remain within our circle as information and mutual advice on current events. On this subject I want to warn you that your last letter to the Party on the recent deliberations of the Presidium was written in too personal a fashion and, if communicated internally to Moscow, it is going to cause you problems if it is read, in some heated discussion, to demonstrate your stubborn refusal to reject a position that you should by now have abandoned. I am convinced that, appearances to the contrary, our minoritarian brethren are continuing to collect facts, little items of information, episodes etc, to be able always to demonstrate that the mentality of the majority has continued and is continuing to hinder the Comintern's political work in Italy. Every time you write a letter you have first of all to give the end of your nose a good pinch and remind yourself of all the rules of diplomacy. This, moreover, will be a very useful habit in the future, we hope in the very near future, when diplomacy will no longer be used just between comrades, but towards the representatives of reactionary States.[8]

THE CHIARINI-PELUSO AFFAIR

I am here reminding you of the following. When you were leaving, you told me that, in your conversation with Z[inov'ev], the two of you agreed that Chiarini would be removed from his present position, even if not immediately, and that in the mean time it would be possible to call Peluso to replace him. Indeed, you left me with the task of renewing the request, initially rejected, for Peluso to come.[9] Since Souvarine was on the point of leaving, I spoke directly with him. He told me that he would raise the question again at the Executive, which was to meet before his departure, that he would quote Z[inov'ev]'s favourable opinion and, as soon as he reached

Paris, he would authorise Peluso's departure. For me, that meant the question was left suspended for the moment because, when Edmondo [Peluso] arrived, the matter would be peacefully solved through administrative channels. Since this did not happen, I am telling and reminding you of the following. I have come to know that Chiarini joined the Party only at the end of 1920; this I learnt when travelling with Chiarini and Doriot to Tula in February 1923 for the ceremonial handing over of the flag to the 16th Fusiliers, a regiment under the patronage of the Comintern.[10] The regimental archives must still contain the questionnaire that Chiarini completed, in which he says that he entered the revolutionary movement in Italy in 1917. I knew for certain that, at least until July 1920, Chiarini was not a member in Italy. I first met him towards the end of 1919 in Turin, where – at least as far as he told me – he had come to study our student movement, at the request of a student group in Florence who wanted to organise a similar one there. I saw him again around May-June 1920 when he came to Turin to invite me to a talk with Niccolini, whom I did not know personally and whom I had attacked in violent terms in *L'Ordine Nuovo*, but who, unknown to me, was the Comintern representative in Italy.[11] I saw Chiarini in Milan at Niccolini's when I went to see this latter. I had every reason to believe after these events that Chiarini was a person whom one could trust since he even knew Niccolini's real name. When, therefore, in July 1920, I went to the conference of the abstentionist fraction in Florence, and the Pieraccini brothers, of whom at least one is still in the Party, asked me 'Why are you always going around with Heller? Have they not told you that there are suspicions about him and that it is even believed he is a spy?', at that point I was not too surprised.[12] And neither was I too surprised when the Pieraccinis, who had been the main people behind creating the student group in Florence that had gravitated around *L'Ordine Nuovo*, told me that Chiarini had never been detailed to go to Turin to study the movement. I remembered all this last February at Tula after having seen the famous questionnaire. At the time I thought only that, since Chiarini was a person of trust and operating in reserved fashion, he might have aroused very plausible suspicions of this kind on the part of those who did not know what I believed was his true role. I still remembered the famous episode at Bologna between Magnelli and Chiarini and the figure of another Chiarini-spy who now seems to bear a strange resemblance to the false Rizzetto. I was very worried about all this and turned to Vujović, telling him my doubts, and asked him, since he knew Russian, and as a member of the Giovintern [Young Communist International], if he could make an approach to Russian Party organs to find out something regarding Chiarini's political career. V[ujović] told me that he himself had never been able to explain to himself the reasons for Chiarini's standing, that he had explained it only as resulting from Bordiga's pronounced tendency to surround himself with woodenheads who never contradicted him when he was expounding his own particular viewpoint. He also said he was very surprised when, a few days previously at a meeting of the Org[anisation] Bureau, in replying to strong criticism made of Comintern foreign envoys, Z[inov'ev] said that, despite all the criticisms that could be levelled and all the deficiencies that they could note, it was however undeniable that these representatives sometimes did a very good job, as for ex[ample] Chiarini had done in Italy. Some days later, V[ujović] informed me of what he had done to bring the matter to the attention of the Party and of Pjat[nickij]. At the Party, he found out that Chiarini had been a member only since 1921.[13] He got rather a stormy reception from Pjat[nickij]. After he had outlined all the reasons why he thought Tomo's past should be looked into carefully, Pjat[nickij] replied that these stories had all been invented there and then to get rid of someone who had always had a clear view of Italian events, while Amadeo's and my policies had led the Italian proletariat to a rout.[14] After June's E[nlarged] E[xecutive] and after a conversation between Tito, Negri, Serra, Balbina and myself, during which, after the derision levelled at us for the errors of the Party, we replied by pointing to the way that other parties were helping us by sending old and tried militants of the Chiarini type, V[ujović] came back to me to complain on behalf of Pjat[nickij] that instead of posing the question clearly against Tomo we were spreading frivolous gossip and that, after having thought about it more, Pjat[nickij] now thought it best to hold an inquiry into Chiarini's past.[15] Naturally, I replied that we wanted to avoid any possible scandal through rev{eal} ing to other members of the Comintern the irresponsible way in which there had been selec{ted} for Italy, right at the most difficult and serious moment of the struggle, the inestimable help {that the} international proletariat was giving the Italian proletariat, and that, after Pjat[nickij]'s demagogic re{ply} to V[ujović] himself, after the steps he had taken in my name, there was little to rejoice over, that in any case if the inquiry were not carried out s{oon} and did not put our minds at least somewhat at rest, then, for the security of our work, it would from time to time have been impossible not to express our judgement {on} Tomo.[16]

I am adding some other episodes so that you will know how to act. I learnt from Verda[ro] that in effect Chiarini was for a time in 1917 an habitué of the Bottegone in Florence, where every day a new secret Committee was hatched and a new insurrection plotted, and that Chiarini formed part of what for Verdaro was a famous committee of seven.[17] When I questioned him about how the members of this committee were chosen, and about some guarantee of seriousness on Tomo's part for being a member of it, Verdaro quite candidly replied that in those times no one ever thought of these things!!! It is probable that Chiarini was referring to this comic opera episode when he was challenged regarding his Tula questionnaire.

Valente told me about the following episode. He had been detailed to go to Genoa by S[edler] to carry out a check on the work of a certain person, and found that this someone, Tomo's brother-in-law, was away, and had gone off to the South of Italy to see to personal business. When this was told S[edler], the brother-in-law was immediately sacked and sent off, after much cursing, in the direction of Tomo, who had had his irresponsible and unreliable relations taken on in paid employment. I remember that, straight after the Fourth Congress, from Rome, you sent Tomo a letter in gentle reproof, since he had chosen for his correspondent from Rome a seventeen-year-old, not even a Party member, whom we absolutely could not trust. Were proof needed of Tomo's great technical ability, this is it.

I'm also recalling to you the affair of the letter to Maffi which came into Mussolini's hands, and on which Mussolini challenged Vorovskij.[18] Yet another demonstration of Tomo's famed technical ability.

Among the various papers, you will have found the declarations made by Sozzi, Cicalini and Silva regarding Tomo's sabotage against our Party.

Before leaving this subject – in the course of a talk with Sedler I reminded him of the episode I think I mentioned to you on the choice of lawyer for the matter of the train.[19] As you know, I had been called to Rome urgently by S[edler], who told me that, for a month and a half, you had been urged to choose a lawyer and you had carried on in such a way that, due to your dithering, a dreadful scandal could have blown up. I had been called on purpose to intervene. The same afternoon I spoke with Ruggero [Grieco] and the matter was settled on the spot. {I thi}nk that the same evening, through the person in Turin, the lawyer was fo{und}. When I spoke to you of all that, you told me that the Party knew nothing about the search for the lawyer and together we thought that we were dealing with an ob{stacle (?)} of Tomo's.[20] Sedler confirms this version. Tomo, who had to serve as c{…} [indecipherable word] said to her that the Party did not wish to compromise itself in the business [indecipherable words].[21] {He} himself then personally insisted on leaving Italy, through fear of {being} arrested. A conversation of yours with Sedler, which you can then find […] Silva [indecipherable words] on the subject. Communist greetings.[22]

Source: AAG; typewritten with the end of some lines torn; unsigned

---

To Terracini[23]

VIENNA 24/12/1923

(Personal)

Dear Urbani,

Regarding the Chiarini affair, I should like to add for you that I think it not inappropriate to state fairly clearly that it will be impossible for us not to make known, at least to the best qualified of our comrades involved in Party questions, the truth – even in detail – about how Chiarini was taken on. The origin of all these questions which arose after Livorno is undoubtedly to be sought in the period that goes from the 1920 National Council in Florence to the formation of the Imola fraction.[24] The introduction of Chiarini into our camp is one demonstration, and not the least of them, of the methods being applied in Italy to organise the opposition, methods that are chaotic, light-minded and irresponsible to the highest degree.[25]

THE MOST RECENT DELIBERATIONS OF THE PRESIDIUM

Your attitude as regards our relations with the terzini and the intentions that, it seems, have been adopted by Our Executive, leads me to warn you that great caution and ability will be needed. It seems to me that you, as much as Negri, forget that there exists a decision of the Presidium, taken after the work of the Commission on Fusion, in which it is stated that, even though the terzini are a minority within the Socialist Party, they will go into the unified Party with the selfsame rights and organisational prerogatives as fixed by the 14 points. I think that the manoeuvres of the terzini to avoid an immediate fusion with us, to create an independent Party etc, are bound up with the following: they are seeking the minimum indispensible conditions to be able to demand from us what I have just stated above, not from an exclusively bureaucratic standpoint. It is undoubtedly the case, however, that Maffi, for example, is very much in favour of that deliberation, and is not hiding the fact, and even more so I think that Serrati holds the same view, however much he may hide it. Chiarini's manoeuvre must be seen in this light. I think that Chiarini has carried the authentic voice of Maffi into the Presidium.

What is to be done? We are still at this point. Negri thinks he can even operate as if the famous decision did not exist. Amadeo is coming out again with the idea of joining as individuals. I think that, if Amadeo is logical, insofar as he is obviously leaning towards creating an ideological conflict that could lead to the revision of the whole doctrine and tactics of the Comintern as developed since the Third Congress, and is seeking to link the present moment back to the Third Congress and to its polemics on the proletarian offensive, Negri, on the contrary, seems to me not to have understood that he seems to want to emulate the famous ostrich. I am of the opinion that nothing will make the Comintern draw back in its wish to demonstrate to Serrati and the rest of the Socialist Party that it is holding firm to the 14 points and their niceties. It is useless to give oneself illusions on this score, and indeed it is extremely dangerous to go on wanting to play around on little questions such as these, which have the sole result of discrediting us and having us thought absolutely incapable of carrying out a political negotiation. In any case, I want to tell you that I no longer intend to continue to play the part I have been doing up to now. I think we have to arrive at a clear and frank explanation with Amadeo. He is maintaining all his opinions unaltered. I do not believe today, just as I did not believe yesterday, that these opinions are all or totally exact, and I think that this is also true as regards both you and Negri. I think the moment has come to put a stop to all this tug of war that we've been involved in up to now. It will be better for everyone, and perhaps even for Amadeo, for him to express right down to the last detail his entire conception, without any smokescreen of ours interposed. We will discuss with him and perhaps that will be useful for the whole Party which, in the course of these years, has suffered more than a little from political and intellectual rickets.[26]

Write to me on this question at length. Everything else is subordinate to it. If, as a group, we arrive at a definitive resolution of this basic question, we shall resolve all the problems of organisation, and of day-to-day tactics. If, on the other hand, we continue to want to act as a cushion between Amadeo and the Comintern, we shall never have a precise overall direction, like children we shall let the minority and the terzini run rings around us and we shall find ourselves completely discredited in the eyes of the Italian workers.

Friendly greetings

G. Masci

Source: AAG; typewritten with handwritten signature

To Mauro Scoccimarro

VIENNA 24/12/1923

Personal –

Dear Negri,

I am sending you copies of the letters I have written to Urbani. I would like you to do the same as regards me. For I have seen a number of very interesting but, for me rather mysterious, side comments in a letter that Urbani sent to you, saying that you had forgotten the agreements made and may not be forwarding all copies to me.

I should have liked to have written to you at length about the manifesto but I have to send off the post immediately. From the enclosed letter to Urbani, you will be able to understand what my thought is. It is certain that I cannot sign the manifesto. I am in profound disagreement with its general spirit and with much of what it asserts in concrete terms. Who took the draconian measure against com. Meunier, who was editor of the *Araldo* [*Herald*]? I think that from all points of view, politically and organisationally, a fairly seriously mistake has been committed. I warn you that if there is to be an inquiry into Meunier, that I too will want to be interrogated, since I was in constant contact with him in '21-22 and know exactly in what situation he found himself, in that shambles of a Party branch in Genoa, and what favours he did. It seems strange to me that you do not understand that old com[rade]s must not be treated like this, while at the same time quite a different treatment is reserved for certain people who then respond as they think fit.

Friendly greetings

Masci

Source: AAG; typewritten with handwritten signature

To Jul'ka

1 – 1 – 1924

Dearest one,

What will the New Year have in store for us? Will we be able to be together for a little, enjoying each other's company, laughing at everyone and everything (except of course at the serious things, which in this great and terrible world are however very few)?

Your letter arrived safely. Here too winter has begun, with the streets covered in snow, the countryside is a white mass as far as the eye can see, reminding me of nothing so much as the salt-pans of Cagliari – and the convicts who work them. But how much sadder and more depressed is V[ienna] than Moscow. Here there are no ringing sleighs ploughing their joyful furrows through the streets, white as bed linen, but just the din of the trams. Life goes on, sad and monotonous. I go out only to eat and for some organisational meeting. I'm working quite a lot and getting back into the methodical routine of sitting down and writing hour after hour. I've already finished a number of articles. I'm translating a lot because translating gets me back into hard work without either discouraging me or giving rise to too strong a shock. I'm translating Rjazanov's notes to the *Communist Manifesto*;[27] I've already done the first 11 notes and I'm now revising and copying them to send them to you for your corrections. I have decided to prepare a complete translation of this edition of the *Manifesto*: it will be very useful and, I think, the sales will go well. Naturally if I did everything by myself it would take too much time, while I would like to finish it off in 3 to 4 months. You will help me, won't you? We'll put our two names together on the cover. I've received the translation of Lenin's article on revisionism, but unfortunately neither the text nor other translations have arrived.[28] If you have time, you can start work on Rjazanov by translating the chapter entitled *The Communist League* in his edition of the *Manifesto*, the third one, which comes straight after the prefaces to the first and second editions.

Has Trotsky's book *How the Revolution Armed* come out yet?[29] Have you bought all issues of *Knigonoša*? And has number 25 of the communist *Sputnik* come out?[30] Have they published any new books that you think might interest me?

Tweak Bianco's ears for me. Tell him I'm now writing at least half a dozen letters a day. I've never written as many of them in my life as I have over the last few days. Letters are becoming a nightmare for me. I'm going to end up badly. I'll write one to Bianco as well.

An embrace of the greatest tenderness for you

Gr

Source: AAG

To Scoccimarro

U.9. VIENNA, 5/1/24

Dear Negri,

I have received your letter of 25/12 and that of Palmi of the 29th of the same month. I'm replying to both of them together. Tell Palmi the contents of this letter of mine and, if possible, do the same for Lanzi and Ferri.

I'll tell you in brief why I'm continuing to maintain that it is impossible for me to sign the manifesto even after having read the second draft.[31] For the manifesto there exists neither the Enlarged Executive meeting of February 1922 nor that of June '22, nor indeed either the Fourth Congress or the Executive of June '23. For the manifesto history finishes with the Third Congress, and it's that Third Congress that we have to refer to in order to go forward. All this may be plausible as the personal opinion of an individual comrade and as the expression of a small group; it is simply mad as the political line of a majority fraction that has been leading the Party from the Third Congress onward and is continuing to lead it.[32] It's mad and absurd because in all the Enlarged Executives, and at the Fourth Congress, the representatives of the majority have always made the broadest possible declarations in favour of centralism, of the single international Party and so on. At the Rome Congress it was stated that the theses on tactics would be approved as consultative documents, but that, after the discussion of the Fourth Congress, they would be set aside and nothing more would be said of them. In the first half of March 1922 the Comintern Executive issued a special statement in which the party's theses on tactics were refuted and rejected, and an article of the statute of the International states that any deliberation of the Executive is binding on all individual sections. This much may be said for the formal and juridical side of the question and, it must be underlined, this has its importance. In actual fact, after the publication of the manifesto the majority could find itself totally discredited and even excluded from the Comintern. If the political situation in Italy were not to militate against it, in my view this exclusion would happen; in the light of the conception of the Party that stems from the manifesto, this exclusion would be obligatory. If a federation of ours were to do just half of what the Party majority want to do vis-à-vis the Comintern, it would be dissolved immediately.

I do not wish to appear an utter clown by signing the manifesto. In any case I am not even in agreement with its substance. I have a different conception of the Party, of its role, of the relationships that have to be established between it and the non-Party masses, between it and the population in general. I remain absolutely unconvinced that the tactics developed at the Enlarged Executives and the Fourth Congress are mistaken either in their overall approach or in their salient details. I think the same holds for you too and for Palmi, and I cannot therefore understand how the two of you are so light-heartedly venturing up such a dangerous blind alley. It seems to me that you now find yourself in the state of mind that I found myself in during the period of the Rome Congress. Perhaps, since in the meantime I've been a long way away from any internal party work, that state of mind has disappeared. But in actual fact it has disappeared for other reasons too. And one of the most important reasons is this: I have become convinced of the absolute impossibility of coming to any compromise with Amadeo. His personality is too strong and he is so deeply convinced he is in the right that to think of hemming him in through some compromise is absurd. He will carry on his fight and continue at every opportunity to put forward his own theses unaltered.

I think Palmi is wrong in maintaining that the moment is not right for starting our own independent action and for giving rise to a new formation, which only 'geographically' would appear as the centre, but which in reality would be situated on the only road which today can be followed. It is undeniable that the official conception up to now regarding the role of the Party has led to its being crystallised in organisational discussions and thus to a total political passivity. Instead of centralism we have arrived at the creation of a morbid minority movement and, if we speak with the comrades who have emigrated in order for them to take a more active part in activity of the Party abroad, we get the impression that for them the Party is in actual fact of very little account and that there is very little they would be disposed to do for it. The experience of the school at Petrograd is very instructive on this. In the real situation I have become persuaded that the greatest force holding the Party structure together is the prestige and ideals of the International, and not by any means the bonds that the specific activity of the Party has managed to bring into being; and it is exactly on this terrain that we have created a minority. And we allow that minority to parade itself as the International's real representative in Italy.

It is just now, when a decision has been made to take discussion to the masses, that everyone must assume a definite position and their own precise profile. While the discussions were still going on within a very limited circle, and it was a question of organising five, six or even ten people in a homogeneous body, it was still possible, although it was not even then totally right, to come to individual compromises and ignore certain questions that were not immediately relevant. Today we are going to the masses, debating, deciding on mass formations that are going to have a life longer than just a few hours. Well then, it is essential for this to happen without either ambiguity or implicit assumptions, for these formations to assume an organic form and be able to develop and become the whole Party. It is for these reasons that I am not going to sign the manifesto. I do not know yet exactly what I am going to do. It is not the first time I have found myself in this condition, and Palmi will remember how in August 1920 I broke away from both him and Umberto. At that time it was I who wanted to maintain relations with the left rather than with the right, while Palmi and Umberto had joined up with Tasca, who had broken away from us as early as January.[33] Today it seems that the opposite is happening. But in actual fact it is the situation that is very different, and, just as then inside the Socialist Party it was necessary to support the abstentionists, if we wanted to create the central core of the future Party, so now it is necessary to fight against the extremists if we want the Party to develop and stop being nothing more than simply an external fraction of the Socialist Party. Indeed, since the two extremisms, of the left and of the right, have confined the Party within the limits of one single discussion, that of relations with the Socialist Party, they have reduced it to an entirely secondary role. In all probability I will remain isolated. As a member of the Party Central Committee and of the E[xecutive] of the Comintern, I shall write a report combating both positions, accusing both of one and the same fault, and basing a programme of action for our future activity on the theory and tactics of the Comintern. Thus much I have wished to say, and I may assure you that no amount reasoning of yours is going to budge me from this position. It goes without saying that I want to go on collaborating closely with you, and I believe that the experience of the last few years has been useful for all of us, at least in the sense of teaching us that, within the Party, we can still have different opinions at the same time as continuing to work together in the utmost mutual confidence.

Urge the comrades you are in contact with to hurry up and send me the articles I've asked them for. Palmi has to let me have immediately a 'Battle of Ideas' piece of at least three columns. (The entire last page.) I don't know what book or series of books or other publications to suggest to him. He could do a critique of the point of view expressed in Gobetti's *Rivoluzione Liberale*, demonstrating how in reality fascism has posed a very sharp and cruel dilemma, that is to say that of the revolution in permanence, and of the impossibility not only of changing the State form, but simply of changing government except by armed force. And he could examine the new current that has sprung up among the ex-combatants and crystallised around *Italia libera* ['*Free Italy*']. I believe that the ex-combatant movement, generally speaking, since it was to all intents and purposes the first secular peasant party in central and Southern Italy especially, has had an immense importance in overturning the old political structure of Italy and in leading to an exceptional weakening of bourgeois parliamentary hegemony and hence to the triumph of the reactionary fascist petty bourgeoisie, itself incapable of reaching any goal, yet full of aspirations and utopian dreams of complete renewal. What is the exact significance of the birth of the 'Free Italy' movement in this general picture? This escapes me and I should be truly happy for Palmi to shed light, for me too, on this subject.

Naturally Palmi must be one of the pillars of the review and send general articles that will make it possible in real terms for the old *L'Ordine Nuovo* to be reborn. I have always neglected to give any indication regarding the collaboration of Valle since I think he will want to have a completely free hand. Tell him however that I would like to have a very condensed article on the subject of Gentile's educational reform, 'condensed' understood of course logically and not in strict terms of length. The article could even be five columns in length and form the core of one of the issues of the review.

And what is Lanzi up to? He too will have to collaborate, especially on trade union affairs. Write to him or let him know I want to know something about his activity and of his opinions on ongoing affairs.

Greetings

Masci

Source: AAG; APC 513-1-248/1-2

To Terracini

U.9. VIENNA, 13/1/1924

Dear Urbani,

I am here giving a more specific reply to the letter in which you pose the question of my attitude in what to a great extent are erroneous and very exaggerated terms.

1) From what transpires, your memory is very much at fault. In the conversation between us I said that I was *on principle* against the publication of a manifesto that polemicised with the International. You assured me that the numerous amendments made to the original that I read were such as to completely modify its general lines in order to make it into a simple historical reconstruction of the events of the last few years and, as such, it would be the necessary and indispensable basis for any fruitful discussion.

2) Here I have seen only the amended manifesto. Since I do not have the original to consult I cannot make any philological judgement on the import of the changes introduced. Politically the emendations have not changed the situation to any great extent. There still remains the absolute negation of the developments brought about in the tactics of the Comintern after its Third Congress. There remains, objectively unmodified, the position assumed by our party as the potential centre of all the left tendencies that may form within the international field. There remains a spirit that is fundamentally hostile to the tactic of the united front, of the workers' and peasants' government, and of a whole series of deliberations in the organisational field taken before the Third Congress or approved at the Congress itself.

3) From what I told you in the conversation I had straight after your arrival in Moscow, it is clear that I could not have signed even the second version of the manifesto. Your surprise at this seems to me, then, to be very much out of place. Much more in place is my amazement at the great simplicity with which you and Negri, whom you helped and with whom you made public declarations at the En[larged] Ex[ecutive] in June, see the future. You must recall that in Moscow, in the conversations that the three of us had with Tasca, we put the following reasoning to him: the internal life of a communist party cannot be conceived of as an arena of a parliamentary-like struggle in which the role of the various factions is determined, like that of the various parliamentary parties, by their different origins, depending on the different classes of society. Within the party there is one sole class that is represented, and the differing attitudes that from time to time become currents and fractions are determined by the differing assessments of events as they unfold, and thus they cannot crystallise into a permanent structure. The C[entral] C[ommittee] of the Party

may have a given overall line at a given time and in a given situation, but it can change the overall line that it has assumed, if the time and situation are no longer what they once were. The minority, by making a conflict of views into something permanent and by seeking to reconstruct and ascribe to the majority some general mentality which will justify this permanent process, and which, furthermore, has put, is putting and will put the majority on a continual conflict course with the Comintern, i.e. with the majority of the revolutionary proletariat, and especially with the Russian proletariat that carried out the revolution, is in actual fact bringing up the first elements of a question which ought surely to lead to the exclusion of the Party majority from the Comintern. But we are denying any basis to this abstractly dialectical procedure of the minority's and are demonstrating, facts in hand, that we are on the grounds defined by the Comintern, that we are accepting and applying its principles and tactics, that we are not becoming crystallised into a permanent oppositional attitude; we know instead how to modify our approach according to the changing balance of forces and to the different basis on which the problems to be resolved are placed. If, notwithstanding this, the minority continues to adopt the attitude towards the majority that it has had up to now, it will be we who look to whether in that attitude there are sufficient elements to demonstrate that the minority is an effect of the liquidationist tendencies that are found in every revolutionary movement after it has suffered a rout, and which are inherent in the oscillations and panic typical of the petty bourgeoisie, that is of a class which is not the one on which our Party is based. It will not be difficult to demonstrate that the minority's orthodoxy vis-à-vis the tactics of the Comintern is just a smokescreen to gain control of the leadership of the party. An examination of the groups comprising the minority offers an easy way to show that the minority is fundamentally opposed to the Comintern and will not be slow in demonstrating its nature. It was in these terms that we spoke to Tasca, and I remember that, together with you and Negri, I repeated over and over again how I regarded this reasoning not as some move to intimidate Tasca momentarily and weaken him in front of the En[larged] E[xecutive], but as a new platform on which the Party must stand squarely in order to liquidate the past honourably and put itself in a position to resolve its internal problems. And I recall that you and Negri were in agreement on this.

4) I think the two of you are still in agreement and I cannot therefore understand your present position. We are in actual fact at a great historic turning point in the Italian communist movement. It is the moment at which, with great resolution and precision, we must define the new bases for the development of the party. And the manifesto certainly does not represent this basis. Quite the contrary, it gives every reason for making the minority appear as the fraction which, at the Fourth Congress and at the [En]larged [Ex]ecutive, saw things clearly, distrusting the goodwill and sincerity of the majority, and making this latter seem like an a clique of small-time politicos that manage time after time to save their situation with some mean little contrivance. And not even the most recent events (the case of Bombacci authentically interpreted by Belloni and Remondino's declarations) will manage to save us. In the current situation, which is still objectively revolutionary in Germany, while being extremely confused in Italy, the Comintern cannot sit back peacefully and allow there to be formed in the international field a Party majority which is both in opposition and demanding a rediscussion of all the decisions taken after the Third Congress. To allow that would be to allow an enormous reinforcement of the extremist tendencies that sprang up in the German Communist Party and thus delay its reorganisation. You too often forget that our Party has international responsibilities and that any attitude of ours has its repercussions in other countries, which often take morbid and irrational forms.

5) I am insisting on this approach of mine because I maintain it is the most appropriate and necessary one. Your letter only confirms me in this decision, especially on what you say regarding the 'bridge' that you have wanted to represent during the recent past. You, Negri and Palmi need to opt for clarity, for a position nearest to your most inner convictions, and not one taken in your role as 'bridge-builders'. By so doing we shall be able to carry out a great task together and give our Party the entire development allowed by the situation. It is useless to want to conserve some semblance of formal fractional unity that is always forcing us into ambiguity and half-measures. If Amadeo wants to insist, as he certainly will do, on this attitude of his, that will maybe be all to the good, on condition that his is the manifestation of an individual position or that of a small group; by becoming, on the other hand, and with your

consent, the manifestation of the majority, this would compromise the Party irredeemably.

I have received the two packs of material that you sent me.[34] They were open, so I would ask you to make them up better in future so as not to lose anything. Try to send me the rest as soon as possible; if it's too much to send all at once, then at least do it in small batches one after the other. You will certainly have seen the proposal I put to the Executive to publish a quarterly review in a big format (250-300 pages every three months) that could bear the title *Critica proletaria* [*Proletarian critique*]. I think the proposal will be accepted and be put into effect within a few months. I've listed the contents of the first number as follows:

1) Manifesto-programme, which I could write.
2) Bordiga. Problems of proletarian tactics.
3) Graziadei. The accumulation of capital according to Rosa Luxemburg.
4) Tasca. The school problem and the Gentile reform.
5) Scoccimarro. Perspectives for a Workers' and Peasants' government in Italy.
6) Longobardi or Pastore. Italian industrial structure.
7) Terracini. The programme of the Communist International.
8) Togliatti. The Vatican question.
9) News items: economic, financial, political, military, international, trade union, working-class life.
10) Book reviews.

(The authors of the articles will also have to send a critical-cum-bibliographical sketch of the publications dealing with the subject matter they are dealing with.)

11) Political diary.
12) Indices of magazines and newspapers.

You ought to get down to work immediately on your article, which should be at least twenty pages; take as a guide the format of a review like *Nuova Antologia*. In it you should make an analysis of the programmatic projects that have been presented and the discussions they have given rise to. I should tell you that in Russia there has been quite a full discussion. Bukharin will be able to give you all the necessary indications and have the press office translate the Russian material for you. It would be good if you had several copies made of the translations so they can be sent to the Parties that have formed commissions to discuss the programme but who are lacking the documentation for the discussion. This question could be put to the Secretariat. Your article however will have to be ready in two months.

Warm greetings to you and Alma.[35]

Masci

P.S. It would be good to have your article on the situation in Germany immediately, which would be the backbone of the first number of *L'Ordine Nuovo*.

What's become of Monti's brother? What's happened to him? If he's not set off yet, give him our home address: Schönbrunner Strasse 236, Apartment 7, right hand staircase, c/o Dr Joseph Frey. He can ask for Gramsci.

Tell comrade Clementina Perrone that, if she has not done the typed-up copies of the famous questionnaire, she shouldn't hesitate but send me the original, which I want to use straight away. I'll then send a number of copies to Moscow.

See if, among the papers I left you, you can manage to find the following ones: 1) an article of Bukharin's in French, torn out of a number of *Clarté*, on the 'Decadence of Bourgeois Culture', or something like that, which, in the absence of other things, I would like to publish as one of the first in the 'Battle of Ideas' series. 2) An article by Pokrovskij, also in French, and that, too, torn out of *Clarté*, on 'History and the Class Struggle'. 3) An article by Umberto Ricci on the 'Myth of Economic Independence' and one by Jannaccone and Catani on 'The Steel Industry', taken from *Riforma Sociale*, which I need immediately to have precise data for an article of mine. In general I would ask you to keep everything I left with you, since it's of importance for me, and is already marked out for future use. I'm therefore sorry that you've sent Martello's *History of the International* to Petrograd, since it will be very difficult to have another copy sent on from Italy, and it's completely wasted in Petrograd. It is in fact a reactionary pamphlet against the International which will make a number of comrades, who do not have the necessary critical approach and who are coming to read a history of the International for the first time, come out with quite a number of stupidities; for me, it served just as documentation. When you think of putting to some other purpose books that we left behind, think seven times seven before doing anything and then remember that we too are living on a pittance, with no material means, but with the need, if we want to carry out serious and scrupulous work, to have lots of books at hand. Greetings once again.

Source: AAG; typewritten except for the handwritten signature and the part after the first sentence of the post script.

To Jul'ka

13. I. 924

Dear one,

And you, how is life with you, how are you managing? You write that you cannot imagine my life, but yours – how is that going on? I try to picture to myself the comings and goings of your daily life, with the coffee maker and the little plate. On that subject, you haven't said anything to me about the plate, about that precious little instrument for ham or cheese omelettes of untold magnificence. Is it still in use?

My life is simple and straightforward, as transparent, according to Rimbaud, as a louse trapped between two lenses. I am always at home, or almost always, in a street far away from the city centre, alone, reading and writing. I am often cold because the stove doesn't produce much heat, and I don't sleep at night much because the bedroom isn't heated – it's six degrees, which gives me a cold every night. The bed is German-style, very hard and uncomfortable and, instead of sheets and blankets, there is an eiderdown that slides off all over the place and so I continually wake up with a foot or shoulder that's absolutely freezing. However life can be lived just the same, especially because you are always, always in my thoughts. Often I'm tormented by not being able to hold you in my arms, not feeling you near me, so gentle, so kind, so dear, not being able to embrace and caress you at length. I can't live without you. My life which, with you and for you, had begun to put out new green shoots, sometimes now seems to me once again to be drying up and becoming oh so bitter. But this will pass, we shall meet again, I'll stick my tongue out at you to annoy you, then I'll hold you oh so close and tight because I love you so much and you too love me so much and I cannot be without you, because I do not seem whole, but it seems there's always a part of me that is detached and far away, and its absence is tormenting me beyond what words can say.

I'm sending you the first chapters of the Rjazanov translation. I don't know what it's like. You'll have to look at it closely and be very severe in your corrections. For the technical expressions you can ask Bianco. Virgili has a technical dictionary in 6 languages, including Italian and Russian.[36] You can make a list of the Russian expressions and then check them off in that dictionary.

I still don't know the exact terms of the discussion that has taken place in the party. I've seen just the C[entral] C[ommittee] resolution on inner-party democracy, but no other resolution. I don't know anything either of Trotsky's article, or that of Stalin. I can't understand the attack of this latter, which seemed to me to be quite irresponsible and dangerous. But it may be that my lack of knowledge of the subject is leading me to mistaken conclusions. This is why I wanted you to give me information and some direct impressions. Is it really so impossible to have something of the kind?[37] To safeguard against any risk whatsoever of possible loss you should write to me in coded form, but the work would be a burden for you and very tiring if what you had to write were very long. If anything, have a word with Umberto and ask him on my behalf to teach you a system whose key you'll then send me; this will in any case then be of use me too, should need arise.

The pack of books that I'd left at the Comintern to be sent on to me has now arrived, but I've only received numbers 14 to 26 of Книгоноша [Knigonoša]. Have you bought the subsequent numbers? Send them on to me and see if you can get numbers 1 to 13. Maybe it's easier through the Rajkom than any other way.[38]

Your last letter, that of New Year's Eve, made a strange impression on me and left me rather disturbed. I can't fully understand your state of mind – it seems to me that you are a little disturbed and disorientated. Does this depend on your still not having a house, on being forced to have a nomad-like existence, on tiredness coming from work and no rest? I hope it is this, but it seems to me it can't be just this and there must be something else.[39] It seems to me that, more than the hard work, there's an inner torment weakening you more than the work. You must write and tell me everything you feel so that at least I have the illusion of having you near me.

A very tight and close and embrace

Gr

Source: AAG

To the Executive Committee of the Italian Communist Party

U.9. VIENNA, 14/1/24

To the E[xecutive] C[ommittee] of the PCI

Dear comrades,

Today I received two parcels at once. Since I want to be in time still to send you something, I'll limit myself to just one subject, namely our publishing activity.

The things I am now going to explain have a relative value. It is self-evident they have been conceived taking account of the situation our Party finds itself in, and of the impossibility that, at any moment, may arise of continuing a given course of action. It is also however certain that, precisely in the situations like the one now attaining in Italy, particular attention must be paid by the Party to the means by which it can establish relations with the widest possible masses of the working population. The absence of legal activity of a certain importance on the part of the Party may, and inevitably does, have the following consequences:

1) The mass of the workers, and thus also the Party members, who cannot be considered as something separate from the masses, are falling prey to the systematic campaign of the leaders of the State, carried on in all the organs that shape public opinion, to destroy revolutionary ideology, to argue that the programme of the revolution has failed and that it will not be on the agenda for at least the next half century. The best we can hope is that this campaign is succeeding in inducing a state of passivity,

with immediate revolutionary work being given up, and the expectation being created that the collaborationist workers' parties will succeed, through the formation of a government consisting of a democratic bloc, in recreating conditions of freedom in which the revolutionary forces might regroup.

2) This state of mind has its reflection in some parts of the most authoritative centres of the Party and may give rise to the birth of fractions that quite clearly liquidate revolutionary ideology. The Bombacci affair, as authentically interpreted by Belloni, has demonstrated that even within our Party the danger is now no longer a mere hypothesis, but a reality whose depth and limits – given the Party's situation – it is impossible to gauge.
3) It is inevitably happening that the Party and the Party fraction that is immediately to the right of our movement, and that, through its ability to manage the situation, has succeeded in keeping its legal status, is automatically inclined to exploit the situation to its advantage by taking over the traditional readers of our press with its literature, which very often has only the slightest veneer of communism. And yet inevitably the organs of this Party or Party fraction end up by exercising a real and proper function as a political directive centre by diminishing or completely annihilating the prestige and strength of authority of our C[entral] C[ommittee] which only irregularly and sporadically can give proof of its existence to the masses.

Another problem posed by the given situation is as follows. The present Party members who have remained faithful and braved all the dangers of reaction must not be swamped by the mass of new members who will throng our ranks as soon as danger has disappeared or on the eve of taking power. We must regard the present Party members as the future cadre force of a mass Party. For at least 5 years after freedom has returned, it is solely and exclusively with these elements that we shall be able to build any Party apparatus. But for that to be possible we must certainly not think that just experience and practice are sufficient: these purely or near purely mechanical forces, which are acting spontaneously with varying results, must be aided and guided by an entire activity of the Party's. This problem is closely bound up with that of emigration. Some thousands of comrades are now abroad, and they must be persuaded to collaborate closely to form the Party's new cadre force, which must therefore be oriented in some way, not only from the general political point of view but through the narrower but no less important one of creating the possibility for a great Party of having cadres that are capable, intelligent and practical.

Resolving these problems means not falling back into the bedlam created in the Socialist Party after the armistice, when the twenty to twenty-five thousand left in the organisation during the war were completely submerged by the hundred and fifty thousand who came in with no ideological training, no spirit of organisation and no discipline.

I have posed the problem in practical, almost schematic, terms because my understanding is that it can only be resolved in practice. But the important thing is for the C[entral] C[ommittee] to bear the problem constantly in mind, and, as the occasion arises and in the light of the possibilities, seek to resolve it, through one single orientation. Schematically I would pose the problem in these terms: encourage, at least, the training of three hundred comrades with the ability necessary for directing the work of an entire province, who will thus provide the environment in which there can be formed a good Central Committee, good commissions for general problems of the Party, of the unions, and in future for work of a State nature.

Encourage the formation of at least three thousand elements suitable for becoming good Party branch secretaries in the towns and therefore also for becoming union and cooperative officials, members of the federal and provincial committees and so on.

I do not now want to go into further detail on these questions, since I reserve the right to deal with them more specifically from the point of view of what we can do today, with the present Party apparatus. I will here deal just with the initiatives of a more strictly intellectual nature, which may be summed up in the following four points.

1) The creation of a quarterly journal capable of encouraging and organising the front-line elements of the Party around a given activity.
2) The creation of party schools, especially abroad.
3) The creation of a correspondence course on party organisation and on the organisational principles that characterise the Party in all fields.

    Numbers two and three seek in fact to create the elements that we may thus call second rank; naturally, the remaining party activity will also contribute to this.

4) Bookshop publications organised according to a given plan which takes account of the need for elementary propaganda for the defence of our principles, of our programme and of our general ideology.

This is a schematic vision of use for overall indications and norms; it is to be understood that each single activity influences and determines the others and that the divisions must not give rise to formation of any closed ranks and to some distribution of certificates guaranteeing future places and positions.

As regards the publication of a quarterly, I do not consider the objections raised by com. Palmi to be entirely well-founded. In any case we can and must always try, with the proviso that we may not be able to publish the second number or that it will be published four, five or even six months after the first.

I have compiled a possible contents list for the first issue:

1) Manifesto-programme, which I myself could write.
2) Bordiga. Problems of revolutionary tactics. This could give rise in subsequent numbers to a high-level debate.
3) Graziadei. The accumulation of capital according to Rosa Luxemburg. While this problem is almost unknown in Italy, it will form the hub of the discussion of the Fifth Congress regarding the Comintern programme. Comrade Graziadei is in my view the best qualified person to do a 30-page outline of Rosa Lux[emburg]'s theory, relating it to that of Marx.
4) Terracini. The programme of the Communist International. An objective summary of the current state of the debate on this question.
5) Scoccimarro. Perspectives for a Workers' and Peasants' government in Italy. This ought to consist of an examination of the relations of force that obtain in Italy and of their eventual developments in view of a campaign around the slogan of a Workers' and Peasants' government. All of this should be preceded by an objective exposition of the theory and practice of this watchword.
6) Tasca. The school problem and the Gentile reform. An examination of the social structure of the school in Italy and of the political significance of the Gentile reform, beyond the nature of scientific utopianism which is its innermost hallmark.

7) Longobardi or Pastore. Italian industrial structure. An examination of the geographical distribution of the factory system in Italy, of the development it has undergone in relation to national wealth and to the system of world trade. The analysis should serve as a preliminary basis for a study of the conditions of industry under a socialisation system.
8) Togliatti. The Vatican. Examination of all the problems and of all the political and social forces grouped together around the Vatican.
9) Book reviews. All authors of articles published should also compile a political-cum-bibliographical sketch of the publications dealing with their subject matter. This could then be of use for different bibliographical reviews on other subjects, asking for such also from foreign com[rades], especially Russian ones.
10) News articles: economic, financial, political, military, international, trade union, working-class life (wages, strikes, labour legislation, social insurance, housing, cost of living). Naturally, these items must not be published all together in all numbers of the review. The only permanent items must be that on the Italian political scene, which could be compiled in each single issue by com. Grieco, and that on international questions, again compiled for each issue by the Italian representative in Moscow. In the first issue, however, all of these should appear, briefly summing up the events of the period under the fascist government. The military question too could be given over to com. Grieco. As for the other items, I myself could have them compiled by people with the necessary expertise if you do not have the possibility of suggesting comrades.
11) The political diary of the preceding three months (not strictly speaking necessary).
12) Index of the main articles published in the papers and reviews of the Communist Parties of all countries, understood 'with a pinch of salt'.

The periodical could be entitled *Critica Proletaria*, each number being about 250-300 pages of a *Nuova Antologia*-type format. I think they could sell at least 3000 copies at a price around 7.50 to 10 lire. Some articles, in a revised and extended form, could be turned into more widely distributed pamphlets. I do not think it impossible, by sending the leaflet that has already been printed, with a contents list, for us to get at least 500 subscriptions of 40 lire each, which would ensure the right to the four issues that comprise the first volume. The subsequent issues should be compiled following the same general make-up as the first one, with the aim of dealing in the first volume, i.e. the first 1000 or 1200 pages, with the most urgent problems especially of life in Italy but also in general of that of other countries too. Only in exceptional circumstances should we have recourse to translations or to reprinting previously published material. Since the first issue should come out by April, it does not seem to me that Palmi's objections are valid. Furthermore, you could draw up a contents index of each article and require each single author to do the same, as a matter of Party discipline. I think the publication will make a very positive impression, not solely on Party members, and will take on a real political significance.

The creation of Party schools and a correspondence course. Here a long discussion would be necessary. Since our office has to have relations with various committees that, outside Italy, deal with Italian emigrants, I would ask you simply to give an opinion as to whether we could take on these two questions. If you think it is possible I will put together circulars on the subject to send off to various countries, subject first of course to your approval of the content.

As regards publishing I would propose: 1) a first series of fifty popular pamphlets (32-64 pages), translated, adapted, or original as may be, that can be used for propaganda and agitation amongst the broad masses. The first ten of them might be as follows: 1) Lenin, *The Teachings of Karl Marx*. 2) Korsch, *The Essence of Marxism*. 3) Adorackij, *Utopian Socialism*. 4) Same author, *The Method of Dialectical Materialism*.[40] 5) Adorackij, *Marx's Theory of History*. (We ourselves could prepare these first five pamphlets. The one by Lenin has already been translated and I would like to publish it in *L'O[rdine] N[uovo]* before it comes out as a pamphlet.) 6) A guide to communist propaganda (advice for small conferences, for small-scale propaganda, outlines for how to make reports, organisational norms etc). 7) Organisational questions. 8) The Workers' and Peasants' government. 9) What a Red Army is. 10) The Southern question.

11) How to organise and direct a party school. 12) Guide for self-educated workers.

All these could come out as *O[rdine] N[uovo]* pamphlets.

An anthology of historical materialism. I have a copy of an anthology with this self-same title which has come out in Russia; it is excellent and, if Prof. Zino Zini is still one of our sympathisers, we could ask him to edit a similar one in Italy. Zini knows both Russian and German (the anthology is composed solely of writings of Marx and Engels) so he could trace the chapters that have already been translated into Italian and revise them, then translate from the German the parts that have not yet been published in Italian.[41]

As in Russia, in Italy too the anthology form could be an excellent system for publications on the following subjects: the agrarian question; the trade union question; the cooperatives; questions regarding party organisation; the cultural and schools question; the national question etc.

---

13) The *Communist Manifesto* with the notes by Rjazanov. Taken in their entirety these notes are an extremely good treatment in a very popular form of all subjects regarding socialism. I am translating them as an exercise but I will of course have the translation looked over by a Russian comrade. We could ask Rjazanov to do a special preface for the Italian edition and the stencils for the portrait illustrations and the reproduction of the handwritten pages published in the Russian edition.

Borchardt, *Karl Marx's Capital.*[42]

Engels, *Antidühring.*

Marx, *Historical Essays* (*The Eighteenth Brumaire*, *The Civil War in France* etc)

Engels, *Socialism Utopian and Scientific.* It would be useful to start by republishing these three works, revising and correcting the existing translations, which are dreadful.

Bukharin. *Historical Materialism.* (This already exists in a German translation and there ought to be one in French.)

The publishing venture ought to be put on an absolutely commercial basis, by looking for someone just as *Avanti!* did with the publisher Bietti, who will then take on the task of organising it from a commercial point of view and who, keeping the earnings, will take on legal responsibility for publication. But this is a question you will already have looked into. I will finish later on some of the parts here just summarised.

Greetings.

Source: AAG; the original version used here – single spaced as was the norm – is also at APC 513-1-248/16-19; a double spaced copy follows on pages 20-26, which also differs in underlining and section breaks; all versions are unsigned

---

Recipient unknown; possibly Ruggero Grieco

[BETWEEN JANUARY AND MARCH 1924][43]

[...] I have read Amadeo's opinion. I think that this Bianco who, together with another person, signs as the 'owner-administrator' of *Prometeo* is someone who is able to lay out money, and financially should be used to the full.[44] For example he could publish the edition of the *Communist Manifesto* with Rjazanov's notes; the important thing is that it should be done and that it should not cost a great deal. Things stand like this – that I am translating the notes and have sent the first part I have translated to Moscow for revision, and they have not as yet sent it back to me. As well as the notes, the volume contains:

1) Two short editorial introductions by Rjaz[anov].
2) A chapter by Rjaz[anov] on the 'Communist League'.
3) A chapter of Engels' on the revolutionary movement of 1847.
4) The 5 prefaces by Marx and Engels to the editions in German (1872), German (1883), German (1890), Polish and Italian.
5) The Manifesto.
6) Rjaz[anov]'s notes to the Manif[esto].
7) The translation of the first number of the *Kommunistische Zeitschrift*, published in London by Marx in September 1847.
8) The *Principles of Communism* by Engels as questions and answers.[45]
9) The Statute of the Communist League.

10) The demands of the Communist Party in Germany.
11) A chronology of the main events in the history of socialism and the working-class movement from 1800 to 1848.
12) 6 illustrations: α) a portrait of Marx; β) likewise of Engels; γ) an extract from the *Manifesto* in Marx's handwriting; δ) a passage in Engels's handwriting; ε) the front cover of the first edition of the *Manifesto*; ζ) the cover of the *Kommun. Zeitschrift.*

Number 1 could be substituted by an original introduction of Rjazanov's for the Italian edition.

We would have to have numbers 2-6-11 translated from the Russian; these comprise exactly 220 pages of the 380 pages of the volume in Russian (the notes occupy 190 pages). Someone else, meanwhile, such as Amadeo himself or someone in Amadeo's charge, could revise the existing translations in Italian of the other numbers and translate what has not yet been translated. The book would really be of great use for the Italian comrades. Taken as a whole it is a simple treatment of the whole of communist doctrine and in part also of the history of the movement up to 1848. I think that as a publication it would be a success and, all told, would not be a bad speculation to make. In Russian it exists in two editions, a small octavo format and a popular edition in a large 32mo format. I think it would be easy enough to obtain the stencils for the illustrations of one of the two formats, the small pocket edition, which seems to me the most appropriate one for our public.

Let Amadeo know the above. The Party ought not to have anything to the contrary regarding a solution of this sort. The important thing is that there should be publications and that there should be a reasonably wide readership, since it is impossible for us to create a Party publishing house.

I am still persuaded of the usefulness of the other initiatives which Amadeo does not think necessary. This persuasion of mine took shape in Russia, in contact with our émigrés and by seeing in the present results what the Russian comrades had done before the revolution. Do you really believe that the simple workers who today are heading sections and divisions of the Commissariats acquired their experience only through the political and economic activity of the Party? The Party schools have had an enormous role in forming this expertise of theirs, they have created what the Russians call 'militant materialism', in other words that phenomenon which I think is the only one of its kind in the world, by which Marx's doctrine became a living thing in the Party, became incarnated in consciousness, gave rise to the birth of an integral movement of a new civilisation. Of course, it has also produced excesses, such as a mania for hair-splitting, interminable discussions, the wish to go right to the extreme limit in an analysis. But all this is of necessity linked to the formation of every new mass current of ideas and, at the start, fanaticism is also a strength.

Write to me, telling me about the more properly technical questions of *L'O[rdine] N[uovo]*. How much does it cost? When has the material to be handed over to the typographers? Could you let me have a copy of the list of subscribers and of the sales?

At *Inprecorr* they tell me they have published all the articles of yours that have arrived; something, then, must have been lost on the way.

Who now is in charge of the women's movement – is there someone? If there exists a 'specialist' tell that person to write an article on the movement, on the difficulties it is experiencing and on its future prospects.

Warmest greetings

Masci.

Source: APC 495-221-8/1; handwritten, with another digitalised copy, not the original and with somewhat disordered pages, in AAG

To Togliatti, Terracini etc.

U.9. VIENNA, 9/2/1924

To Palmi, Urbani etc.

Dear comrades,

I am sending two copies so that you can send one straight away to Milan to the comrades who are now there. I would like what I am here outlining to be passed on to the following comrades: Palmi, Negri, Ferri, Lanzi, Platone, Montagnana, Gennari.

Dear comrades,

I am very happy to accept com. Urbani's invitation to set down, at least in general terms, the reasons why at this particular moment I think it necessary to open up a discussion, before the mass of the Party membership, on basic issues dealing not only with our internal situation but also regarding a new alignment of the groups aspiring to the leadership of the Party. Certain reasons of appropriateness will however oblige me not to go into too much depth on a number of questions; I know the psychology that is widespread among our movement and know that the absence up to now of any internal polemic and any forceful attempt at self-criticism has led, even among ourselves, to an excessively carping and irascible mentality, with comrades flaring up for the slightest reason.

THE INTERNAL SITUATION OF THE INTERNATIONAL

I am not at all persuaded by Urbani's analysis of the new positions that in his view would come to the fore in the Comintern after the events in Germany. Just as, a year ago, I did not believe the International was going to the right, according to the widespread opinion among our E[xecutive] C[ommittee], so today I do not believe it is shifting to the left. The political terminology itself that com. Urbani is using seems to me absolutely mistaken or, at the least, extremely superficial. As regards Russia, it has always been my understanding that, in the geography of the fractions and tendencies, Radek, Trotsky and Bukharin occupy a left position, with Zinov'ev, Kamenev and Stalin on the right, while Lenin was in the centre holding the ring during all situations of serious tension. All this is, of course, according to the political language now being used. The so-called Leninist nucleus, as is known, maintains that these 'topographic' positions are totally illusory and deceptive and, in its polemics, has continually shown how the so-called lefts are nothing other than Mensheviks who make use of revolutionary language while being incapable of assessing the real relations of objective forces. It is well-known that, throughout the whole history of the revolutionary movement in Russia, Trotsky was further to the left than the Bolsheviks, while on organisational questions he often formed a bloc with or even was indistinguishable from the Mensheviks. It is well-known that as long ago as 1905 Trotsky maintained that there could be a socialist and workers' revolution in

Russia, while the Bolsheviks intended solely to establish a political dictatorship of the proletariat in alliance with the peasantry which would serve as the shell within which there could develop a capitalism whose economic structure was not to be attacked. It is also well-known that in November 1917, while Lenin and the majority within the Party had gone over to Trotsky's conception and intended to lay hold not only of the political government but also the government of industry, Zinov'ev and Kamenev remained anchored to the Party's traditional opinion, wanting a government of revolutionary coalition with the Mensheviks and the Social Revolutionaries, and thus resigned from the Party C[entral] C[ommittee], publishing statements and articles in non-Bolshevik journals and only by a hair's breadth avoiding a scission. It is certain that, had the coup d'état failed in November 1917, as the movement in Germany did last October, Zinov'ev and Kamenev would have left the Bolshevik Party and probably gone with the Mensheviks. The recent polemic in Russia shows that Trotsky and the opposition, in general, given the prolonged absence from the Party leadership of Lenin, are seriously worried about a return to the old mentality, which would be harmful for the Revolution. By demanding a greater intervention of the working-class element in the life of the Party and a reduction in the powers of the bureaucracy, they basically want to safeguard the working-class and socialist nature of the Revolution and to prevent it from slowly taking on the nature of that democratic dictatorship, the shell of a developing capitalism, that was still the programme of Zinov'ev and com[rade]s in November 1917. This, it seems to me, is the situation in the Russian Party, which is much more complicated and more substantial than Urbani sees it; the sole novelty is the passage of Bukharin to the Zinov'ev, Bukharin, Stalin group.

As regards the German situation, too, it seems that affairs are unfolding somewhat differently from Urbani's description.

The two groups contending for the leadership of the German Party are, both of them, inadequate and incompetent. The so-called minority group (Fischer-Maslow) undoubtedly represents the majority of the revolutionary proletariat, but it has neither the organisational force necessary to lead a victorious revolution in Germany, nor a firm and sure political line that would be a guarantee against still greater catastrophes than that of last October. It is composed of elements who are still inexperienced as regards party activity, who have found themselves at the head of the opposition only due to the absence of leaders, a situation characteristic of Germany. They represent the great masses like a cork bobbing on the surface [represents] the sea.[46] The Brandler-Thalheimer group is stronger than the first one as regards ideology and revolutionary preparation, but it too has its weaknesses [and] in certain ways some of these weaknesses are much greater and more serious than those of the other group.[47] Brandler and Thalheimer have become the Talmudists of the revolution. In wanting at all costs to find allies for the working class, they have ended up by neglecting the role of the working class itself; in wanting to win over the working-class aristocracy controlled by the Social Democrats they have thought they could do this not by developing a programme of an industrial nature, focused on the factory councils and on the question of control, but, instead, their desire to compete with the Social Democrats on the terrain of democracy has led to a degeneration of the watchword of the workers' and peasants' government. Which of the two groups is right and which is left? The question is all rather Byzantine. It is natural that Zinov'ev, who cannot attack Brandler and Thalheimer for being incompetent and nonentities as individuals, should pose the question at a political level and, in their errors, seek indications that allow him to accuse them of rightism. The question then, moreover, becomes accursedly more complicated. In certain respects Brandler is more a putschist than a rightist and one might even say he is a putschist because he is a rightist. He had guaranteed that by last October it would be possible to carry out a coup d'état in Germany, and had assured us that technically the party was equipped for this. Zinov'ev instead was very pessimistic, and of the opinion that the situation was not politically ripe. In the discussions at the Centre in Russia, Zinov'ev found himself in a minority and Trotsky's article 'Is it Possible to Fix a Definite Time for a Counter-Revolution or a Revolution?' appeared instead.[48] In a discussion at the Presidium this was said fairly clearly by Zinov'ev. Now, what is the nub of the question? As long ago as July, after the Peace Conference at The Hague, on his return from Moscow after a *tournée*, Radek made a catastrophic report on the German situation.[49] From this it appeared that the C[entral] C[ommittee], led by Brandler, no longer had the confidence of the Party; that the minority, although consisting of incapable and at times very shady elements, had the majority of the party behind it and, at the Leipzig Congress, would have had the majority, if centralism and Comintern support for Brandler had not made this impossible;[50] that the C[entral] C[ommittee] was only formally applying the Moscow decisions, that for the United Front and for the workers' government there had been no systematic campaign, but just newspaper articles of a theoretical and abstruse nature which were not read by the workers. It is obvious that, after this report by Radek, the Brandler group got to work and, in order to avoid the minority getting the upper hand, prepared a new March 1921.[51] If there were errors they were committed by the Germans. The Russian comrades, that is Radek and Trotsky, were mistaken in believing the fine words of Brandler and comrades, but in actual fact even in this case, their position was not of the right, but really more of the left, to the extent that they risked being accused of putschism.

I have thought it useful to discuss this subject in some detail since we must have a fairly clear orientation in this field. The statute of the International assigns *de facto* hegemony to the Russian party for world-wide organisation. In consequence we have to be acquainted with the various currents that form in the Russian party in order to understand the orientations that from time to time are demanded of the International. One must further bear in mind the superior situation of the Russian comrades who, as well as having at their disposal the mass of information which more properly belongs to our organisation, also have information which, on certain questions, is more abundant and precise and which belongs to the Russian State. Their orientations are therefore founded on a material base that we could have only after a revolution, and this is what gives their supremacy a permanent and not easily assailable nature.

THE MANIFESTO OF THE COMMUNIST LEFT

I now come to questions that are more strictly speaking our own. Comrade Urbani writes that my assessment of the general nature of the manifesto was greatly exaggerated. I still maintain it represents the beginning of a battle without quarter against the International and that, contained in it, there is the demand for a revision of the whole tactical development that began with the Third Congress.

Among the conclusions of the manifesto, point b) says that a discussion must be initiated within the appropriate organs of the International on the conditions of the Italian proletariat's struggle over the last few years, a far-reaching discussion going beyond the purely contingent and transitory nature that has often suffocated the examination and solution of the most important problems. What does this mean except not just the demand for a revision, and the view that it is possible to revise not only the Comintern's tactics in Italy after the Third Congress, but also a discussion of the general principles on which these tactics were founded? It is not true, as claimed in the last sentence of the section 'Communist tactics in Italy', that, after its Third Congress, the International did not say what it wanted done in Italy. Issue 23 of the review *Communist International* published an open letter from the International E[xecutive] to the C[entral] C[ommittee] of the PCI, written towards the middle of March 1922, in other words after the E[nlarged] E[xecutive] of February. The letter refuted and rejected the whole conception of the theses on tactics presented at the Rome Congress, going on to say that the conception was in flat contradiction with the resolutions of the Third Congress. It dealt in particular with the following points: 1) the problem of winning the majority; 2) the situations under which the battle becomes necessary and the possibilities for the struggle; 3) the united front; 4) the watchword of the workers' government.

The third point defines the question of the united front in the trade union and in the political fields. In other words it was explicitly stated that the Party had to go into and be part of joint committees for struggle and agitation. The fourth point attempts to trace out an immediate tactical line for the struggle in Italy leading the way to a workers' government. The letter concludes with this sentence: it is preferable for the party to content itself with the theses laid down by the Third Congress and at the E[nlarged] Ex[ecutive] of February, and for it to give up its own theses, rather than present the theses in question, which would force the E[xecutive] to combat the conceptions of the Italian C[entral] C[ommittee] openly in the most forceful fashion. After this letter of the E[xecutive], which has a very precise meaning and value, I do not know whether one may ask, as the manifesto does, for the whole discussion to be reopened over and above the existence of contingent events. This would mean stating openly that, after the Third Congress, the Italian Party has found itself in systematic and permanent disagreement with the Comintern line, and wants to launch a struggle over principles.

THE PARTY'S TRADITION

I categorically deny that the Party's tradition is what is reflected in the manifesto, which instead deals with the tradition, that is the conception, of one of the groups that initially constituted our Party, and not at all with a tradition of the Party. In the same way I deny that there exists a crisis of confidence between the International and the Party in its entirety. This crisis exists only between the International and one part of the Party leaders. The Party was born at Livorno, not on the basis of a conception that then continued to persist and develop, but on the concrete and immediate basis of the separation from the reformists and from those who sided with the reformists against the International. The wider basis, which brought the sympathies of one part of the proletariat to the provisional committee of Imola, was faithfulness to the Communist International. One may therefore assert as true the complete opposite of what the manifesto maintains. With justification its signatories may be accused of not having been able to interpret, and having gone outside, the Party tradition. But this is a purely verbal and Byzantine question. We are dealing with a political fact. When Amadeo found himself leading the Party, he wanted his conception to predominate and become that of the Party. Still now, through the manifesto, he would like the same thing. That we allowed this attempt to succeed in the past is one thing, but that today we should continue to want this and, by signing the manifesto, should approve an entire situation and encapsulate the Party within it, is something quite different. In actual fact we have never in any absolute sense allowed this situation to become consolidated. At least before the Rome Congress, in my speech at the Turin assembly, I stated fairly clearly that I accepted the theses on tactics only for the contingent reason of Party organisation, but I declared in favour of the united front right up to its normal conclusion of a workers' government. Moreover, the whole set of theses had never been discussed in depth by the Party and, at its Rome Congress, the question was clear enough: if the E[xecutive] had not reached a compromise with the Comintern delegates, by which the theses were presented as a consultative document to be changed after the Fourth Congress, it is not very probable that the majority of delegates would have backed the Ex[ecutive]. The majority, if faced with an ultimatum from the Comintern, would not have hesitated and would have followed its tradition of international loyalty. Certainly I would have done so, and so too would the Piedmontese delegations, with whom I had a meeting after Kolarov's speech and with whom I was in agreement on the points of preventing the minority from winning the party in a surprise move, but of not giving the vote a significance going beyond the organisational question.

THE MANIFESTO'S CONCEPTION

Except for these more or less juridical questions, I am of the opinion that the time is ripe to give the party a different orientation from the one it has had up to now. A new phase is opening up in the history, not only of our Party but also that of our country. We therefore need to enter into a phase of greater clarity in the relationships inside the Party and between the Party and the International. I do not wish to discuss this at too great a length, but will deal with just a few points in the hope these will shed light on the problems that have been left on one side.

One of the most serious errors that have characterised and still characterise the activity of our Party may be summed up in those same words that express the second of the theses on tactics: 'It would be mistaken to consider these two factors – of consciousness and of will – as faculties that may be attained by or expected from single comrades, since they are realised only through the integration of the activity of many individuals in a collective unitary organism'.

This concept, correct if applied to the working class, is mistaken and extremely dangerous if applied to the Party. Before the Livorno Congress the concept was held by Serrati, who maintained that the Party in its entirety was revolutionary even if socialists of different political species and hue cohabited within it. At the Congress that marked the split within Russian social democracy, the same concept was held by the Mensheviks, who maintained that it was the Party in its entirety that counts and not single individuals. As regards the individuals it was sufficient for them to declare themselves Socialists. In our Party this conception was only partially responsible for the danger of opportunism. Indeed one cannot deny that the minority was born and has gained supporters through the absence of discussion and polemics within the Party, that is through not having given importance to the single comrades and not having sought to give them a somewhat more concrete orientation than through statements and binding decisions. In our Party there have also been complaints

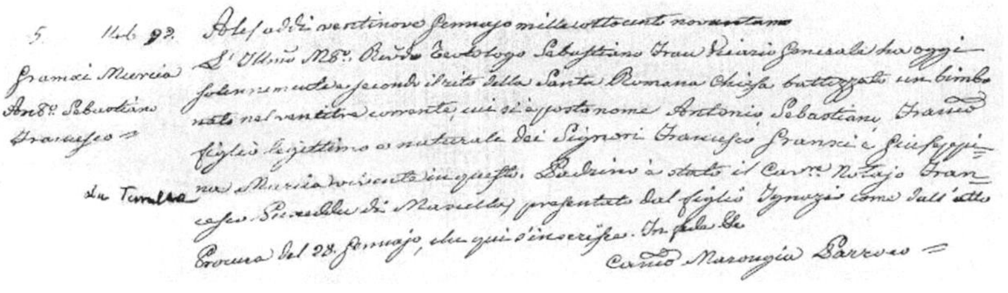

1. Gramsci's baptism certificate in the name of Antonio Sebastiano Francesco (Francesco after his father).

Numero Secondo

Gramsci Antonio Francesco

Morto in Roma il 27 Aprile 1937 (vedi atto trascritto nel 1937 al n° 2 - Parte II S. A del Comune di Ales)

Gramsci Antonio ha contratto matrimonio in Mosca il 23/09/1923 con CHOUKHT JOULIA APOLONOVNA atto matrimonio n. 907 Parte II Serie C.7 Anno 1994 del Comune di Roma. Ales, lì 04-01-1995

* S'indichi la professione o la condizione.

Delio Gramsci

Giuliano Gramsci

Firme dei figli di Antonio Gramsci di passaggio, provenienti dalla Russia (URSS)

Ales 29/12/1947

L'anno milleottocento novanta uno, addì ventisette di Gennaio a ore anti meridiane nove e minuti trenta, nella Casa Comunale.

Avanti di me ... Ufficiale dello Stato Civile del Comune di Ales, è comparso Gramsci Francesco, di anni trenta, * ..., domiciliato in Ales, il quale mi ha dichiarato che alle ore anti meridiane undici e minuti ..., del dì ventidue del corrente mese, nella casa posta in Via Cattedrale al numero Ventitre, da Marcias Giuseppina ... sua moglie ... è nato un bambino di sesso maschile che egli mi presenta, e a cui dà il nome di Antonio Francesco.

A quanto sopra e a quest'atto sono stati presenti quali testimoni ..., di anni sessantuno, * ..., e ..., di anni trentacinque, * ..., entrambi residenti in questo comune.

...

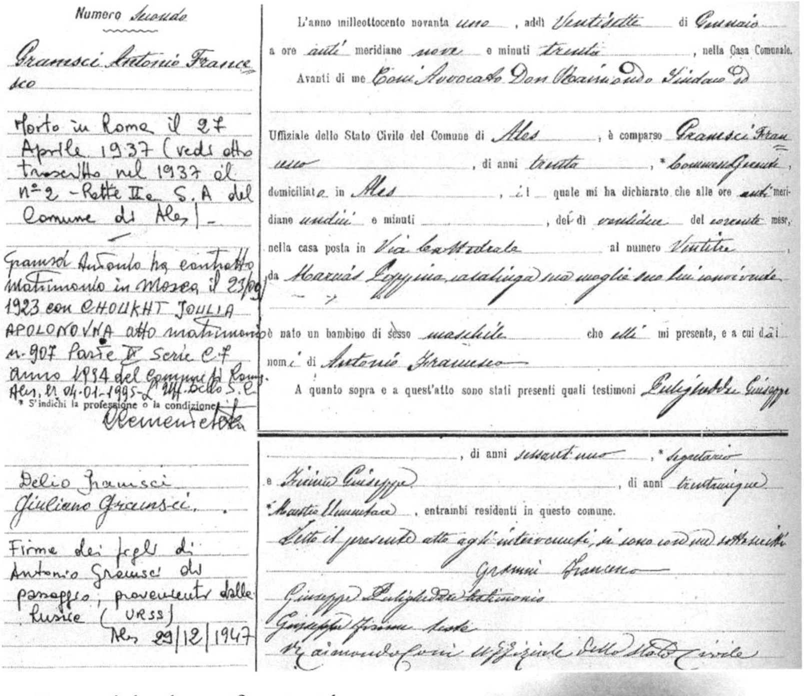

2. Gramsci's birth certificate, with a note in the margin about his marriage. Also in the margin are the signatures of Gramsci's two sons, Delio and Giuliano. A note at the top of the margin says when and where Gramsci died.

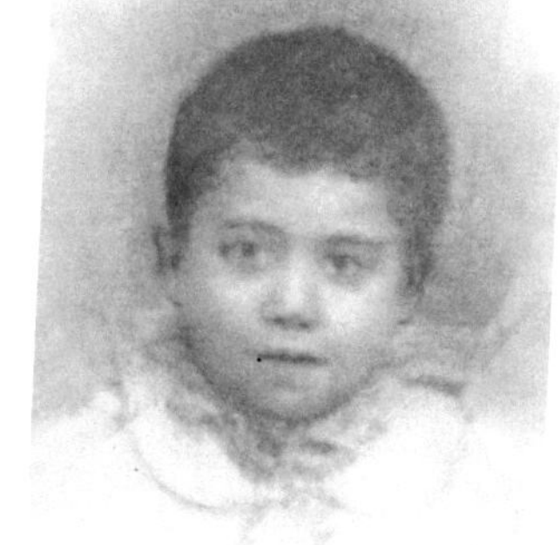

3. Gramsci as a small child.

All photographs are courtesy of the Gramsci Institute in Rome except Number 8, which is courtesy of the Gramsci House Museum at Ghilarza.

4. Franscesco Gramsci, Gramsci's father

5. Giuseppina Marcias ('Peppina'), Gramsci's mother

6. Gramsci at middle school

7. Teresina and Carlo (Gramsci's brother and sister)

8. Sardinian cart (see p45 and letters on pp125, 128, 129) in its glass case in the Gramsci house in Ghilarza (now a small museum).

Свидетельство о браке № 2817

Выдано в том, что Гражданин (фамилия его до брака) Грамши Антон (имя) Францискович (отчество), гражд. (фамилия ее до брака) Шухт Юлия (имя) Аполлоновна (отчество) вступили в брак, о чем в книге записей актов гражданского состояния О БРАКЕ за 1923 год 23 числа сентября месяца произведена соответствующая запись.

Место для штампа: 12 января 26

Фамилии после заключения брака	его Грамши	ее Шухт
Особые отметки		

Заведующий

Делопроизводитель

9. Russian marriage certificate, dated 12 January 1926, which gives the date of Gramsci's marriage as 23 September 1923.

10. Jul'ka Schucht in 1922, around the time she and Gramsci first met.

11. At fourth world Comintern congress, 1922. Gramsci is seated.

12. Gramsci in Moscow with Italian delegates to the fourth congress of the Comintern, November or December 1922.

Российск. Социалистич. федератив. Совет. Респуб.

УПРАВЛЕНИЕ ДЕЛАМИ

СОВЕТА

НАРОДНЫХ КОМИССАРОВ.

Москва,

КРЕМЛЬ.

ПРОПУСК № 704

Выдан т. Грамши

члену Президиума И.К.К.И.

сроком по 1-е Января 1923 г. на право свободного прохода в помещение Совета Народных Комиссаров и во все учреждения Р. С. Ф. С. Р.

Управляющий Делами Совета Народных Комиссаров

Начальник канцелярии

13. Gramsci's delegate's card as member of the Presidium of the Comintern, dated 1 Jan 1923.

14. Gramsci, Vienna 1924. To his left, Victor Serge is holding a child.

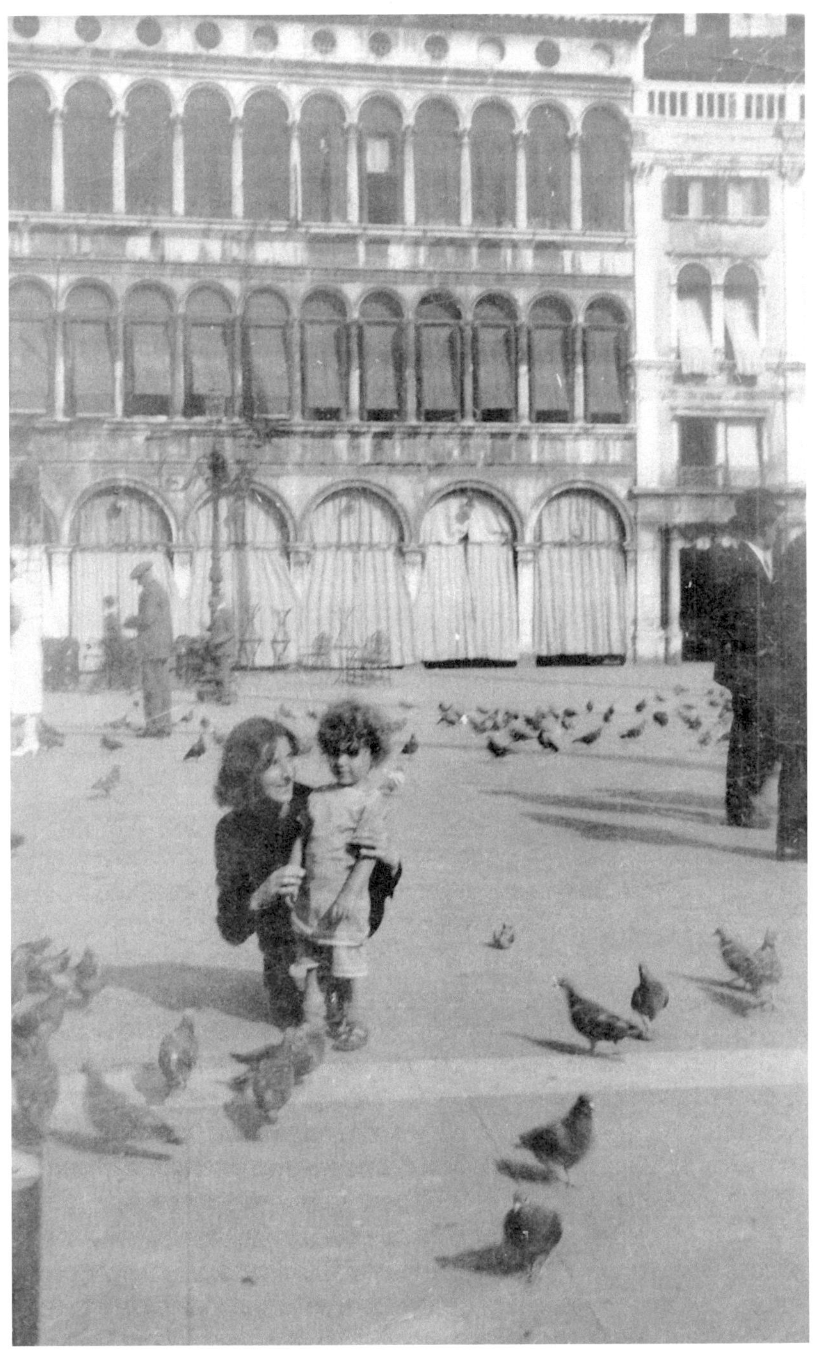

15. Jul'ka's elder sister Evgenija, in 1925 or 1926, with her nephew Delio, in St Mark's Square, Venice

16. Amadeo Bordiga around 1921

17. Palmiro Togliatti around 1921

18. Umberto Terracini around 1921

19. Piero Sraffa

regarding another aspect of the danger: the progressive impoverishment of the entire activity of individual members, the passivity of the mass of the Party, the unthinking certainty that it doesn't matter because there's always someone who has thought of everything and taken the appropriate measures. This situation has had the gravest repercussions in the organisational field. The Party did not have the possibility, using rational criteria, of choosing the trustworthy elements to whom it could assign given tasks. The choice was made on an empirical basis, according to the personal knowledge and acquaintanceship of individual leaders and, in the majority of cases, fell on elements that did not enjoy the confidence of the local organisations which thus saw their work sabotaged. And it may be added that the work carried out was never subject to any but the most minimal control, thus producing within the Party a veritable separation between the mass and the leaders. This still remains the situation, in my view full of countless dangers. During my stay in Moscow, I did not find one single political émigré (and they were from all over Italy and were among the most active elements) who understood the position of our Party and who did not criticise the C[entral] C[ommittee] bitterly, at the same time – let it be understood – as making the most wide-ranging promises of discipline and obedience. The Party's error has been to put the emphasis, and abstractly at that, on the question of Party organisation, which then has meant just the creation of an apparatus of functionaries who were orthodox as regards the official conception. It was, and is still, believed that the revolution depends solely on the existence of just such an apparatus, arriving at the point of believing that this existence can bring about the revolution.

The Party has lacked an organic activity of agitation and propaganda, which is what should have received the whole of our attention and have given rise to the formation of real specialists in this field. We have not attempted, at every single opportunity, to create among the masses the possibility of expressing themselves in the same sense as the Communist Party. Every event, every anniversary of a local, national or international nature should have served as an instrument for the communist cells to carry out agitation among the masses, by having resolutions passed, distributing leaflets. This has not happened purely by chance. The Party has even been against the formation of factory cells. Any participation of the masses in the activity and internal life of the Party, except for the big occasions and as a result of a formal order from the Party centre, has been seen as a threat to unity and to centralisation. The Party has not been conceived of as the result of a dialectical process in which there is the convergence of the spontaneous movement of the revolutionary masses and the organisational and directive will of the centre, but only as something suspended in mid-air, which develops in itself and for itself and to which the masses will arrive when the situation is favourable and the crest of the revolutionary wave reaches its height, or when the Party centre is of the opinion that an offensive should be undertaken and brings itself down to the level of the masses to spur them on them and lead them into action. Of course, since affairs do not proceed in this way, centres of opportunist infection have been formed unbeknown to the centre. And these have found their reflection in the parliamentary group, and found another one, in a more organic form, within the minority.

This conception has had its influence on the fusion problem. The question that was always asked of the Comintern was the following: do you think that our Party still has a nebulous form, or is it a fully-fledged formation? The truth is that, historically, a Party is never definite in form and never will be, since it will be defined only when it has become coterminous with the entire population, in other words at the moment of its disappearance. Right up until this disappearance, when it reaches the highest goals of Communism, it will go through a series of transitional stages and will from time to time absorb new elements in the two historically possible forms, i.e. through individuals and through groups of a bigger or lesser size joining the organisation. The situation was made even more difficult for our Party, given its dissensions with the Comintern. If the International is a world Party, understanding this with many pinches of salt, it is obvious that the development of the Party and the forms that it will be able to assume depend on two factors of the will, and not just one.

In other words it depends not only on the will of the National Executive but also, and especially, of the International Executive, which is the stronger one. To repair this situation, to succeed in giving the development of our Party the impetus that Amadeo wants, it is necessary to win over the International Ex[ecutive], in other words to become the fulcrum of an entire opposition. Politically this is the result reached, and it is natural that the International E[xecutive] should to seek to break the back of the Italian E[xecutive].

Amadeo has a whole conception regarding this: in his system everything is logically coherent and consistent. He thinks the International's tactics are affected by the influence of the Russian situation, in other words they were born on the terrain of a primitive and backward capitalist civilisation. For him these tactics are extremely voluntaristic and theatrical, since only with an extreme force of the will could one obtain from the Russian masses a revolutionary activity that was not determined by the historical situation. He thinks that for the more developed countries of central and western Europe these tactics are inadequate or even useless. In these countries the historical mechanism works according to all the Marxist hallmarks: there is a determination that was lacking in Russia, and thus the absorbing task must be that of organising the Party in itself and for itself. I, instead, believe the situation is very different from this, in the first place because the political conception of the Russian communists was formed on an international, and not on a national, terrain; and in the second place because, in central and western Europe, the development of capitalism has created not only broad proletarian strata but also, and for that very reason, an upper stratum, the working-class aristocracy, with its appendages of trade-union bureaucracy and social democrat groupings. The determination which in Russia was direct, and which launched the masses into the streets in a revolutionary assault, becomes complicated in central and western Europe by reason of all these political superstructures created by the greater development of capitalism. Indeed it slows down and urges caution on the action of the masses, and thus requires the revolutionary Party to have a strategy and tactics that are much more complex and of longer range than were necessary for the Bolsheviks between March and November 1917. However, it is one thing for Amadeo to have this conception, and to try to have it triumph not only at the national level but on the international scale: he is convinced and is fighting with great skill and elasticity to obtain his goal, not to compromise his theses, to delay any sanction from the Comintern that would stop him from carrying on right up to the successful confluence with the next historical period, when the central and western European revolution will take away from Russia the hegemonic nature that it today enjoys. But it is quite another thing for us, who are not persuaded of the historicity of this conception, to continue to give it credit politically, and thereby to give it all its international value. Amadeo has adopted the standpoint of an international minority. We must adopt the standpoint of a national majority. We cannot therefore want the government of the Party to be given over to the representatives of the minority, on the grounds that they are in agreement with the International, even if, after the discussion opened through the manifesto, the Party majority remains in the hands of the present leaders.[52] This, in my view, is the central point that politically must define our approach. If, then, we were in agreement with Amadeo's theses, naturally we would have to pose the question of whether, having the majority of the Party with us, it would then be appropriate for us to remain within the International, and be led nationally by the minority, in order to play for time and arrive at a reversal of the situation which would confirm that theoretically we were right, or whether it would be appropriate to split the majority. But if we are not in agreement with the theses, to sign the manifesto means taking upon ourselves the entire responsibility for this ambiguity: if Amadeo's theses obtain a majority, we – who are not in agreement with these theses and could therefore resolve the situation organically – accept the leadership of the minority; if not, we remain in a minority, when by our conceptions we are in agreement with the majority, which would align itself with the International.[53] This would mean our political liquidation: a separation from Amadeo, subsequent to such a state of affairs, would take on the most objectionable and obnoxious aspect.

INDICATIONS FOR FUTURE WORK

I do not want to spend much time on this since it would require much more space to be dealt with adequately; I shall content myself with just a few indications. The future work of the Party needs to be overhauled in two fields: the organisational and the political ones.

In the organisational field I think it is necessary to enhance the role of the C[entral] C[ommittee] and, insofar as is possible, given the situation, have it work more. In my view it is necessary to establish more clearly the relations that have to exist between the various bodies of the Party, defining responsibilities and the division of labour more exactly and rigorously. Two organs and two new activities must be created. The first is a Control Commission, constituted in the main of old workers who must in the last instance judge controversial questions not having an immediate political repercussion, for which an immediate intervention by the Executive is not therefore necessary; the Commission will have to keep under continuous examination the situation of Party members for periodic revisions. The second is an agitation and propaganda committee, which will gather together all the local and national material that is necessary and useful for the Party's agitation and propaganda work. It must study the local situations, propose agitational activities, and write leaflets and documents to give an orientation to the work of the local bodies: it must base itself on a whole national organisation, whose central nucleus for the big urban centres will be the city ward and for the countryside the rural district.[54] It will have to begin work by carrying out a census of Party members, who must then be divided for organisational ends according to seniority and the official positions they have filled, the capabilities they have shown, as well, obviously, as their moral and political qualities. A precise division of labour will have to be established between the E[xecutive] and the UI: precise responsibilities and spheres of activity must be established in this field that may not be violated without serious disciplinary sanctions.[55] I think that this is one of the weakest aspects of our Party, the one that, more than any other, has demonstrated how the centralism that has been set up has been more a bureaucratic formality and a banal confusion of responsibilities and spheres of activity than a rigorous organisational system.

In the political field we have to establish with precision the theses on the Italian situation and on the possible stages of its future development. In 1921-22 the Party's official conception was that it was impossible for a fascist or military dictatorship to come to power; it was only with great difficulty, by radically changing theses 51 and 52 on tactics, that I managed to have removed this prediction in written form from the theses. Now it seems to me that we are falling into another error strictly linked to the error of that time. Then we did not take into account the covert and latent opposition to fascism of the industrial bourgeoisie, and we thought that, of the various possibilities, a social democrat government was to be ruled out, leaving only one of these three solutions: the dictatorship of the proletariat (the least probable), a dictatorship of the general staff acting on behalf of the industrial bourgeoisie and the court, and a fascist dictatorship. This conception tied our hands politically and led us into committing many errors. Now once more we are not taking account of the emerging opposition of the industrial bourgeoisie and especially the one that is taking shape in the South, which is of a more decidedly territorial nature and is thus broaching some aspects of the national question. There is a certain current of opinion that a proletarian revival can and must come about with our Party as the sole beneficiary. I, on the other hand, think that, in any revival, our Party will still be in a minority position, that the majority of the working class will go with the reformists and that the liberal bourgeois democrats will still have much to say. I do not doubt that the situation is actively revolutionary and that therefore, in a given period of time, our Party will have the majority on its side; but if this period will perhaps not be long in terms of time, it will undoubtedly be dense in secondary stages, which we shall have to foresee with a certain precision in order to be able to manoeuvre and not fall into errors that would prolong the experiences of the proletariat.

I believe moreover that, in practical terms, the Party must pose certain problems which have never been faced up to, and whose solution has been left to elements that were closely bound up with the problems themselves. The question of winning over the Milanese proletariat is a national problem for our Party, which must be resolved with all the means at the Party's disposal and not just those of Milan itself. If we do not have the overwhelming majority of the Milanese proletariat firmly on our side we cannot win and cannot maintain the revolution throughout the whole of Italy. We must therefore bring to Milan working-class elements from other cities, get them into work in the factories, strengthen the legal and illegal Milanese organisation with the best elements from all over Italy. Roughly speaking, I think that in this way we have to introduce at least a hundred comrades, all ready to put their entire effort into working for the Party, into the body of the Milanese working class. Another problem of this type is that of the seamen, closely bound up with the problem of the military fleet. Italy lives from the sea and not to deal with the problem of the seas, as one of the most essential problems, one to which the Party has to devote its greatest attention, would mean not thinking in concrete terms about the revolution. When I think that for a long time our policy vis-à-vis the sailors was in the hands of a youngster like Caroti's son, I get the shudders.[56] Another problem is that of the rail workers, whom we have always considered from a purely trade-union point of view, whereas the question goes beyond this and is a national and political one of prime importance. The fourth and last of these problems is that of the South, which we have misunderstood just as the socialists did, believing it could be resolved in the normal course of our general political activity. I have always been of the opinion that the South would become the graveyard of fascism, but I also think that it will turn out to be the main reservoir and training ground of national and international reaction if, before the revolution, we do not study the questions adequately and are not prepared for everything.

I think I have given a fairly clear idea of my position and of the differentiations that exist between it and what is in the manifesto. Since I think that, to a great extent, you are more in agreement with my position, on which we have found ourselves side by side for quite some time, I hope that you still have the possibility to decide differently from what you were about to do.

With the most fraternal greetings

Masci

Source: AAG; also APC 513-1-248/40-45 and 46/51; typewritten with interpolations in Gramsci's handwriting in the copy on pages 46-51. All copies bear the handwritten signature 'Masci'; the copy on pages 40-45 has Gramsci's handwritten request in the first lines to pass on the copies to the comrades listed at the start

---

To the Executive Committee of the PCI

U.9. VIENNA, 10/2/24

To the E[xecutive] C[ommittee] of the PCI

Dear comrades

I will send the outlines of the articles for *Critica proletaria* with the next courier. I am very pleased that, at least in principle, you have agreed with the idea of such a publication; I think that we shall be able in any case to try and bring it to fruition, maintaining an occasional basis for publication, but each issue having a strictly organic approach to a single subject.

As for the pamphlets, it is obviously not going to be possible to publish them straight off. The *Communist Manifesto*, with Rjazanov's notes, is still being translated and I think will be ready only in a few months' time, since I have to have the translation revised. With this letter I am including the one to Zini, for you to send after having put his address on; I will send the book directly to Zini if he is willing to take on the work.

Here is what I am thinking of as the correspondence course for Party organisers. Each week we would publish, according to the number of subscriptions, a guide of 8-16 pages either lithographed or printed (eight if in medium-size type, sixteen pages if done by lithograph with handwritten text like university handouts). The first course ought not to last more than six months and would therefore correspond to a volume of 200-400pp. It will be available on subscription, with a price to be set only slightly above production and postal costs; the service must appear as devised by the Party for its members and not as some business venture. The Party has the moral obligation to provide its members with certain notions, but not, given its general conditions, to do this free; we can however take account, on a case by case basis according the indications of the local groups, of whether there are comrades whose personal circumstances (unemployment etc) mean that we should provide the service free. The service is to be carried out internally through Party channels with, for any future eventuality, a record being kept of the subscribers. The course will be strictly private in nature and the subscribers will not be able to give away the material and pass it on to anyone outside the Party. We will take account of any loss of material, just as is done in military schools for study material that, while not being secret, is however classed as reserved.

The course will deal with the most important organisational notions, taking particular account of the decisions of the Congresses of the International, especially the Third Congress. Given the Italian situation, we will also deal with other parts of work that the Party must undertake in the organisational and propaganda fields. These include, for example, how to carry out basic level propaganda, e.g. how to write leaflets, how to make use of all occasions and all existing worker and peasant organisations to get our Party's slogans and watchwords across, how to make political reports to groups of comrades that exist and meet together, even in the smallest centres. How one must assess a given local situation in order to make best use of it for propaganda and agitation. Or why it is necessary to collect, as from now, all possible information on individual reactionaries to prevent them from infiltrating our movement tomorrow, and, if common criminals, from escaping the penal sanction that today's oppressed population will demand just as soon as they have reacquired their freedom. More than anything else the first issue must be an attempt to have the necessary material, and the more rational criteria given by experience, in order then to compile a second more complete and comprehensive one. In each instalment the last page will be devoted to correspondence with the subscribers; in this way we will answer in brief the general questions that the subscribers ask, while a reply will be given directly by letter to individual questions. In its general lines, then, the course will be divided in the following way:

1) An introductory part outlining the limits and purposes of the course itself and a short exposition of the main principles of Marxism that underlie the Party's entire activity.
2) What a Party is and what the general organisational criteria of the International are for the various stages of the class struggle and civil war.[57]
3) Trade union organisation.
4) Work among the peasants and the organisational relationships between the working class and the peasant class, with mention of the religious question.
5) The problem of education and the general preparation of Party members.
6) The general questions of propaganda and agitation with discussion of the more general criteria of a less reserved nature that lie at the basis of the preparation for insurrection.
7) Lithography for women comrades.[58]
8) Demonstration of how and why pre-revolutionary organisational form and necessity is closely bound up with the needs of the victorious revolution.

Comrade Monti and I can take on the duty of compiling the first course. It will naturally be compiled from week to week according to the needs of publication; we can however always send three issues in advance, so that the Ex[ecutive] can check as needed and suggest additions and amendments.

The course will be able to have a distribution especially abroad and give some oxygen to the Party schools that ought always to be promoted everywhere there are elements capable of carrying out even elementary work; but a certain distribution will be possible in Italy too. The Party representative and the central groups of emigrants in the various countries should order copies in advance, and should receive the weekly parcel of course instalments and distribute them. In Italy this can be done by the Organisational Office.[59]

From the viewpoint of the Party schools and the course, the comrades should be organised in groups, each one of which will have a Party tutor, the choice of whom will initially fall upon the comrade who, to a certain degree, unites in his person three qualities – that of seniority in the movement, of participation in the organisational life of Party and trade union committees, and that of morality and dedication. We must pay special attention to creating this type of comrade who must become the Party tutor. Above the level of the tutor will be a type of inspector who initially will be defined by the propaganda experts sent to do rounds, and to whom special instructions and directives will be given for this special work. The Party will have to collect together very carefully all the data necessary to reconstruct the personal qualities and characteristics of this stratum of comrades who demonstrate they have willingness and spirit of initiative; this will be an extremely useful archive to be used as a basis for choosing personnel and trusted representatives. By following this path, if circumstances allow, we ought eventually to reach two results. One will be the convocation on a regional and provincial basis of something similar to the social weeks of the catholics, that is to say lectures and courses of lessons on chosen subjects taught by capable elements for groups of comrades who have already reached a higher level of general preparation. The other is the formation of a sort of communist college, such as existed in Bulgaria and as they want to create in the United States, in which for a period of six months a certain number of carefully chosen comrades, housed and paid for, follow regular courses on the most important subjects of communist doctrine and the science of State administration. Obviously we cannot think of putting these initiatives into effect immediately but is also true that to reach these aims we shall have to go through a whole series of successive stages and experiences through which a selection will take place, and a fairly secure base will be created for the choice of the best comrades who will be able, in the shortest possible time, to give the best results.

We know that in the development of the working class the same experiences and attempts are repeated an infinite number of times, and this, unfortunately, is a necessity inherent within the mode of existence of the proletariat. But we also know that none of these experiences and these attempts is ever completely lost and that it is absolutely necessary to pass through them if we want to reach the goal.

I hope that, as I write, the work for bringing out *L'Ordine Nuovo* has been completed and that the first number is already being printed. I would inform you that part of Ruggero's correspondence was sent on to Moscow and from there it was sent back to me, thus leading to a certain amount of anger and loss of time.

I am also informing you not to make any further use, for any reason whatever, of Dr M's address or of his business company. Experience has proved this to be too slow.

Greetings

Source: AAG; APC 513-1-248/52-3; unsigned

To Jul'ka

28. II. 924

Dearest one,

A fortnight has now passed without any news from you, just when I was more anxiously expecting some. I think your tiredness is more serious than appears from your words. Every time you can, send me just a single word to reassure me on your state of health. I don't know – and maybe this happens to you too? – whether not being able to be in constant contact and receive news from each other weighs down on you. At least as far as we can, let's try and lessen this distance. I am sending you my address so you can write to me directly: Floriangasse, 5 – Door 20 – III Floor Vienna / VIII Austria.

My dear

Gr

Source: AAG

To Scoccimarro and Togliatti

1 · 3 · 924

To Negri and Palmi

Dearest friends,

The bankworkers' strike, which made it impossible to cash a bank draft, means that we still cannot buy a typewriter for our office.[60] I cannot therefore carry out all the work I would like to in the Party's current situation, since I cannot keep copies of the material prepared. It seems to me most useful and appropriate therefore for me to briefly explain to you my opinion on the general lines to give to our activity.

Your letters have been very gratifying and have put new heart into me. I was very pessimistic about the future of our movement. We were going straight towards the event that in words we said we were trying to avoid, that is with our own hands we were preparing the conquest of our party by the terzini. My impression was the following: that the Party centre, absorbed by its organisational work, is not taking account of the fact that, in all this time, a certain work and a certain political propaganda have indeed been carried out. This work and propaganda have been carried out through the action of the International, according to a given line, and it is beyond doubt that they have created states of mind, currents of opinion and attitudes that are at work within the masses and are establishing a given situation. It would be childish to deny this: the struggle to conquer the PSI has been the *one single* concrete political action over the most recent period that has kept us in some sort of relation with the masses, that has allowed us to say we were alive. Can you find another action that can be counterposed to this? Maybe parliamentary action? Maybe trade union action, which itself has in any case been effective only insofar as it has been directed at the conquest of the PSI? Organisational work, the tenacious and difficult struggle to maintain the Party apparatus, are certainly important, but it is not on these things that we can draw up a balance sheet of the Party. It is not enough just to live: we must have a history, we have to move and develop in order to be able to say that we are a political organism with a base of its own and the future for itself, as we desire.

Your decision improves the situation greatly and avoids any definitive isolation.[61] Obviously there are still going to be many difficulties ahead, but they will not be as inextricable as before. We can constitute the centre of a fraction that itself has every chance of becoming the entire party. I want to recopy for you an extract from a letter written me by a worker who has emigrated to Moscow, and who, having heard of our discussions, has lost no time in telling me his opinion. (He was one of the minority before June's E[nlarged] E[xecutive] and then passed over to the position we have assumed, not so much in public as in the meetings that have been held with the émigré group, in opposition to Tasca.) He writes that 'There are two people in Moscow who, it appears, want to revolutionise the Party. To hear these ex-parliamentary deputies, it seems that the C[entral] C[ommittee] and the E[xecutive] C[ommittee] are a sect governing the Party without any control, without any ability, without any intelligence, it seems that the police know everything and let things be since they have no orders; when the orders do arrive, according to them a brake is put on the P[arty]. One report after another is being sent to the Comintern, we hope with some result. What I am hoping is that, within the limits imposed by legality, there is life in the P[arty] from the level of the base and not from the top; that it is taking account of the thought of comrades and that it is not hindering the expression of ideas contrary to the policy lines indicated just by a group of comrades who may have all the intelligence you want, but who are still people who err; that we are not going to ape the Russians too much since not everything that it was and is possible to do in Russia can be done at home. There is too great a difference in character; here, there was a whole underground life that was also extended to the masses, while with us I doubt whether illegal work has got to the point of being made fully its own by the P[arty]; this is one more reason for not believing that the voice of the P[arty] is reaching the masses. To my mind, the illegal side of the P[arty]'s life is still very legal and there are still lots of shortcomings, which are elementary but which are unseen. These are doubts which, in any case, I am expressing without any proof, but they come to mind after having heard complaints that are too exaggerated, but ones that maybe contain some grain of truth. And another thing. It seems to me that there are three currents forming within the P[arty], a left, a right and a centre one. I am afraid of the one headed by Bombacci, which is even against the Tasca-Graziadei current, so that we shall no longer have just one but two right wings. I wouldn't want you to be the centre, taking on – without wanting to – the whole ballast we are saddled with on the right as well as on the left. So, if you engage battle, fix the terms of it clearly and demand the greatest degree of clarity and purpose from everyone. And if there is some congress or conference and these 'crows' flock around you, make sure you know how to use them, but then drive them off straightaway with a shotgun. These are thoughts I had when I got to know you hadn't signed the manifesto of the left (whose content however I don't know) and so I thought that you would have been forming a centre so as to have done with the baying of the left and the right and grouping around yourself a good number of comrades who have learnt something from past events in Italy, have understood the R[ussian] R[evolution] and know how a Party is organised and must work when its task is to lead the proletarian mass to power.' I wanted you to read this extract since it seems to me very significant from a number of points of view, and shows the interest with which the émigrés (who are perhaps the biggest reserve of organisational strength for our Party) follow events, making use of every crumb of information for making their judgements.

The most serious question for us is undoubtedly that of differentiating ourselves from the rightists, but this does not seem to me insurmountable, and I think that to a great extent it is one of the people involved. Differentiation from the left will, unfortunately, come about automatically through the sole fact of our position.

In my view it is indispensable to draw up a series of theses on the situation in Italy defining our platform. They will be published under the signature of comrades solely of our group, in order to establish a first line of demarcation: the other elements eventually wishing to sign will do so afterwards and be forced into this action, which will have its political significance, even if they will not be led into differentiating themselves to avoid this; it would be useful for our theses to be published before those of the others. The signatories will be myself, Palmi, Negri, Leonetti and some others of the majority who are in agreement with us (for example what do Tresso, Gennari, Montagnana, Marabini think?); I don't know what stance Urbani will adopt but I hope he will join us. It will be useful to have Gennari and Marabini because of the authority they enjoy among many vast strata of the masses, through their history and their experience (unfortunately experience and seniority are always confused!), even if this might sound dangerous. Furthermore, we shall have to have the signatures of the workers' groups from the biggest centres. Who could sign from

Turin? Maybe Oberti? The comrades I knew best have emigrated: of these we shall certainly have the support of Bernolfo and maybe Ravazzoli from Milan, both of whom I have talked with at length in Moscow. From Milan I hardly know anyone. From Genoa, what are the thoughts of Arecco and Franzone, whom I know and who are two extremely good comrades? I know hardly anyone from Trieste, Rome, Naples, Messina, Bari, Florence, Palermo, and would not know what steps to take. We must try to have on our side comrades from all these centres; if we succeed in this we shall have made a great stride forward and this demonstration of ours will assume first rank importance. I think we shall have Germanetto on our side. And Gnudi, what does he think? And Arecco, our schoolmistress from Alessandria? And Azzario, Bellone (Virgilio), Betti (from Bologna), Ferrari (from Modena), Longo (from Turin), Peluso, Polacco (from Udine), Roberto, Scaffidi (from Girgenti), Tarozzi?[62] This work will have to be done by you, probably assigning the task to some comrade in whom you put the utmost trust: it is extremely important and carries great responsibility. If done well it will bear magnificent fruit. When the theses are ready, and we are sure of a good collection of signatures from the P[arty]'s traditional majority, I think we shall have to try to win the assent of some comrades of the right, such as Pastore and Mersú, but only after the work is already finished and our nucleus put together. We shall also need the signatures of émigré comrades, especially those in France; as I said, I think we have those of Bernolfo and Ravazzoli. I will write to Bernolfo for him to give me information and the names of comrades we can be sure of, such as for example Bonino and some others. Among the émigrés in Russia, Bianco (author of the letter quoted above) will be on our side and maybe Parodi, together with others.[63] The situation among the émigrés in Russia, however, is in total chaos, and I think has got worse since I left.

As for the content of the theses, I want to hear your opinion, since the lack of direct contact with events in Italy, which I know only through reading the more important newspapers, always gives me doubts about possible flaws in my conclusions. I'll state here briefly what I think.

We must dwell little on the past especially as regards our P[arty]. We shall mention the exceptional confusion that has been produced in Italy by the phenomenon of fascism, caused by the lack of national unity, by the dissolution of the State through the entry into historical life of the enormous popular masses who did not know against whom to fight, and by weakness in the development of capitalism, which has not in actual fact brought the economy of the country under its control, given that there are a million handicraft-artisan workers in Italy, and agricult[ure] is overwhelmingly pre-capitalist. Further, through the Southern question, the question of the relations between city and countryside is being posed on a clear-cut territorial basis, giving rise to the birth of autonomist parties or parties like social democracy, of an original type. This confusion serves us for explaining the uncertainty of many approaches adopted by the P[arty] and a certain sectarianism that had paralysed the P[arty]. The situation has now become clearer, of that there is no doubt. Fascism has defined its nature.[64] The elections have offered the way for the situation of the P[arties] to be driven towards a certain clarity. Examination of the petty-bourgeois P[arties]: the Popular and Republican Parties for Nor[thern] and Central Italy, representatives of the peasantry and the artisans, of social democracy in the South, with its appendages of Nitti and Amendola's positions etc; significance of the entry into the fascist list of Orlando and De Nicola, great Southern saints who represent the attempt of bourgeois capitalism to find a certain unification within fascism or to stop unity from seeming, even momentarily, to be broken.[65] Distinction between fascism and those traditional bourgeois forces which are not letting themselves be 'occupied', such as the *Corriere*, *La Stampa*, the Banks, the general staff, the General Confederation of Industry.[66] These forces, the ones that ensured the success of fascism in the 1921-22 period in order to avoid the collapse of the State, the ones that, in other words, created for themselves with fascism those forces of a mass popular nature which they did not have with them in 1919-20, with the bursting onto the scene of history of the most elementary and passive masses, these forces are today feeling the effect of the international situation, they are an Italian aspect of the leftward-tending international situation, an instrument for the bourgeoisie to reconquer dominion of itself. Two currents have sprung up: one of them, that of *La Stampa*, is openly posing the question of collaboration with the Socialists, and would not be averse to a 'MacDonald'-type experiment in Italy, in the ways and forms that the Italian situation allows; the other is that of the *Corriere*, which is more attached to bourgeois conservatism and which would form an alliance with the Socialists, but only after the latter have been subject to numerous utter humiliations. In a nutshell, *La Stampa*'s tendency is to maintain

Piedmontese-Northern hegemony over Italy and, in order to reach this goal, is not even averse to allowing the working-class aristocracy into its hegemonic system. The *Corriere*'s conception of the situation on the other hand is more 'Italian' and more 'unitary' – more commercial and less industrial – and just as it supported both Salandra and Nitti, the first two Southern Heads of Government (the Sicilians are South[erners] in a manner of speaking), so it would now support Amendola, that is a government in which the Southern petty bourgeoisie rather than the Northern working-class aristocracy would participate in the really dominant forces.[67] How will the situation develop? The sole fact that fascism exists as a big armed organisation is determining this development. Will the forces I have described stage a coup d'état? Not in my view. They have no trust in the reformists, that is they have no confidence that, in the event of a coup d'état, the reformists will be able by participating in the government to put a brake on the mass movement that will inevitably be unleashed. The reformists have not had the courage to unite with these forces, who wanted to act in September-October 1922 and who entrusted General Badoglio with the task of opening fire against fascism. Certainly the reformists are even more hesitant now that the fascists are stronger militarily and have the government in their hands. Maybe Modigliani in practice and … Rigola in theory are the only two reformists who favour this solution.[68]

This deployment of the relations of political forces in our country indicates the direction to follow.

1) Detailed unceasing propaganda around the watchword of the worker-peasant government, which must spring from the Italian situation in its entirety and must no longer be some theoretical formula.
2) Struggle against the working-class aristocracy, that is against reformism, for the alliance of the poorest strata of the Northern working class with the peasant masses of the South and the islands. Creation of an organisation committee for the South to conduct the struggle in the most forceful way possible. Study of the military possibilities for an armed insurrection in the South and the islands. Study of the possibilities of giving these populations certain political concessions with the formulation of a 'Federated Republic of the Workers and Peasants' instead of a workers' and peasants' government.

3) Reorganisation of the Party: saturation with political education to avoid discussions and disagreements of a serious nature at culminating moments of our activity. Expansion of the leadership sphere of the Party, and creation of a higher level within the Party obtained through the formation of an organis[ation] and propaganda committee which will draw up an inventory of the membership and compile a dossier for everyone, ask everyone for their political biography,[69] make sure of contacting the best people, spur them on, keep an eye on them, guide them without pause with circulars and brief political documents.
4) Greater care to be taken of the emigration question. Creation of Party schools in every major centre abroad, coordinated by a central leadership. Put three or four émigrés in the new C[entral] C[ommittee] as either full or alternate members to keep the Party's prestige high abroad and work effectively.

In our international relations we must be explicit insofar as is possible. We have to assert our loyalty to the E[xecutive] C[ommittee], explaining that we maintain that, for Italy too, the decisions from the Third Congress onwards are the only ones capable of allowing real contact with the masses in the period of capitalist offensive.[70]

As regards the PSI we have to assert that it is our task to resolve the question, which will remain until there is a S[ocialist] P[arty] independent of the unitary Socialists. We shall resolve this by all means possible, bar none. On this subject I will tell you quite frankly what I think: only our organisational weakness, our tenuous contact with the masses of our P[arty], has prevented us from accepting the deliberations of the Comintern. All the theories and conceptions that we have come up with were just the result of our weakness. If our P[arty] becomes stronger, as we wish, and as will happen if we know how to give it the right orientation, if we succeed in creating a vast and politically well-educated central nucleus, what dangers will the Comintern tactics present us with? None other than the following: that outside the Party there might exist groups who are more revolutionary than our constitutive nucleus and who, if they enter our organisation, might take over the leadership, a danger that would be a stroke of luck from the revolutionary point of view … unless one fell into the childish stance that the Revolut[ion] is guaranteed only because the proletarian Party is headed by certain people called Tom and Dick, instead of Harry or Jim.

I have written to you in a somewhat disordered fashion, among other things because I don't know what decisions have been taken on how discussion is to be organised. Will there be individual articles or is it foreseen that groups and fractions may publish their common platforms? This is of course important but only up to a certain point. Obviously, both at a Congress or Conference and at the Comintern Ex[ecutive], at a certain point one has to present group platforms. In consequence, we must begin straight away to prepare and obtain support for our theses, as I have said, in a private and confidential way. The points established will serve as guidelines for compiling articles if discussion is necessarily individual in nature.

I would ask Palmi to draw up an analytical scheme of the theses, to be sent on as soon as possible to me and to Negri (and to others, if thought appropriate) for revision and additions. The structure of the theses should in my view be as follows: 1) A brief mention to be made of the international situation, characterised by a recovery of the proletarian movement based on two factors: a) the bourgeoisie has partially taken back control over the forces of production; b) social democracy has shifted even further to the right and the bourgeoisie has tended to let itself be partially represented by it – on account of which the bourgeoisie is returning to liberalism, and for this very reason the revolutionary forces are advancing, though without having with them the majority of the working people. The tactic of the Comintern, when put to the proof, has shown itself capable of interpreting and directing events. – 2) A much more extensive part of the theses to be devoted to the Italian situation from the analysis of which there should emerge the watchword of the Workers' and Peasants' Government. – 3) Organisational questions, in all fields and according to the situation: the Party, the trade unions etc, internat[ional] relations, relations with other parties. The theses, overall, should not be very long, should not contain any theoretical treatment except merely as a mention, and should be exclusively political and current in nature. If theoretical questions do crop up, they should be dealt with separately in articles in specialised reviews.

I think I have been fairly exhaustive, albeit rather disordered, in the presentation. Many things I haven't said since it seemed to me they were obvious. A fraternal embrace

Masci

I should say something about the question that Palmi has brought up regarding my past approach.[71] I will say only that I too came to know of the P[arty]'s most serious problems at the Rome Congress and, as for the others, I was aware of them earlier in such a form that made any judgement impossible. Further to this, in 1921, before the publication of *Il Comunista* I was invited to Rome by Chiarini who, without explaining much of the question, invited me to join the Executive as a counterweight to Amadeo's influence and to take over his place.[72] I told him I did not want to be party to such intrigues and that if a new leadership was wanted then it should be posed as a political question. Ch[iarini], who had never adopted any position, but who at Rome posed as a follower of Bordiga, while sending reports to M[oscow] against the P[arty], did not insist and gave me no more details about the matter. He told me it was just because of Urbani's weakness and the complete absence from the work of the E[xecutive] of Luigino and Bruno, that Amadeo's tendency gained the upper hand, which went against the spirit of the decisions of the Com[intern] to have the Turin group prevail within the P[arty].[73]

At the Fourth Congress I had only been back for a few days (a few numerically and not just metaphorically a few days) from the sanatorium, after a stay there of about 6 months, which had been of little use, but merely stopped the illness getting any worse and prevented a paralysis of the legs that would have kept me bedridden for several years. From a general point of view the breakdown continued alongside the impossibility of working due to periods of memory loss and insomnia. The Penguin, with his typical diplomatic tact, buttonholed me with another offer to become Party head, getting rid of Amadeo, who would be excluded from the C[omintern] if he carried on with his line. I replied I would do anything in my power to help the Int[ernational] Ex[ecutive] resolve the Italian question, but I did not think that Amadeo could in any way be replaced (much less so in my person) without preliminary work to give the P[arty] a new orientation. Further, to substitute Amadeo in the Italian situation, more than one single person would be needed given that in effect, as regards his capability generally and for work in particular, Amadeo is the equivalent of at least three people, granted that one could replace a man of his value in that way. I was walking on live coals and this certainly was not the most congenial sort of work for my condition of chronic weakness. I realised that the majority of the delegation did not have a guideline of its own; it was sufficient to make even the vaguest comment to any of them regarding the situation for them immediately to give vent to their feelings and show themselves to be potentially minoritarian. It was a pitiable and politically disgusting affair. If the Penguin, instead of being stupid, had had an ounce of political intelligence, the P[arty] would have cut one of the sorriest figures of all because the majority, at least in its congress delegation, would have shown itself totally lacking in substance. The mere fact that Negri and I spoke with the comrades on these questions raised Amadeo's hackles and, if I am not mistaken – Negri should remember this – he had some very strong things to say against us. What would have happened if I had not answered evasively, which is what unfortunately I had to do? The majority of the delegation would have been with me, except for some individuals like Azzario, and there would have been a crisis in the P[arty] at long range, with no agreement with you.[74] Urbani, Bruno, Luigino, Ruggero, Amadeo would have resigned, the C[entral] C[ommittee], unused to working, would have collapsed, and the minority, even less prepared than it was later on, would have taken hold of … a will-o'-the-wisp. Was I perhaps too pessimistic? Maybe, given the conditions I found myself in. But I don't think so. Fascism was torn between, on the one hand, Mussolini's tendency, which saw all the dangers of a civil war unleashed to satisfy the power lust of its followers wanting a complete hands-down victory, and, on the other hand, the tendency of the mass of those very followers, who wanted a romantic 'revolution' with firing squads, summary tribunals, and so on and so forth – in a nutshell, a chapter out of Michelet. It was easy to foresee, then, that having gained power unexpectedly and being forced by a pressure of events that gave it no other way out, fascism would have found a certain equilibrium by pounding down on us, by stopping us doing anything, which would have put power back in the hands of the General Staff. I was not even pessimistic in my predictions regarding the attitude of the members of the E[xecutive] at that time. I will say, rather, I would not have believed what I have seen today: Luigino's attitude has been disgraceful while Bruno, although having many good reasons for his actions, has shown a desolating lack of political passion.[75] When one does not manage to have one's own opinions prevail, in a P[arty] like ours, which is able to overcome the different situations facing it only by miracles of political dialectic, this tactic of retreat is suicidal, and, with all my pessimism, I had not foreseen it. In reality, a knot had formed which could be cut only by a will and capacity for work like Amadeo's. I had neither the capacity nor the will that were necessary, and could not take on my own shoulders the burden of determining the new situation in the conditions I found myself in. Today, after your letter, I am of a different frame of mind: we can constitute a strong group capable of working and of taking a forceful initiative. I will give this group all the collaboration and contribution that my strength allows, in so much as these are of use. It will not be possible for me to do everything I would like since I still go through entire days of appalling weakness, that make me afraid of a relapse into the stupefied and comatose state in which I found myself in previous years, but this notwithstanding, I will put in all my effort. I have confidence in you for our movement and think that, through our common work, we will succeed in getting the majority of the P[arty] on our side and creating a healthy, robust organism, capable of development and struggle, as the Italian working class has the right to have after so many sacrifices and so many hardships.

M.

You would do me a great favour if you found the way to make a copy of the parts from this letter that seem to you the most important to send to Urbani.[76] If you can, send a copy to me too as a record.

Source: AAG and APC 513-1-248/60-70; handwritten

To Jul'ka

6. III. 924

My dearest one,

I want to kiss your eyes so as to dry the tears that I can imagine, that I seem to feel on my lips, just like other times when my thoughtlessness made you cry. We hurt each other, we torment each other in turn, because we are far away from each other and we cannot live like this. But you give up hope too easily. Why? You have promised me lots of times that you would be strong and I have believed you, and I still believe you are strong, stronger than you think. Lots of times you are stronger than I am, but because of my life apart from other people, a way of life that I have had since I was a boy, I have been used to hiding my states of mind behind a hard mask or behind an ironic smile, and it's here that the entire difference lies. For a long time this has been a source of hurt; for a long time my relationships with other people were enormously complicated, with every real feeling multiplied by seven or divided by seven, in order to avoid other people understanding what my real feelings were. What really saved me from becoming just some wretch in a starched shirt? The instinct of rebellion, an instinct that from childhood was against the rich, because I couldn't go on and study, I who had got top marks in every single subject at primary school, while the son of the butcher, the village chemist, the clothier went with no problem. That instinct extended to include all the rich who were oppressing the peasantry in Sardinia and I thought then that we had to fight for national independence for the region: 'Into the sea with the mainlanders!'. How many times did I utter those words. Then I got to know the working class of an industrial city and I understood the real meaning of those things of Marx which I had first read out of mere intellectual curiosity. It was in this way that I acquired a passion for life, for struggle, for the working class. But how many times did I ask myself whether it was possible to bind oneself to a mass when I had never actually loved anyone, not even my own relatives, whether it was possible to love a collectivity if I did not love the single human individuals themselves. Would that not have had a reflection on my life as a militant, would it not have sterilised and reduced to a pure intellectual fact, to a pure mathematical calculation, my nature of being a revolutionary? I have thought a lot about all this and I thought about it again over the last few days, because I have thought a lot about you, you who have come into my life and have given me love and have given me what I have always lacked and which often has made me rude and intemperate. I love you so much Юлька that I do not realise that sometimes I hurt you, since I myself am not sensitive to it.

I've written to you, I've told you to come, because, reading between the lines of your letters, it seemed that you yourself wanted to come. I too have thought about your family: but can you not come for a few months? Do you think it's impossible, or just difficult, for you to leave them just for a short stretch? How beautiful it would be to have a life together again for a time, the everyday joy, that of each hour, of each minute, of loving each other, of being close to one another. I seem to feel your cheek next to mine, and my hand stroking your head and telling you I love you even if the mouth remains silent.

I had a rush of blood when I read your letter. You know the reason. But your mention was vague and I am tormenting myself, because I want to hold you tight and I too want to feel a new life uniting ours even more than they are now united, my dearest, dearest love.[77]

I am now receiving lots of letters from the Italian comrades. They want faith, enthusiasm, willpower, strength from me. They think I am an inexhaustible source, that I am in a situation such that I cannot but have these gifts, and have them in a quantity such that I can freely distribute them to everyone. And they are in Italy, in the white heat of the struggle, and besides that they are demoralised and feel lost. Sometimes I get a feeling of anguish. I have received a letter from a Russian comrade living in Rome who was a comrade of Rosa Luxemburg's and of Liebknecht's, and who then by pure luck or by an incredible effort of will escaped the massacre, and she too has written to me, discouraged and disillusioned;[78] and she is not even Italian, with the justification of that temperament. They are asking too much of me, they are expecting too much and this leaves a sinister impression with me. The situation in the Party has deteriorated a great deal over the last few months. Bordiga has retired to the Aventine, and his attitude has cast a spell over the whole mechanism of the commonly-shared life of the comrades.[79] I've managed to win over some of them from this situation but will this be enough? I always have in my mind the picture of a scene in Turin during the occupation of the factories. The Military Committee was discussing the need, that maybe would have presented itself the next day, of a sally forth out of the factory by the armed workers; they all seemed drunk, they were about to come to blows, they were weighed down with a responsibility that was crushing them to the very marrow of their bones. One of them got to his feet – one who had done five years of war, as an airman and had faced death a hundred times – swayed from side to side and nearly fell. With an enormous nervous effort I intervened and brought a smile to their faces with some witticism and brought them back to their senses and to some sort of useful work. Today however I would not be able to do this. In our Party they are all young, and reaction has worn down their nerves and will, instead of strengthening them. And I too, why was I so ill for such a long time and why do I still feel it? For me too, life, which for two years I always felt to be hanging by a thread, all at once just broke when I arrived in Moscow, when I was safe and could feel calm. Today I would need to be very, very strong, but how can I, if you are not here, you who are so much part of me? Come, Jul'ka, come, even if only for a short time, just so I can feel you still close to me, and launch myself into work once again with greater enthusiasm than I've been able to up to now. I kiss your eyes, my dear, a long, long kiss to give you strength, to drive away all the dark clouds so that you may be so strong, just like you can be, like you must be, my comrade.

Gr

I'm sending on to you the 'absolutely precise' address:

Floriangasse, 5 A, Door 20, 3rd floor.

I would like to have a more recent photo of you, one taken over the last few days. I'm afraid of forgetting you, of having only the impression that has been left with me of the last evening I spent with you, when I was so nervous, irritable because I didn't know what to say to you. You had promised me another photograph. Send it to me as a sign that you are coming.

Have you corrected Rjazanov's notes? Can you send them to me? Have you found the booklet of Keržencev's on organisation? Can you let me have extracts of some of the best pages written regarding the death of Lenin? You see that I believe you are strong because I'm asking you to work for me.

Source: AAG

To Jul'ka

10.III.24[?][80]

[...] I understand the whole weakness of such a state of affairs. It is however also a source of strength. Among the masses one can never avoid the Revolution being summed up in a few names that seem to express all the aspirations and the painful feeling of the oppressed working class masses. In a village in Italy the following thing happened. Three days after the death of Lenin an agricultural wage worker died, a communist who, together with his workmates had been forced to become a member of the fascist trade union Corporations. He had himself buried, dressed in red, with 'Long live Lenin' on his breast. Lenin was dead, and he wanted to be buried like that. His workmates took his body by night to the cemetery and sang the *Internationale* over his grave. The grave digger told all this and the fascists dissolved all the local organisations, formed in the main of poor revolutionary peasants, terrified by their isolation and by the knout. These names, in a great part of the poor and backward part of the masses, become almost a religious myth. And this is a force that must not be destroyed.

G.

Source: typed transcription in AAG; earlier transcription in the Comintern Archive, fascicules 519-1-95 and 519-1-104

To Jul'ka

15. III. 924

Dearest one,

My imagination is dried up and dead. I can think only of you and the probabilities of your coming. It's an idea that is an obsession with me, always dominating my mind, and leading me to build one castle in the air after another. At one moment it seems that, at least for a certain period, you'll be able to decide to come, then at another moment I think this too is an illusion, and you are never going to find enough strength to come to the decision. Obviously I am still very weak and my brain is still working very badly, but that's how it is. Your image is always in front of me, and the memory of our happiness is torturing me like a red-hot iron. You once almost took offence because I said that life is short, but in actual fact this idea always has me in a vice-like grip. I am old – I seem to have been born at the age of eighty like the Chinese sage Lao-Tse, and everything in front of my eyes is racing on without letting itself be caught even for an instant.[81] And yet the life I lead ought to make me feel every minute, given its sameness and monotony. I'm staying in a boarding house run by a lady who is, I think, a Social-Christian, who didn't give me a moment's peace until I bought a pair of something like slippers that don't offend the ears of the other boarders, don't wear out the shine on the floor and don't wear out the carpets in the room. I have a big room, with a fine figure of a saint over the bed (it must be St Agnes, though she doesn't have her traditional lamb) and lots of little pictures on the walls; there's even one of a parrot with real feathers attached to it, an idea that moved the very bowels of me, but I don't have any semečki [seeds]. Since I changed house I've again been sleeping very little, even though I get up early (at 9 o'clock and often even at 8). All these items of news will (not) I think be of great interest to you, but they do in fact represent the normal texture of my life, which is very empty because you are not here. All I have is your photograph that one of these days I'm going to cut into little pieces: how can I keep next to me some piece of card that's trying to compete with the St Agnes up on the wall? I'm going to turn Christian, go to church every day, make my confession and receive Communion next Easter. In that way the disintegration of my brain will have run its full course, because you are constantly delaying the moment of interrupting the race with your will.

Over the most recent period I've worked less, with no real appetite for it. I've been sleeping little, as I've already said, my brain is tired and my eyes are burning. I'm sending you the first number of *L'O[rdine] N[uovo]*, which I'm not very satisfied with. It had been ready for a month when it was published, and had been put together in a hurry because it seemed it had to come out straight away, immediately. It was very successful, had a print-run of 6500 copies (1500 more than in 1920) and sold out completely on the first day. From Turin, Milan and Rome there were requests for another 2000 copies that we couldn't meet. This should spur me on to work. I've received letters from comrades that demonstrate how great was people's attachment to this paper that we began to bring out in 1919 with little enthusiasm and no great hope in the future, in which we still saw too clearly, so very clearly, what eventually turned into a millstone; everything seemed to us to be doomed to plunge into the void, as indeed did happen. I am now being oppressed by this very attachment and by the hopes that many comrades are putting in the work that the reborn *Ordine Nuovo* will be able to carry on; more and more I feel my own weakness, my own inability. One would need a will of iron, a mind that is always clear and ever present, an effective capacity for work, which are exactly the things that I'm missing. And I'm missing you too, you who had given me back some of this strength. You see – I've become a whinger, always whiningly going back to the same note. You understand, however. You must also feel, really feel in your bones, that, in coming to me, you will work and help me to work. Your work is not going to be of no use, quite the contrary; I think that from a revolutionary standpoint it will be much more useful than what you're doing at the moment – think of how many initiatives, how many things we could do together. That ought to give you strength and bring you to a decision. I can moreover assure you that if it were only a question of our love, I would not have insisted as I have done, but our love is and must be something more than that, it must be a full working collaboration, a union of energies dedicated to the struggle, as well as being a question of happiness. Maybe happiness, then, lies just in that. An embrace with all my tenderness.

Gr

Source: AAG; handwritten

To Togliatti, Scoccimarro, Leonetti etc.

21 · III · 924

To comrades Palmi, Negri, Ferri etc

Dearest friends,

I still haven't received your reply to my last letter, to provide me with an indication, at least roughly, of the practical work that you've decided to undertake.[82] I shall therefore, in this letter too, deal solely with general questions, which I don't know if you've already discussed and, if so, how.

I have received, amongst other things, two letters which have made an impression on me and which I think are a clue to a general situation to which we must give serious consideration. Sraffa has written to me, and one part of his letter you will be able to read, suitably commented on, in the 3rd number of *L'O[rdine] N[uovo]*, and Zino Zini has also written to me.[83] Both of them write they are still with us, but both are extremely pessimistic. Sraffa is oriented towards a position that in my view seems exactly that of the maximalists; Zini remains, in principle, with the communists, but writes to say that he feels old, tired, no longer having confidence in anything or anyone and completely given over, as well as to his professional occupations, to putting his thoughts in order in book form, which, from the indications in the letter will be a pure reflection of this state of political passivity. Sraffa will collaborate with the *Review* and I also think that, from what he has written to me, that his collaboration will be of great interest. In his regard, I don't think we have any difficulty; he has remained isolated after the contacts he had with us in Turin, and has never worked in the midst of the workers, but he is certainly still a Marxist, and it will be necessary only to keep in contact with him again in order to put him back on the right track and make him an active element within our Party, to which he will be able to offer many useful services now and in the future.[84] His letter also contains an extremely interesting section, not to be published. In speaking to me of the trade union question, he asks me why the party has never thought of creating unions along the lines of the American IWW, exactly the type appropriate to a situation of illegality and violent repression by the State and private capitalist organisations. He has promised me an article on the trade union bureaucracy, in which he will, I think, outline this subject too, which seems to me to warrant our greatest attention.

It is a fact that we have not up to now posed in practice the problem of whether it is possible to create a clandestine, centralised trade union organisation that would work towards creating a new situation in the working class. Our groups and our Trade Union Committee have maintained a Party character, a Party fraction within the CGL, something necessary, but it does not resolve the whole question. And it cannot even be resolved by taking the IWW as a model, since in actual fact they were, more than anything, the organisation of so-called 'migrant' workers, but the organisation of the IWW may however give us some indication and help define the question.

After the June Executive meeting, I proposed, and Negri and Urbani were in agreement with me (but Tasca was completely against), that we should try to organise, at a conspiratorial level, a small conference of representatives of the biggest Italian factories, with 20-30 workers from Turin, Milan, Genoa, Pisa, Livorno, Bologna, Trieste, Brescia, Bari, Naples, Messina, as factory representatives and not in the name of a Party, to study the general situation, vote resolutions on the different problems and, before breaking up, nominate an Italian factories C[entral] C[ommittee]. It goes without saying that the conference would have a solely propaganda and agitational value. Our Party, which will organise the conference, will prepare the ideological material necessary for it and ensure that the decisions taken will have the greatest possible repercussion among the masses. The C[entral] C[ommittee] to be nominated will be a useful channel for many agitational demands, and, if we know how to support it, it will become the embryo of a future organisation of the factory councils and the Internal Commissions, which will become the alternative necessary to the CGL in a changed general situation. I think that on this basis we can undertake an exceptional task of reorganisation and agitation. In the present situation the P[arty] must systematically avoid appearing the inspirer and leader of the movement. Locally and at the national centre the organisation will have to have a conspiratorial character. After the decisions of the national conference are made known through our manifestos and newspapers, the follow-up will be local town, provincial and regional Conferences. In this way we will be able to breathe life into the action of our Party groups. We shall have to study the problem of the feasibility of being able to pay contributions, however small, to the national C[entral] C[ommittee] for general propaganda and the like. Of course there is the problem that we shall be accused of creating another organisation so it will be indispensable to: 1) simultaneously intensify the campaign for a return to the unions belonging to the Confederation, and 2) insist on the fact that it is not new unions that we are proposing but a factory movement, along the lines of the factory Councils and I[nternal] C[ommissions].[85] This in general is my plan, which was accepted by Negri and Urbani, but until now it has remained at the level of mere intentions. It does not seem to me it is now anachronistic, anything but. A letter from Losa (Turin), to be published in no. III of *L'O[rdine] N[uovo]*, demonstrates that, after interference in the Land Workers' Federation, the masses are still wary about going back into the unions because they are afraid that union membership lists will become black lists.[86] The situation, already favourable to a conspiratorial union movement, has therefore become even more favourable. The important thing is to be able to find an organisational solution that will adapt to the circumstances and give the masses the impression of a collective group work, of a centralisation. The question appears to me of the greatest importance and I would therefore like a detailed joint discussion of it, with you sending me your judgement, your impressions, the future perspectives you think probable or possible.

It is Sraffa's letter that made me think of this, while Zini's made me think of another problem. Why, among the intellectuals who were actively with us in 1919-20, has this pessimistic and passive state of mind now become so widespread? It seems to me that it is connected, at least in part, to the fact that our Party does not have an immediate programme, based on the perspectives of the probable solutions that the present situation may have. We are for the workers' and peasants' government, but what does that mean in concrete terms in the Italy of today? No one would know how to explain it, because no one has taken the trouble to say what it means. The great masses, of whom the intellectuals automatically become the spokesmen, have no precise orientation, do not know how to get out of their present straits, and they therefore accept the solution demanding least effort, the solution given by the constitutional-reformist opposition. Sraffa's letter is clear on this point. Zini is an older militant, and certainly does not believe that fascism can destroyed by Amendola or by Giolitti or by Turati or by Bonomi;[87] he doesn't believe in anything. For Sraffa we are in the situation of 1916-17, while for Zini we are hardly in 1915, when the war had only just broken out (his comment), when everything was in a state of confusion and darkest shadow.

I am therefore convinced that much work has to be done along the following lines: political propaganda work and research on the economic bases of the situation. We must illustrate all the probable solutions that the current situation may give rise to, and for each one of these probable solutions we must establish guidelines. I have, for example, read Amendola's speech, which seems to me very important; there is a hint in it that could be developed. Amendola says that the constitutional reforms suggested by the fascists pose the problem as to whether, in Italy, it might be necessary to divide off constitutional activity from normal legislative activity. It is likely that what he says here contains the germ of the political orientation of the opposition in the next Parliament. Parliament, already discredited and deprived of any authority through the electoral mechanism on which it is based, cannot discuss constitutional reforms, which can only be done by a constituent assembly. Is it likely that the watchword of a constituent assembly could again come onto the agenda? If so, what would our position be on it? In a nutshell there must be a political solution to the present situation: what is the most likely form for such a solution to adopt? Is it possible to think that we can go from fascism to the dictatorship of the proletariat? What intermediate phases are possible or probable?[88] We have to carry out a political examination, we have to do it for ourselves, for the masses of our Party and for the masses in general. In my opinion, in the crisis that the country is going to go through, the party that comes out on top will be the one which has best understood this necessary process of transition and will therefore give the masses the impression that it is serious. From this point of view we are very weak, without doubt weaker than the socialists who, for better or for worse, are carrying out a certain amount of agitation and who, moreover, have an entire popular tradition backing them.

It is in the light of this general problem that the question of fusion is now being posed. Do we believe we can arrive at the eve of the revolution with a situation like the current one? With three socialist parties? How do we think this situation will be resolved? Will there be a fusion between the maximalists and the reformists? This is possible, but I think not very likely: maximalism wants to remain independent so as to exploit the situation to its own advantage. And so? Do we make an alliance with the maximalists for a sovietist government, just as the Bolsheviks did with the left Social Revolut[ionaries]?[89] It seems to me that, should this situation come about, it will not be as favourable for us as it was for the Bolsheviks. We have to take account of the tradition of the S[ocialist] P[arty], of its three-decade-long links with the masses, which cannot be resolved either by machine guns or by small-scale manoeuvres on the eve of the revolution. It is a big historical problem that can be resolved only if, as from today, we pose it in all its breadth and if, as from today, we make begin to solve it. I think that if we give our group a solid foundation, if we undertake political and organisational work capable of holding the present majority of our Party together firmly, leaving aside the die-hard left and the liquidationists of the right, in this way we shall be able to accept and therefore autonomously develop the Comintern tactic of the conquest of the majority of the S[ocialist] P[arty]. This, then, is our horizon, our overall direction, certainly not something to be achieved in the here and now. The aim is to win influence over the majority of the masses who today are influenced by the S[ocialist] P[arty]; the aim is to have it such that, if there is a recovery of revolutionary fervour among the workers, that upsurge is organised around the C[ommunist] P[arty] and not around the S[ocialist] P[arty]. How is this to be achieved? We have to exert pressure on the S[ocialist] P[arty] until its major[ity] either comes with us or goes with the reformists. It is an entire process that must be led by us, that must give all its active benefits to us – it is not a mechanical fact. In my view, therefore, the most recent attitudes you have adopted are very dangerous; we are falling back into the same situation as there was from the Fourth Congress up to June. The episode of the circular sent round is highly instructive. Circulars of that type should be sent to a small number of totally reliable comrades, not to organisations as such;[90] in the current situation, the only circulars to be sent to the organisations are 'political' and 'diplomatic' ones.

Has the Rome trial not taught us anything?[91] And have you not considered that, in many centres, the terzini have become the real leaders of our movement? And have you not taken into consideration that Vella and Nenni may have tried to introduce their own trusties among the terzini who have left the Socialist Party? I am of that persuasion, indeed I am sure of it. Nenni was in the R[epublican] P[arty], which has a certain experience of intrigue, and furthermore has learnt for his own ends the organisational methods of the Comintern. In '21-22 I visited many of our organisations, and in Como, for ex[ample], the centre of fairly industrialised zone, we had not even one single organisational comrade, so the administration of the federation had to be done from Sondrio. In Como, because of the attitude adopted by Roncoroni at Livorno, the mass of communists stayed with the S[ocialist] P[arty] and then became terzini. I would swear the most solemn oath that in Como, for example, our Party is more or less directly in the hands of the terzini, and that among them are Momigliano's trusties.[92] I even have proof of this. The Tortona local branch was reorganised, and who was it that was given the task of reorganising it? A terzino, thought to be a communist, who is not liked by the masses. This at least is what a well-informed friend has written me. The terzino is making use of a communist for the effective work of reorganisation but the fact demonstrates: 1) that the Party apparatus has many organisational flaws, and 2) that it is possible for socialist trusties to enter the Party, who then leak out documents. I hope the post brings me some communication from you, which I will reply to straight away.

Affectionate greetings

Masci

If possible, send me a copy of this letter too, and send on a copy to Urbani. In my new flat I cannot type a great deal, which causes lots of complications.

Source: AAG and APC 513-1-248/73-77; handwritten

To Jul'ka

21. III. 924

My dearest one,

The weather has become much milder here too. It seems we've got to the end of the daily ups and downs in temperature (and the attendant snow, sun, fog, rain, cold, warmth, dampness) that over the last few weeks have weakened my nerves and brain. I've caught myself singing – just think, it's something that hasn't happened to me for ages. I've become somewhat more optimistic or less pessimistic. I'm no longer tormented by the doubt that I'm a complete idiot who does nothing but commit stupidities and blunders; I think sometimes that a little intelligence is still there and I'll be able to carry out some useful activity. Sometimes I still think that maybe I did wrong in telling you one particular evening that, yes, it really was you that I loved passionately; I think that I'm a monster for having created such a great turmoil in you and since now I've become so idiotic and stupid, it will be a serious and awful thing to go ahead. But sometimes I also think that you're not a child (except on occasion), that if I've really become stupid you will recognise me as such, and so on and so forth. In a nutshell I feel that I really am close to you, more and more all the time, inexplicably, and I feel that you too also love me, and that fills me with happiness. Today I'm sure that we're going to be very happy, that together we're going to do lots of fine and beautiful things, at the same time that every so often we'll be just like children playing. I would like however to have the impression that you are at peace, that you still know how to laugh. But I seem instead to see you always in such a serious mood, with a dark countenance. I would like, then, to have you near me; it seems to me I would find the most ingenious things to make you happy, to make you smile. I'd make watches out of cork, papier-maché violins, two-tailed wax lizards, in short I would exhaust my whole repertoire of Sardinian-type memories. I would tell you other stories, even more wonderful ones, of my somewhat savage and primitive childhood, so different from yours. And then, I would embrace you and kiss you over and over again to feel you alive within me, life of my own life, just as you really are.

You see, spring is softening me up, in a different sense from winter. In a few days' time, I think, I'll be writing you poetry, sonnets and sestinas, although I won't be able to find a rhyme for Юлька; I'm going to write a whole songbook, that's for sure, in praise of you. In short, winter or spring, I miss you and this is torturing me in different but similar ways. My dear,

Gr

Source: AAG

To Jul'ka

25. III. 924

My dearest Юлька,

I've received your last letter (of the 20th), which has made me think in a way that I've never done before. I have understood nothing, absolutely nothing of this letter. I am absolutely convinced that you have no intention of going into flights of fancy and I believe that every word of yours is the sincere expression of how your thoughts are directed. What then is the meaning of 'a shadow is lengthening, lengthening ever more: shall I still find you?' I don't understand, I simply do not understand. I've sought to calm myself by giving rein to my imagination, as if I were near to you and wanted to make fun of these scarecrows of yours:[93] – the idea that Юлька has seen Serapidovič again and that his sombre shadow 'should once more begin' to cast itself over our life? – the idea that up to now Юлька has been an agent of the Čeka sent to sound out how corruptible I am and that, today between us two and the person behind this, a situation is being created similar to that of the famous Siberian couple who appeared before the Control Comm[ission] at the time of the Party *čista*?[94] – that the shadow is in fact that of the Čeka? – that we are dealing with an unexpected manifestation of the much-famed 'Slav soul'? – But today I no longer want to indulge in these imaginings; again I do not understand, I just do not understand. And instead I really want everything to be totally clear between us, even though we might really bleed in the process. Why did you write that you've made the two of us bleed too much? I remember only that I was happy as I've never been before in my life; I just do not remember having bled. Loving you is a joy to me, it has brought peace to my thoughts, it has given me the impetus to live and work: all my feverish activity, all the disorderliness that often characterises my thoughts, has found equilibrium and calm in my love for you. I understand from your letter, or at least I think I understand, that for you it is not the same. This also seemed to me the case some time ago, when I wrote to you to ask you to come and be near me. I felt there was this fleeting shadow (but does it really flee?) that represented a threat and I wanted to take a club to it, even from afar, seeking to do violence to your will. But you have made no more mention of any possible decisions about coming, and the shadow has come back, more threatening than before. I want there to be total clarity between us even if that means blood-letting. You must never again write to me in such a vague fashion. You must tell me what you think really, the reason behind these doubts, this lethargy that to my mind seems unhealthy and morbid, in you whom I appreciate and love for the health of your mind and spirit. You must be frank and tell me everything, not being afraid of hurting me; do you think it's better like that, with these hints of yours that are like so many drops of molten metal falling on the flesh? You must tell me what you think of the practicality of your eventually coming to join me. I love you Юлька, but it is essential that there should be no veil of any kind separating us. I feel that if you came here, everything would vanish. A great part (though certainly not everything) depends on your tiredness, of that I am sure; I want to hold you in my arms, so close and so tight, so as to conquer this tiredness, to make you feel the full life of our love, just as once it already has been.

Gr

Source: AAG

To Terracini

27-3-24

To Urbani, Moscow

Dearest friend,

I'm sending you at least a short letter every week so as not to break the habit and also because I always have something to say in reply to some question of yours or, indeed, to ask you something. If on the 20th you didn't receive anything, that means it has gone missing.

As agreed, the job of writing the theses will be Palmi's and he will send them to you immediately. From his last letter you will already have learnt what lines the comrades in Rome have decided on for the discussion; I'm here including my reply to this letter.[95]

In a few days' time I will see Riedel, who is here, and will ask him for explanations regarding what he says on the military section. I remember there was talk about this business but nothing was done. There was never a meeting in Turin of Samorè, Chiarini, Pieraccini, Riedel; Pieraccini never came to Turin; Samorè was distrustful of Chiarini, who introduced himself to us around October 1919 as a non-party student, just to see how the student circle was organised, and showed he did not understand a great deal about general questions. In July 1920, when I went to Florence to attend the conference of the abstentionists, Pieraccini warned me against Chiarini, whom he even regarded as a spy, and told me he had been kept at arm's length by the socialist students. Riedel is evidently referring to the conversations that took place, which maybe, in his intention, should have resulted in the formation of a committee. I would ask you to look back and see whether some time ago you received a long letter from me about Chiarini, in which I told you everything I know about this fine specimen; from what you say, it would seem that this letter never arrived.[96]

On the subject of the united front and of the workers' and peasants' Government, in my opinion the material we have had up to now and the overall direction given by the Comintern correspond, in their general lines, to the situation and are to be approved en bloc. The problem in my view is to be posed in the following terms: 'have the various Parties been able to apply these guidelines in concrete terms in their different countries, each with their specific conditions?' And to this question, the answer is 'no'. In no country has there been carried out a systematic and consistent campaign on this watchword and, to my way of thinking, it is here that the weakness of the movement lies. Let's take for example Germany, which has even, for this purpose, been the best-placed and most appropriate field of manoeuvre. The offers of a united front made to the leaders of the opportunist P[arties] were not accompanied, every day and everywhere, by all that systematic action among the great masses that the situation required. Theoretical articles were written in favour of the united front in general, in favour of the workers' and peasants' government in general, but these watchwords were never incorporated into the situations that rapidly succeeded each other. This, in my view, is a general fault, which all our Parties have, and we have to seek the causes in order to combat them. One cause, without doubt, is the way in which the so-called centralism of the Comintern has been understood. Up to now indeed we have not been able to arrive at a situation in which there exist Parties capable of carrying out an autonomous, creative policy that automatically is centralised, in that it responds to the general plans of action outlined in the various Congresses. I think, then, that it is difficult to change the current situation by laying down mandatory tactics, because that is actually what has been done, but to no avail. Italy is one example. The problem is very difficult; in the last analysis it is bound up with the development of the general situation which is very slow and tortuous; it seems to me that in this interim period there is objectively not a great deal to do different from what has been done up to now. What attitude should we adopt politically? That is another question and it is a very knotty one. I think it boils down to the solidity or otherwise of our Party. If before the fifth Congress our Party recovers from the crisis, if it builds a constituent nucleus of comrades and a centre that, through its own action and not because of any international reflection, enjoys the confidence of the Italian masses, then we shall be able to adopt an independent position and even allow ourselves the luxury of being able to criticise. Currently it seems to me that it is to our advantage to keep on tacking for some time, so as not to increase the confusion and crisis of confidence and prestige that is already widespread.

I do not know the Bulgarian theses so cannot make the comparison you suggest; in general I have little information at my disposal. Neither do I know whether the German and Bulgarian theses are international ones, or whether they deal just with their respective countries. Indeed, given the strength that the Peasant P[arty] still has in Bulgaria, it seems to me difficult to be able to get away from the assertion of a workers' and peasants' government as a necessary 'stepping stone' to the dictatorship. In Germany, in contrast, it seems that the immediate watchword adopted has been that of the dictatorship; I cannot judge whether that is normal and allowed by the situation, but I doubt it. In my view Maslow is right in saying that a return to the open letter is not to be excluded.[97] But, I repeat, I have little material to go on. The German situation seems to me still not very clear, both in the Party and in the country. Obviously the left is to be supported, as representing the real movement of the revolutionary masses; has the left, however, found the right political and ideological expression in the current leaders? That is the nub of the question, it seems to me, and it could give rise to acute and profound crises as yet unknown to the P[arty]; it could even lead the Party to the brink of disaster. Nothing is more dangerous than a radical change of leadership on the eve (or presumed eve) of the revolution. The mention you make of the question asked of Serrati by Kuusinen appears to show that there are doubts about the left, that it is being surrounded by a *cordon sanitaire*; what is your explanation for all this? What is the reality, then, lying behind this upheaval in the German leadership? Is it a manoeuvre or a state of necessity that they are trying to cure by homeopathic means?

I would be grateful if you informed me about the present state of the Trotsky-Zinov'ev question. It seems to me it is going to have a bearing on the fifth Congress, and it will perhaps be necessary to assume a position on it. On this subject, how has the discussion gone with the Polish, French and Bulgarian P[arties]? In my view the question is of the utmost interest and full of unknowns. A whole series of problems, both of principle and organisation, spring up, problems that sooner or later will have to be resolved since they just cannot be avoided. I would like to have information on this and your opinion. At any rate, I am more and more convinced that it is we ourselves who have to work, in our country, to build a Party that is strong, politically and organisationally well-equipped and resistant, with such a stock of clear general ideas, well-lodged in the consciousness of each individual, that there will be no possibility of these questions disintegrating with every blow aimed at them – and these questions will arise more frequently and in a more dangerous form with every day that passes, with the development of the situation and the objective strengthening of the revolutionary movement. On the subject of such questions, it would perhaps be best for us to discuss these problems at length between ourselves, so as to be able to resolve them, one at a time, as they emerge, in a spirit of unity and with the certainty of having the backing of the entire group. That is certainly one of the great strengths of the Russian comrades, just as, on the opposite side, the lack of coordination is a weakness of the other Parties, who run the continual risk of disintegrating, including even the disintegration of what seemed their most solid constituent nuclei.

Warm greetings

Masci

Source: AAG and APC 513-1-248/81-82; typewriten with handwritten signature

---

To Togliatti

VIENNA, 27/3/924

To be communicated to Negri etc
To comrade Ercoli
(copy to Urbani)

Dearest friend,

I'm first of all replying to the current questions that you raised in your last letter.

On the theses – I am in agreement with you and Alfonso. It seems to me that Negri and Silvia are making a purely formal question of the matter. In actual fact there exists a fraction even when only two or three comrades agree in advance to put together a common platform that involves the whole activity of the P[arty]. This being the case, from all points of view we must try to ensure that the formation of the fraction bears the greatest fruit and involves the smallest crisis possible for the entire organism. That seems to me especially indispensable in our situation. To take part in the general discussion as an already conspicuous group, with representatives of the main organisations, with if possible the majority of the present C[entral] C[ommittee], is a political fact of prime magnitude that has its repercussions on the whole mass; it is already an organisational start. I even believe that, if it were possible to have with us the majority of the C[entral] C[ommittee] (I do not know with any precision the opinion of the single members), it would be appropriate to convene the majority and present the theses as its theses. To my way of thinking, the influence of such a fact on the Party and on the Comintern would be enormous; in itself, it would be the beginning of a solution. I can't imagine what reasons of any substance Negri and Silvia may put forward against a choice of this type, given that the party, in deciding that discussion should take place, has not decided that it should have the exclusive form of individual contributions. Everything boils down to a question of numbers – is 5 better or 50? Does 50 constitute a fraction and 5 not? This is absurd, nothing more than absurd. Since however you have decided to carry out the necessary campaign of persuasion among comrades, so as to have them add their signatures at least some time later, in my opinion the situation is not compromised, nor is the question closed. I still maintain my point of view and since we are three against two, our opinion should triumph 'democratically'.

Ottavio. I'm mentioning his name as I could have done with many others, whose attitude I have not been able to catch up with for some time. What you write does not come as any great surprise, because it is normal from everything I know about the line he has followed in the past. The key point is not his name, but the question of our attitude to the minority. When I mentioned Ottavio's name, I was bearing in mind that Negri or Urbani, in describing to me the attitude of individual comrades about whom I was asking for information, said about him 'Ottavio is with the minority but says that he would like the present majority to continue to lead the party, adopting as its own the programme of the minority on its defining questions'. This position of Ottavio's seems to me highly significant for understanding the strength and composition, in general, of the minority, and for this reason I mentioned his name. It may be changed, as in general for all the names I may mention, which should be understood in the sense of their overall approach, not literally. Indeed, in the case of many comrades, I do not know what has happened regarding their initial lines and initial positions.

Amadeo. The question you pose is very difficult;[98] I have often asked myself what could be done regarding him and never been able to give an answer. We shall in fact have to discuss a whole series of questions of principle and organisation with him, questions on which I know he is absolutely rock-solid and immovable. With the minority we do not in general have questions of principle that divide us; they can be absorbed as a mass by us, together with the residual liquidationists, who had entrenched themselves in those positions so as to carry out their work more effectively. With Amadeo the position is very different and much more taxing. I am convinced he cannot be budged and convinced even that he would not hesitate to walk out of the Party and the International, rather than work responsibly against his own convictions. If this were not the case, if I had not always had this firm conviction, long ago – since '21 – I would have taken another stance. I have not yet read Grieco's article in *Prometeo* with my profile, but in March 1923, after the arrests, I did read an article in *Il Lavoratore*, again by Grieco himself I believe, containing completely wrong assessments of me.[99]

My approach, which in that article was characterised in parallel with the personality of Amadeo, was not autonomous, but always stemmed from the preoccupation about what Amadeo would have done, had I gone over into opposition to him. He would have withdrawn, would have caused a crisis, would never have been able to adapt so as to reach a compromise; Chiarini's attempt, which I mentioned to you elsewhere, shows that if I had gone into opposition, the International would have backed me, but what would have been the results, then, when we were having great difficulty in organising the party, in a civil war and under attack by *Avanti!*, which was exploiting each and every dissent in our ranks in order to disintegrate our ranks?[100] Today the situation has not changed as regards what I believe Amadeo's position to be. I too think the Party cannot do without his collaboration; but what should be done? Writing him a letter seems to me to be too little and I wouldn't even know what to write to him, so banal does this seem to me to be. As a general line I think that opening a polemic with him is useful to us, to him and to the Party. The important thing is to remain on a politically principled line and not go beyond that, which it appears to me will undoubtedly happen. There is another important aspect in my estimation, that is we must not let the question of Amadeo hypnotise us into thinking that we cannot work if he is in opposition.

By his very nature he is inflexible and tenacious to an extreme, which in consequence obliges us instead to pose the question of constructing the Party and its centre even without him and against him. I think that, on questions of principle, we must no longer make compromises as we have done in the past; it is preferable, instead, to have a clear and loyal polemic going to the basics, which will be of use to the Party and prepare it for all eventualities.

Of course the question is not closed; this is my opinion as of now. What you write is correct, but what is to be done in practice? You yourself, if you want, can write the letter, even in my name, if you think such is useful. But in my view, we must not have too many illusions and we must prepare ourselves for the worst so as to be ready for every eventuality.

I think it would also be as well to let Amadeo know of the mention made of him in one of the last reports that H[umbert]-D[roz] sent to Z[inov'ev] (to be exact the talk with Ruggero).[101] Through this report a completely false judgement of Amadeo and the situation will be made, and its repercussions will be damaging to the P[arty]. Ruggero has been very foolish in backing up the stupidity that H[umbert]-D[roz] has written, something that will be believed to reflect Amadeo's state of mind. I think Amadeo is completely innocent in all this.

I know him well enough to be sure that he has never thought such stupidities about himself, anything but.

L'Ordine Nuovo. I would like your judgement on the first two numbers. The isolation I've been in for so long, and which I'm still in, has very much blunted my sense of self-criticism. At times I seem to be doing something completely artificial, detached from real life. We must moreover look seriously at how to organise our collaborators, otherwise it is inevitable that *L'O[rdine] N[uovo]* will go downhill. It must be borne in mind that the review now comes out fortnightly and not weekly, and that it does not form part of a specific movement, as it did in 19-'20 with the factory councils. This determines its present nature, which has to be organised. This new nature must also be reflected in the impagination. I think that the leading article should be followed by a detailed political review of the fortnight's events, which will – let's say – occupy the whole of the third page, and which, from the standpoint of our immediate programme of a workers' and peasants' government and according to our overall doctrine, will comment on Italian events in all their various aspects. I think that you ought to assume responsibility for this current events sector, which should be open, right up to going to print. You can do this very well if you have the time and are willing.

The specific programme of the review, in my opinion, ought still to be the factory and factory organisation. If it is acceptable, we could ideologically and in practice undertake the programme that I outlined in my last letter to you.[102] I feel I am at something of a loss – I am always afraid of being rather detached from actual reality and of building castles in the air. I should therefore be grateful if you would always write, giving an analytical judgement on my proposals and opinions, which I send you not as directives but as suggestions that always await your detailed confirmation, so that I can take them seriously and develop all their implications and all their aspects. We ought, with the means at our disposal, to try and rebuild a common feeling between us, just like that of 1919-20; then, no initiative was undertaken if it had not been tested against reality, if we had not sounded out beforehand, through various channels, the workers' opinion on it. For that reason our initiatives almost always had a wide-ranging and immediate success and appeared as the interpetation of a widespread and heart-felt need, and never as the cold application of some intellectual scheme. I am used to working in this way; my absence for so long from Italy has stopped me from getting used to the new environment, to the new methods of work, from creating for myself those other possibilities of communicating with the masses and keeping my finger on the pulse of the situation, which you instead have been able to obtain for yourselves. I am strongly conscious of this weakness of mine, which at times is demoralising.

Il Seme. Before I finish I still want to mention another proposal I would like to put forward and which, alongside the others, will be of use for the preparation of our future movement. I am of the opinion that, on its own account, our Party ought to revive the old S[ocialist] P[arty] paper *Il Seme* [*The Seed*] as a fortnightly or monthly.[103] It should be done like the old one was, with a modernised content, but of the same type. The cost should be very modest, so that it will have a circulation even among the poorest peasants, it should contain lots of simple cartoons and lots of short articles, and so on. It should be directed at popularising the watchword of the workers' and peasants' government, taking up again something of an anti-clerical campaign, which to me seems necessary since I think that four years of reaction must have once more thrown the masses in the countryside back into a state of superstitious mysticism, as well as at popularising our general propaganda. I don't know why the socialists themselves have not thought of reviving this journal, which had a very wide distribution and in the past brought in lots of votes. For that reason I think it best not to speak of it publicly until we are already at the pre-publication stage, otherwise the socialists are capable of grabbing it and bringing it out themselves. It would instead be necessary, here and now, to draw up a sort of inventory of our organisational and intellectual forces so as to be able to use them at the appropriate moment. This is a job which, to our great harm, we have never undertaken. I think there is more ability and expertise in the party than we think, and it would be good to set these forces in motion, forcing them to work, constantly spurring them on. Only thus can we broaden and strengthen our movement.

Fraternal greetings

Sardi

Source: AAG and APC 513-1-248/83-85; typewritten with 'To be communicated to Negri etc.' and 'Ercoli' handwritten

---

To Jul'ka

29. III. [1924]

Yes, it really is necessary for you to write to me in all sincerity and clarity. For some days now I have no longer been able to think about you without everything seeming misunderstandings and lies. My imagination goes off in two directions: when I am at peace with myself, my mind gives free play to bizarre and clownish situations, but when I am tired and embittered, it invents cruel and unhealthy ones. I cannot not think of you: you are too much part of myself, of my most intimate life, for me not to think of you. Right now I am disturbed as I never have been before. I am tired, embittered, miserable. The life that is born with the spring, all around me, is emptying me completely, totally destroying me. In 1911, in a period when I was seriously ill because of the intense cold and of malnutrition, I used always to imagine a huge spider that each night lay in wait to ambush me and suck out my brain while I was asleep. I seem to be returning to that time. But all this state of morbid affairs will disappear as soon as you have written to me frankly, leaving aside all vagueness and uncertainty.

On February 24th you wrote to me with a mention of your pregnancy, filling me with joy. I had a burning desire for you to be a mother and thought that that would strengthen your personality, allow you to overcome a crisis which I thought was latent within you, bound up with your past, to your girlhood, to the whole of your intellectual development, that it would have allowed you to love me with a more complete abandon. I hesitate to put these things down to you in writing since I would prefer to tell you them in person, so as to avoid any misunderstanding, any shadow of doubt, any semblance of my being domineering towards your personality. Your love has strengthened me, has really made a man of me, or at least has made me understand what it is to be a man and have a personality. I don't know if my love for you has had similar consequences for you; I think it has, since I have felt this creative power very strongly in you too, as in myself. I thought intensely, in the brief period of our complete happiness, about how your motherhood would contribute to crowning all this. You have mentioned it only once, then nothing more. Юлька, любимая [Jul'ka, ljubimaja – darling], I feel so much that you love me as I love you, and that we shall still be so very happy, because in all our activity, in all our work we shall carry forward the strength and the courage that is born of the happiness and joy of creation.

Gr

Source: AAG

To Zino Zini

2. IV. 924

Albeit after a long delay, I too received your reply, and took great pleasure in receiving your news directly.[104] I had received different and contradictory information about you, as also about many other friends, and was not able to form an opinion on their current way of thinking and looking at the future. The differences between us now depend, I think, to a great extent on the fact that in 1920 I was very pessimistic about the solution that the course of events of that time would take. The coming to power of fascism and the destruction that preceded and succeeded those events surprised me, relatively speaking. Certainly what has contributed to my current state of mind has also been my not being in Italy in the most recent period and thus not having experienced the horrendous spiritual pressure that the daily round of mortifications and violence has exerted on many of our comrades and friends. On the other hand, the daily demonstration that I witnessed in Russia of a people creating a new life for itself, new patterns of behaviour, new relationships, new ways of thinking and posing all life's problems, today makes me more optimistic regarding our country and its future. Something new exists in the world and is toiling away under the surface, molecularly I would say, in an irresistible fashion. Why should our country flee from this process of general renewal? The attitude that a great number of Italian emigrant workers have in Russia demonstrates that we would not have maintained power in 1920 if we had conquered it; they do not understand how the Russian workers, after six years of revolution, can endure willingly the great suffering they are still subject to; they, the Italians, want to be exempt from this, and are trying to banish it with all means at their disposal. Fascism, from this point of view, has transformed our people and we have daily proof of this; the people are more strongly tempered thanks to fascism, they have a healthier morality and a previously unknown resistance to evil, a depth of feeling that had never existed before. Fascism really has created a new permanently revolutionary situation, just as tsarism did in Russia. The pessimism that dominated me in 1920, especially during the occupation of the factories, has today disappeared. Of course this does not mean that I am looking at the Italian situation through rose-tinted spectacles. I believe that there are many trials and tribulations still lying in wait for our proletariat, more bloody than those of the past, but also that today there is a sure line of development and this appears to me to be an observation of great importance for our country. Today we may make predictions with a certain degree of confidence, we can work with greater vigour than in '19-20. This is the source of my optimism, which I would like to communicate to all the friends and comrades with whom I am coming back into contact, and who have, it seems to me, been oppressed by the spiritual pressure of fascism.

As I see it, the masses are much less pessimistic than the intellectuals. They are looking for a point of reference, of concentration, and today the most important question for our country is just this – providing the masses with a reference point. The intellectuals of the older generation, who have had such a long historical experience, who have seen the whole tormented development of our people over these last decades, would be failing in their duty and their mission if, exactly in this culminating phase, they were to hold themselves aloof, not wanting to contribute to clarifying, to organising, to concentrating the forces of ideas which already exist, which have no need to be spurred on (which would be utopian), but only concentrated and oriented. You see the development of our periodical.[105] Today it is being printed in twice the number of copies that it was in '20, and this is an index that confirms what I am saying. In '20 the situation appeared enormously favourable; it was running fever high. Today on the other hand there is a deeper understanding, a greater solidity, even if the landscape seems as if a whirlwind has hit it.

I would be very happy to recreate the work group that formed around the journal in '19-20. For this, I think your collaboration would be precious; you would of course sign with a pseudonym since we have already too often committed the error of sending our defenceless or near-defenceless forces down to defeat against a well-equipped and implacable enemy.[106] The idea of your collaboration with a number of Russian reviews could also be taken in hand again and put into effect through me. In Russia a whole series of great literary, artistic, philosophical reviews are being published which need regular collaborators from Italy on our cultural and intellectual movement. The articles and commentary on current events would also be well-rewarded, since in Russia literary activity is appreciated to a great (maybe to an excessive) extent. That would, in any case, give you the opportunity to procure Russian periodicals and books, whose publication in all fields, that of the natural sciences especially and also of Marxist philosophy, is becoming enormous.

I wanted to reply immediately to your letter and have therefore merely touched on the many matters on which I should have wished to write to you. I should indeed be grateful if you would write to me again, at the same address as last time, and also tell me something of

Prof. Cosmo, with whom I had an interesting conversation in Berlin in May 1922.[107]

Please accept my warmest and most affectionate greetings.

Gramsci

Source: AAG; handwritten

To Togliatti, Scoccimarro etc

VIENNA, 5-4-24

To comrades Palmi, Negri, etc (copy to Urbani)

Dearest friends,

I have received the communication from comrade Silvia. I must however confess that it has caused me great embarrassment since the situation is still very complicated and I do not understand what exactly you want me to do. What is the Agenda of the C[entral] C[ommittee] session? In the motion I should write, what specific problem or discussion point should be addressed? I thought of writing an open letter to the C[entral] C[ommittee] to make a personal statement, but I have given up this idea, thinking that I might in this way have divided myself off from you and thus left the situation open to being exploited. The article written in the 2nd issue of *L'O[rdine] N[uovo]* may be assumed as my statement to this session, and as having given my position. And in this sense I would ask you to make a declaration in my name if necessary.[108]

Our work is still far too disjointed. I really do not know exactly what you want in concrete terms. Do you accept all my proposals *en bloc*? But, then, is it not possible that in some detail, that may however be of paramount importance, there is some disagreement? How, under such conditions, can one put forward a motion? I think you know fairly completely what my view is, but I only know yours somewhat imperfectly. If someone can formulate a motion, given the wish to carry forward our work collectively and organically, it is among you, who can discuss and find harmony among yourselves, that this person exists.

In general, if problems of tactics and of the Party's orientation are discussed at the meeting, as you tell me, I think it is necessary to take up a decisive and unhesitating position: the one that I have indicated, if you are in complete agreement with it. In that case I think a short motion is all that is required, which should round off a speech by Palmi, for ex[ample], outlining our position from the Rome congress to now. In Rome we accepted Amadeo's theses because they were presented as an opinion for the fourth congress and not as a line of action. We maintained that by so doing we were keeping the Party united around its fundamental nucleus, we thought we could make this concession to Amadeo, given the immense importance he had had in the organisation of the Party, and we do not regret this. Politically, it would have been impossible to lead the Party without the active participation in the central work of Amadeo and his group. The situation has now been modified by what has happened since, and we find ourselves faced with a new wave of events which have also had their reflection in Italy. We then retreated and had to do so in an orderly fashion, without new crises and without new threats of splits in our movement, without ever adding any new ferments that would add to disintegration, over and above the ones that the resounding defeat itself caused within the revolutionary movement. Today we have to lay the foundations for a big mass Party and have to be clear in the extreme on their theoretical and practical positions. We have found ourselves in partial disagreement with the Comintern, not so much in the assessment of the general situation in Italy as in that of the repercussions that the measures proposed would have had within our Party, whose initial constitutive weakness and fragility we were aware of. We have been somewhat sectarian, as happens when the movement is on the ebb, as a reaction to the overwhelming optimism of the previous period. In principle, we have always been in agreement with the Comintern, but our attitudes have had repercussions that have given rise to reflection among us. Meanwhile we note that, in the ranks of the minority, a clarification has taken place that has contributed to orienting us. The minority is divided into two tendencies, one of which has shown its true liquidatory nature, which we foresaw and which had frightened us. With this wing we can never have anything in common; we shall fight against it. The other part, represented by com. Tasca, has changed by accepting in practice many of our points of view. With this tendency, in other words with the politics that it claims to represent, it is possible to work fruitfully. With the left there is still a need for much further discussion to see exactly where the difference lies. We must however put blame on Amadeo's attitude, which has harmed the Party.

We are differentiated from the left on a number of organisational principles, which will have to be examined in depth to see where they extend to. With the approach of Amadeo the world Party is in practice denied, i.e. in the only way in which that it can become a concrete reality in the present situation. In the national field there is an obstacle in the way of the Party's development and we are moving towards political passivity. It is, however, our continuing conviction that Amadeo's collaboration in the work of the Party is necessary. We believe that a man like him cannot become a simple militant, a rank-and-file member. In practice that would mean a permanent state of malaise in the mass of the Party, the permanent existence of a fraction, even if not an organised one, since at any instant, faced with any difficulty, any member of the Party would pose the question 'What does Amadeo think? If he were there, maybe things would be better'. The assertion that a leader might remain in the ranks as an ordinary member is false in both theory and practice.[109] Amadeo's insistence on this point would be enough for us not to be able to help him in anything, but we should foresee the need to take up the fight against him to prevent crisis and confusion in the Party. It will be necessary to be clear on these points and to be extremely frank. Only by so doing shall we be able to get the Party out of its present predicament and put it on the right lines. If you agree, you can say that my article in *L'O[rdine] N[uovo]* roughly represents our position and that our further statements will be a follow-up to the outlines contained in the article: 1) a firm desire to put an end to the crisis by liquidating fractional activity; 2) concrete work in agreement with the Ex[ecutive] C[ommittee] of the Int[ernational], whose deliberations we accept *en bloc* (i.e. not excluding that they may be open to improvement in part); 3) an impetus to be given to the Party so as to make it better able to face up to the serious tasks awaiting it.

On these elements, if you are in agreement, you yourselves can write a brief motion, putting my signature to it, too, and saying that it also represents completely my point of view.

Warm greetings.

Sardi

I have received Negri's letter, which persuades me even more that there is still far too much disconnectedness amongst you. His observations are, it seems to me, to be taken into consideration, at least as regards our group and its organisation, since, among other things, too much time has been lost. I am not in agreement with him on the minority: I believe it is absolutely indispensable, vital, to try and tear Tasca away from the minority, split the minority whatever the cost of any formal concessions. Do not put any trust in Tasca's verbal statements, which is one more reason for detaching him from the others.[110] Greetings.

Source: APC 513-1-248/87-8 with copy in 513-1-250/3-4; typewritten except for the handwritten last paragraph after 'Sardi'

To Terracini

13 · IV · 924

Dearest friend,

You will now be aware that I have perhaps been elected for the Veneto constituency, at least if there has not been yet another change in the preference votes, as is possible and as, moreover, I hope. If I have to go back to Italy, I do not therefore know if it will be easy for me to get out again for the Fifth Congress.

The elections have in my opinion gone very well for us – from all points of view. I was afraid that the terzini would have headed the preferences everywhere, but this has not happened. Indeed, I read today that they will have only 5 seats to our 13, since it appears that Fortichiari is in front of Buffoni in Lombardy. Our Party has emerged with immensely increased prestige. Here everyone is agape. It was a widespread belief that we no longer existed and that our influence was minimal. We shall have to give wide currency to the outcome of the election, demonstrating especially the importance of the preference votes, which are the index of the real influence of the organisation. I shall write a special article on this for *Inprecorr* as soon as I have all the data.[111]

For *L'Ordine Nuovo* things are not going too well. There's a lack of collaboration, and any postal mishap causes a hold-up in the review.[112] I think we need to bring our original Turin editorial group together again. You have to collaborate, writing on the subjects that you feel closest to; I think it would be very interesting to have something from you on the Russian Congress, with a brief summary of the recent polemics. For our P[arty] too, this Russian experience lends itself to lots of reflections and many lessons are to be drawn from it. Fraternal greetings

Masci

Source: AAG and APC 513-1-248/91; handwritten

To Jul'ka

13. IV. 924

Dearest one,

I have received your letter of the 4th (the week before I received Keržencev's book and the issue of *Rabkor*).[113] I don't know which letter of mine you received before you wrote to me, given that you speak of having received three of them all together, but I have been sending you one a week; the last one was very serious, not to say almost solemn.[114]

Now in one way I am calmer because I have heard your sweet voice, I have seen your love, I know more than ever that you are mine. In another way I am anxious (life is terribly dialectical): it appears I have been elected as a deputy for the Veneto constituency and I think that if I return to Italy it will not be all that easy for me to get out again to go to the Fifth Congress. How then can I expect you come and visit me? You will now have to wait so that our child does not suffer, but I would have liked so very much to have you near me now, to share with you all your new life, to share joy and suffering with you. My mind is continually swirling with different and contradictory thoughts, which I want to tell you day by day, hour by hour. But I hope everything is going to go well. The new Italian Parliament opens only on May 25th and, even if I really were elected, maybe it would not be necessary for me to move from here, because on the 25th I should already be in Moscow. Will I still be able to stick my tongue out at you? We are serious people now, shortly we shall have a child and we must not give little children a bad example. Do you see how many new horizons are opening up? The world is undeniably a great and terrible place.[115] Over the last few days I've re-read Pascarella's sonnets which I had sent to me so I could then send on to you, and *The Discovery of America* still proves to me the preciseness of the point of view contained in the sayings of the old Tibetan lama. Who then knows whether, with modern armed warships, Colombus would be able to discover twenty Americas; the world etc. I think, among other things, that straight after the birth of our child, we are really going to come to blows, because we're always going to be disagreeing about lots of things. The name to start with: do you remember my penchant for Nebuchadnezzar, Simeon, Ermengard, Prudenziana, Veneranda, Parallelepiped etc, etc? There are going to be some serious set-tos, I can assure you. You've never opened up on this subject, but your present tactics seem nowadays to me opportunist and full of threats.

I'm playing the fool a bit, I know, though I haven't got any great desire to. The truth is I love you very much, that I think of you all the time, and every so often it seems to me that I hold you in a tight and close embrace. Strange things are happening to me. Right after your last letter had hardly got here, it seemed to me you must have already arrived in Vienna and that I would meet you in the street. I had been ill yet again, hadn't been able to sleep, and your letter had really set me aflame.[116] When I do actually hold you again I think I'm going to feel ill, because I'll be overcome by passion. Dear Юлька, you are my whole life, as if I had never felt life itself before loving you, it's something great and beautiful that is filling every minute and every vibration of my being. I want to be strong today like I've never wanted to be before, because I want to be happy in your love, and this wish is reflected in my whole activity. I think that when we are once more living together we shall be invincible and we'll find the way to conquer even fascism; we want a world that is fine and free for our child and we will fight to achieve it like we've never fought before, with a cunning that we've never had, with a tenacity and with a strength that will overcome all obstacles. Write to me at length. If I could be with you in a month's time … Maybe however that might just happen.

A long kiss любимая [ljubimaja: darling]

Gr

Source: AAG

To Jul'ka

16. IV. 924

Dear Юлька

I have received your letter of the 8th which has blown away all the clouds and all the misunderstandings. We must no longer talk of 'morbidity' or other such silliness. We must simply love each other and be patient, wait until we are together again and try to find the way of being together as long as we can. This is the sole cause of all our malaise, which is leading us to search deep inside ourselves, or in other words to tear ourselves apart quite uselessly in search of some hidden cause. I am certainly not going to allow myself to be again dragged into this appalling game. I am calm, collected, I no longer have any doubts, there is no drop of molten metal threatening to burn into my tender flesh. It is not going to be easy to have patience, but, in short, I am not going any longer to create a metaphysics of impatience. And you too must do as I do, you must not let yourself be tortured by scarecrows. I acknowledge that to a great extent the fault is mine because, in short, I am older and more experienced; I should not have written to you the letter I did because, now that I have thought about it, I did not really believe a great deal in what I was writing, and I was just translating into words the unease of my nerves and the beetles crawling through my brain.[117]

We have been together too little, and that little has been time we have stolen from destiny; our happiness has been contraband we have smuggled in day by day, enjoyed in a mysterious hut in the forest. That left us with too much regret in all our being, too many unsatisfied vibrations that have continued and are still continuing to disturb us. Here lies the cause of our fleeting malaise. Deep down we have not had the time to feel ourselves husband and wife, we have just been lovers on our honeymoon (do you remember my proposal for the Party Rules?). I cannot think without deep emotion about this period, one which both made us happy and united us morally and intellectually. Do you remember your hesitation? You were in the right and I felt it; but even more so I was right. If I had left without our lives being fused into one, without the happiness of belonging to each other that had made our whole being vibrate more strongly would we have overcome this crisis, which after all has been such a trifle? I don't know. I have changed so much that I can't even imagine what would have happened otherwise, but nothing to the good. Even more so with the distance that separated us, ours would have been a little novel, a blancmange à la Matilde Serao.[118] At least that is how it seems to me, in as much as I am able to reconstitute events through absurd hypotheses.

Today I think like this, that even if, for some cursed hypothesis, I might have to be far away from Юлька for a long time, what would happen? Certainly I would suffer a great deal and the thought of other lives going on far away from me would be a continuous torment, though not for that reason would I despair or be less strong. I would wait because there would be sure to come the day we were together again, when once again we would be like children, sticking our tongues out at each other, and at a single stroke all the past would seem cancelled from our memory. That is what I think today, because I am sure of seeing you again soon, holding you in my arms once more, to kiss your eyes, to kiss your wrists, your neck, to kiss all of you, passionately, like a greedy child. Because my love for you is immense, and I understand how a real meaning may be taken on even by expressions that seem to have become banal through people over-using them. Everything is renewed, because our love is something new and we are original to the highest degree in loving each other as we do, even at the cost of tormenting ourselves a little, sometimes.

It seems that this time cruel fate has willed it that I should be a parliamentary deputy for … Venice. I am therefore going to Italy for a few days, but then I will come back out again to go to the E[nlarged] E[xecutive].[119] The elections went very well for us. The news that the Party has received from various places is extremely good; officially we have received 304,000 votes, but in actual fact we certainly obtained more than double that, the fascists thinking well to get the extra for themselves by rubbing out the communist symbol and putting in a fascist one instead. When I think of what it cost the workers and peasants to vote for me, when I think that in Turin, 3000 workers wrote my name under the threat of getting beaten up and in the Veneto region another 3000, mainly peasants, did likewise, and, for that, lots of them were beaten until the blood ran, my judgement is that for once being a deputy has value and meaning.[120] However I think that in order to be a revolutionary deputy in a Chamber where 400 drunken apes are yelling continuously, you need resistance and a voice far superior to those that I possess. But I'll try to do my best. A number of strong, forceful workers have been elected, whom I know well and can count on to carry out work that will not be entirely useless. Some fascists of my acquaintance will be writhing in anger on more than one occasion. But we'll speak of all that in person, since there will be time, given that the Chamber assembles only on May 24th and I shall not be able to be there since I shall be close to you, to stick my tongue out at you, in the expectation of sticking it out at … Mussolini.

A kiss for you, хорошая, славная, любимая, родная [khorošaja, slavnaja, ljubimaja, rodnaja: my good, my sweetheart, my darling, my own one]

I am also sending on to you two articles by Prof. Alaleona.[121] As an antidote I want to copy out for you something of Pascarella's:

'I wouldn't want to take the time to list – Each bush and tree, but what made going hardest – Was how, with every step into the forest, – They came upon another savage beast. – They were surrounded by a curious herd – Of more wild beasts than at the Roman zoo. – The elephant appeared before them, too. – (You'll find his statue in the Piazza Minerva.) – With every step, be careful as you can, – Or when you least expect, unless you're cautious, – You'll stumble into the jaws of the Wild Man. – He's worse than lions, worse than a grizzly bear. – He'll eat you up in little bites and crunches – You're lucky if he leaves your bones and hair. –

"*But what about them*?" – Huh? Them? Oh, yeah, as they – Were wading through deep moss with knives to hack – The tangles weeds and vines that held them back – From making even slow and hard headway – Suddenly they stumbled on a face – Painted all colours like a spinning top. – Its head was covered with a feather mop. – It had no clothes in any other place. – They halted, trembling, tried to shed their fear: – "Hey you, who are you? Who sent you here?" – "You'll find out soon," they answered, "by St. Peter. – But first you have to take us to your leader."'[122]

I would like to send you the book by post, but I'm not sure it would arrive. I'll try to send you an issue of a children's magazine which was sent to me as an exchange subscription for *L'O[rdine] N[uovo]*, but which cannot however be compared to Vamba's *Il giornalino della domenica*, which I think you saw in Italy.

When I come to Moscow, will it perhaps be possible for us to spend a few days together in the country? We'll read the whole of Pascarella and do all sorts of mad things, won't we? You will have to laugh a lot, just to forget all the dreadful time we've spent apart. I'm thinking what I can bring you from Italy, but I still can't decide; I'll decide on the spot. Another kiss on your sweet and dear eyes, dear Юлька

Gr

Source: AAG

To Terracini

VIENNA, 19-4-24

Dear Urbani,

I want to explain better what I meant to say about the trade union action we have to undertake, so that there can be no dangerous misunderstandings or ambiguities. Given my absence from Italy for so long, and given the lack of concrete and detailed impressions indispensable for these questions, I am always very chary about suggesting given forms of organisation, especially illegal ones.[123] I am only putting before the comrades this precise problem: in Italy there no longer exists even a minimum level of centralised trade union activity. The CGL and all its organisations have gone into hibernation, are applying to the letter the tactic of passivity, of playing for time and so on. As a matter of principle, and for a whole series of practical considerations upholding that principle today, we do not want to create a new trade union confederation. But even so, something must be done; the masses of the workers are relatively quiet: isolated strikes go on continuously. If, in all their breadth, we put into practice the norms for the organisation of factory cells, if – as you too agree – we convene the conference of factory workers, at a certain point, even though we may not want to, we are going to find ourselves faced with the need to undertake real and proper trade union activity. If we create a political force within the factory, we will not be able to avoid it automatically becoming the centre, the representative body of the whole factory, from which the workers will expect advice and leadership. This action will be real and proper trade union action, will have to face up to the self-same problems that the councils of leagues were faced with in the past.[124] Given the absence of official bodies, it will be up to us to satisfy all the needs posed by the masses. What then have we to do? Do we have to give up even on organisation and agitation, since it is from these latter that, at a certain point of their development, there springs the need for real and proper action? Certainly not. Consequently we have to resolve the problem and find a form that contains this substance in the conditions existing in Italy. This is the terrain of the discussion that I have defined in its most general terms. Since we do not want to create a new central trade union body, the organisation will have to be illegal, so much is evident. In practice, then, we shall have real and proper illegal trade unionism. Is this dangerous? Undoubtedly so. But in general it cannot be avoided if we want to work. Do you believe the broad masses are very interested in the exchanges of letters between the trade union committees of the various parties? That serves for the committees themselves, and for a small circle of worker sympathisers who, in less bitter times, would be in the Party: it is of no use at all for influencing the broad masses. These latter can feel the effectiveness solely of practical activity, which can be undertaken only by an organisation that extends into the heart of the great masses themselves. What is the main weakness of the working class in Italy? Isolation, dispersion; we have to fight this state of affairs. We cannot immediately hope for great results, that is clear. But let me give an example: if we already had an extensive factory organisation, it is certain that, through methodical and systematic campaigning, we would manage to get a good result on May Day.[125] How can we create a conviction among the workers that some sort of centralisation already exists, that the same work is being carried out in all factories, that we are attempting to form a movement, without any factory fearing it will remain isolated and therefore crushed? This we can do in many ways that, taken together, give the desired feeling. In my view we must have our groups vote resolutions on the events taking place, in the name of the whole body of workers of factories A, B, C etc; our papers will publish them, the workers will read them and they will know. And so it will go on. I believe that a whole new technique of agitation and propaganda, and also of organisation, must be devised. We shall have to succeed in getting a great part of the masses to become used to illegal action, used to keeping things secret, etc. I think that harsh experience has taught Italian workers to take quite a number of steps forward in this field, so much so that, in my view, now we should even pose the question of whether in Turin, in Milan, and in some other big cities, to organise a public demonstration. You'll say that I'm exaggerating, but I have no wish to joke. I believe that if in Turin and Milan we managed, through good organisational capacity, to bring together 50,000 workers in a given part of the city, no catastrophe would occur, and the thing would have an immense repercussion. Certainly, to think of doing such a thing today would be hare-brained, but I am saying that, in carrying out the activity that I mentioned above, we must ask ourselves how we can arrive at just such a result.

I think I've made myself quite clear on this. In any case bear in mind that I'm putting forward these ideas for discussion by the comrades and nothing more than that. I think that by no stretch of the imagination are they utopian. We have to get out of this dead end we're in.[126] We have to get out of the present situation which then ends up in exchanges of letters and meetings of Committees. Certainly we have a lot to reflect on and weigh up, we have to find the best forms of organisation, get the comrades used to concrete work, and so on and so forth.

But, in conclusion, we really must make a start, and make a start at least by discussing things among ourselves in order to have our ideas clear and our guidelines precise. On that at least I think you are in agreement.

Fraternally

Sardi

Source: AAG and APC 513-1-248/92-93; typewritten

To Togliatti

VIENNA 19-4-24

Dearest Ercoli,

I am sending you a copy of the letter to Urbani. Up to now I have received little from you. Because of the long time that has passed since we were last together, I am unable to imagine up to what point we are in agreement. Even if it had to be rushed, I would like there to be a more detailed exchange of impressions between us. Why am I saying this to you? Because I have seen, from two letters from Veneziani, especially from the second of these, how one may get misled. Veneziani there wrote that he had understood that I wanted expulsions on the left.[127] Sheer fantasy; it leaves me aghast to think that there might be communicated and circulated among comrades the claim in the schematic form: Sardi wants to expel Amadeo from the P[arty].[128] Enough to make one commit suicide, on my word of honour. This is why I always want there to be great discussion, even amongst those who seem to be nearest each other and in agreement, even between us. We have to pose the question of the Party in all its breadth, in all its ramifications. The result of the elections, wonderful in my estimation, is something we have to analyse in all its significance. It seems to me to pose in a fairly serious way the danger from the right; it is not to be excluded that, after three years without discussion, the Party might fall into rightism; it is not to be excluded that, through our current action, we are contributing to this. We have to pose the question and see what can be done so as to skirt round all dangers. Given my isolation and lack of direct impressions, I can only make hypotheses, which is tiring for me without bearing fruit.

Germanetto has written to me, saying he is in agreement with our line. I am sending you my reply to his letter. With the agreement reached with Urbani, I think we have taken a great step forward and that we can really face the future with our minds more at rest.

I believe we shall soon meet up again since I think you will write to me asking me to come to Italy.[129]

Warm greetings

Sardi

I have read the two articles of yours on the elections, which are good as analyses. I think however that you should follow them up with practical indications to orient the comrades in their propaganda work. Was it you who wrote the introduction to the article by Gobetti? In his concept of winning the municipalities, obviously naïve, like that of parliamentary obstructionism and like the whole of the article in general, there is however a measure of truth. Obviously, a new power must be organised, in the factories and in the villages, the development of which might suffocate the fascist State.

Source: AAG and APC 513-1-248/27; typewritten

To the Central Committee of the PCd'I

19-4-24

To the C[entral] C[ommittee] of the PCI

STJEPAN RADIĆ AND THE SITUATION IN YUGOSLAVIA

Dear comrades,

You will already know from the newspapers the general nature of the present political crisis in Yugoslavia. Given the close relations that exist between the Balkans and Italy, because of which every important event in one country has its repercussion in the other, I think it is useful to give you some specific information on the situation in Yugoslavia and especially on the movement of the Croatian peasants under the leadership of Stjepan Radić.

1. The national question

The Yugoslav crisis is taking on political form within the national question. Since the great majority of Croatia supports Radić's Party, which says it is republican and federalist, the two chief players in the crisis have become Pašić, head of the Serbian Radical Party, a centralist and monarchist party, and Radić himself, who latterly has tended to put himself forward as the champion of all the Yugoslav nationalities crushed by the military and administrative hegemony of the Serbs. The social root of the national question lies in the agrarian question, complicated by the following political factors:

1) Serbia is the least industrialised of the three main nationalities that give their name to the Kingdom of Serbs, Croats and Slovenes.[130] For strategic reasons, Serb industry would like to concentrate the industrial apparatus of Croatia and Slovenia on Serb territory – less exposed to Italian, German and Hungarian invasions – and, in this, finds powerful support in monarchical centralism.
2) The Yugoslav Bureaucratic-military apparatus is in the hands of the Serbs, who have extended the old apparatus to the new territory, systematically excluding members of other nationalities. This Serbian hegemony makes its presence felt strongly in the army, whose numerically enormous officer corps, organised in a secret organisation called the 'White Hand', is the strongest instrument of the monarchy and of centralism.

3) International relations. Pašić's government and the monarchy are being aided by France, which wants to see a strong militarist State east of Italy to take the place of Austria-Hungary as the force of equilibrium both among the Balkan influences and in the case of a war between Italy and France. The movement of Radić and of the nationalities is supported by Britain, which looks askance on Serbian nationalist militarism, from which a new Balkan war and a new European war could arise.

2. Who is Stjepan Radić?

I have had a conversation of about a couple of hours with Radić, who outlined his conception and his political plan to me at great length.[131] It is difficult for me to sum up my impression. Radić is very cunning and able, but I don't think he is a great statesman, which is what would be required for putting his policy into action. I would say he is a consummate tactician, able to resolve immediate questions by means of compromises that always leave him a great deal of room to free himself after a successful operation, but he is no strategist. On general questions he adopts utopian stances, abstracting from the real relations between the conflicting forces, giving an overwhelming importance to ideology and, what is more, to an ideology that is nebulous, humanitarian, democratic, something that may be of use in public speeches to whip up waves of mysticism among the Croatian peasantry, but certainly cannot be of use for giving substance to a State. Naturally, this impression has to be corrected in a relative sense by two orders of considerations: 1) that even when Radić outlines his conception, he is engaging in politics, that is to say aiming at creating a favourable political situation for himself; 2) that he knows the real weakness of his own forces in the game of international politics that focuses on the Balkans and tends, as he thinks fit, to exploit the conflicts between the big powers to his own ends.

3. The role of Croatia.

The Pašić government has managed to keep constitutionally afloat in the present legislature only because the Radić fraction, consisting of about 70 deputies, has systematically boycotted Parliament. When Radić, in evident agreement with the other oppositional forces, changed tactic, and an initial group of his deputies went to Belgrade to have their mandate recognised and swear the parliamentary oath, the situation was overturned, thus producing a ministerial crisis. The government ought to have passed into the hands of the opposition, under Davidović as parliamentary leader, but that would have officially meant the opening up of a far-reaching crisis, with no clear and sure way out for the Serbian monarchy. Moreover, in the opposition ranks, the work of fusing together the various programmes has obviously not been completed, there is much hesitation, much wavering, from which Pašić has profited greatly in order to stay where he is and have the possibility of new elections. The crisis has however shown that, in the play of parliamentary forces, Croatia can put Serbia in check and that Croatia is the main danger for the current state of affairs since it is tending to put itself forward openly and officially as the leader of all the anti-Serbian and anti-monarchist forces.

4. Radić and fascist policy

You will recall how for some time both D'Annunzio and Mussolini were favourable to Radić's movement. In a document of D'Annunzio's that I saw with my own eyes in July 1920 when I was invited to go to Rijeka for the first time, there was written more or less as follows: 'Stjepan Radić is my (D'Ann[unzio]'s) spiritual brother and Rijeka will always give his movement all the aid and comfort its forces can offer. Like me, Stjepan Radić wants the basis of the new life to be the peasantry, this pure and virgin force of history etc, etc'. In the period of his campaign to win power, Mussolini too seemed favourable towards the oppressed nationalities in general and especially towards those of the Balkans. The *Popolo d'Italia* published articles by the Egyptian nationalists and the paper's editorial staff received frequent visits from émigrés from Montenegro, Macedonia, etc, to whom Mussolini promised support and gave advice.

Before the treaty with Yugoslavia, Mussolini sent Attilio Tamaro to Radić, I believe with some concrete proposals: Mussolini would not have concluded the treaty had Radić and Croatia gone over to revolutionary opposition against Serbia. In other words Mussolini would have come to an agreement with Radić and materially aided Croatia to gain independence if Rijeka and other concessions in Dalmatia had been granted to Italy. In the opposite case Italy would have come to an agreement with Serbia, and Croatia would have had to bear the cost of it. But then, as things have turned out, Radić is sure that within the Italo-Yugoslav treaty there are secret, military, clauses against Croatia. The Italo-Yugoslav treaty has in my view been very important in persuading Radić to overhaul his political plan and drive him leftward. Before the treaty Radić counted especially on British help and therefore, secondarily, on Italy. His own opinions on fascism were intentionally vague and uncertain and he systematically sought agreement with the bourgeoisie of the other Yugoslav nations rather than with the working class and the peasant parties; on Russia he was agnostic. Britain, which is using Radić for its own foreign policy, and nothing else, has shown itself satisfied with the Italo-Yugoslav treaty. Radić has been promised that if Pašić, profiting from his strengthened position, carries out a coup d'état and instals a military dictatorship, the British government would not recognise the legality of the new state of affairs. This is meagre consolation for Radić, and even this, in its meagreness, is by no means certain.

5. *Radić's new orientation*

In consequence Radić is today looking in Russia's direction and towards the working class – at least apparently for the time being. He is saying that the peasant masses can have no other ally than the proletariat, that there is no democracy other than a democracy of the working classes. He is saying he is willing to join the Peasant International, based in Moscow, while he is against the Green International based in Prague and is against international Sturzism.[132] In his view, Stambolijski's fundamental error (over and above his crass materialism) was to have counterposed countryside to city, not at all the peasants to the bourgeoisie, but the peasants to the city in its entirety, and thus also to the proletariat. He admires Soviet Russia and believes that the sole permanent reality in present day history is that of Russia, and the sole army that is strong, since it is based on popular will – the Red Army. *On the basis of Russian conditions, he also justifies the dictatorship and red terror*, but of course believes that in civilised Europe one will be able to do without both.

Within the Yugoslav political framework this new orientation of Radić's has caused the Pašić cabinet crisis. The Croatian Republican Party, which has now left its localist particularism behind, has sought to form a coalition with the Slovene clerical party (Korošec), with the Muslims of Bosnia and Herzegovina (Dr Spaho's party) and with the democrats of Davidović's party. In the Belgrade parliament all this means putting Pašić's radicals in the minority. Outside parliament Radić intends however to bring peasant movements and organisations into being in the various countries (Slovenia, Bosnia-Herzegovina, Vojvodina, Montenegro and Macedonia); these would be of the same type as in Croatia, in other words anti-Serb, republican, federalist ones. He also hopes to create a similar movement in Serbia. He is justifying the agreement with bourgeois representatives like Davidović, with clericals like Korošec, with representatives of the Muslim *beys* like Dr Spaho, as immediate tactical necessities in order to create new situations favourable to the development of the popular movement as properly understood: that of the workers and peasants.[133]

6. Possible Outcomes of the Crisis

The parliamentary situation created by this new orientation of Radić's is extremely serious and full of unforeseen circumstances. The political structure of the new kingdom is weak, and only with great difficulty is the set-up kept on is feet by the administrative apparatus and by military coercion. If Radić's plan comes to fruition, if in other words he really does manage to put together the intended coalition, the monarchy will carry out a coup d'état to save itself.

That the situation is serious is demonstrated by the fact that the king in person called in both Messrs Davidović and Korošec and showed them an alleged receipt of Radić's for sums received from Russia. The thing in itself is monstrous. The king, who is by law 'sacred and inviolable', and cannot be … sued by Radić for falsehood and libel, and who moreover does not have to give proof of his assertions, has lent his authority to putting this fraud into operation. Even taking into account that Yugoslavia is in the Balkans and that the Serb dynasty is not a babe in arms in such plots and intrigues, the episode is serious and significant. They will have few constitutional scruples in attempting to destroy the opposition's plan. The use of corruption, blackmail and intimidation in the first instance, and then the open use of armed force in the second are the means by which the Serb dynasty's militarist gang will seek to maintain power.

It would be naïve to think that Radić has not seen these dangers or that his humanitarian ideology is hindering preparations equal to the task represented by such dangers. As already pointed out, I maintain that Radić is too able to let himself be embroiled in ideologies that for him seem to me to be, more than anything, weapons in the struggle. The difficulties are to be sought in the very nature and social character of Radić's movement, a movement of the great peasant masses, but without any strong cadre forces, and dispersed as it is among a myriad of villages. Radić states he is not opposed in principle to armed insurrection and revolutionary methods, but would have recourse to them only in the last analysis. He says that if and when needed he has access to lots of weapons, even without accepting the not disinterested offers of Hungary or of Italy. But it is not difficult to foresee that he may find himself in check in this field. He does not believe it possible that a fascism like that in Italy can arise in Yugoslavia, and to a great extent he is right in this opinion. But this optimism of his does not hold up when measured against the Serb army and gendarmerie, and even less so when one is dealing with a foreign army, e.g. that of Italy or the fascist national militia.[134] He thinks that no army of today (with the exception of the Red Army) is capable of waging a regular war, especially against a people that has given itself free (almost soviet) institutions, such as the Croat people will do. He says he has replied to Tamaro's veiled threats with counter-threats, in other words, if the Italian army dares invade Croatia, the Croat people in arms will sweep away the invader, and the Slavs that have now been annexed to Italy will be liberated. I think that, even if he is hiding much of his true opinion in all this reasoning, there is still a great deal of utopianism in it, similar moreover to the utopianism prevalent among many Russian comrades at the time of Brest-Litovsk, who, because the German Army was composed of proletarians, excluded the possibility of its marching against the workers' State. One cannot, furthermore, see how Radić could resolve the problem of the armed force necessary at a certain point to parry the inevitable counterblows caused by his political tactics.

7. *The Yugoslav Communist Party*

The sole solution ought to be an alliance between the peasants and workers, between the working class of the whole of Yugoslavia and the various peasant movements of the constellation of nationalities. It is however difficult even simply to pose this problem to Radić, since the Communist Party in Yugoslavia is a metaphysical entity rather than an organisation in the proper sense of the term, except in the sense of the influence of Communist ideas. But exactly what counts most in the present situation is the effective organisation in all its ramifications. It is precisely on the national question that the Party is divided into two fractions, that of Sima Marković (this comrade is at the moment in prison) and that of Kazlerović, who currently has the majority of his Party's Executive behind him. Sima Marković provides a partial solution to the national question, a constitutional one, in my view, that satisfies no one. Kazlerović's fraction accepts on paper the Comintern solution but is incapable of working since it is thoroughly corrupted by bureaucratic attachment to office and the spirit of fractionalism, and is holding on to power in order to sabotage any useful and revolutionary initiative. Thus in actual fact there exist as many Communist Parties as there are historical regions in Yugoslavia, though the acute situation requires the highest degree of centralisation. The movement is especially weak in Serbia, where it ought to be strongest; in Belgrade, whose city council was Communist in 1920, the illegal section of the Party is composed of twenty members, of whom 14 are intellectuals and full-time Party workers and 6 are working-class and, of these latter, 4 are Trade Union full-timers. The Serbian Communists deny there is a national question, while the Slovenes on the other hand say that if, in their country, there were to be a plebiscite, 80% would vote to return to Austria, and so on. The Marković fraction says that the Comintern ought to stop any subsidy to the party and limit itself just to financing the deficit of the weekly, which, however, ought to have just one paid member of the editorial staff and not 4 as at present. Only in this way, by cutting off the means of subsistence at source, would the bureaucratic incrustation be eliminated and the Party start to work among the masses. The Kazlerović fraction is retorting with other accusations. Meanwhile the Party is paralysed while the ground is scorching under its feet.

In such a situation it is no wonder that Radić has become the main leader of the opposition and is not able to detach himself once and for all from the democratic bourgeoisie.

8. Some duties facing our Party

More than anything else, I have wanted to inform you of a number of specific points regarding the situation in Yugoslavia. I think however it is fitting to mention a number of other points that involve our Party more closely.

1) We have never stated clearly what our policy is towards the national minority, Slav and Germanic, populations that were annexed to Italy after the war. I think it would therefore be useful to have an exchange of views with the Yugoslav Party, so as to arrive at a line of conduct by common accord.
2) In general it would be useful to have greater contact with the Balkan Communist Federation, given the importance of the Balkans in the politics of the Italian State. During the Corfu affair the Greek Party tried unsuccessfully to make contact with us in order to launch a joint manifesto; this manifesto was launched just the same by the Greek comrades with our signature appended and I still do not know whether even to this day you are aware of it. Likewise, in agreement with us, it is wished to set up a Communist movement in Albania where there are many Italian workers (many in a relative sense). We have to remember that in Southern Italy, especially in Puglia, Calabria and Sicily [there] are a lot of Albanians (about 300,000) and that there are lots of contacts between Albania and Puglia, so much so that the *Giornale delle Puglie* used to publish a page in Albanian (I don't know whether it still does). Do we have comrades among these Albanian-Italians, do we have comrades among the sailors going between Bari and Albania etc, etc? It would be useful to know these things in order to work effectively if the Balkan Communist Federation invites us to take part in the initiative.
3) Our newspapers should always reprint the articles from *Inprecorr* dealing with Yugoslavia and the Balkans in general. They should then avoid falling systematically into errors of judgement, as recently happened with *L'Unita*, which presented the party of Stambolijski, which was working with the Communists, as a band of adventurers or something of the like. We have to try to create within our movement a more exact knowledge of Balkan affairs and an awareness of the vital importance that the Balkans have for our revolution. Greetings.

Sardi

Source: AAG and APC 513-1-248/97-100; typewritten

NOTES TO CHAPTER 5

1. This is a paraphrase, rather than a direct quote from *L'Ordine Nuovo*, of the aims of the Turin group and review.
2. Monti was the pseudonym of Carlo Codevilla, who often appears in Party documents as secretary to PCI groups in Moscow, and whom Gramsci preferred as his secretary in Vienna over Guido Zamis, whose fluent German made him the Party centre's choice.
3. Codes, composed of equal numbers of groups of letters, were used for sending sensitive information.
4. Initially Gramsci lodged in Schönbrunner Street, then on the south-west outskirts of Vienna, with Joseph Frey, the general secretary of the Austrian Communist Party.
5. The Party Committee of a District ('rajon'); see also the letter to Jul'ka of 13 January 1924.
6. Almost certainly the Politburo meeting of 5 December, then reported in *Pravda*; the 13 January 1924 letter to Jul'ka takes up the question again.
7. The 'Rabkor' were the worker correspondents, and the book is probably *Principles of Organisation*, first published in 1922, by P.M. Keržencev, now better known for his work in the theatre and Proletkul't movement of that time.
8. Up to this point, the letter is in Togliatti (1962) and in Gramsci (1992), but the rest of the letter remained unknown, as also did the following two letters, until publication in Giasi (Giasi et al, 2009).
9. Togliatti made this request in a letter of 23 September 1923 sent to the Comintern secretariat and to Gramsci (APC 513-1-178/1); Edmondo Peluso arrived in Moscow a few days after Gramsci's departure from there for Vienna.
10. Since Gramsci thought that the current letter had not arrived, he repeated much of the content in another letter to Terracini not included here (27 March 1924; see Gramsci APC 513-1-248/86 and Gramsci (1992)), for clarity adding at this point his transliteration of the Russian for fusiliers ('strelki') after the Italian word.
11. The unsigned attack was in the 3-10 April 1920 issue of *Ordine Nuovo*: see the reprint *L'Ordine Nuovo* (1976), p340, and continuation on p345, or Gramsci (1987), pp493-6.
12. Gramsci was not abstentionist, but he and Bordiga were united in favouring a 'national communist fraction' in the Socialist Party to prepare the formation of a Communist Party (Spriano 1967, pp72-3). Chaim Heller (or Haller) was the real name of Chiarini.
13. It turned out that Chiarini had joined the PCI at or shortly after its foundation, claiming – falsely – that he was a member of the Russian Party, which he was later able to join – without a preliminary candidate membership period – only in 1922, by transferring from the Italian

Party (cf letter from Terracini to Gramsci, undated but early 1924: Comintern Archives 513-1-251/88).

14. Tomo is a nickname used for Chiarini which, as well as a book volume, also means a bizarre person.
15. The typescript list of names reads Tito, Negri, 'Scura' – rather than 'Serra' (Tasca), as written here – but Serra is in fact the only possibility.
16. Where the sense is obvious, words or letters missing in this letter due to a torn manuscript have been editorially added in brace brackets.
17. Like the Italian Angelo Valente, mentioned in the next paragraph, Virgilio Verdaro, a Swiss citizen, took refuge in Russia in the early 1920s. The other three named in the latter part of the letter, Gastone Sozzi, Arnaldo Silva and Antonio Cicalini, also found their way to Russia at about the same time, the first two then going on to attend the Party cadre school in Petrograd. The Bottegone was a well-known café bar in the cathedral square in Florence.
18. Vaclav Vorovskij, the soviet government representative in Italy from 1921 to 1923, was 'killed by the bullet of a fascist bandit' (Comintern Executive motion, *Inprecorr*, No 52, 23 July 1923); *Inprecorr* No. 45, 22 June 1923, carried an article by Beruzzi (Manuil'skij) criticising the PCI for not having exploited this incident to the full.
19. 'Sedler', referred to earlier in the letter by his initial, has now been identified almost certainly as the artist and aviator Nikolaj Nikolaevič (also known as Gerbert or Herbert) Zedler; other variants of his surname are also found. Formerly a member of the Italian Socialist Party, as a Russian citizen he became a member of the Russian Communist Party and worked for the Comintern Executive, but left the Russian Party in 1925.
20. The word may be 'intralcio' ('obstacle') but only the first three letters are legible.
21. Perhaps because of a slip, the feminine pronoun is used here, whereas the masculine form seems needed.
22. Terracini acted on the Chiarini/Tomo question, confirming in two letters of March 1924 that Chiarini had been relieved of Italian duties (Comintern Archives 513-1-251/60-61).
23. Another copy of this letter exists, written to Negri (i.e. Scoccimarro) and unsigned, of which the next letter is the covering letter.
24. The 'Imola fraction' of the Socialist Party, it may be recalled, favoured the immediate formation of a Communist Party (see the appendix to Chapter 3).
25. Gramsci is referring to the internal right-wing opposition within the PCI leadership.
26. A few days after his release from three months in prison, Togliatti wrote of 'the rickets you complain of' in his letter to Gramsci dated 29 December (see Togliatti, 1962, p141), confirmation that a copy of the present letter had reached Terracini and, through Scoccimarro, been

forwarded to Togliatti. This letter, reproduced here and first published in Giasi (Giasi et al, 2009), resurfaced only much later.

27. The English title of this book is *The Communist Manifesto of Karl Marx and Friedrich Engels. With an introduction and explanatory notes by D. Ryazanoff*, trans. Eden and Cedar Paul, Martin Lawrence: London 1930. Gramsci had told the PCI Executive (letter of 20 December) that, with the aid of a 'Russian comrade' (i.e. Jul'ka), he was working on a translation for partial publication in *L'Ordine Nuovo*. The sole extracts known to have survived are now in the only two parts completed of the Party educational correspondence course (Gramsci 1988, pp107-15 and 187-97).
28. Almost certainly *Marxism and Revisionism*, now in Lenin: *Collected Works*, Vol. 15, Progress Publishers: Moscow 1973, pp29-39.
29. For *How the Revolution Armed, see The Military Writings and Speeches of Leon Trotsky*, ed. and trans. Brian Pearce, New Park Publications: London 1981. It is not known which particular volume Gramsci is here referring to, but probably Vol. IV (published in Russian in 1924), which deals, among other things, with the failed German uprising of autumn 1923; other volumes were however also published in 1924.
30. *Knigonoša* (*Bookseller*) was a magazine of the period carrying book reviews. The title *Sputnik* is not a mistake or misreading; the word's basic meaning is 'companion', hence by extension a satellite (the moon) and therefore a natural choice for the name of the Soviet artificial satellites.
31. This is the 'Manifesto of the Party left' (Merli, 1964, pp515-21), drafted in prison by Bordiga in the first part of 1923 and subsequently modified, albeit very little, in Gramsci's opinion.
32. The verb used here also means 'administer'; 'lead', used as a translation here, should not be confused with the way 'lead' ('dirigere' in Italian, or 'leading role' = 'funzione dirigente') is used in the *Prison Notebooks*.
33. Cf Gramsci's letter from Moscow to Togliatti, dated 18 May 1923 (see Chapter 4), where reference is made to the dissent with Angelo Tasca, representing the right of the Turin group.
34. The following part of this letter, regarding publications, to a great extent duplicates the more detailed letter of the 14 January to the PCI Executive. Given the importance of these letters, and in line with the decision to publish the fullest form available of letters, both of these are reproduced in their entirety.
35. Alma Lex, a Latvian-born soviet citizen; she and Terracini met two years previously at the Third Congress of the International and later married.
36. Virgili was a self-taught engineer who, after not having been able to interest anyone in his projects in Italy, on the advice of Bordiga (also an engineer), emigrated to Moscow, where his aviation projects attracted more attention.

37. See the Introduction for more on Trotsky's criticisms of bureaucratisation and the rift with Stalin. The motion mentioned by Gramsci is that of the Politburo of 5 December, published (*Pravda* 7 December and *Inprecorr* 31 December) under the names of the Central Committee and Central Control Commission who, in a joint meeting on 25 October, deputed the Politburo, Trotsky included, to reach the final form (cf. Carr (1954), pp107 and 300-301, and Daniels (1960), p222).
38. For the 'Rajkom', see the note to the 16 December 1923 letter to Jul'ka, p187.
39. The tiredness was presumably due to Jul'ka's first pregnancy, which Gramsci says (letter of 29 March 1924) that she first told him of in her letter of 24 February.
40. Probably an earlier edition of V. Adoratsky, *Dialectical Materialism*, Martin Lawrence: London and International Publishers: New York, 1934.
41. Gramsci had already sent a letter to Zini on 10 January to re-establish contact and ask him to undertake this Italian-language anthology.
42. This compendium had only recently been published. A literal translation of the Italian title is used here for what in English is *The People's Marx: Abridged Popular Edition of … 'Capital'*, ed. Julian Borchardt, trans. Stephen L. Trask, International Bookshops: London 1921.
43. The first page of this letter, including the name of the recipient and the date, has not come to light. From the closing lines, the person must have been a frequent contributor to *Inprecorr*, which suggests Ruggero Grieco, who had various articles published in 1924; the attribution is however not definite. The letter was discovered and first published by Francesco Giasi (Giasi et al, 2009).
44. This Bianco was Michele, not Vincenzo, who in Moscow often liaised between Gramsci and Jul'ka.
45. *Principles of Communism*, part of the *Communist Manifesto*'s preliminary material, is now available in Paul Sweezy's English translation (Pluto Press: London 1971).
46. This sentence, included in the 513-1-248/46-51 copy, was added by hand, probably somewhat hurriedly, before the letter was despatched. The meaning is as given here, but both Gramsci's verbs are in the plural; for sense, the second one (here in square brackets) has been made singular to agree with 'cork', glossed as 'foam' by Dante Germino in his *Antonio Gramsci. Architect of a new politics*, Louisiana State University Press: Baton Rouge, p155).
47. The phrase 'some of these weaknesses' is a handwritten addition by Gramsci in the 513-1-248/40-45 copy, adjusted here by substituting 'and' before the words 'in certain ways' for Gramsci's 'that', left unchanged in the typescript from the original wording.
48. The article was published in *Pravda* on 23 September 1923, then in *Inprecorr* on 11 October, No. 66 [42], pp731-2, and in the January 1924 number of *Labour Monthly*; see also Vol. 2 of Trotsky's *The First Five*

Years of the Communist International under the title 'Can a counter-revolution or a revolution be made on schedule?' and elsewhere sometimes under a slightly different title.

49. In December 1922 there was a Peace Conference called by the Social Democrat-oriented International Federation of Trade Unions, to which – for once – Bolshevik delegates were invited.
50. 'For Brandler' is a handwritten addition.
51. As a consequence of the defeat of the attempted insurrection in Germany in March 1921, encouraged by what was then the left in the Russian Party, the International shifted its position, adopting a united front policy.
52. Minority here, and in the rest of this paragraph, means Tasca's right-wing in the PCd'I, who were ostensibly in agreement with the International (see p199).
53. To 'accept the leadership of the minority' refers again to Tasca, while 'if not' gives the opposite case, namely that Bordiga does not get a majority and that the group around Gramsci remains with that minority despite its convictions that Bordiga's position is mistaken. In this part of the letter Gramsci's meaning becomes difficult to interpret. He sees an 'ambiguity' in the Manifesto as consisting, first, in the fact that if Bordiga were to gain a majority for his theses within the Italian party, the group being created by Gramsci would find itself having to accept the leadership of Tasca's minority, in order to be in line with the position of the International; but if Bordiga were outvoted, then the group supporting him would also comprise the one around Gramsci, notwithstanding the latter's basic opposition to Bordiga's theses. At that point, a break with Bordiga would take on a 'most objectionable and obnoxious aspect'. The implication is that such a situation could be avoided only through the centre group – forming around Gramsci and *not* in agreement with Bordiga – openly breaking with Bordiga more or less immediately and attempting to win a majority within the party. The interpretation given here is a consensus view arrived at with colleagues from the Gramsci Institute.
54. What is here translated as 'city ward' (*rione*) is not to be understood electorally, but simply as the traditional quarter into which many Italian cities are divided; while 'rural district' is the *mandamento*, having more limited judicial and administrative functions than the municipality (*comune*); the *mandamento* was quashed by Fascism's hostility to local administrative autonomy.
55. The 'UI' was the 'Ufficio Illegale', the bureau that dealt with illegal and underground work. 'Must be' and 'in this field' are Gramsci's handwritten additions to the typescript.
56. The father referred to is Arturo Caroti, a socialist member of parliament who joined the infant Communist Party but was soon expelled for shady financial dealings.

57. That the PCI had published incitements to civil war formed part of the accusation against Gramsci and other leading communists at their trial in 1928. Terracini was able to show in their defence, however, that an authoritative fascist legal journal had already published in full the text of the International's guidelines on civil war tactics; see D. Boothman, 'The British Press on Gramsci's Trial', *Counter-Hegemony*, No. 8, cited in endnote 16 to the Introduction.
58. Point 7 was added by hand, after the list was written, as is also the numbering of the points themselves.
59. The only two completed parts of the correspondence course, inspired by the Party School in Petrograd (mentioned in various letters), is reprinted in Gramsci (1988), pp59-209. They included sections on the theory of historical materialism, elements of general politics (much of it on economic questions), the working-class Party and its organisational principles, and appendices with notes on the *Communist Manifesto*, leading revolutionaries and a Marxist-Leninist anthology.
60. Due to a shift in office (brief letter from Gramsci to Terracini of 24 February, not included here), there was no typewriter available. In the current letter Gramsci initially writes 'letters' in the plural, but towards the end of the long postscript writes 'letter', as if there were just one joint letter from Togliatti and Scoccimarro.
61. Writing to Gramsci on 23 February 1924, Togliatti outlined moves in Rome to work towards a new majority.
62. The 'Longo' referred to is indeed Luigi Longo. Girgenti is now Agrigento (the Roman Agrigentum), overlooking the Valley of the Temples in Sicily; 'Roberto' was possibly Rodolfo Fobert.
63. It seems, however, that approval by signature to a document or letter did not take place.
64. The Italian is somewhat ambiguous, but the meaning appears to be that fascism had defined its own character, not that of the situation.
65. This was the fascist-constructed and fascist-dominated list, which was awarded 356 out of 535 seats in the Chamber of Deputies in the elections of 4 April, and which included many liberals and others regarding themselves as democrats. Both Orlando, head of government 1917-19, and De Nicola (see the 'Main people' appendix), went into opposition to fascism, although sometimes a wavering one.
66. Then, as now, important press organs – the *Corriere della Sera* representing the Milanese bourgeoisie and *La Stampa* FIAT interests.
67. Similar arguments appear in 'Some Aspects of the Southern Question' in (Gramsci 1978b, pp441-62) and in Gramsci's article 'The Mezzogiorno and Fascism' in *L'Ordine Nuovo* of 15 March 1924, now in Gramsci (1994b), pp260-64.
68. Rinaldo Rigola was the first general secretary (1906-18) of the CGdL trade union confederation, but later collaborated with the fascist regime.

Giuseppe Emanuele Modigliani, like Rigola a leading member of the reformist Unitary Socialist Party (PSU), led the case against the regime after the murder of the PSU secretary Giacomo Matteotti.

69. Although now mainly forgotten, this used to be the norm in the Communist movement.
70. I.e. the Comintern Executive.
71. In his letter to Gramsci of 23 February 1924, cited above, Togliatti reproaches him for not making his views explicit earlier and conducting an open battle within the PCI for a different line from Bordiga's.
72. Cf Paolo Spriano (1967), pp160-1 for this little known episode.
73. Luigino and Bruno are Repossi and Fortichiari respectively.
74. 'At long range' is a reminder that these events were taking place in Moscow, while the majority of the Central Committee were in Italy.
75. At around the time of this letter, Bruno Fortichiari sent a number of written requests to the Party centre, now in the Party Archives, asking to be relieved of political responsibilities.
76. In a separate letter of the same date to Urbani, i.e. Terracini (not included here), Gramsci gives a very succinct summary of this long letter to Scoccimarro and Togliatti.
77. Antonio had only just received the news, in a letter from Jul'ka of 24 February, that she was pregnant with their first child, Delio; see also the letter to Jul'ka of 29 March.
78. This is Fanny Jezierska (the Polish form of her name that she is best known under).
79. For the Aventine secession both in fifth century BCE and Rome in 1924-5, see introduction, p37.
80. The letter fragment in the typescripts of both the Rome and the Moscow Archives is dated 10.I.24, an obvious mistake since Lenin died on 21 January. The date may have been 10.II.1924 or, as conjectured here, 10.III.24, a few days after Gramsci's previous letter to Jul'ka in which he asks for 'extracts of some of the best pages written regarding the death of Lenin'. We use the Moscow and current AAG versions beginning 'capisco' ('I understand') rather than another one in Rome beginning 'spiace' ('I'm sorry'), which does not make sense and is, in any case, open to further transcription errors since it was done later, as seen from the use of an electric typewriter.
81. Gramsci had referred to the legend of Lao-Tse (Lao-Tzu), born at the age of eighty, in an article in *Avanti!* of 13 July 1916. It then appears in the *Prison Notebooks*: see e.g. Gramsci (1985), pp34, 118, 179, 401; Gramsci (1995), pp125-6; and Gramsci (1996), pp72, 291 and 472-3.
82. The letter referred to is that of 1 March 1924 to Scoccimarro and Togliatti (p236).
83. Sraffa's letter, with the title 'Problems of today and tomorrow' from an

'old subscriber and friend of *L'Ordine Nuovo*', was published under the signature 'S' on p4 of the 1-15 April 1924 issue of *L'Ordine Nuovo* (referred to as the *Review* a few lines later in this letter); the extract, with Gramsci's reply, is in Gramsci (1978b), pp229-36. Sraffa's promised article on the trade union bureaucracy, mentioned by Gramsci at the end of the part of the letter on Sraffa, was probably never written.

84. After writing an article on the Italian banking system in the *Manchester Guardian Commercial* supplement (7 December 1922), Sraffa was attacked violently in a telegram from Mussolini to his father, then rector of Milan's Bocconi Commercial University. Piero wrote that as a result he felt obliged for a time to 'interrupt all contacts I had with the Italian communists': cf. the appendix ('Piero Sraffa e il marxismo') to Luca Meldolesi's *L'utopia realmente esistente – Marx e Saint-Simon*, Laterza: Bari, 1982, p110.
85. In other words, of a similar type to the ones in Turin of the 1919-21 period, for which see Spriano (1975), especially pp32, 35, 59 and Gramsci 1978b, pp11-22; see also 'The Programme of *Ordine Nuovo*' in Gramsci, *The Modern Prince*, trans. Louis Marks, Lawrence and Wishart: London, 1957, pp22-7.
86. We have translated as interference the ambiguous term 'manomissione'. Losa specified in his letter to *L'Ordine Nuovo* (1-15 April 1924, p8: see *L'Ordine Nuovo* [reprint, 1976]) that a Royal Commissioner had been sent in to 'different organisations' for purposes of 'government control'; here we have chosen the generic term 'interference', which in Gramsci (1978b, p220) is interpreted as 'takeover' of the Federation.
87. Bonomi, initially a socialist, was expelled from the Socialist Party as an ultra-reformist in 1912; he was prime minister from July 1921 to February 1922, then allying himself with Giovanni Amendola. He retired to private life under fascism, but again became prime minister from June 1944 to June 1945 during the allied occupation of Italy.
88. These lines foreshadow the position Gramsci was to adopt in prison on a Constituent Assembly, opposition to which among fellow Communist prisoners caused him to interrupt the joint political discussions they were having.
89. With 'sovietist', of course, having its meaning of 'councils'.
90. Togliatti (1962, pp231-3) explains that the Socialist Party daily *Avanti!* had got hold of and printed the main part of an internal Communist Party circular on the question of fusion with the terzini.
91. Various communists, including many of the top leaders, were tried in mid-October 1923, some, like Gramsci, in their absence. The court, still maintaining liberal principles of law, admitted the legitimacy of the Party, and freed all but one minor defendant: see Spriano (1967), pp315-23.

92. Saverio Roncoroni, a leader of the peasants at Como and initially an anarchist, sided with the communists when the PCd'I was founded but then was one of the terzini who remained in the Socialist Party: see Detti (1972), especially p405. Riccardo Momigliano initially signed the pro-Comintern maximalist motion at the Socialist Party Congress where the Communists broke away, but later opposed any type of fusion with the PCd'I: see Spriano (1967), pp106 and 274.
93. See also the letter to Jul'ka of 16 April in which he writes of the scarecrows tormenting her.
94. The *čista* was the membership purge decided at the Tenth Congress of the Bolsheviks in March 1921; Serapidovič (name misremembered by Gramsci) seems to have been Jul'ka's local Party functionary.
95. I.e. a carbon copy of Gramsci's letter to Togliatti (see below, p264), sent in reply to a letter from Togliatti of 20 March.
96. The letter to Terracini (probably the one marked 'personal' of 23 December 1923) did arrive, but Gramsci told him to destroy it after reading it, as Terracini reminded him (letter to Gramsci of 11 April 1924: Comintern Archives 513-1-251/65). Gramsci goes into further detail on Chiarini in another letter to Terracini (not included here) on the same day as the present one.
97. The German Communist Party's 'Open Letter' of January 1921 is taken by many (cf. Hájek 1972, p60 and note) to herald the birth of the United Front policy, with all the variants and often conflicting interpretations of this policy. The International's Third Congress (1921), which gave official currency to the United Front, held up the 'Open Letter' as a model to be followed on tactics.
98. In Togliatti's letter the previous week (see Togliatti, 1962, p237), referred to by Gramsci at the start of the current letter, Togliatti emphasised that Bordiga's 'collaboration in the party leadership with us, and in general with the groups that are not completely in agreement with him, is something that all of us greatly desire', and that this should take place on the 'clear and explicit basis' of recognising that due to the differences 'at certain moments a separation of responsibility might be indispensable'.
99. The two articles were in *Il Prometeo* (Naples) of 15 February 1924 (on Gramsci) and in *Il Lavoratore*, the Trieste journal of Bordighian outlook, published without an author's name on 7 March 1923.
100. For 'Chiarini's attempt' see the letter to Scoccimarro and Togliatti of 1 March and also the personal letters to Terracini of 23 December 1923 and of the same day as the current one.
101. Humbert-Droz quotes a talk he had with Grieco (Humbert-Droz Archives 0020: see Spriano 1967, p335): '[Grieco] told me "The International and the Party are currently following an anti-communist line and it is the duty of certain leaders, when they note such deviations,

to be indisciplined. Certain comrades ... are predestined, so to speak, to be leaders. Bordiga, like Lenin, is one of these. You cannot apply discipline to these men as you can to other Party members. Their historic mission is to apply it to others and not to follow it."'

102. The change from a singular form of 'you' (Togliatti) in the previous sentence, to the plural form here means that the 'last letter' referred to is that of 21 March 'to Togliatti, Scoccimarro, Leonetti etc'.
103. This was indeed set up as the fortnightly organ of the National Peasants' Association ('Associazione Nazionale dei Contadini') under Romano Cocchi, who went against both catholic and previous socialist tradition by arguing that smallholdings could only be guaranteed, and their agricultural production developed, within a workers' and peasants' state.
104. See Gramsci's letter of 21 March addressed to Togliatti, Scoccimarro, Leonetti and others for comments on Zini's letter.
105. I.e. *L'Ordine Nuovo*.
106. The idea of Zini using a pseudonym is also mentioned in a letter to Scoccimarro of 10 December 1923 (not included here) about organisational matters and possible contributions to the first issue of the new *L'Ordine Nuovo*: Gramsci asks for information on Zini's political position and suggests that articles of his could appear under a pseudonym.
107. See Gramsci's letter from prison to Tanja of 23 February 1931 (Gramsci 1994a, Vol. 2, p14). Gramsci had followed Cosmo's course in Italian literature at university and also mentions him in his own original interpretation in the *Prison Notebooks* of the tenth Canto of Dante's *Inferno*. After a period of tension between the two, due to an article by Gramsci that attacked him, they were reconciled on meeting again in Berlin, where Cosmo was the Italian cultural attaché.
108. Togliatti (1962, pp297-326) contains the partial minutes of this key Central Committee meeting (18 April 1924) with the motions (pp318-26) of the right minority, the left, and the new centre group, which now had a wafer-thin majority there. His opening statement later came to light and was published, together with another part of the debate, by Stefano Merli (Merli 1964, cit., pp527-40). The article mentioned by Gramsci was his unsigned editorial in the 15 March issue of *L'Ordine Nuovo* ('Against Pessimism': see Gramsci 1978b pp213-7). It gives a dispassionate run-down of the strengths and weaknesses of the PCI, and analyses the changes in the national and international situation since the PCI's foundation.
109. Due to a slip, instead of 'leader', a word that had already found its way into Italian, the typescript has the similar-sounding 'lieder', i.e. the German for 'songs'.
110. Tasca had said he wanted to resign from the PCI Executive and, later in April, when the political task set by the Comintern of bringing about the fusion between the PCd'I and the terzini had in principle been

resolved, he and another representative of the right, Giuseppe Vota, did resign from the Executive: Scoccimarro's letter, referred to in Gramsci's postscript, is in Togliatti (1962), p269.

111. This article, signed G. Masci, was published as 'The Results of the Elections in Italy' (*Inprecorr*, 1924, Vol.4, No. 25, p231, now in electronic form in the *International Gramsci Journal* No. 3 March 2011, p34). The working class, he claimed, had resisted beyond expectation, with the combined vote of the Communists, Maximalists and Reformists in Milan having 'surpassed those which the Socialist Party polled in 1919, i.e. the period of highest revolutionary development'. The Communist Party, 'strengthened from the elections … must continue and intensify the campaign for the proletarian united front and the workers' and peasants' government, to this end taking advantage of the parliamentary tribune'.
112. The first issues of the new series came out regularly, two in March and a double issue dated 1-15 April, after which the only other issues were those of September 1924, two in November, and a last one in March 1925.
113. Cf Antonio's letter to Jul'ka of 16 December 1923.
114. Unless a letter has gone missing, this seems to refer to the letter of a fortnight previously (29 March).
115. A couple of days before this letter, Jul'ka had written using their common phrase 'Today I feel my love is no longer that of a girl who needs a hand to caress her eyes to shield her from the great and terrible world and make her forget her feelings of anguish, because that hand is giving me the courage and consciousness to conquer them' (*L'Unità*, 18 October 2007). The Tibetan lama mentioned a little below is the character in *Kim* who often uses the phrase 'great and terrible world'.
116. A mistaken transcription in Gramsci (1992) gives the meaning 'I have been ill again' rather than 'I had been ill again'.
117. In Gramsci's imagery, the reference to insects recalls the spider of the 29 March letter to Jul'ka while the reference to molten metal, a few lines above, might also implicitly recall the red-hot iron of his 15 March letter.
118. See also the letters of 13 February 1923 to Evgenija and of 12 July 1925 to Jul'ka that mention Matilde Serao.
119. This seems a slip by Gramsci, for the Fifth Congress, which was then scheduled; the Fifth Enlarged Executive, which he attended, took place a year later in spring 1925.
120. Gramsci was elected to parliament for the Venetian regional constituency, officially obtaining 1,585 preferences in a communist vote totalling 32,383: see Detti (1972) pp470-2.
121. Domenico Alaleona had been a teacher of Jul'ka's at the Santa Cecilia Conservatory in Rome.

122. John DuVal's 'free' translation captures very well the spirit of the original.
123. This takes up again the subject already broached in Gramsci's letter to various Party leaders of 21 March.
124. Councils of workers' leagues organised on territorial basis.
125. On 14 April, the PCd'I Executive proposed to the PSI and the PSU a joint demonstration for May Day, whose celebration had been abolished by the fascist government; the PSI was favourable, but only in words, while Matteotti, secretary of the reformists, rejected the proposal disparagingly (Spriano 1967, pp347-8).
126. Gramsci's expression ('morta gora', the 'dead canal') is more colourful, and is used in Canto VIII of Dante's *Inferno* to mean the River Styx; here it also picks up politically a use of the phrase made in Bordiga's Manifesto of the Communist Left.
127. In a letter not included here (dated simply Vienna, IV.1924), signed 'Sardi' and replying to one of 11 April 1924 from 'Lanzi' (Tresso, here under the pseudonym 'Veneziani'), Gramsci wrote 'I don't know from what statement of mine you have drawn the conclusion that I want to assimilate on the right and expel on the left. That is fantasy'.
128. The Italian is badly expressed here, a literal translation being at best a stylistically strange 'such a communication may be communicated and [may] circulate among the comrades'. Santucci in Gramsci (1992) reads the passage as 'such a communication may have begun to circulate among the comrades', substituting 'begun' (*cominciata*) where Gramsci or his secretary writes 'communicated' (*comunicata*). The version suggested here simply tidies up the wording by suppressing the 'communication'/'communicated' repetition.
129. The plural 'you' is used, meaning the Party, not Togliatti, will write to Gramsci.
130. The country's official name from 1918 to 1929.
131. Radić was not present at the Comintern Balkan Conference in late 1923, attended by Gramsci, so the two probably met when Radić passed through Vienna a couple of months after Gramsci's arrival there.
132. A reference to the catholic priest, Don Luigi Sturzo, leader of the centrist, peasant-based Partito Popolare Italiano, forerunner of the post-World War II Christian Democrat Party.
133. Muslim *beys*: Gramsci's actual words here are 'beg mussulmani', not 'bog mussulmani' as transcribed in Gramsci (1992). 'Beg' (in its more modern form 'bey') is now usually a title of respect, but it formerly referred to the head of a province in the Ottoman Empire; while in the Slav languages, 'bog' is, instead, the root of the word for the divinity.
134. Fascism's notorious 'blackshirts', or Voluntary Militia for National Security (MVSN).

6. Rome I: Political upheaval, family matters

To Piero Sraffa

ROME, 3 JUNE 1924

Dearest friend[1]

I have been out of Rome for a few days and have not been able to write to you since I would not have been able to say anything definite regarding my stay here. I shall now be in Rome at least until 10 June; could you find a day to come and see me so that we may have some exchange of views? I am living at number 6, via Andrea Vesalio, and shall be at home near continuously over the next few days. It would however be as well that you wrote to me at the Chamber of Deputies to say when you are coming, and not use my address for letters.

Warmest greetings

Gr

Source: AAG; handwritten on Ordine Nuovo headed notepaper

To Giuseppina Marcias

ROME, 7 JUNE 1924

Dearest mother,

Your letter has arrived and I thank you for your kind words. I was very pleased to hear the news about how all of you are getting on – that father is working and his mind is at rest, that Carlo has found work, and that Teresina has persevered to become financially independent so that her marriage is now a freely-chosen union and not some family slavery.

I am quite happy with my present situation, with all the risks attached to it. I'm proud not to have changed anything in my line of conduct over the years and to always have been in the front line in defending the interests of the people who work and suffer. My partner shares my ideas completely. She is not Italian but for quite some time lived in Italy, while she was studying in Rome. She is called Giulia (Jul'ka in her language) and has a diploma from a music lycée.[2] She is brave, has a strong character, and I am sure that you will all appreciate and come to love her when you know her. Next summer or autumn I would like to come to Sardinia with her for a few days.

In the press I have sometimes read rather scanty news items about Ghilarza. I've seen that Nino Meloni has taken up the theatre, but have not been able to understand what his position is. I've seen Felle Toriggia mentioned as a big name in the town. What has become of Nessi? And what of Luigino Oppo, the ex-serviceman who lived near to Uncle Agostino's mill? And the family of Aunt Margherita, Igino, Giovannino, etc, what are they doing? Write to me about everyone, especially my closest friends, like Daniele Putzolu, so that I can form an idea of the current situation in the town.

I will try to get some precise news about Nannaro and persuade him to write. I am pleased that his daughter is well and has made herself well-liked.[3]

The tickets I have can be used just by direct relations (for Teresina but not for Paolo) and, since there are not many of them, it's best to use them for journeys that are longer than just Abbasanta-Cagliari.[4] I hope to be able to put them to use for you for a trip to Rome and would ask Carlo, who seems to me more decided than the rest, to find the best combination.

In a few days' time I shall have to go off out of Rome into the mountains to get over the last effects of nervous exhaustion. I will be away maybe for more than a month and will write to you from my new address.

A heart-felt embrace for everyone

Nino

Source: AAG; handwritten on Ordine Nuovo headed notepaper

To Jul'ka

22 JUNE 1924

My dearest Юлька

I have waited to be able to leave, with my departure being put back from day to day, and so I haven't written to you, thinking that I would have arrived before the letters. Will I leave, that is, will I be able to leave in a day or two's time? I don't know and therefore I want to write to you, so that you will feel me all the same near to you, my dear, so that you feel my love binding you close and tight.

The days that I have lived and am continuing to live through are unforgettable.[5] From the newspapers it is impossible to form an exact impression of what is happening in Italy. We have been walking over a smouldering volcano and suddenly, when no one was expecting it, especially not the fascists, who were totally sure of their own infinite power, the volcano erupted, shooting out an immense river of molten lava that has engulfed the whole country, sweeping away everyone and everything belonging to fascism. The events developed at lightning speed, totally unprecedented. From one day to the next, from one hour to the next, the situation was changing, every single part of the regime was shaken, fascism was being isolated in Italy and was feeling its isolation through the panic that struck its leaders, through the desertion of its rank-and-file. Work reached fever pitch; from hour to hour we had to give instructions, issue directives, attempt to give guidance to an overflowing popular torrent. Now the acute phase of the crisis is apparently over. Fascism is desperately trying to rally its forces which, however reduced in number, are continuing to dominate, because of support from the whole State apparatus and because of the conditions of incredible dispersion and disorganisation that the masses find themselves in. But our movement has taken a great step forward; the paper has trebled its print run and in many centres our comrades have taken over leadership of the masses and have tried to disarm the fascists. Our watchwords have been taken up enthusiastically and used time and again in the motions voted on in the factories; over the last few days I am convinced our Party has become a real mass Party. I have taken part in the meetings of all the parliamentary opposition groupings, which for public opinion have become the leading centre of the general movement. Grand words but no desire to put them into practice, with an incredible fear of us taking matters into our hands, and therefore manoeuvres to force us to abandon the meeting. How many experiences I've had over these few days! I've seen the face of the 'petty bourgeoisie' with all its typical class characteristics. Its most sickening part was constituted by the Populars and the reformists (not to speak of the maximalists, poor kaša eaters gone to the dogs);[6] the most likable were Amendola and General Bencivenga of the constitutional opposition who said that in principle they were in favour of armed struggle and (at least in words) disposed to put themselves under the orders of the communists if these latter showed themselves able to organise an army against fascism. A deputy of the social democrats (a Sicilian party uniting landowners and peasants) who is also a *Duke*, Colonna di Cesarò, one of Mussolini's ministers up to last March, claimed he was more revolutionary than I am because he was carrying out propaganda in favour of individual acts of terror against fascism.[7] Everyone, of course, was against the general strike that I proposed and against an appeal to the masses of the proletariat.[8]

The situation is still very acute. There has already been an attempted coup d'état by the extremist sectors of the fascists, thwarted by a huge concentration of soldiers and carabinieri, and bizarre rumours are flying around everywhere. Certainly over these next few days, something is going to happen that might even be a military coup. Politically the situation has not been resolved because the opposition parties do not want to return to Parliament before certain of the fascist leaders responsible for these events have been arrested. For this reason I shall still not be able to think of leaving for a number of days yet. But I will come all the same, so that in Moscow they will be informed of the real situation and the needs of our movement, which finds itself having to face up to immense tasks.

My dear, how many difficulties are blocking our happiness! But we will overcome them all, at the same time as carrying out our duty. How happy I would have been to have you here with me in these last few days; you would have helped, your caresses would have calmed my nerves and my continual headaches. We must resolve this situation of ours: you must come to a decision, just as soon as you are able to do, to come to Italy to be with me. I would have wished for news of your state of health in this period, just before the birth of our child, to be sure that you are well, that you are strong and that my delay has not unsettled you. How I would like to embrace you, Юлька, how I would like to hold you tight in my arms, so dear you are, and hold you for ever so long, so as to stroke your hair, kiss your eyes, feel myself as one with you. How happy we will be when we see each other again, a new life will begin for us, now that we have become stronger and better in these months of waiting and expectation. A kiss to you, my dearest one.

Gr

I have managed to get hold of your sister's address and will go to see her as soon as possible.[9]

Source: AAG

To Piero Sraffa

27 JUNE[10]

Dearest friend

I will wait for you at home, where I shall be until 8 o'clock.

Greetings

Gr

Source: AAG and also in the Sraffa archives at Trinity College, Cambridge; handwritten on Chamber of Deputies notepaper

---

To Vincenzo Bianco

30 JUNE 1924

Dearest Vincenzo,

I'm expecting a letter from you. The situation has stabilised but the break that has come about between the country and fascism is irreparable; fascism is in its death agonies.[11] Of course it can't be at all ruled out that there may be a last lash of its tail. But its fate is sealed. If the opposition parties weren't such a heap of cowards and weren't scared of the proletariat more than of fascism, by this time Mussolini would be miles away from government and a good number of his butchers in gaol. Our positions have improved enormously; from 20,000 *L'Unità* has jumped to 60,000; our slogan of a general strike has been adopted by lots of workers and has received favourable comments from the others. But there's still great disorganisation, which makes any action very difficult.

Let me know how you're getting on. Have you been to see comrade Schucht? Write to me to say whether she needs anything and what I can do. Tell me the tiniest details as far as you can. I'm really sorry I haven't been able to come, but my presence here was absolutely indispensable, given what the situation has been. The comrade is a communist and will have understood this, of that I'm sure. Tell me about her state of health and ask her when she'll be able to come to Rome, given that I can no longer come there, and tell me what I have to do to make everything easier.[12]

A fraternal embrace and greetings to all the friends

Gr

Source: AAG; handwritten on Chamber of Deputies notepaper

To Jul'ka

30 JUNE 1924

My dearest Юлька,

Have you received my letter of last week? I have thought a lot about you over these last few days. I've re-read a lot of your letters, going back in my thoughts to all the memories of our life together, from the first day I saw you at Serebrjanyj Bor when I didn't dare come into your room because you had intimidated me (really true – you had intimidated me and now I smile when I remember this impression), up to the day that you left on foot and I went with you up to the big road that crosses the forest and then I stayed there stock still for such a long time to watch you going off all alone, with your wayfarer's burden, off along the big road, towards the great and terrible world, and then, and then, all our love; today you are about to become a mother and our lives are bound up together even though we are far away from each other.

My dear, I have suffered a great deal over these last few days thinking about you and the fact that you are far away. I was working, but just because of that I was suffering, because in my mind I wanted you to be working alongside me, next to me. I can't manage any more to picture myself alone, I seem to be smaller and not to be able to do everything I would like – one part of my will is far away from me. And then, for over a month now, I haven't heard anything about your life. I know that you must have been expecting me, but what have you been thinking about and doing all this time, as well as waiting for me? I want you to tell me all the little details; there are so many things I'd like to do for you and the impossibility I find myself in makes me sad.

Maybe in a week's time I'll leave for Moscow. I'll be able to tell you something definite with the next post. The situation has stabilised but remains tense. It's such that it might take a sharp turn for the worse from one moment to the next. Within a week's time there will be a decision on whether it will be possible for me to leave. Write to me or send me news through Bianco. Will I be able to embrace you again only when you've become a good mummy or will it be possible to be near you when our baby is born? I love you so much, Юлька, and embrace you very, very tightly.

Gr

Source: AAG; on Chamber of Deputies notepaper

To Jul'ka

7 JULY 1924

Dearest one,

I have received your letter of 29 June, after nearly two months of enforced silence due to the uncertainty about my journey. I have been a little anxious about you, about your strength, about your health, objectively, not because I had doubts about your strength, I wish I could have been near you in this period, to share with you the happiness and emotions of having a child uniting us and recalling for us a brief moment of common intense joy.[13] You must now write to me anew every week, or at least send me your news through Bianco, who I hope has been to see you and given you two letters that I sent you last week and the week before. You must write a lot in your letters to me, tell me about your life, tell me when the baby will be born and whether there's some way I can help you. You must write to tell me what you have decided to do. It seems it has become impossible for me to come to Moscow for some time ahead; you, my dear, will have to come to Italy as soon as your health allows it. I'll come and meet you, maybe as far as Vienna, or at least as far as some station in the Venice region if it's not possible for me to go abroad. Who knows, maybe we'll be able to spend a few days together in Venice. You have to write to me about all these questions and give me your opinion on them and on the possibilities that you are mapping out for yourself. I cannot live far away from you, separate from you, dear Юлька, I won't be able to wait as long as an Enlarg[ed] Exec[utive] or the Sixth Congress; the only solution is, then, for you to come to Italy, to work with me, and in this coming period we'll need that, we'll need people who can work.

My life is proceeding fairly quietly, despite the general very turbulent situation. I'm living in one of the narrow little streets off the main one, the via Nomentana, in the house of a German family who do not know who I am. I am suffering a lot from the heat. I can move about the city and meet the comrades doing illegal work, because the police apparatus does not work, just like the other organs of the fascist State, sabotaged as it is by State officials. I don't know how long such a state of affairs can last. Events are forcing the Party into a very difficult apprenticeship, after three years of illegality and pure defence of the organisation. We have to move, carry out agitation, come out into the open; the comrades, unready for this unexpected jump, have been a little unsure of themselves. For me, after more than two years out of Italy, it's been a great lesson and a great experience, necessary so as to be able to feel safe in our work.

I await your news. Can you send me a photo of yourself and, as soon as possible, of our child too? Will you write to me if you need something, so that I'll be able to see to it? Will you tell me when we'll be able to see each other, and be happy together once more? When will I really feel your lips joined with mine and my hand caressing your hair? Dear Юлька, the memory of your caresses brings a fever on, brings on a feeling of great sadness and loneliness, does not allow me to appreciate the beauty of Rome. I would like to wander around with you, to see things together, to remember them together afterwards and, instead of that I shut myself up at home; it seems I've become a bear in its lair. Write to me, tell me when I'll see you again. Many, many kisses.

Gr

Source: AAG; Chamber of Deputies notepaper with, on a separate plain sheet, 'Comrade Julia Schucht' – 'Julia' written in that form – and Bianco's telephone number

---

To Jul'ka

14 JULY 1924

Dearest Юлька,

I haven't received any letter from you with today's courier. I don't know if the letters that I send through Bianco get through to you, because there's been no word from him. How are you? This is an ever-present question of mine to which I would like to have an answer each week, in this period when our baby is due. My imagination just will not stay calm but gallops off of its own accord and creates a whole series of pictures. How long will this uncertainty last? The world truly is great and terrible – it surrounds us on all sides with an immense great wall of space and time, against which we beat our head to no result. Through your strength and determination I remain just relatively calm. But how I would like to be near you, so that I would be the first to caress you after the birth, to feel with you all the sweetness of having created a new life, to make you forget the suffering you've gone through. Dear Юлька, write to me as soon as you possibly can, take this uncertainty away from me, make me feel your love. Lots of long, long kisses over the whole of your body, so dear to me.[14]

Gr

Source: AAG; on Chamber of Deputies notepaper

To Jul'ka

21 / VII. 1924

Dearest Юлька,

Your letter of 6-13 July has arrived, as has also one from Bianco, who tells me about you. I'm going through drab and depressed days. Events have coagulated in a jelly-like mass; an enormous amount of work is going on in the country among the masses of the population, among all classes, but results are being produced only molecularly, in a non-visible form, and all of that demands an enormous tension and effort to be understood, to be dominated. We can make really serious mistakes (and, unfortunately, we do so) even without wanting to, because the situation differs from region to region, and in order for it to be under control and channelled we would need a big Party, used to systematic work, with all its constituent elements able to respond to the stimuli arriving from the centre. The temperature is scorching and I'm again suffering from insomnia and weakness; thinking tires me, and work is reducing my nerves to shreds. There are so many things that I should do and which I can't manage to do. I think about you, about the sweetness of loving you, of knowing that you're near to me even though so far away; dear Юлька, even from afar your thought helps me to be stronger. But my life cannot become normal again while we are separated; my love for you is too much part of my personality for me to consider myself normal without your presence. Maybe what is adding to this is a little tiredness on my part, as well as the memory of the equilibrium that was created within me in the period we were happy together. But it also seems to me that this is right in general: it isn't possible to cut oneself into pieces and let only one section work at a time; life is unitary and each activity feeds off, is strengthened by the other; love strengthens the whole of life (isn't that so?), creates a balance, a greater intensity in the other passions and the other feelings. But I don't want to lay down doctrine. I would like to tell you about lots of episodes, lots of little things which would give you an impression of the situation and the actual moment that Italy is going through. I had lots of memories stored up to tell you, at first hand, when we're together, and I can't make up my mind whether to write them down since I think they'd just become insignificant and stupid. Maybe I'll try another time and begin it like a diary, starting from my entry into Italy, from my train journey from Tarvis [Tarvisio] to Milan by way of Venice; about my conversation with a fascist who wanted to annex to Italy Nice, Savoy, Malta and the Canton Ticino, and who I drove wild by playing the part of a Sardinian nationalist and proving scientifically that a fascist Italy would have lost Sardinia – the poor fellow didn't know how to reply to my arguments as a Sardinian fascist, and was desperately tying himself in knots trying to convince me that I was wrong. I really went to town at his expense. Then I listened in on the conversation that a silk factory owner from Schio was having with a landowner from Padua, which left me with a sinister feeling because of the strength and self-assuredness the two of them demonstrated. And then again an illegal Party conference, held under the guise of a trip to the mountains by employees of a firm from Milan:[15] the whole of the day passed in discussions about the various tendencies, on tactics and, then at meal time, in a mountain refuge full of hikers, fascist speeches, hymns to Mussolini, a general farcical affair so as not to give rise to suspicion and not to be disturbed in the meetings held in beautiful valleys, white-carpeted with daffodils. And then again and again, the flowering of red carnations on the chests of Roman workers the night the Party's call for a general strike started spreading; going back home towards midnight through the Porta Pia area, the whole quarter was swarming with workers, red carnations in their buttonholes, totally blocking the streets. There was an air of revolt in the outlying parts of the city, while in the centre the fascists were attempting to sow panic with their squads, bayonets at the ready, squads that disappeared whenever a company of soldiers arrived ready to fire. Just the same … it was rather sad for me to come back into Italy and straight away afterwards see the situation so improved, only hearing from others accounts of the impressions of the terror that had reigned during the most acute moments of fascism, knowing from the voices of others of the hunt by the fascists, who thought I was in Turin, and were chasing my shadow, and of the beatings and the bayonetings that my brother received, leaving him with a finger missing and half his blood shed, all on my account. I'm sure that they wouldn't have got me, but I would have liked to feel this emotion of being the prey, hunted down in rage and then escaping the impotent rage.

And now just look at me, living in a comfortable house on via Vesalio, a side-street off the via Nomentana, with a German family who don't yet know my exact name and don't know I'm a communist member of parliament. I put on a very serious professorial air, and they hold me in the greatest respect and, exasperatingly, leave me completely on my own.

How many things I'd like to tell you, but I'll tell you them when we're together, won't I? You'll have tears of laughter streaming down your face and I'll tell them, pausing every so often to give you a little kiss on your ear or the nape of your neck, to give you a hug, because I can't do without that, because for me it doesn't seem possible that we can be together without remembering every minute that we love each other so much, while at the same time we're serious people who are fighting and working and we have a child, too. My dearest Юлька I love you very much and embrace you closely and tightly.

Gr

Your sister is well. I haven't yet been able to speak with her because she's off at a spa somewhere. She's recently been unwell and was in the Bastianelli clinic at the hospital.[16] By the time I got to know her address and went to the hospital she was already better and had gone off to the spa, some told me in Pescara and some Tuscany. I'll send her the address as soon as I manage to track her down again; she's known at the Russian Embassy where I think she's registered herself as a citizen of the USSR (that is to say the SSSR).

Do you still remember that a long time ago I sent you, for you to correct, a translation of mine of Rjazanov's notes on the *Comm[unist] Manif[esto]*? I've heard nothing more either about the corrections or about the translation.

Publication of *L'O[rdine] N[uovo]* has been interrupted, but we'll start up again within days.

Source: AAG

To Jul'ka

4 / VIII. 924

Dearest one,

I've received your letter of 28 July and I think that by the time you receive this maybe your whole life will have changed. I'd like to write to you about lots of things, but already this last week I've torn up one letter in which I would have come over to you as having gone a bit soft in the head. But don't let that disturb you, nothing serious has happened. Sometimes, thinking about you and the happiness that, together, we could have shared, I start to feel rather sad, and I pass from the 'sentimental wolf' phase to the 'bear in its lair' phase. But the events I'm immersed in will make sure I get shaken out of this. The situation is clearer today and is getting ever clearer with every day that passes. In my view there are going to be some really big novelties. In October there's an anniversary for which already there's talk about guns going off, and everyone is in breathless expectation.[17] The fascists, in their death throes, are making one blunder after another, and it's probable that before October comes they're going to commit that of provoking a movement in order to then crush it. In any case, we've entered an active phase and I have the impression that it's the fascists who are going to be crushed, but … not to our immediate benefit; we're going through a stage of fanatical democraticism, a psychological reaction to three years of terror that is having its repercussions against us too, even though our Party is getting stronger and new members are joining our ranks by the day.

Then I want to say that I love you so very, very much. And I want to tell you that your expression 'shortly even you personally are not going to be alone', got me very annoyed as if I had not thought about that in my letters. You've shown yourself to be terribly selfish in your joy and it seemed to me you were giving my ears a good tweak. But I'll wait, I'll be able to wait, and when we're together, I'll decide to run off with the baby and stay with it by myself for just as long as you'll be alone with it. I want to force you to run after me like you once followed the famous beds along the lines of a famous picture of mine painted in prehistoric times or almost that, back in the age of the … mummies.[18]

What are you going to call the baby? Ottilija is what your father has suggested if it's a girl; I think it's better than Prudenziana, or Veneranda, or Cunegonda and so on.[19] And if it's a boy? You've thought about Ninel, but, when he grows up, is he really going to call himself Ninel? When he's got a beard for example? I can't suggest anything to you, because too many names are going through my mind; I've thought about Elio, meaning 'sun', or Delio, which again is also 'sun' in the form of Delian Apollo, or yet again … but no, I don't want to start a parade of names.[20] I think it would be good to have a name that's suitable for all ages of life, and not just for when a baby is tiny and nestling in mummy's arms. I always remember a friend of mine at university, with great heavy-framed glasses and the bushy moustache of a Hun, who was called … Amorino, since his mother had thought that he would always remain a graceful little baby.[21] I am convinced that our child will be really beautiful and become ever more so, because you are its mother, but I think the child is also one day going to be a serious person, even though he'll still remain something of a child, and is going to lead the revolution in Madagascar, since by then everything else will have been done in Europe, Asia and America. Don't you too think a revolutionary leader should have a solid-sounding first name, such as to make an impression on the Malagasies? You choose then; I put myself in your hands. And what about the surname? I don't know the soviet laws very well on this point. Do I have to make a written declaration to recognise the child or is a statement from you sufficient? The world is great and terrible, but I love you very much, indeed I love you both so very much and console myself by thinking that the day is going to come when I'll be able to embrace both of you so tightly. My dearest Юлька I love you and kiss you passionately.

Gr

Source: AAG; on Chamber of Deputies Notepaper

To Giuseppina Marcias (AAG; handwritten on Chamber of Deputies notepaper).

ROME, 15 / VIII – 24

Dearest mother,

Your last letter was waiting for me when I got back to Rome. For reasons of peace and calm I haven't been able to send you the address I've been staying at over the most recent period; I didn't want to be known and for that reason couldn't receive any correspondence.

In the letter I got the news of Teresina's wedding and send her my most affectionate good wishes. I would like to do something more but I don't know exactly what; I'd be glad if you can give me some suggestion that doesn't go beyond my financial means, which, as you can imagine, are not very great.

My child should be born any day now, but I still haven't received any news, given the distance that separates me from my comrade; I knew the doctors were expecting the birth any time between 8 and 15 August. I think everything has gone well and hope to have news by next week.

I have never met Uncle Cesare and don't know where he lives. I'm not going to seek him out either at his office or at home, even if I should happen to come upon his address. I still remember his fright when I looked him up in 1917, given that I was in Rome as witness in a political trial; he was afraid of being compromised and told me a pack of lies to make me believe that the police had gone to his house to find me, a story he'd completely invented out of fear. He knows I'm in Rome and that he can come and see me in Parliament; if he hasn't done so, that means he has his own good reasons, which I'm going to steer clear of discussing or putting to the test.

I haven't managed to have any news of Nannaro. The address that was left me by a common friend in London has got lost.[22] As soon as I can get back in contact with him, I'll ask him to contact you too. I think that the child, whom he has recognised, should be in your care officially. The threat her mother has made is of no consequence; she is not thinking of taking the child back with her at all, but just wants to use this as blackmail. I know her very well because of the amount of trouble she plagued me with in Turin. Before coming to me, whom she didn't know, she'd gone to the police headquarters to kick up a fuss, and the officers there thought she was a lover that I'd abandoned. That was the story given to the press. I don't know what she's doing now and how she's behaving.[23]

I am quite well and my life is proceeding peacefully. I am waiting for my comrade and our baby to be fit to undertake a long journey and then have them come to Italy, so as to be more at ease. I'm sorry to hear what you tell me about Grazietta. Give her lots of caresses from me, and ask her to write to me and send me a photograph if she has one. I would like to make a trip to see you in September; maybe it will be possible for me to decide on one.

Kisses to everyone. Tell Teresina and Paolo I'm expecting their news.

An embrace for you

Nino

Would it be possible to have some photographs of the Tirso basin?

Source: AAG; handwritten on Chamber of Deputies notepaper

To Jul'ka

18 / VIII. 924

Dearest Юлька,

I have received your letter of the 6th, on the eve of a new life for us. How I would like to be near you. While I'm writing perhaps our child has already been born, is already clinging to you and you are able to caress it, after the suffering of giving birth to him. My joy is tinged with sadness because of that. What a lot of things I cannot know but would like to know. But what does it matter to know them if I wasn't there to suffer alongside you? I seem to myself to be privileged because fate has left me precisely the thing which cannot but make me happy. But my love for you is too strong, too intense, and I feel I live so much as one with you that I cannot free myself of these oppressive phantoms. And my happiness has something of a long face and feels just a little sad.

There's lots of work to do, but the form the work takes is not the best for absorbing one's entire life and thoughts. Events are unfolding inexorably and meanwhile we have to reorganise the P[arty], which is weak and overall is working very badly. I am part of the central political leadership and am now general secretary.[24] I should also be editing the paper but I haven't got the physical energy for everything. I can still work only a little. You have to keep an eye on everything, follow everything. Tomorrow I leave for Milan and then for Turin to see how these, our biggest two organisations, are working. We are lacking in cadre workers, especially in Rome; from the meetings I take part in, I'm satisfied as regards the framework of good will and the enthusiasm of the comrades, but pessimistic as regards the lack of general preparation. The situation is very much in our favour; the opposition forces are organising a military movement and are arming ... our comrades. Fascism is falling to pieces and seems to have gone crazy, it cannot find even one political measure of any use to it. Everything is turning against it. But events are going to develop relatively slowly, because there are still too few of us and we're too badly organised.

Perhaps next week I won't be able to write to you because I'll be travelling. Write to me always or make me write. I want to know about every moment of your life and that of our child. I love you more and better than before. I would not know how to explain how I feel; maybe the new life that we are feeling means that at last we have become ourselves, since we've left behind lots of encumbrances of our previous life. We would have to be together to see things more clearly. How can our happiness be more intense? And yet I feel it will become more intense and more alive. I have written to my mother to tell her that we shall shortly have a child and she is anxious to have news about it. If you can send me photographs, send me two copies; certainly I will give my mother great joy since, like all Sardinians, she feels family ties in a quite violent and impassioned way.

My dear Юлька, you must feel my lips on your eyes, in your whole being you must feel yourself locked in a tight embrace, you must feel all my happiness in loving you, of being one with you in the joy of having created a new life.

Gr

I still have not managed to get the address of your sister, who must still be out of Rome. Her illness wasn't serious, since at the Bastianelli clinic, where I went to look for her, they do not take seriously ill patients, and your sister was there only for a short time. As soon as I can, I'll send her your address and ask her for news.

Source: AAG

To Giuseppina Marcias

ROME, 5 / IX. 924

Dearest mother,

I've been out of Rome for about a fortnight. I found your letter and the news of the birth of a son. He was born on August 10th and both he and his mother are doing well, because she was already writing to me on the morning of the 11th and again on the 18th. The baby weighed 3 kilos 600 grams, had lots of brown hair, the little head was well formed, the forehead was broad and he had very blue eyes – I'm copying this for you from the description of his mother's, who also adds, very poetically, that he seems to have been bathed by the sun like a fruit still on the tree. Already 25 days have passed since he was born and by now he must have grown. He's called Lev, which in Italian means Leone [Lion], rather exaggerated in my opinion for a baby who weighs only three and a half kilos and doesn't yet have even one tooth.[25] It's very hard for me to be so far away from my comrade at this time; I also think I'll have to postpone her visit here for some time since a rail journey of 5 days is very difficult with a baby only a few months old. In the meantime, she's staying with her family. As soon as possible, she'll send me a photograph of the baby which I'll send on to you, so you'll be able to see your new grandson, who, for the moment, at a distance of 3000 kilometres from Italy, is tormenting only his mummy, who is writing the craziest things about him. She's saying that he's sticking out his tongue just to annoy her, which to me seems rather exaggerated. Don't you think so too? But maybe all mothers see these miracles in their first child.

Greetings and kisses to everybody.

Nino

Source: AAG; handwritten on Chamber of Deputies notepaper

To Jul'ka

18 / IX. 924

Dearest Юлька,

I've now received your letter of 4/IX. The difficulty I have in writing to you is really oppressive. Why is this? Maybe I'm afraid of upsetting you, of involuntarily causing you some worry. I've made you cry so often, when I have been near to you, and able to tell you everything I wanted to tell you, being able to put misunderstandings right straight away; and I'm afraid of hurting you from afar, without realising it and without being able to correct myself. Now I think I might harm, not just you alone, but the two of you, and I've become more strangely timid. I'll get used to things, and you'll help me with your letters, won't you? At times, my mind is invaded by lots of sad thoughts. I'm thinking of all this long time that we've spent far away from each other, of the intensity of your life, and of my absence, so many times, from lots of things. The worst is that I don't see any solution at hand for this state of affairs, and it's going to be very difficult for quite a while for me to leave Italy, and, at the same time, I understand all the difficulties in your way for coming to Italy. Let's then wait for the unexpected to turn up.

Here I should work a lot, but I don't always manage to do everything I ought to. Up to a few days ago I was quite calm, I could move around with a certain ease, albeit with all due caution. Every week I was able to hold three or four meetings both with the leading organs of the P[arty] and with the local organisations of the comrades. These were very interesting meetings, especially the ones with the working-class masses. Conversations, discussions, information, problems to resolve, questions of principle and of organisation to sort out. There has been a huge shift towards our P[arty], and through the propaganda month, we've almost trebled our membership, the paper has grown by 120% as compared with three months ago, everyone is seeking out our literature; trade union organisations being rebuilt around our cells.[26] The reception our propaganda has found among the peasantry is amazing. Our agrarian section had had 2000 membership cards printed for a national peasants' defence association, but the province of Siena alone asked for 5000. Naturally this doesn't mean we're out of the woods yet. The P[arty] continues to be outlawed de facto, although not juridically; every time a meeting is discovered, it's broken up and the comrades arrested and kept in gaol for a few days. We have to be very cautious in our relations with comrades who work in the offices of the P[arty] to avoid the discovery, seizure and dispersion of the archives and documentation. Although I had first been left alone, after the fascist deputy Casalini was killed I was put under surveillance;[27] just at that time I was recognised by one of the Turin fascists, who pointed me out to a group of his friends. 'To defend me' the police began to follow me, that is they made it difficult for me to make any movement, which has forced me to spend money on taxis instead of travelling by tram when I have to go to some meeting. I can't write a heap of things to you since I don't trust the post; the experiences we're having in Italy are of very great interest and are posing new problems to be resolved one after another. In this current period, we're holding lots of provincial congresses which will give us a picture of our strength and of our fighting capacity. We shall thus be able to establish a concrete programme of work that is more precise and systematic than that followed up to now.

Have you gone back to work? How is your life organised now, under your new conditions? I think Bianco will have put the thumbscrews on you, a bit at my instigation. But why did you not want to accept the money that he had the job of giving you?[28] I don't think there's anything in that which goes against the principles and our norms of life; for me it would have been a great pleasure had you accepted it. I often think there's nothing I can do for us, for the child; yet I would like to do something. It seems to me that if I knew that in your lives my work had any importance of some kind, or helped to overcome some difficulty, I would be very happy; it would seem to me that some new bond had been created to unite us, to give the illusion that we were nearer to each other. For example, I've found the famous Marseille soap, but not a way of sending it off so it would arrive safely; I'll pick it up and send it off by ordinary post, hoping it will arrive.[29] This is something that has plunged me into real despair. Let's hope for the best.

You must always write to me at length and tell me lots of things, about every moment of your life. You'll have to be very frank in telling me what you intend to do. Don't be afraid to cause me displeasure. I too have become much stronger than I was some time ago. I want only to feel you joined together with me, with all your sincerity and your love. All the rest is just a matter of time. I'll think our happiness will be overflowing when we are able to see each other again. And that moment will indeed arrive. A close and tight embrace, my dearest one.

Gr

Source: AAG

To Vincenzo Bianco

[SEPTEMBER 1924]

Dearest Vincenzo,

This week I have not received letters from you and not even from comrade Schucht. It's best if you do not speak any more to the comrade, either about her coming to Italy or about money questions. I know that her family situation is very difficult and I don't want to cause any greater displeasure. What you've written to me about her father doesn't surprise me; I know he has become embittered about his situation and that for some time now he has been surly and obdurate.[30] There's no great seriousness in what he has told you, of that you can be sure; I manage to work quite a lot, even though the P[arty] is illegal, I can hold meetings, be in contact with the masses and so on. The limitations on my political activity are, more than anything else, those imposed by my physical weakness. If I were able, I could be continually on the move and have contact with comrades from all over Italy. In Rome I've held meetings with comrades and workers from all the different areas of the city. I was in Turin for only two days and held three meetings; in Turin however I'm very well-known and was immediately shadowed by … Bagnasco, who met me by pure chance in via Goito. In Milan I held at least 10 meetings.[31] As you can see, it isn't the impossibility of holding meetings that is holding back my work. As regards the other subject, the question is more difficult. Fulfilling my duties towards the child does not depend on me: I can't do anything other than send money, which is then refused. But that is a matter for me and my comrade more than for her father, don't you think?

The situation is very difficult and complicated. You say the opposition groups and fascism must end up in an armed conflict. But let's be clear on this. The opposition groups are carrying out a great manoeuvre to detach the king, in other words the army and the carabinieri, from fascism.[32] The opposition groups do not want a direct armed conflict, but rather want the army and the carabinieri to put the fascists in their place, in other words they want to overthrow fascism without popular intervention. They have been carrying out this plan so far without any great difficulty because the maximalists and the reformists belong to the opposition groups, and the majority of the workers, disorganised as they are, remain passive. Our task therefore cannot but be that of organising the masses and carrying out agitational activity, and in this field we have already had a lot of success. We must not however nurse any illusions: 1 – because as a whole the P[arty] is still working badly and moving sluggishly. 2 – because the situation is still clearly dominated by the fascists, by the army and by the carabinieri, that is to say by the armed bourgeois forces in their entirety, the basis of which has not been notably disorganised (once the first crisis had been overcome, over the last few months the fascists as an armed force have gained in relative strength). 3 – because the masses are terribly disorganised and think the opposition groups will be able to eliminate fascism without a bloody struggle. They want peace, they want calm, and any prospect of a new period of great struggle frightens them. The most active part of the population is still the urban petty bourgeoisie and especially the southern peasantry, whose orientation is clearly democratic.

Warm greetings

Gr

Source: AAG; handwritten on Chamber of Deputies notepaper; the internal evidence suggests the date of September 1924

To Jul'ka

6 / x. 924

My dearest,

Last week I was in Naples for the congress of the provincial federation and wasn't able to write to you. I'm truly sorry when I can't send you a letter and I have to overcome a mass of psychological barriers when I do decide to write. It seems to me, and I think you feel the same, that putting things on paper impoverishes all our feelings, that it acts as a reverse filter, muddying what was clear and transparent. That's why, you see, I can't think in concrete terms about our child. I think about children in general, about their weight, their weakness, the dangers they are in at any given moment, but I can't manage to think about our child living as an individual. Is this a failing on my part? I don't know. I think of you, but I imagine you as you were when I left you; you must have changed in the intervening period. I feel there's been a development in you, but I am here on this side of the wall, and the wall is stopping me from seeing things concretely. I don't want to torment you, there is a great feeling of calmness in me, but I can't avoid thinking of these things. Why is it that I wanted Bianco to go and give you something on my behalf? I wasn't thinking about anything of what you had written to me; the mention of the rights of man and of woman was a joking one.[33] I thought only of this, that I would be happy to know that something of your life and that of the child was due to me; that it was due – just think of this – to the fascist State that pays my wage as a parliamentary deputy, and represented a small sacrifice on my part, let's say a packet of cigarettes or one coffee less. Why is this? I think it's a memory of my childhood, bound up with material sufferings and hardships, overcome with my mother and brothers and sisters, hardships which bound us together, which created bonds of solidarity and affection that nothing will ever be able to destroy. Do you think that the best of communist society will be able to fundamentally modify these conditions of individual relationships? For quite a time yet it certainly won't. And in my view these feelings are exactly those of the exploited classes, not those of the bourgeoisie – those of the classes for whom oppression comes out precisely through an instability of life, through insecurity regarding bread, clothing, a roof over the heads of the children and the old folk. You think that, because you live in a sovietist State, that gives you a cast-iron guarantee, but at the same time you have to admit that even in a sovietist State these conditions still exist for a great many people, and then and then … You know, I really wanted to get you angry. When you described to me the scene of the babies, all crying inside a great wagon, then being given out to their mothers who have to feed them, the scene seemed so vivid to me that I thought of getting you angry by writing to you that maybe each time they give the mothers a different baby, given that sovietist discipline is not so perfect as to ensure that the conscientiousness of the hospital njani [paediatric nurses] is really above reproach.[34] I then thought better of it, not wanting to inflict this bout of anger on you, after reading what you wrote about the sovietist laws that defend the rights of the child regarding the care taken by the whole of society, not only that of the father, the mother etc. You know that this seems to me to be Rousseau rather than Lenin? In saying that, I'm stirring up your anger just the same …

But why am I making you angry? Just because I love you so very much. You know, this makes me think of a famous night we spent together in Serebrjanyj Bor. Do you remember? You had just got back from Moscow, I think, and they'd put other beds in your room, and somebody else was already asleep there when we went into the pavilion. Do you remember? You stayed in my room; first of all I showed you the owls haranguing each other on the veranda, then we talked about all manner of general things, but especially a line of Dante's: 'Love, that exempts no one beloved from loving'.[35] Then we had to sleep and there was only one bed, so at that point, cynically, I made you cry. I made you cry on purpose out of callousness; I loved you very much and I wanted to kiss your eyes, but I didn't believe that you could love me, so then I wanted to hurt you, just because I was being so bad. Do you remember? You lay down in my bed and neither of us slept a wink, but in the morning you got up as quietly as you could so as not to wake me and I let you do so, I let you do everything right to the moment when you were gently opening the door, and then I made you angry, but I wanted to hold you closely and tightly. I remember all the details, because it seems to me that that night was so important for us and that for too long afterwards we were playing a game of blind man's buff with each other. Well! Sometimes that makes me suffer; the memory of all these little but great things, while you are so far off and I can't embrace you, I can't feel your body near to me so as to be able to caress all of it, to feel you as one with me. But we shall see each other again and we'll be so happy. It's just such a pity that I have not been able to share with you the anxieties and the joys of the first moments of our baby's life, and that will always be something missing from my life. I love you so much, Юлька.

Gr

I've carried on looking for your sister Tat'jana and I think I saw her once on a tram, it was certainly a lady who looked very much like you. I found out the other day that she is teaching in a private school in via Savoia, but I still haven't managed to find this street, which is a new one. Next week I think I'll finally be able to tell you something precise.

Source: AAG

To Jul'ka

10 / XI. 924

My dearest one,

I've been back from Sardinia for three days and found two of your letters waiting for me.[36] I would need to write a whole volume to give you all my impressions of the last few days. Events are developing headlong and yet they are so unpredictable and immature in form that, to give them a reading that can be understood by someone who does not live in Italy and is not immersed in the situation, one would need a systematic treatment of the psychology of fascism, the acute phase of a bourgeois civilisation in galloping decomposition when the proletariat still is not sufficiently organised for taking power. Demoralisation, cowardice, corruption, criminality are taking on unheard-of dimensions; youngsters and idiots find they are the political expression of the situation and break down into tears or are driven mad under the weight of the historical responsibility that all at once they are weighed down with as ambitious, irresponsible amateurs. Tragedy is alternating with farce on the stage, with no connection between them, and disorder is reaching levels that once seemed beyond the wildest imagination. I sometimes think that I too am like a straw in this historical hurricane, but I have enough strength to maintain all possible composure and do whatever I think duty requires. At moments like this I think of you, of the greater force I would have if you were near to me and of the sweetness that will infuse new strength into all my vital energies when, despite everything, I manage to see you again and to be happy in your love. I no longer find it possible to imagine your life. I think of you as rather isolated from the world around you, near to our child, but can't imagine what you do, which it seems to me ought to be different in practical terms from the similar things that all mothers do with their babies. I don't know why but it seems to me that, externally, in the gesture of your caress, in the faint smile on your face, in the way you hold your head, there must be something different when you draw close to the child as compared with everything I know of you, of what has remained in my blood, in my nerves, of what has become an essential part of my life. My dear, maybe I'm not able to imagine myself as a father, maybe that depends on all this. In my village I played a lot with my four-year-old niece; since she was afraid of some boiled crabs, I got her to act out a story I invented where there were 530 bad crabs, under the command of their general, Soupchewer, aided by his brilliant general staff (schoolmistress Leech, schoolmaster Beetle, Captain Bluebeard and so on) and a small group of good crabs, Coltsfoot, Clatter, Whitebeard, Blackbeard and so on. The baddies pinched her legs using my hands, while the goodies arrived on their tricycles armed with skewers and brooms to defend her; the chuff-chuff of the trikes alternated with the knocks of the broom handles, with my ventriloquist's dialogue, and the whole house was filled with a mass of crabs hithering and thithering, to the absolute amazement of the child, who believed everything and really entered into the story, inventing new episodes and new and funny comments of her own. I lived again something of my own childhood and enjoyed myself for three whole days, more in that way than in receiving visits from the village notables, including the fascist ones, who came to pay their respects in great solemnity and pomp, congratulating me on being … a parliamentary deputy even if a communist one. The Sardinians pay due honour … eh! Onward together! Onward Sardinia![37] Sheer enjoyment, no doubt about it. But as well as these, there came along the members of the local self-help Society of the artisans, workers and peasants, dragging along with them their President, who did not really want to jeopardise the Association's political neutrality, and all asking lots of questions: on Russia, on how the soviets work, on communism, on the meaning of capital and capitalists, on our tactics towards fascism etc. This meeting was very interesting because, while it gave me a measure of the widespread prejudices, of the backwardness of the Italian village, it also gave me a demonstration of the refusal to put up with things as they are, of the immense force of attraction of Russia. 'We all want to be Russians' they were saying, even the president with much humming and hawing finally ended up by agreeing. When I manage to get my thoughts in order I'll write to you with some typical episodes of the life I found: I'm up to my neck in various tasks and am able to snatch only a moment from my comings and goings between one end of Rome and the other. There's a comrade who is leaving in a few days' time and he'll take with him some Marseille soap for you (I sent you some by parcel post and I sent some more with someone making the trip); he'll also bring with him a Sardinian bonnet for you, from the village of Desulo, which to my mind demonstrates some strange relationships between the Kyrgyz and the hill people of the Barbagia (Barbagia = Barbaries). A warm and tight embrace, my dear.

Gr

Source: AAG; on Chamber of Deputies notepaper

To Vincenzo Bianco

25 / XI. 924

Dearest Vincenzo

Marco must by now have arrived over there. I've spoken with him about the question of the emperor.[38] I'm sure he will try to put things right as far as is possible.

Also through Marco you'll be able to have detailed news of how the P[arty] is working. We have reached about 30,000 members, excluding emigrants; we can say that, from the organisational point of view, we have regained what we lost after '22. Politically we have made great advances. My impression is as follows. The overall policy of the P[arty], as carried forward by the C[entral] C[ommittee], has earned us a lot of support, but this support remains a state of mind and is not being converted into concrete political activity. Why is this? The intermediate bodies, federations and city branches, are not yet functioning as would be desirable, even though great progress has been made in this field too; there is a widespread passive mentality of 'waiting for orders', namely the ultra-leftist conception that the P[arty] serves only for direct action and, while waiting for the great day, as a mass it has nothing to do but wait.[39] Thus the fruits produced by the overall policy are not stored up at a local level, and the great mass continues to remain spiritually disorganised. The active and skilled elements are few in number; they have to work at the Party centre, on the newspaper, and have to continually break away from the periphery in order to help and extend the work of the various organisations. The old guard has emigrated, as you well know; the yields are scanty and unorganised; the lack of financial means does not allow us to put a satisfactory organisational plan into effect. It's a patient and tiring period, so the success obtained from time to time is all the more marvellous, as for example when a meeting of 4000 workers in Milan was dominated by enthusiastic cries of 'Long live the C[ommunist] P[arty]'. The shortcomings that you note are exact; on *L'Unità* the only old journalists are Leonetti and Amoretti; the others are comrades still being trained, still undergoing their schooling. We consider these shortcomings with great dispassion; I can tell you that there has never been an Exec[utive] that has worked, and that is making comrades work, as much as the present one, one that studies everything, right down to the small problems of the various local organisations, trying to advise comrades, to spur them on with letters and circulars, with visits and inspections, sending capable cadres to the spot.[40] All this has already borne fruit from the point of view of tendencies, with a reduction of the left's influence and a strengthening of the authority of the C[entral] C[ommittee] and the Int[ernational]. Even in Naples the workers are beginning to criticise Amadeo, not at all for his personal position but for his overall political conception. In short, we have worked and worked quite well too. You know me and you know I'm not given over to facile enthusiasm: I just observe that the P[arty] in its entirety is more respected and appreciated by everyone, even by its most strenuous opponents; it comes over as a serious force that is developing relentlessly. Once again, we are of the opinion that it can take power earlier than we thought.

I'm sorry to know that your health is not good. I think it would be a mistake for you to leave M[oscow] without having a sure and precise task. I've seen before how adventures of this type have ended up.

The celebrations for November 7 at comrade Schucht's made me smile rather than laugh. Dear Bianco, do you maybe think that men can change as quickly as you want? I think moreover that in Marabini and Peluso there is a basic sincerity and friendship towards me such that cannot make me laugh. I would have been happy if Delio had done a big wee-wee on them, which would have made the party even better.

A fraternal embrace

Gr

Source: AAG; on Chamber of Deputies notepaper

To Jul'ka

26 / XI. 924

Dearest one,

I have had no word from you for nearly a month. I had to leave Rome just when the post was due so I missed a letter. In a few days' time I'll be leaving for Milan where I'll be for at least a fortnight. We are working hard. Politically, the situation for the moment means our activity is necessarily detailed but, when taken in its entirety, gigantic. The proletariat is re-awakening and regaining consciousness of its force; still greater is the reawakening among the peasantry, whose economic situation is frightful; mass organisation is however still difficult and the Party in its overall cell and village group structure is slow in moving and working. The P[arty] centre has constantly to intervene in the various places, spur on and check the work done, aid the comrades, get them moving in the right direction, work alongside them. We've become very strong, we've managed to hold mass meetings outside factories with 4000 workers present, all shouting their support for the Party and the International. The fascists no longer instil fear as they once did; already it's been the case that, after a public meeting, the mass goes off and besieges the house of some leading fascist. The bourgeoisie is in disarray and no longer able to give itself a government in which it has confidence; it has to cling on desperately to fascism; the opposition groups are languishing and are really just working to obtain greater respect of legal forms from Mussolini.

I have received a letter from a group of Italian comrades who wanted to celebrate the anniversary of the November Revolution with you. The letter had a certain air of solemnity that amused me; furthermore it was undoubtedly sincere. I would like to know from you how the celebrations went, and would be really satisfied if, to show his joy, the baby had left some trace on the celebrators. I don't think in saying this I'm at all offending the dignity of the little one or doing wrong to the good manners that you have tried to inflict on him. Have you finally received the real Marseille soap? A packet was taken there by comrade Elanskij who was here as 2nd secretary at the Emb[assy]. Bianco could be given the job of finding it if it has got lost. Another packet has been brought by an Italian comrade who by this time should have arrived. A third packet was sent on by parcel post. I would like to do something for you, not 'to help you' but to feel myself closer to you, to feel myself thoroughly part of your life.[41] This thought assails me and I feel it physically. Already a year has passed with us far apart from each other. How long this has been! We've fashioned ourselves better in this intervening period, but at what a price. I'm waiting for the spring; I have the impression that, one way or another, *we must* see each other again. But I force myself not to think too much about this possibility, so that the torment won't afflict me and wear out my nerves. I don't know how to measure my love for you: it seems different from what it was a year ago. I can't imagine the impression that I will feel in seeing the baby actually alive and real and not some slight impression on photographic paper. I think of these things thanks to your letters and your feelings, but reality has to be something else, deeper and more beautiful.

Write to me always, even if some weeks I will not be able to write to you. That is essential for my life. A very close and tight embrace, my dear.

Gr

Source: AAG; on Chamber of Deputies notepaper

To Jul'ka

20 / XII. 924

Dearest Юлька,

I haven't had any news from you for more than a month. Why is this? Does it depend just on the disorganisation of the services, which has got worse in the last few weeks, or are there other reasons? I need your news like I need the air I breathe, especially over this most recent period when I'm ever more tormented by the thought that maybe in a short while I'll be seeing you again.[42] I would like to know if you need anything. Bianco hasn't written to me either, after in his last letter he said he'd found you rather down in health. Why then haven't you written to me? Lots of things go through my mind and I am assailed by doubts and fears. When we're together I'll be able to explain to you all the phases of my life in relation to my love for you. Just think: maybe in a month and a half we'll see each other again, and how much we'll have changed; will I be able to poke my tongue out at you again? But meanwhile I don't have any news from you and that saddens me. The thought that maybe in a short while I'll be seeing you isn't enough, and this thought is embittered by strange doubts and fears that I can't in any way get rid of. They're like a chain round my head, stopping me thinking about anything else.

A tight and close embrace, любимая [ljubimaja: darling]

Gr

Source: AAG

To Mauro Scoccimarro

5 JANUARY 1925

Dearest friend

Just a couple of words at the last moment. The situation is deteriorating.[43] Ottavio has been arrested. Felice and Romano are wanted by the police. The government is hunting for any potentially scandal-producing documents. *Italia Libera* has been dissolved. There is talk of our P[arty] being dissolved.[44] We still have no news from Milan about the *U[nità]* journalists. We already had news of these measures and everything had been got ready. Benito wanted to dissolve the Chamber or at least close the session so as to arrest a number of deputies. It's said that the Crown denied its permission. A purely fascist cabinet will be formed through the withdrawal of Salandra and the Casati-Sarrocchi resignation.[45] The situation cannot last for long. Opinion is on our side. In the country things are increasingly being set fire to and there are assassination attempts. The opposition groups are panic-stricken: there is talk of the Committee dissolving itself; this would be suicide. I think that the situation, although extremely serious, will still not end up in a head-to-head clash; the government has an impressive military apparatus and the Militia has reared its head again in no uncertain terms: the great masses are not moving, since the government has forced a crisis because it wants to have these scandal-producing documents back, and therefore perception of the gravity of the crisis is limited to restricted circles. Of course an assassination attempt or some chance conflict may precipitate everything. We are working to gather all the fruits of the situation and possibly to broaden the movement through mass action.

An embrace

Antonio

Source: AAG; other copies in APC 513-1-309/5-6 and the Comintern Archive 513-1-309/4-4a; handwritten

---

To Jul'ka

12 / 1 . 925

Dearest Юлька,

A couple of hurried words. I haven't had any news from you for several weeks and I don't know if that depends on general reasons or on your state of health. Bianco had written to me, saying you were not very well, and this got me worried. I am living through a very intense period because of the continual succession of events, which however are not such as to lead us to foresee a very early end to fascism as a regime except as a government. I ought to come over there, but will events let me? For the moment, I think so. In Italy we are living through a stage that in my view has not happened in any other country, a totally unpredictable situation – since fascism has succeeded in its task of destroying all the organisations and thus all the means by which the masses can express their will – and a situation that has shown itself clearly to the great majority.

At this moment I'm seeing Stučevskij who is leaving tomorrow or the day after and will be able to bring you a letter and something else.[46] I embrace you

Gr

Source: AAG; on Chamber of Deputies notepaper

To Jul'ka

2 / II. 925

Dearest Юлька,

I haven't had any news from you, either directly or from Bianco, for a number of weeks. In a few days (towards the 10th) I'll be setting off, if I can get all the necessary documents, and I'll be there towards the 20th of February. I hope to find you and the little one both well.

I have met your sister Tat'jana. We spent yesterday together from four in the afternoon to nearly midnight; we talked of lots of things, of politics, of her life here in Rome, of her job possibilities. We also went to eat together and no wonder she's so weak. She eats so little, even though she doesn't have any type of illness, and, rather, can be said – and appear – to be the picture of health. I think we've already become firm friends. Before I go, we'll talk again at length (we live very close, only a couple of hundred yards from each other); she's promised to tell me about all her various adventures so that I can then tell you in person. I really think you can rest assured about her health and her general conditions of life. I'm very happy to have made her acquaintance, because she resembles you very much, because politically she is much closer to us than I was given to believe. The first time that I went to look her up, in her absence I had to undergo a long interview with Mr Isaac Schreider, SR, a lugubrious fellow entrenched behind the preconceived idea that nothing of any good can exist in Russia.[47] For him the revolution cannot be anything other than a coming together of fine intellects and, from that point of view, historically the communists are losers in that they cannot put into the field anyone that matches Mikhajlovskij. This too is a point of view … Your sister has only the exception of the freedom of the press denied to the 'SRs', and the tribulations that a certain Izmailija (I think) and Spiridonova have to suffer in some prison: she would like to work for the Soviets, but they've made her believe that the Soviet representatives in Rome are all corrupt rogues and she wouldn't want to have anything in common with them. She wouldn't want anyone to believe that by working with them she wants to enjoy the benefits of the Revolution without having undergone the sacrifices. Your sister is very likeable however, and has nothing in common with the SR gravediggers such as Isaac Schreider. In Russia she would be an exceptional worker, understanding all the necessities of the struggle. I've given her one of the little photos of Delio that you sent me, a photo with a woman in the background that could be you, although a number of doubts may arise on that score. She's said that you've changed a lot, but I said it could be one of those games that you get children to play at like 'Look for the hunter and look for the hare', and it might be that the hunter was yet another person still more invisible.

I'd like to write to you about lots of other things but I'm rather tired. For a few days I've been suffering from neuralgia and, through that, from insomnia: my mind is confused and my head feels like lead. And yet you're being naughty and not writing to me, you're not telling me anything about either yourself or the baby. I'm certainly a very bad father, but I hope your sister is going to give me some good advice. What can I bring from Italy for the little one? It has to be within the limits of my few pieces of luggage and must be really appropriate. Left to myself, I'd be like that old woman who, with her house on fire and wanting to save what was dearest to her, couldn't decide and, in the end, managed to get herself to safety along with the fire tongs. Anyway, we'll see.

A firm and strong kiss, любимая [ljubimaja: darling], in the expectation, in a matter of days, of seeing you again actually living beside me.

Gr

Source: AAG; on Chamber of Deputies notepaper

To Jul'ka

7 / II. 925[48]

My dear,

My trip has been put back again by a fortnight, but now, it seems, it is certainly on. They're even going to give me a normal passport – a small consolation for having had to wait.[49] I think however I'm already going to find some herald of spring; who knows whether we may have the joy of a bonfire in the snow and at the same time a meadow bursting into flower. Will we be able to go out for walks at the end of March or beginning of April? I've forgotten when the seasons start and just remember events outside their time reference, so I can't actually envisage the sequence for myself.

You know, your sister Tat'jana is already giving me a foretaste of your presence: she's very much like you in some ways and certain of her movements. The intonation of her voice is an echo of your voice (she'd be happy if she knew I'd written 'echo', because once she almost got offended at the thought that her voice could be compared to yours, which she says is extremely beautiful). I often go to see her and she's often come with me to some trattoria or other in Rome, but I've managed to get her to eat only just a little more than usual. I've had a lot of practical advice from her on what may be useful and at the same time lovely. She's found a dress model that can be made up in half an hour, a record for dresses in the communist regime, I think. I don't know if you know it, but for me it's a marvel, and I think its introduction into Russia will mark a new era in the art of sovietist clothing. She's wanted me to bring you some light shoes with a certain Nep-type heel which have terrorised me.[50] I've put up a strenuous resistance, arguing that you would never wear such horrors. I don't know if I'll manage to get across the sovietist frontiers with a suitcase of such assortments. I've got a vague fear that it's going to end badly, with doubts being raised as to my social identity.

And then, and then, I'm going to see the baby. I don't want to pause over that because it is disturbing me in a strange way and destroying all the memories of the past without helping me to create new images. I've already found a colour print of the cherubs of Correggio; I'd also got hold of some mandarin oranges but I ate them myself, given that they would have gone bad during the wait. Maybe the baby will put his toes in his mouth for the first time when I'm there to see it? That really would be really lovely. Tat'jana wants to buy some little shoes for him too; that sister of yours really is an awful woman, with her mania for shoeing the whole world.

I'll have to write you another letter before setting off. How badly this work is organised, though. You always have to put your own hopes off to a later date, writing instead of seeing, instead of kissing so firmly and strongly the one you love so dearly. But …

Gr

Source: AAG; on Chamber of Deputies notepaper

To Christophe (Jules Humbert-Droz)

25.4 [1925][51]

Dear comrade,

We found on our return a situation that has changed very unfavourably for us, not from the point of view of our influence over the masses, but because of the greater difficulties that, on the one hand, the government and, on the other, the General Confederation of Labour are creating for our work.

The Confederation has declared any initiative we undertake in its regard among the masses to be illegal, in that it cannot but have its reflection in the trade union organisation, or insofar as the comrades who assert such an action or attempt to undertake it are in the unions. This is then a ban, under threat of expulsion, on factory congresses, a ban on taking part in the elections for the internal commissions and so on. These threats have been successful among a number of groups of comrades, causing a tendency toward passivity in some and in others a conviction that a split is inevitable and so, in that case, one might as well work towards that. We are putting up a resistance to both tendencies. We have however had to take some action that is serious as regards formal trade union discipline. We put forward Communist candidates in the elections for the internal commission at FIAT in Turin, despite the Confederation's ban. And we did well: the workers gave us a majority. It is probable that this will give the Confederation leaders food for thought, by demonstrating that any split would not be completely to our disadvantage, since by now we have established a broad base. If we had given in without reacting, I think the Confederation leadership, believing we were weaker, would have put yet more pressure on us, putting us in an even more serious situation.

The government is undertaking systematic activity to uncover our organisation. The new law against organisations will be a dreadful instrument of persecution against us. We are studying what the most appropriate measures are that will allow us to maintain some minimal degree of legality and, at the same time, a mass organisation.

The opposition groups are in disarray. We must have a whole complex plan ready to hasten the detachment of the masses from their influence. With the next post I will give you a more detailed report on the situation and the possibilities it offers us.

Communist greetings

Gramsci

Source: Handwritten on Chamber of Deputies notepaper, published in J. Humbert-Droz, Il contrasto tra l'Internazionale e il P.C.I. 1922-1928, Feltrinelli: Milano 1969, p237

To Jul'ka

25 / V

Dearest one,

I have found again the letter that I wrote to you as soon as I arrived back in Italy.[52] But I'm not sending it to you, because for me it has lost all significance. It was just a nondescript, drab little letter about the slight problems experienced – nothing of any importance. However, at the frontier, they seized your translation of Stalin's speech, with the promise that it would be returned after it had been examined, but I don't think they are going to give it back.

Work is proceeding in a disorderly and unconnected way, which reflects on my state of mind, already disordered enough. Difficulties are multiplying and now we have a law on (against) organisations, which is a prelude to a whole systematic action by the police aimed at breaking up our Party. I made my parliamentary debut on this law.[53] The fascists reserved special treatment for me and, from the revolutionary viewpoint, I therefore got off to an unsuccessful start.

Because my voice does not carry, they gathered around me in order to hear me, and they let me say what I wanted, interrupting me only in order to drive me off the point, but with no attempt at sabotage. I was amused to hear what they said, but I couldn't restrain myself from replying and thus fell into their trap, because I got tired and could no longer manage to follow the lines that I'd thought of giving my speech.

In this situation, I feel even more strongly your absence and that of Delio. I seem to be shipwrecked, at the mercy of the waves. I see now, more vividly, lots of difficulties that before I was only aware of at the intellectual, intuitive level, and I feel despairingly insufficient. Yours and Delio's news are a consolation for me, but they increase my general state of perturbation. I don't want to hide any of my feelings from you, but at the same time I can't bring myself to tell you everything I would like to.

Tat'jana is well, better than when I left. She told me she's considering having you come to Italy with Delio and Ženja. I'm left without any will on this subject, because just thinking of it and studying the difficulties tires me out a lot. I feel that I love you a great deal, more than before, certainly, because I can think of you as a mother, and I can see you in flesh and blood with our child.

A close and tight embrace,
my dear

Gr

Source: AAG; on Chamber of Deputies notepaper

To Jul'ka

I – VI. 925

Dearest one,

I have received your letter of 10-21/V and I don't know if you have received two letters of mine that have already been sent. I think there's been some disorder and confusion lately, as much for me as for you, in the mail deliveries.

On the surface my life is going on calmly and there are no great dramatic scenes. Events are however moving on relentlessly and all one's attention has to be fixed on them in order to follow them, understand them and attempt to guide them. Nationwide, the effective social forces are ever more lined up, either with the fascists or with us; the centre parties are dying a slow death. The crisis is involving everyone. Already in some intellectual circles, where it seemed we could in no way get a hearing, voices demanding a united front with the revolutionary workers are beginning to make themselves heard. We are making ever more marked progress in the organisation of the working class. We thus find ourselves ever closer to a series of decisive points: 1) the threat by the reformists – who do not want to allow us any public demonstration that it is we who are the relatively stronger working-class party – to arrive at a split in the trade union movement; 2) the threat by the fascists to break our ribs, for the same reason; 3) internal work by the Party's extreme left to create fractionalism.[54] We are too strong not to have initiatives that lead to our forces coming into the open, and still too weak to be able to sustain a head-on collision.

The apparent calm is therefore shot through with anxiety and continual tensions. And I am alone my dear … Over and above everything else I feel my loneliness, even in the illegal organisation of the P[arty], which means one has to carry on individual and independent work. I try to escape from this purely political desert by frequent visits to Tat'jana, who reminds me of you. But in no way can this make up for your absence. All the scenes that in the world around me pass before my eyes remind me of you and Delio and make my unhappiness even more acute. And, furthermore, I can't dive into P[arty] work as much as necessary, or as I would like. The heat here is beginning to make itself felt and is knocking me out, once again giving me chronic insomnia. But that doesn't matter … I'll get over everything, because I'm sure you'll come to Italy and it will be possible for all our forces to expand, for our entire personality to assert itself, for us to see together Delio's life developing. A close and tight embrace, my dear, together with our baby.

Gr

Source: AAG; in pencil on Chamber of Deputies notepaper

To Jul'ka

22 / VI. 925

Dearest one,

I have received your two letters and the photograph. I'm expecting a photo of Delio. This week too, I haven't found the right moment to write to you at length, summing up my thoughts in my love for you, putting them in order around the feelings that the memory of you brings to life. My life is lived in the expectation of you, interrupted by the practical activity that absorbs me. The internal struggles within our Party against Bord[iga] are beginning, struggles that do not seem difficult in themselves, but in the given situation they require a great sense of responsibility. How much calmer and more peaceful I would be if I had you near me, if during the struggle I could rest and once again temper myself in your love. My dear, I love you very, very much. A close and tight embrace for you and Delio.

Gr

Source: AAG

Gramsci to Zinov'ev

25 JUNE 1925

In fact no ban exists. Possible to consider exclusion from the party of Girone, demonstrated to have gone beyond all limits in [his] speeches against the Party. Permission for free discussion not needed. First of all submission to Ispolkom decision [is] needed.[55] Request for suspending disciplinary action implies discredit of authority of Party C[entral] C[ommittee]

Gramsci

Source: AAG; 25 June is the date on which the telegram, in its typed-up Russian translation, was sent to Zinov'ev; the name 'Girone' was added by hand in Cyrillic

To Jul'ka

12 / VII. 1925

Dearest Юлька,

I have been away from Rome and lost two opportunities of writing to you. I've travelled and been to Venice and Trieste to discuss with the comrades up there the Party's internal situation, which is very good, better in absolute terms than I myself thought. At the Congress, we shall have an overwhelming majority; the Party is much more Bolshevik than might have been supposed and has reacted very strongly against the fractional activity of the Bordiga extremists. Our political line has already won out within the Party, in that the extremist tendency has disintegrated and the majority of its responsible elements have gone over to the theses of the International, and it has also triumphed amongst the working masses, insofar as our Party has acquired great influence and is even directing the masses of the other parties from the outside.

I have received your latest letters, which have rather worried me. I don't know how to reply to you; the only possible reply would be for us to be near each other, experiencing together the feelings that are troubling us, seeing together how our child is developing, how he is wholly ours even in his tiniest movements. Don't you think so? I know from T[at'jana] that you are not too well, that you tire yourself out too much; I've also heard from T[at'jana] about the progress Delio is making in talking and moving around. You write to me saying that you always find yourself with very little time; I feel my love for you and your love for me and that is enough for me, or rather I try to make it enough. But it isn't sufficient for me. I seem to be growing older quickly, today to be more tired, if not physically like before, then in a different and more depressing way than before. I miss your company next to me. I feel that sometimes without our realising it we could find ourselves far away from each other and I could find myself far away even from my child. You see, even I sometimes fall into these Matilde Serao-type states of mind! Write to me more at length, if that is possible, and make me feel your love and the life of Delio from closer up.

A strong and tight embrace

Gr

Source: AAG

To Zinov'ev from Gramsci and Humbert-Droz

13/VII-25

Peremptory telegram to presidium has brought results. From last information Liaison Committee has announced its dissolution in writing to C[entral] C[ommittee].[56] Date of convening congress not yet fixed. Opposition's links with abroad obvious. Internal state of the Party good.

Christophe. Gramsci.

Source: AAG; telegram in Russian translation

To Zinov'ev

28-VII-1925

Dear comrade Zinov'ev,

I have received your letter with some delay and have had to delay even further the reply since, over the last few days, I have been forced to go off on urgent Party business.

The Party's internal situation is fairly good. The attempt at fractional activity by Bordiga has not succeeded in causing confusion in the mass of the Party. One can now say that the battle has been lost for Bordiga and that this defeat will exert a certain influence on the whole of the discussion and voting for the Congress. In actual fact the Party has gone through a very serious crisis in its leading stratum, not in the mass, but it is clear that if the majority of the leading stratum had not shifted towards the ground occupied by the C[entral] C[ommittee] and the International, the C[entral] C[ommittee] would have lost contact with the mass of the Party, that is to say it would have lost the Congress battle.[57] Bordiga was wrong in wanting to precipitate the situation by enforcing fractional constraints on those elements who in the past were favourable to him, and who, he felt, through a thousand different signs, were shifting. After several days of crisis, these elements broke with him in a more radical way and to a greater extent than would have happened through normal discussion. That may be seen from the letters that the C[entral] C[ommittee] and each one of us have been receiving from the comrades in the local organisations. Certainly, we should have no illusions in thinking that everything has been resolved; we still have much work to do, but what is sure is that a big step forward has been taken. I have personally taken part in three information conferences, in Rome, in Venice and in Trieste, attended by the members of the provincial Committees, the secretaries of the various sectors and of the most important cells, as well as of our trade union fractions: the overwhelming majority came out in favour of the C[entral] C[ommittee], against Bordiga's ideology, which received a lukewarm defence from some individuals, more for sentimental than for political reasons (since Bordiga is a good and capable comrade, courageous, forceful, etc). I think that, in the discussion, the articles by the Russian comrades and a manifesto from the International will be of great use in explaining the importance of Bolshevisation and of Leninism in the current stage of development of the C[ommunist] P[arties].[58] If you think that it is better to have the International intervene on the eve of the provincial Congresses, which will begin in the second half of August, then it might be useful to have an immediate letter from the C[entral] C[ommittee] of the R[ussian] C[ommunist] P[arty].

The situation of our newspaper has not worsened over the present period, but it had become worse before the Enlarged Executive and perhaps the news that you have received referred to that period.[59] All the anti-fascist papers have had to reduce their print-run because the government and the fascists are systematically blocking distribution. The paper is being seized every day, one may say, in either one province or another, and it is often being seized country-wide. In the factories the workers' pockets are searched and our readers are being beaten up. Bundles of the newspaper are continually being set fire to in those centres where fascism is strongest. Sellers are being threatened and their news-stands burned down or their vending licence taken away if they sell *L'Unità*. We can react only by multiplying the illegal press, which, however, is very costly and can lead to a year's prison sentence to whoever reads it; already we have had a lot of people sentenced. The drop in print-run is due to this reactionary situation, not to any reduction in the popularity of the party; in fact funds raised for the paper are very high (260,000 lire on 24 July), higher than those to *L'Avanti!* (240,000 lire): a very large number of workers contribute money to the paper. In some provinces where the paper is being boycotted by the fascists and only a few dozen copies arrive illegally, hundreds upon hundreds of workers and peasants have sent money, which means that every copy circulates from hand to hand and we thereby reach a fairly large mass.

The Maximalist Party is going through a fairly serious crisis. Our C[entral] C[ommittee] has made a proposal to this Party and at the same time also to the Republican Party, to the Reformist Party and to the Sardinian Party to have a united front on the basis of 'Down with the fascist monarchy! Land to the peasants, control of production to the workers to break the backs of the landowners and the capitalists supporting fascism'.[60] The reformist Party immediately answered no, *the Maximalist Party did not even inform the mass of its members of our proposal*, the Republican Party is split, with one part wanting to accept our proposal while another is against, and meanwhile its Party Executive is trying to delay any official reply.[61] We reacted with action from below and by having the youth sector intervene. We have managed to obtain the support of a series of local organisations, even of the reformists, so much so that the Reformist Party has debated the 'Monarchy or Republic?' question in its Milan organisation. A conflict broke out there between Turati (who wants no talk of a republic) and Caldara, a former mayor of Milan and a very popular figure among the Milanese workers, who wants the reformists to declare for a republic. Our campaign will continue on this terrain, too, in parallel with the trade union action that is developing satisfactorily and will bring over a lot of people, especially from the maximalists.

Warm greetings

Gramsci

Source: AAG; also in APC 513-1-309/67-70 and 74-77, and Comintern Archive 513-1-309/57-60; handwritten on Chamber of Deputies notepaper with date on last page

To Jul'ka

15 / VIII. 925

Dearest one,

I've received your letter of 7 August. I hadn't had any news from you for about a month and a half. I know that some letters of yours had arrived but they fell into police hands following a search. For that reason, many of the things you tell me are new; I didn't know that Delio had been ill, what he had and how serious it was.

I have been and still am a long way from Rome. I have to travel a lot to hold meetings and continually have to try to shake the police off my tracks, so for this reason I haven't been able to write to you over the last few weeks, so as not to complicate the work of the comrades and for fear that my letters to you might fall into the hands of the police.

Lots of things struck me in your letter of 7 August. You use the words 'I want' next to the other ones 'to be near you' and this desire on your part has made a strong impression on me. Lately I've travelled far and wide and seen places that they tell me are very beautiful and countryside that, it seems, is splendid, so much so that foreigners come from far afield to admire them. I have been to Miramare, for example, but it seemed to me an aberrant fantasy of Carducci's;[62] the white towers looked to me like smokestacks whitened with a touch of lime; the sea was a dirty yellow because the workers who were building a road had thrown down ton after ton of rubble; the sun just seemed to me like some out-of-season radiator, left there forgotten. But it came to mind that all these impressions must have been linked to the 'apathy' that has overcome me, and, as your mother said of me, to having lost the taste for the nature and the life around me, because I'm always thinking that you are far away, because, from the moment that I began to love you, I could feel no joy other than what is bound up with you, no joy that does not cease immediately if I think that you are not next to me and cannot see what I see, cannot feel with me. And it is because of this that your 'will' has left such an impression on me. I think that something like this must happen to you too, with the difference that you have Delio near at hand, and his existence, his development, the way he relates to life in general, must bind you to the world and make you see it every day with new eyes, with a renewed and purified sensitivity. For me Delio really has really been one of St Lawrence's shooting stars.[63] And has our love, too, not had something of the same nature? It's true that it has still kept its infinite possibilities, even that of making us weep, hasn't it? And that of bringing us lots of surprises when we are together again once more, and together shall be able to feel the same life.

And meanwhile Delio is now a year old, and is beginning to talk. But doesn't it seem strange to you that you see time really divided in years and you think that Delio is beginning to live for the second time? This vision of time as something solid that has an end and then begins again seems to me intimately bound up with the physical sense of motherhood, something which escapes me since I have not physically seen the development of the creation of a new life bound up to mine. And Delio now has his pram … I received the news in a rather roundabout way but the important thing is that there is a pram. I thought that the famous wheels had been made quite some time ago and it was only from Tat'jana that I found out that this was a myth; consequently I wrote to M. for him to see to things.[64] So it is that I got to know that Tat'jana has not yet sent you the underclothes and the rest that should have arrived ages ago. I had given Tat'jana the job of doing this because I thought she was more decisive and precise than I am … What a disappointment: but then Tat'jana belongs to the … Schuchts and her will suffers from its ups and downs. Some time ago she bought some Sasso oil and some small pasta with gluten for Delio but then she left it in a cupboard, and as for the underclothes she's decided to wait until you send her … the sizes.[65] Now everything will be sent to you (so Tat'jana has assured me) with approximate sizes.

I'll wait expectantly for new letters from you. You'll have to explain to me the exact meaning of your words 'I want'; Tat'jana is certain that you will come in September and has already booked rooms where we will go to live. You will write to say 'yes' won't you?

A close and tight embrace, любимая [ljubimaja: darling], for you and Delio

Gr

Source: AAG

To Amadeo Bordiga[66]

18 – 8 – 25

Dear comrade,

The delay in this reply is due to the arrest of comrade Terracini.[67] We have looked in vain for the letter from you of which you spoke to Com[rade] Morelli. It is possible that it was in the possession of comrade Terracini at the time of his arrest.

In any case, we are here communicating to you that the E[xecutive] C[ommittee] has reconfirmed its decision not to publish your statement of 19 July.[68] The reasons? These are intuitive.

Personal reasons do not come into the matter. We do not feel that the far-fetched accusations you levelled against us have touched us in the slightest. It is instead a political reason, the general interest of the party, that has induced us not to go back on our previous decision. The document you drew up seems designed on purpose to scatter the seeds of disintegration in the party. You demand the right to defend yourself from an alleged attack by us, which in your view would have followed up the declaration of dissolution of the Liaison Committee.[69] You are requested to re-read that declaration: in it, you will find more than sufficient reasons to understand our reply.

We referred the question to the Control Commission, among other reasons to put an end to the incredible and incomprehensible denigration to which we have been subjected in what you have written. The publication of your declaration would have frustrated this intention, which was inspired not by personal reasons but by consideration of the real interests of the party. We would have been obliged to make an even more detailed reply, and put many more dots on the i's. It is easy to foresee what conclusions we would have reached and what consequences would have stemmed from them. Had it been a question of a defence or a rectification contained within the terms and limits allowed in a discussion between militants of the same party, no barrier would have been raised regarding its publication. But that declaration goes further, much further indeed … … …

Might one know, for example, what factual element authorises you to speak of 'those who go to Moscow for family reasons'? Are you aware of the significance that this assertion would have in the party or among the mass of the working class? You more than anyone know that there is not a shred of reality in this claim. So why then do you have recourse to such means?

And with what right do you expect that what you have written should be published in the party organs? The assertion is not even a response to our criticism of your not having gone to Moscow, a criticism that was duty-bound, and necessary for attacking the sceptical state of mind you find yourself in. This state has made you consider of little value – while instead it was of the greatest importance – your participation in the recent E[nlarged] E[xecutive], subordinating your fulfilment of a precise duty to family reasons.[70] All this is a long way from the accusation of corruption implicit in your reply, even if this was not in your intentions. Do you not realise how your accusations link up in a stupid chain with the campaign of defamation mounted against the communist movement, which is depicted as the work of mercenary adventurers in order to discredit it in the eyes of the masses? And would you like we ourselves to become the means by which similar false and stupid legends gain currency, falsehoods that are the more serious in that they originate within our own ranks and, even worse, from precisely the person who was once the head of the party?

Ah yes, but we are 'petty bourgeois who accidentally find themselves in the communist ranks' otherwise we would not be speaking of moral questions, of corruption, etc. These [']expressions are not to be found in our texts' – you claim – and this, according to you, ought to suffice for demonstrating your pretensions to Marxist orthodoxy. But you, in your texts, speak of falsity, disloyalty, deception of the party, of speculation etc ... Do you really think that by changing the words you change the essence of the thing? And then it would be we who had dragged political divergences onto the personal terrain in order to exacerbate them. Bare-faced audacity is needed for such a claim.

On the question of morality we would have you note that, if we do not care two hoots about bourgeois morality and all its prejudices, for us there is a communist morality, a party ethic towards which a communist cannot and must not be found wanting.

And then, what does it matter if, in what you write, the words 'corruption, immorality etc' do not figure, when what you write means exactly the same thing, and authorises the readers to seek even wider interpretations?[71] We could even give no importance to what you have written if we did not again find those expressions and those accusations in the language of your followers. You cannot escape this responsibility: a leader is also responsible for the interpretation put on his acts and his words by his followers. In this specific case, this was easily predictable.

As regards the rest of your statement, we limit ourselves to the following simple observations.

1) To the list of the dates of the various documents sent as proof of our disloyalty we could demonstrate that the reality is quite different and that the date of the document, in the conditions in which we are forced to work, demonstrates and justifies nothing whatsoever. But in order to do this, we would have to indicate aspects of our organisation which must remain absolutely reserved.
2) Our reply to the statement announcing the dissolution of the Liaison Committee demonstrates that the initiative in exacerbating the dissent began from our side. To write that is sheer effrontery. The way in which the declaration of dissolution was received has been determined by the way in which the declaration was formulated. One could then go back to previous documents bearing your signature which can give a reply to this question.
3) According to you, we based the campaign on personal insinuations. Our reply would have you note that it was our wish and intention not to discuss names and people, some of whom also figure among the members of the Liaison Committee and on whose account we have many, and then even more, reservations. The reservations we have and the exceptions we take regarding these personages are even more necessary in that they presented themselves as leaders of the opposition. Had it been necessary, we would have spoken of this in closed session should party interests have required this. All this does not regard you personally. Anything but insinuations; we did not even make use of hard facts.
4) According to you, we 'disloyally organised the deception of the party'. We could have demonstrated exactly the contrary, citing factual data which are BEST left buried for ever. It is the C[entral] C[ommittee] that – according to you – acted disloyally; what then should we call the conduct of those who for around two months were working in secret in the party, exploiting the positions of trust assigned to them in order to organise a fraction? and deceiving the leading organs about their activity? In your view is this called loyalty?

And how are we to define the conduct of not a few of your followers who go about spreading lies within the party, knowing that they are lying? Of all the others who all over the place are talking about high salaries, of the enrolment of hundreds of party officials whose political opinions have been bought for cash, of time-serving and venal officials, of the ambition and careerism of the leaders? Some very serious events have taken place in the party. And do you really want us to continue to publish what you have written, from which comrades derive in good faith the reasons for their stupid accusations?

We have to tell you quite frankly that these documents of yours have gone beyond any possible acceptable limit. Those who have read the latest documents that have come to us from the Liaison Committee cannot draw any other conclusion than that, at the head of the Communist Party, there is a group of unscrupulous adventurers, both corrupt and corrupters, fairground charlatans, clowns capable of all sorts of contortions, ambitious careerists, etc.

Can you say that the same conclusions can [be] drawn from the C[entral] C[ommittee] documents on your account?

It is essential to get out of this quagmire into which you have plunged headfirst and return to political discussion.

Giving publicity to what can only be called this ignoble document of yours means jeopardizing the very discussion underway, whereas what is instead needed is to put on all speed to arrive as soon as possible at the Congress.

Having reconfirmed its decision, the E[xecutive] C[ommittee] now considers the question closed.

Communist greetings.

Source: APC 513-1-341/1-2; unsigned

To Jul'ka

3 / IX. 925

Dearest Юлька,

I have received a letter of yours dated 7 August and then nothing else. I have been waiting anxiously for you to clear up some things you mentioned too fleetingly and for you to give me some news of Delio's illness. I have been away from Rome for quite some time and am off again tonight, after being back here for only a few days. Just as soon as I had reached the friends up there, they wanted to know if you had arrived in Rome: when I showed my surprise they replied that, according to news that had been received quite some time ago, you should have been coming to work in Rome. I don't know what to make of this news, and in the absence of any mention you've made of it, I told T[at'jana] this rumour, and the poor thing was so unsettled she did not sleep a wink. She is sure that you will in any case be coming and is waiting for you anxiously.

I remain in my state of apathy. I've been up in the mountains for a week, holding a series of lectures for a group of young communists. I enjoyed myself quite a bit, throwing stones in all directions and beating everyone at who could throw farthest, much to the amazement of the youngsters who couldn't credit such an ability in a … parliamentary deputy, who has to be a serious person. I saved myself from dishonour by 'revealing' that I had taken a special course in stone-throwing for … the civil war, so as to be able to launch grenades. I have further discovered that in our mountains there are a great number of the same small carnations as there are at Serebrjanyj Bor, and I picked a few bunches. But then I got caught in a downpour and was soaked to the skin, and developed a toothache in consequence that left my face swollen for 10 days. I began thinking at that point that I am getting old, that these ailments are destroying me, and that you are far off, and maybe you will remain far away while I move forward into the stage of being decrepit.[72]

I wanted to send you with this letter my share for Delio's summer camp, in accordance with the arrangement we reached peacefully in Moscow. However, I haven't been able to take out any money and so of necessity I will have to send it next time. I await a long letter from you, with lots of good news that will make me forget I'm growing old. I want to hear lots of news about Delio, about the progress he's making, about his life in general.

My dear, a tight and close embrace so as to feel myself happy with you

Gr

Source: AAG; on Chamber of Deputies notepaper

Gramsci and Grieco to Zinov'ev and the Comintern Executive

29.09.25

OMS for Gennari. We expect to see from Krestintern preparation of conference of Italian peasant movement under control of Krestintern and [its] Italian section. We think Miglioli may be obtained as specialist for this work but without autonomy and under leadership of Italian section. Transmit immediately conditions for our congress

Gramsci, Grieco.

Source: AAG; from the Russian translation of the telegram

NOTES

1. This is the first extant letter from Gramsci to Piero Sraffa and testament to the growing bond between them. Sraffa, then aged twenty six, was at the time lecturing in political economy and finance at the University of Perugia. Although he had contributed to the first series of *L'Ordine Nuovo* and the two men were fairly close in age, here as also in the note of three weeks later, Gramsci still uses the formal mode of address – 'lei' or 'ella' – rather than the familiar 'tu'.
2. More precisely the conservatory in Rome.
3. Gennaro had had a daughter, Edmea, with a factory worker, Rina, but they did not marry. In any case, he was forced into exile after having been severely beaten up in December 1922 at the Turin Trades Council by fascists mistaking him for his brother (see Antonio's letter to Jul'ka of 21 July 1924). Edmea immediately won everyone's hearts in Ghilarza by saying, on her first appearance at the Gramsci home, 'Good evening signor grandfather. How are you signora grandmother?': see Paulesu Quercioli (2003 [1991]), p98 and also Gramsci's letter to his mother of 15 August 1924.
4. Paolo Paulesu, husband of Gramsci's sister Teresina. Their daughter, Mimma, was instrumental in having various family letters published.
5. See the Introduction for the events following on the kidnap and murder of Matteotti.
6. Kaša is Russian buckwheat porridge, synonymous with the food of the poor.
7. For Colonna di Cesarò see 'Some Aspects of the Southern Question' (Gramsci 1978b, p456), where he is described as typical of the southern and Sicilian landowners who controlled local parties not directly themselves but through local intellectuals.

8. Gramsci had made this proposal at the meeting of all opposition parliamentary groups on 14 June, the week before this letter.
9. The sister is of course Tat'jana (Tanja), who would later visit and, as much as was possible, help and care for Gramsci in prison. The two, however, met for the first time only several months later (see the letter to Jul'ka of 2 February 1925).
10. The letter is dated 27 June, not 25 June as appears in Gramsci (1992).
11. In a letter the previous week (not included here) Gramsci had told Bianco of much regarding political events that he had written on the same day (22 June) in his letter to Jul'ka, including comments about living through 'very serious days that will perhaps be decisive for our movement, now in full development'; he also reiterated his wish to attend the Fifth Congress of the Comintern in Moscow, which did not happen, perhaps because of the Matteotti crisis.
12. However see the next letter to Jul'ka, dated the same day, where Gramsci gives Jul'ka some hope he will come.
13. The phrase 'about your strength' is in Gramsci (1992), but through an oversight is omitted in Paulesu Quercioli (1987).
14. This last sentence is omitted in Paulesu Quercioli (1987), but is in the autograph letter in the AAG, the typed-up copies in the Moscow Archives, and in Gramsci (1992).
15. See the Introduction for this conference held near Como, between Milan and the Swiss border.
16. The Bastianelli brothers were leading doctors and surgeons, with whom Tat'jana came into personal contact during her studies for a degree in medicine in Rome, a course that she never actually finished (cf Aldo Natoli's 'Introduction' to Antonio Gramsci-Tatiana Schucht, *Lettere 1926-1935*, Einaudi: Turin 1997, pXLVII).
17. The reference is to the second anniversary of the Fascist 'March on Rome', where they arrived on 28 October 1922.
18. For the references to 'beds' – a word left undeciphered in Gramsci (1992) – and Egyptian mummies, see the postcard to Evgenija of 16 October 1922, p125.
19. Ottilija was the name of Apollon Schucht's mother.
20. Since Jul'ka's father was called Apollon, Delio would have a name related to the Schucht family (and here also to Antonio's, through his cousin, Delio Delogu).
21. Amorino translates in one sense as 'little love', and in another a cherub.
22. Almost certainly Piero Sraffa.
23. By family request, while the daughter, Edmea, was still alive, this paragraph was never published; it is printed here for the first time.
24. See the Introduction, p35, for the official confirmation of his nomination.
25. In actual fact he was named Delio (see the letter to Jul'ka of 4 August).

26. The same situation is described in a letter, not included here, to Vincenzo Bianco, dated 8 September; there Gramsci speaks of a thousand Party members in Turin, despite strong police and fascist repression; Milan too had reached about the same numbers, up by 50% or more compared with the previous year. The movement was growing everywhere and publications were springing back into life.
27. Casalini was assassinated by an apolitical worker of unbalanced mind; see Spriano (1967), pp403-4.
28. Gramsci recalled his annoyance at this refusal in a letter from prison to Jul'ka of 9 February 1931 (Gramsci, 1994a, Vol. 2, pp11-12). He had donated 8,200 lire, far more than the comparatively trifling 12 rubles Jul'ka needed, to the new paper *L'Unità*.
29. The meaning 'pick it up' is as written here, but Gramsci slips up by repeating a syllable in his letter, thereby leading Mimma Paulesu Quercioli (1987, p107), to invent a non-existent (and incomprehensible) word.
30. For quite some time Jul'ka was the family's financial mainstay, and it was hard for her, and for the family, to make ends meet. As early as 1920 Apollon had written to Nadežda Krupskaja, Lenin's wife, requesting help in finding work (Antonio Gramsci jr, 2008, pp50-51). Jul'ka's refusal of the money offered by Antonio seems to have been partly due to family pride and partly to the argument that the money was more needed for the movement in Italy.
31. The sentence about Milan is in the manuscript, but through an oversight is not in Gramsci (1992). Bagnasco, to a high degree of certainty, was Domenico Bagnasco, the secretary of the fascist trade unions in Turin.
32. A transcription in Gramsci (1992) mistakenly has the bourgeois opposition try to detach fascism from the king, rather than the king from fascism, the historically and logically correct version.
33. This reference to the rights of fathers under soviet family law, taken too seriously by Jul'ka, was in a letter from Gramsci to her of 8 September (not included here).
34. In the phrase written here as 'not so perfect' Gramsci (1992) accidentally omits the word 'not', which is included in Mimma Paulesu Quercioli's edition; the latter thus corresponds to the original and to the typed-up version in the Comintern Archives.
35. From Dante's *Inferno*, Book V, line 103: 'Amor che a nullo amato amar perdona', here cited in H.W. Longfellow's translation, Ticknor and Fields: Boston and Routledge: London, 1867.
36. In a previous short letter of 20 October, not here included here, Gramsci said he was due to go to Sardinia. The reason, not stated, was to preside over the second regional congress of the PCd'I, held in secret near Cagliari. Afterwards, he went to see his family at Ghilarza for the first time since, four years earlier, he had attended the funeral of his sister

Emma, who had been a victim of the Spanish influenza epidemic in Europe after the First World War.

37. Slogan of Sardinian nationalism; Gramsci writes 'Onward together!' in Sardinian: 'Forza paris!'.
38. Marco is Mauro Scoccimarro and the emperor is Ferruccio Virgili, for whom see p169.
39. 'Sinistroide', translated here as ultra-leftist, carries extremely pejorative overtones.
40. Through an oversight the phrase 'that has worked' is omitted in Gramsci (1992).
41. While in the rest of the letter, the 'you' is singular, referring to Jul'ka, here it is plural, meaning Jul'ka and the baby.
42. In a letter to Jul'ka two weeks previously (not included here), Gramsci had mentioned for the first time that he was hoping to be able to take part in the Enlarged Executive of the Comintern in 1925, as indeed did happen. And, yet again, in that letter he says 'the world is... etc, etc.', without needing to add the familiar 'great and terrible'.
43. When Parliament reopened on 3 January 1925, Mussolini arrogantly accepted responsibility for all the crimes and aggressions committed by fascism, including the murder of Matteotti, and the Fascist Party secretary simultaneously pressed for repressive measures against all opposition forces. Freedom was reduced to a minimum and the dictatorship really dates from this time. Paolo Spriano (1967, p425) defines what happened at this point as a coup d'état.
44. The letter was unduly pessimistic about the situation and Gramsci corrected his views in a brief letter, not included here, written the week afterwards to Scoccimarro. The three communist journalists, Pastore, Platone and Romano Cocchi respectively, were released nearly immediately; the Party organisation around Florence was however dissolved and the Party press had to come out illegally for almost a fortnight. *Italia Libera* was an armed anti-fascist group of ex-combatants.
45. Antonio Salandra was a southern conservative, who as Prime Minister, against a parliament favouring neutrality, had led Italy into the First World War. He supported the early phase of fascism, but like his cabinet colleagues, the liberals Casati and Sarrocchi, resigned at this juncture and retired to private life, though he was nominated Senator in 1928.
46. Stučevskij was a Ukrainian-born communist who, a few days later, located the Rome address of Jul'ka's sister, Tat'jana (mentioned in Gramsci's letter to Jul'ka, not included here, of 16 January).
47. Not a title, but Gramsci's joking way of saying he was a Russian Social Revolutionary. Tat'jana lodged with the Schreider family during much of Gramsci's imprisonment.
48. By mistake Gramsci wrote '924'; until the next letter there is a gap of

almost three-months, during part of which Gramsci was in Moscow for the Fifth Enlarged Executive.

49. From Rome on 9 March 1925, Togliatti confirmed to the Comintern Secretariat and to Scoccimarro that 'MASCI, member of the E[xecutive] C[ommittee], left via Vienna, crossed Italian frontier legally' for the Fifth Enlarged Executive (Comintern Archives, 513-1-285/4).
50. A reference to the New Economic Policy (NEP) that followed the harsh years of 'war Communism'.
51. The date in Humbert-Droz's book reads 25 May, but Antonio Santucci corrects this in Gramsci (1992) after having consulted the manuscript.
52. This was a letter that Gramsci had earlier mislaid; he refers to it in a short note to Jul'ka of the previous week (not included here).
53. His first and only speech to the Chamber, made on 16 May 1925, now transcribed in Gramsci 1978a, pp75-85).
54. On the day of this letter, the Party left, under Bordiga, gave notice to the Party Executive that it was forming a Liaison Committee ('Comitato d'Intesa'), through which it then attempted to rally its forces: see the Introduction and various subsequent letters in this chapter.
55. The Ispolkom was the abbreviation, based on its Russian name, often used for the Comintern Executive Committee; see the Introduction for other information on Girone's case.
56. Here the Comintern translator merely transliterated into the Cyrillic alphabet the Italian words for Liaison Committee (Comitato d'Intesa).
57. Due to a misreading in Gramsci (1992), 'lost control' is written instead of 'lost contact' as in the original.
58. 'Explaining the importance' replaces the phrase 'explaining the question' (crossed out by Gramsci).
59. Zinov'ev's information seems to have been based on the news at the start of the year before the Enlarged Executive of March-April 1925 (cf the letter to Scoccimarro of 5 January and its note regarding the arrests of *L'Unità* journalists).
60. Through an oversight the words 'to the Reformist Party and to the Sardinian Party' are omitted in Gramsci (1992).
61. Emphasis – through underlining – present in the originals.
62. 'Miramar', a poem by the late nineteenth-century poet, Giosuè Carducci, begins by praising the 'white towers' of Miramare on the Northern Adriatic, towers that are the object of Gramsci's cynicism. For an English translation, in a sombre style rather than the florid one of the original, see David H. Higgins's *Giosue Carducci: Selected Verse* (Aris & Phillips: Warminster 1994).
63. Delio was born on 10 August, St Lawrence's day, when the Earth passes through the Perseid meteor shower, giving rise to 'shooting stars', seen very clearly in Italy.
64. Mauro Scoccimarro ('Marco' or 'Morelli'), the PCd'I representative in Moscow since the previous autumn.

65. Sasso is a famous brand of olive oil.
66. The use of 'we' in the letter indicates that, following on the correspondence with Zinov'ev, Gramsci is writing to Bordiga not personally but officially on behalf of the PCd'I Executive (confirmed by a protocol number on the letter).
67. Terracini had been arrested in Milan and was not released until February 1926, only to be rearrested later that year and tried, along with Gramsci and others, before fascism's 'special tribunal' in 1928.
68. For this statement, from which Gramsci quotes (in inverted commas in the present letter), see APC 513-1-340/32-36; it is also available at www.quinterna.org/archivio/1924_1926/bordiga_falsificazione.htm.
69. The demand from the International, in the person of Humbert-Droz, to dissolve the Liaison Committee was published in *L'Unità* on 18 July, the day before Bordiga wrote the statement that is here the object of Gramsci's and the Party Centre's harsh criticism. The Committee's dissolution was accepted with no more than formal protests by its founders, and by Bordiga himself, with the Centre guaranteeing full freedom of expression and debate, although the Left later shed doubt on the genuineness of this promise.
70. Bordiga had said he could not attend the Comintern's Enlarged Executive because his wife's state of health kept him in Italy.
71. In his 19 July statement Bordiga writes explicitly that 'the expressions moral unworthiness and corruption are not to be found in our what we have written …'; later on, in point 4, Gramsci again picks up Bordiga's wording in his claim that the Party leadership had attempted 'disloyally' to 'organise the deception of the Party'.
72. This phrase ('Maybe you will remain far away') is used by Mimma Paulesu Quercioli (1987) as the title of her edition of Gramsci's letters to Jul'ka, *Forse rimarrai lontana*.

7. Rome II: The last months of freedom

To Emilio Lussu

12 July 1926

Dearest Lussu,

Together with this note is the promised questionnaire. Reply as you best think fit and if you think some other questions are necessary politically, please do not hesitate to add them, and modify and delete some of those you find here.

Greetings

Gramsci

It would be best for you to give your reply personally to the *L'Unità* correspondent in the Press Room.[1]

1. What real success has been obtained by the economic policy that the fascist group of the Hon. Paolo Pili is trying to carry out in Sardinia?[2] Has it succeeded in winning consent for fascism and for the government of at least part of the Sardinian peasants and shepherds? And if it has not won active consent, has it however been able to form some sort of passive expectation that objectively could be judged as being favourable to fascism and to the government?[3]
2. What is the reaction of the old groups of speculators and sharks, whether Sardinians or mainlanders, against the activities of the Hon. Pili?
3. What is the real attitude of the Sardinian Party faced with this policy, given that the Hon. Pili is trying to put into effect some of the demands of the traditional programme of Sardism?[4] Has

the Hon. Pili's policy led to a shift to the left in the ranks of the Sardists through the attempt to seek wider support for fascism?

4. Has the fascist regime's policy of compression – resulting in the suppression of the representative regime in 90% of the municipalities of Sardinia – led objectively to making the regionalist problem more acute and to posing the question of autonomy on a more radical terrain of demands of a national type?
5. Since the post-war experience has demonstrated that it is impossible for the Sardinian regional problem to be resolved by the popular masses of Sardinia alone, if these masses are not allied to given social and political forces of mainland Italy – with what social and political forces does the S[ardinian] A[ction] P[arty] think it necessary to ally?
6. Since the Sardinian regional question is indissolubly linked to the bourgeois capitalist regime that, in order to exist, needs not only to exploit the class of industrial workers through wage labour, but also to make the peasant masses of the South and the Islands pay a bounty in customs and tax, and since a coalition of left democrat and social democrat parties cannot contain in its programme the expropriation of the industrial bourgeoisie and the big landowners,[5] does it not seem clear to the S[ardinian] A[ction] P[arty] that the sole possible mainland ally of the Sardinian working population is the workers' and peasants' revolutionary bloc, supported by the Peasant International?
7. What are the widespread opinions among the Sardists regarding the programme of the Peasant International? How is it that the Executive of the S[ardinian] A[ction] P[arty] has not replied, even through internal channels, to the Peasant International's Manifesto, sent to the Macomer Congress in 1925?[6]
8. What is the common opinion of the Sardinian peasants and shepherds on the workers' and peasants' Revolution that has come to victorious fruition in Russia? Is there a popular current that judges the Russian Revolution to be a political victory of the peasants of the whole world, and therefore of the most advanced Sardinian peasants too?

Source: AAG; covering note and questionnaire both handwritten on Chamber of Deputies notepaper

To Jul'ka

19. VIII. 26

Dearest one,

I got back four days ago but it was only yesterday that I managed to see T[at'jana] who gave me the news about your journey back and arrival.[7] I haven't received anything personally; if you've written, your letters have got lost. I set off again this evening and this time I hope to go and see our child without any problem intervening, but over the last few weeks that's been impossible.[8]

My dear, I still cannot persuade myself that you're no longer with me. Every evening I feel rather lost, I just can't think that I'm alone once more.[9] And then I think about lots of things that I can't succeed in expressing, maybe because it's not possible to express them in words. For that I would need to be near you and have you feel all my tenderness directly. Write me a long letter. A close and tight embrace.

Gr

Source: AAG

To Jul'ka

15. IX. 26

Dearest one,

I've received your letter of 29 August. I haven't received any news since then, not even indirectly. I'm waiting patiently, but with a little trepidation too.

I went up to Trafoi at the end of August and stayed there five or six days, all the free time I had. I got the impression that Del'ka was much better than in Rome; I think he's stronger and more robust. He's also developed intellectually, made contact with the world outside and come to know an infinite number of new things. I think his stay in Trafoi, in a magnificent setting of mountains and glaciers, will leave very deep impressions in his memory. We played together. I made a few playthings for him, we lit fires out in the countryside; there were no lizards around so I couldn't teach him to catch them. I think he's now entering what for him is a very important stage, a stage that will leave very long-lasting memories because during his development he's going to conquer the great and terrible world. For that reason I'm rather sad; you're far away and so too is Del'ka. I feel rather at a loss. I'm waiting expectantly for news from you that will bind me even closer to you and Del'ka. I would like to feel you close to me and hold you ever so tight against me. You must feel me close to you and feel my hand caressing you.

An embrace for you, my dear

Antonio

T[at'jana] has let me know the contents of the telegram about Del'ka's arrival and the birth of the new baby. I am very moved, my dear, and can't manage to tell you all my feelings. Together T[at'jana] and I tried very hard to interpret the telegram, which could be understood that two babies were born; this possibility did indeed unsettle me, making me think of the sufferings you've gone through and the effort it could involve you in. But you're going to be strong, aren't you? You know that I absolutely can't make head or tail of things? I love you very much: that's the one guiding light that supports and directs me. I would like to tell you lots of things but they are not yet clear in my own mind. I'll write to you at greater length next time, since I want to reflect better on these things. A very close and tight embrace.

Antonio

Source: AAG

To Alfonso Leonetti

[17 OR 18 SEPTEMBER 1926][10]

SERVICE NOTE FOR LEONETTI

The form in which Friday's leading article was published is indecent and unworthy. The leading article of our paper must be something serious, very serious, not only for the paper's readers but for the journalistic staff too. It is not therefore a waste of time and effort if a knowledgeable, well-informed leader writer is given the permanent responsibility of taking on the care needed for the editorials in general to be published in correct and precise language, above reproach as regards their grammatical and literary aspect. In the case in question, the fact that we are dealing with a lack of professional scruple, inseparable from political irresponsibility, is undeniable from the incomprehensible and stupid title attributed to the article published in *Il Mondo*. Yet this article from *Il Mondo*, which the article in question cited, was in fact available to the journalists, who could have checked it. It beggars belief that *L'Unità* journalists should be inclined to think that the paper's collaborators are total idiots, capable of filling their writings with the most appalling banalities and blunders. It is understandable why in this way our collaborators are dropping off. No serious person is going to lend himself willingly to be jeered at in such a disgusting way. As regards Friday's article it would have been preferable to throw the original in the waste paper basket if no journalist was able to correct its howlers. It was therefore just stupid to change the title, modest but adequate for the subject matter, to the pompous, high-sounding one dreamed up with no regard for the content. This is not revolutionary journalism, it is simply irresponsibility and adventurism, typical of a band of political gypsies. I am here requesting you to print on the front page the enclosed correction.[11]

Antonio

Source: APC 513-1-440/1; Comintern Archives 513-1-440/2; typewritten

---

To Jul'ka

30 SEPTEMBER 1926

My dearest Юлька

T[at'jana] has given me the news I'd been expecting. Very little news, it's true, which has merely sharpened my desire to read something from your, your impressions, your feelings. I'll still have to wait, I realise that it must be difficult for you to send letters and I'll be patient.

A close and tight embrace for you and the children too.

Gramsci

I'm sending with this letter a small amount that I think is really going to be very necessary for you. I'd like to send you something periodically on a regular basis and certainly I'll manage this, because I've made it a firm and definite aim. I'll write to you at greater length when I get a letter from you.

Source: AAG

To Jul'ka

7 OCTOBER 1926

My dearest Юлька,

I've received your letter of 13 September. I think you'll have had a good laugh over the last-but-one letter I sent you.[12] I'm very happy and love you very, very much. I'm waiting anxiously for news of Delio's meeting with his little brother and for your impressions. You haven't written to me about what name you've chosen for the baby; Giuliano, I believe, as you had thought here. I wanted to write you an extremely long and very, very serious letter as a real father who feels his responsibilities; I've been very busy and I'm writing to you now at the last minute. I'll put this off for another week. I just want to repeat that you are my very dearest one, that I always feel you close to me and that I want to embrace you together with our children.

Antonio

Source: AAG

To Jul'ka

14. X. 1926

My dearest Юлька

I've had no more news from you since 14 September, exactly a month ago. For this reason I'm rather worried and sad. Over this last period I've been able to work a lot more than I managed to in the past. Once again I've written with a certain intensity for our papers, overcoming a sort of mental block that had had the upper hand for quite some time. I had seemed no longer to be able to write anything interesting or acceptable from a literary point of view, and this feeling had even become morbid. I tried to overcome it in some way, even though I was convinced that I would have to wait quite a time before once again being master of my means. To obtain this result I've been helped a lot by the contribution made by the continual, insistent thought of you and our two children. You know that at certain moments I've been well and truly crushed by worry. If I think that up to now you've had the whole weight of two children on your shoulders, as well as other responsibilities weighing you down, I feel humiliated and sad. Notwithstanding everything, it will seem I don't love you enough, or love the two children enough either, until the day I manage to change these conditions once and for all. I take revenge on these dark thoughts as best I can, inflicting the heaviest wounds I can on those enemies of ours who in the papers depict us as Nabobs knee-deep in gold.[13] But I don't want to say anything more to you about this, because I don't want you to imagine that I'm always out of humour and in a black mood. I am, instead, fairly well and want to tell you of something serious and at the same time amusing. Like, for example, the competition organised by the newspaper *Il Piccolo* on happy wives, which certainly you'll remember. The winning reply was framed more or less like this: 'Happy is the wife who married the man with whom she would have willingly betrayed her husband'. The paper found this reply to be the quintessence of profundity in the realm of wifely psychology. To me too, it seems that the reply has a certain psychological and historical significance for characterising the customs and ways of thinking of a certain class in a certain era. One would have to communicate the findings to some specialist in erotic questions (Koll[ontaj] for instance) for her to write some tome of palpitating actuality.[14] Have I managed to make you smile? Well then, I want to give you, just while you're smiling, a close and tight embrace, together with the two children (our first- and second-born offspring as we may now with great formality call them).

Ant.

I'm asking you to let Ercoli have the note included here, which otherwise is going to be delayed by a week.[15]

I've just received this moment your letters of 26.IX and 3.X. – I love you very much and embrace you

A.

Source: AAG

To Togliatti

[14 OCTOBER 1926]

Dearest friend,

I am here sending you the document spoken of in another letter.[16] You will have to have it recopied and translated, if you wish adding our names which, in any case, should not be published. You may revise the text as regards changing some matters of detail and form, given the haste in which it had to be written. The essential terms must however be kept unchanged. Since we want to help the maj[ority] of the C[entral] C[ommittee], you can come to an agreement for these changes with those in charge. Send on immediately a copy of the text as finalised. Our impression is somewhat pessimistic and it is for that reason that we have considered the letter to be necessary.

I'm waiting for the corrected and collated text of Antonio Labriola's letters, with Rjazanov's preface. It is needed for the 1st number of *O[rdine] N[uovo]*. We absolutely must hurry this along.

I'll send the articles for the C[ommunist] I[nternational] very soon, as I've been hoping.

Greetings to everyone.

Antonio

Source: AAG and APC 513-1-410/1 with copy at APC 513-1-410/5; handwritten

To the Central Committee of the All-Union Communist Party (Bolsheviks)
To the C[entral] C[ommittee] of the CP of the USSR

[14 OCTOBER 1926][17]

Dear comrades

The Italian communists and all conscious working people of our country have always followed your discussions with the greatest attention. On the eve of every Congress and every Conference of the R[ussian] C[ommunist] P[arty] we were sure that despite the sharpness of the polemics, the unity of the Russian Party was not in danger. Rather, we were sure that, once a greater ideological and organisational homogeneity had been reached through these discussions, the Party would be better prepared and equipped to overcome the many difficulties bound up with the exercise of power in a workers' State. Today, on the eve of your Fifteenth Conference, we no longer have the certainty we had in the past.[18] We feel an irresistible sense of anguish and it seems to us that the present attitude of the bloc of the opposition groupings and the sharpness of the polemics in the CP of the USSR call for the intervention of brother parties. It is out of this precise conviction that we have taken it upon ourselves to direct this letter to you. It may be that the isolation in which our Party has been forced to work has led us to exaggerate the dangers regarding the situation inside the C[ommunist] Party of the USSR, but in any case our judgements on the international repercussions of this situation are certainly not exaggerated, and as internationalists we wish to carry out our duty.

The current situation of our brother Party of the USSR seems to us to be different and much more serious than in previous discussions since today we are seeing a split taking place and widening in the central Leninist group that has always been the leadership core of the Party and the International. A split of this type, *independent of the numerical results of the votes at the Congress*, may have the gravest repercussions, not only if the opposition minority does not accept the basic principles of revolutionary Party discipline with greatest loyalty, *but also if, in conducting its polemics and its struggle, it goes beyond certain limits, higher than those of all formal democracies*.

One of Lenin's most precious teachings was the need for us to study closely the judgements made by our class enemies. Well, dear comrades, it is certain that internationally the top newspapers and strongest statesmen of the bourgeoisie are relying on this organic character of the conflict that exists within the basic nucleus of the C[ommunist] Party of the USSR,[19] are relying on there being a split in our brother Party, and are convinced that such a split will lead to the disintegration and the slow death-agony of the proletarian dictatorship, and produce a catastrophe for the Revolution such as the invasions and insurrections of the white guards did not manage to bring about. The same cold circumspection that the bourgeois press is now using to try to analyse events in Russia, the fact that it is trying, insofar as it is capable, to avoid the violent demagogy that characterised it in the past, *are symptoms that should make the Russian comrades reflect and be more aware of their responsibilities.*

For yet another reason the international bourgeoisie is relying on a possible split or on a worsening of the crisis inside the Com[munist] Party of the USSR. The workers' State has now been in existence in Russia for 9 years. It is certain that only a small minority not only of the working classes, but of the Communist Parties themselves of other countries, is able to reconstruct in its entirety the whole development of the Revolution and to find, even in the details in which everyday life consists in the State of the Soviets, the continuity of the red thread that leads right up to the general perspective of the construction of socialism. And this is the case not only in the countries where freedom of assembly no longer exists and freedom of the press has been completely suppressed or has been subjected to unheard-of limitations, as in Italy (where the courts have seized and banned the publication of the books of Trotsky, Lenin, Stalin, Zinov'ev and most recently even of the *Communist Manifesto*), but also in those countries where our Parties are still able to provide their members and the masses in general with sufficient documentation. In these countries, the masses of the people cannot understand the discussions that are taking place within the CP of the USSR, especially if these are as violent as the current one and involve not only a minor aspect, but the entire political line of the Party. Not only the working masses in general, but the masses themselves of our Parties, see and want to see in the Republic of the Soviets and in the Party that is in government there *one sole fighting unit* that is working in the general perspective of Socialism. Only insofar as the western European masses see Russia and the Russian Party from this standpoint will they accept willingly and as a historically necessary fact that the CP of the USSR is the leading Party of the International, only on account of this are the Republic of the Soviets and the CP of the USSR today a formidable element of organisations and of revolutionary drive.

For the same reason the internal polemics and conflicts in the CP of the USSR are being exploiting by the bourgeois and social democratic parties, who wish to combat this influence of the Russian Revolution, to combat the revolutionary unity that is being built the world over around the CP of the USSR. Dear comrades, it is of the utmost significance that in a country like Italy, where the state and party organisation of fascism is managing to suffocate every notable demonstration of autonomous life among the great masses of workers and peasants, it is of significance that the fascist newspapers, particularly those in the provinces, are full of articles, technically well written ones from the propaganda aspect, with a minimal degree of demagogy and insulting attitudes, in which the authors try to demonstrate with a quite evident effort at objectivity, through the declarations of the best known leaders of the opposition bloc in the CP of the USSR, that the State of the Soviets is now without doubt becoming a pure capitalist state, and therefore that, in the worldwide duel between fascism and Bolshevism, fascism will gain the upper hand. This campaign, although demonstrating how widespread is the sympathy enjoyed by the Republic of the Soviets among the great masses of the Italian people who (in certain regions) for six years have received only scanty and infrequent illegal Party literature, also demonstrates how fascism, which knows the real internal Italian situation very well and has learned how to deal with the masses, is attempting to utilise the political attitude of the bloc of the opposition groupings to break once and for all the firm opposition of the working people to the Mussolini government and to create at least a state of mind in which fascism will appear at the very least as an inevitable historical necessity, despite the cruelty and evils that go hand in hand with it.

We believe that, within the framework of the International, *our Party is the one that most feels the repercussions of the serious situation within the CP of the USSR*. And this is not only due to the reasons outlined above which are, so to speak, external ones and touch upon the general conditions of revolutionary development within Italy. You know that every single Party of the International has inherited, both from the old social democracy and from the different national traditions existing in the various countries (anarchism, syndicalism etc), a mass of prejudices and ideological motifs that represent the matrix of all deviations, both right and left. Over the last few years but in particular since the Fifth World Congress, our Parties, through painful experience, through laborious and extenuating crises, were arriving at a secure Leninist stabilisation, were becoming real Bolshevik parties. New proletarian cadres were being formed from below, from the workshops; the intellectual elements were being subjected to rigorous selection and ruthless and rigid tests on the basis of practical work, on the terrain of action. This re-elaboration was taking place under the guidance of the CP of the USSR in its overall unity and that of all the great heads of the P[arty] of the USSR. Well now, the acuteness of the present crisis, and the threat of a latent or open split that this crisis contains, is bringing to a halt this process of development and elaboration being carried out by our Parties, is crystallising right and left deviations, is once more making more remote the success of the organic unity of the world Party of the working people. It is on this element especially that we believe it is our duty as internationalists to recall the attention of the most responsible comrades of the CP of the USSR. Comrades, in these last nine years of world history you have been the organisational element and driving force of the revolutionary forces of all countries. The role you have played has no precedent in the entire history of humankind that equals it in breadth and depth. *But today you are destroying your own work, you are degrading and running the risk of nullifying the leading role that the CP of the USSR* had gained through the impetus of Lenin. In our opinion the violent passion of the Russian questions is making you lose sight of the international aspects of the Russian questions themselves, is making you forget that your duties as Russian militants can and must be carried out only within the *framework of the interests of the international proletariat.*

xxxxx

The Political Bureau of the PCI has studied with the greatest diligence and attention of which it was capable all the *problems currently under discussion in the CP of the USSR.* The questions that today are being posed to you, may be posed tomorrow to our Party. In our country, too, the rural masses are the majority of the working population. Furthermore, we shall find ourselves faced with all the problems inherent in the hegemony of the proletariat in a form that will certainly be more complex and acute than in Russia itself, since the density of the rural population in Italy is enormously greater, since our peasants have a very rich organisational tradition and have always succeeded in making their specific weight as a mass felt very considerably in the political life of the nation. This is because in Italy the organisational apparatus of the church has two thousand years of tradition behind it and is specialised in propaganda and the organisation of the peasants in a way that bears no comparison with other countries. If it is true that industry is more developed in Italy and that the proletariat has a substantial material basis, it is also true that this industry has no domestic raw materials and thus is more exposed to crises. The proletariat will therefore be able to fulfil its leading role only if its spirit of sacrifice is highly developed and only if has managed to rid itself completely of any last residue of reformist corporativism or syndicalism. It is from this realistic and we believe Leninist standpoint that the Pol[itical] Bur[eau] of the PCI has studied your discussions. We, up to now, have expressed an opinion as a Party only on the strictly disciplinary question of fractions, wanting to conform to the request you made after your XIV Congress not to carry the Russian discussion into the Sections of the International.[20] We declare now that we believe the political line of the majority of the C[entral] C[ommittee] of the CP of the USSR is fundamentally correct and that the majority of the Italian Party will certainly take this stance if it becomes necessary to pose the question in its entirety. We do not wish, and we do not think it useful, to engage in agitation and propaganda with you and with the comrades of the bloc of the opposition groupings. We shall not therefore draw up a register of all the individual questions with our judgement by the side. We repeat that we are struck by the fact that the attitude of the bloc of the opposition groupings calls into question the whole political line of the C[entral] C[ommittee], involving the very heart of Leninist doctrine and of the action of our Party of the Union. It is the principle and practice of the hegemony of the proletariat that are being questioned, it is the fundamental relationships of the alliance between the workers and peasants that are being upset and thrown into jeopardy, in other words the pillars of the workers' State and of the Revolution. Comrades, it has never been seen in history that *a dominant class, in its entirety*, has been subject to living conditions that were lower than given elements and strata of the subjected and dominated class. History has reserved this unheard-of contradiction to the lot of the proletariat. And it is in this contradiction that there reside the greatest dangers for the dictatorship of the proletariat, especially in those countries where capitalism has not had any great development and has not succeeded in unifying the productive forces. It is this contradiction, already manifest moreover in certain aspects in the capitalist countries where the proletariat has objectively reached a social role of a high level, that gives rise to reformism and syndicalism, that gives rise to the spirit of corporativism and the stratifications characteristic of the working-class aristocracy. And yet the proletariat cannot become the dominant class if, through the sacrifice of its corporative interests, it does not transcend this contradiction, it cannot maintain its hegemony and its dictatorship if, even when it has become dominant, it does not sacrifice these immediate interests for its general and permanent class interests. Certainly, it is easy to be demagogic on this terrain, it is easy to insist on the negative sides of the contradiction: 'Are you, the badly dressed and underfed worker, the dominator, or is it rather the Nepman in his furs with *all the goods of the earth* at his disposal?'[21] In the same way, after a revolutionary strike that has increased the cohesion and discipline of the masses, but due to its length has impoverished the individual workers even more, the reformists say '*To what end did you fight? You have ruined and impoverished yourselves!*' It is easy to be demagogic on this terrain, and it is difficult not to be demagogic when the question is posed in terms of a corporativist spirit and not in terms of a Leninist one, of the doctrine of the hegemony of the proletariat, which historically is found in one given position and not in another.

This for us is the essential element of your discussions, it is in this element that there lie the errors of the bloc of the opposition groupings and the origin of the latent dangers contained in its activity. In the ideology and practice of the bloc of the opposition groupings there is the rebirth in its entirety of the whole tradition of social democracy and syndicalism, which up to now has hindered the western proletariat from organising itself as a ruling class.

xxxxx

Only firm unity and a firm discipline in the Party that governs the workers' State can ensure proletarian hegemony in the NEP regime, in other words in the full development of the contradiction that we have mentioned. But unity and discipline in this case cannot be mechanical and forced, they must be loyal and expressed out of conviction, not those of an imprisoned or besieged enemy detachment, always thinking of escape or surprise sallies out of its confinement.[22]

This, dearest comrades, we have wished to tell you, in the spirit of friends and brothers, albeit *younger brothers*. Comrades Zinov'ev, Trotsky, Kamenev have contributed powerfully to educating us for the revolution, sometimes they have corrected us very forcefully and severely, they have been among our teachers. To them in particular we turn as the people most responsible for the current situation, because we want to *be sure that the majority of the C[entral] C[ommittee] of the C.P. of the U.S.S.R. does not intend to be all-conquering* in the struggle and *is willing to avoid excessive measures*. The unity of our Russian brother Party is necessary for the development and triumph of the world's revolutionary forces. *For this necessity every communist and internationalist must be willing to make greater sacrifices*. The damage of an error committed by the united Party is easy to overcome; the damage caused by a split or a prolonged condition of a latent split may be irreparable and lethal.[23]

With communist greetings

The P[olitical] B[ureau] of the PCI

Source: AAG and APC 513-1-410/6-15, handwritten on Chamber of Deputies notepaper[24]

To Giuseppina Marcias

15 OCTOBER 1926

Dearest mother,

I haven't had any news from you for several months. Carlo hasn't written to me since I told him I couldn't send him the tickets, because I'd had them all seized. I would like to have news of everyone. Could you write me a couple of lines? I am fairly well. I'm sending you some photographs of Delio taken in St Mark's Square in Venice, surrounded by the doves; he's there with one of his aunts. A month ago he again left to go back to the land of his birth. As soon as I have a copy, I'll send you a really nice photo of him, which shows him to be a very attractive child. An embrace for everyone

Nino

Source: AAG; handwritten on Chamber of Deputies headed notepaper

To Jul'ka

20 OCTOBER 1926

Dearest one,

As I wrote in great haste at the end of my previous letter, last time I received two letters of yours, 26.IX and 3.X; this week, however, I've received nothing.

I'm sure my letter of 15 September produced a rather comical effect on you. To be very honest, the fault was entirely due to T[at'jana]'s interpretation (you see how chivalrous I am!), and before I'd read it, she'd already given me her interpretation. I kept to the opinion that the telegram was very simple, in that it was psychologically entirely natural for the grandfather to see the two children together, even after having spoken of Del'ka first. T[at'jana] on the other hand referred to impressions of yours while you were still in Rome, to that suffering of yours that I knew nothing about. The reference to this disturbed me greatly, because it gave me a very live impression of your physical condition. Now I'm calm and at peace, even more so now that it seems very probable that we'll be meeting again soon.

I think everything you've done for the baby is good. I already knew the name and had already told it to T[at'jana] because we'd talked about that (had you forgotten?). As regards the rest we'll deal with things as we feel it best, given the fact that we have to leave all possibilities open for our work and our future. I don't know if you get our newspaper. I go on working with a will, I'm finishing off a work that has taken up much time and effort and which maybe will turn out to be interesting and useful.[25]

A close and tight embrace for you and the two little ones.

Antonio

With this letter you'll find 40 dollars enclosed; this is said so you can be certain.

Source: AAG

To Togliatti

26 OCTOBER 1926

Dearest Ercoli,

I have received your letter of the 18th. My reply is a personal one, although I'm convinced that I am also expressing the opinion of the other comrades.

Your letter seems to me too abstract and too schematic in its way of reasoning. We started from the point of view, which to me seems exact, that in our countries there exist not only Parties, understood as a technical organisation, but there also exist the great working masses, stratified politically in a contradictory way, but tending in their entirety towards unity. One of the most forceful elements of this unitary process is the existence of the USSR, bound to the real action of the CP of the USSR and to the widespread conviction that in the USSR the road to socialism has been undertaken. Insofar as our Parties represent the whole active entirety of the USSR, they have a given influence over all the political strata of the great mass of people, they represent its tendency toward unity, they are moving on a fundamentally favourable historical terrain despite the contradictory superstructures.

But it should not then be thought that this factor, which makes the CP of the USSR the most powerful mass organiser that has ever appeared in history, is a stable and decisive gain: anything but. It is always unstable. Thus, it should not be forgotten that the Russian revolut[ion] has already been in existence for nine years and that its present activity is an ensemble of partial actions and acts of government that only a highly developed theoretical and political consciousness is able to comprehend in its entirety and in its movement as an entirety towards socialism. Not only for the great masses of the working people, but also for a notable part of the members of the western Parties, differentiated from the masses only by one fact, namely the radical but initial step towards developed consciousness represented by entry into the P[arty] – the overall movement of the Russian rev[olution] is represented in concrete terms by the fact that the R[ussian] P[arty] is moving in a united fashion, that the people who represent it, whom our masses know and are used to knowing, are working and moving together as one. The question of unity, not only of the R[ussian] P[arty] but of the Leninist core, is therefore a question of utmost importance in the international field; *from the point of view of the masses*, this is the most important question in this historical period of the intensified contradictory process towards unity.

It is possible and probable that unity may not be preserved, at least in the form it has had in the past. It is also certain however that the world is not going to collapse about our ears, and that we shall have to do all in our power to prepare the comrades and the masses for the new situation. This does not take anything away from our absolute duty to recall to the political consciousness of the Russian comrades, and recall to them forcefully, the dangers and weaknesses that their approaches are about to bring into being. We should be totally pitiful and irresponsible revolutionaries if we were to allow *faits accomplis* to come about, justifying their necessity *a priori*.

That our carrying out such a duty may, as a secondary consequence, *also* help the opposition must be of concern to us up to a point. In fact it is our aim to contribute to maintaining and creating a unitary plan in which the different tendencies and different personalities may once more come closer together and fuse together even ideologically.[26] But I do not think that in our letter, which quite obviously must be read as a whole and not in extracts detached from and set against one another, there is any danger whatsoever of weakening the position of the majority of the C[entral] C[ommittee]. In any case, precisely with this in view and with the possibility of its appearing as such, in an additional letter I authorised you to modify its form. You could quite easily put the two parts later on and begin instead with our affirmation of the opposition's 'responsibility'. This line of reasoning of yours has therefore left me with an extremely bad impression.

And I want to tell you that there is no trace of alarmism within us, but simply considered and cold reflection. We are sure that in no case will the world collapse about our ears, but it would be foolish, so it seems to me, if we moved only if the world were about to collapse about our ears. No set phrase is going to budge us from the conviction that we are following the right line, the Leninist line as regards the way of considering the Russian questions. The Leninist line consists in the fight for P[arty] unity, not only for external unity but for that somewhat more intrinsic unity that consists in there not being within the P[arty] two completely divergent political lines on all questions. Not only within our countries, as regards the ideological and political leadership of the Intern[ational], but also in Russia, as regards the hegemony of the prolet[ariat], that is to say the social content of the State, P[arty] unity is an essential condition.

You confuse the international aspects of the Russian question, which are a reflection of the historical fact of the link between the working masses and the first socialist State, and the international organisational problems at the trade union and political level. The two orders of factors are closely linked, yet distinct. The difficulties that are being experienced and produced in the more restricted organisational field, are dependent on the fluctuations taking place in the wider field of widespread mass ideology, in other words the shrinkage of the influence and prestige of the R[ussian P[arty] in certain areas of the people. For methodological reasons, we have preferred to speak only of the more general aspects, and wished to avoid falling into lessons learnt by rote, which can unfortunately be seen in some of the documents of other parties, and which detract from their seriousness.

Likewise it is not true, as you claim, that we are too optimistic regarding the real Bolshevisation of the western P[arties]. Anything but. The Bolshevisation process is so slow and difficult that every, even small, obstacle halts and delays it. The Russian discussion and the ideology of the opposition groupings are playing a much bigger role in halting and delaying this process insofar as that, in Russia, they represent all the old prejudices of syndicalism and class corporativism that weigh down the tradition of the western proletariat and delay its ideological and political development. Our observation was wholly directed against the opposition groups. It is true that the crises of the various P[arties], including the R[ussian] P[arty], are bound up with the objective situation, but what does that mean? Does it maybe therefore mean that we should stop struggling to modify the subjective factors in a favourable direction? Bolshevism consists precisely in keeping one's head and being ideologically and politically firm, even in difficult situations. Your observation is inert, and has no value, as is the one found at point number 5, since we have spoken of the great masses and not at all of the proletarian vanguard. Secondarily, however, there exists a difficulty on this point too, a difficulty represented by something not abstract but closely bound to the mass: and it exists so much the more, in that reformism – with its tendencies towards class corporativism, in other words towards an incomprehension of the leading role of the vanguard, a role that has to be preserved even at the cost of sacrifices – is much more deeply rooted in the West than it was in Russia. You easily forget, then, the technical conditions which many Parties have to work in, which do not allow for a widespread discussion of the higher level theoretical questions, except in restricted circles of workers. The whole of your reasoning is vitiated by 'bureaucratism'. Today, nine years after October 1917, it is no longer *the fact of the seizure of* power by the Bolsheviks that can revolutionise the Western masses, because this is already taken for granted and has had its effect; today the conviction (if it exists) is politically and ideologically active that, once the proletariat has taken power, *it can build socialism*. The authority of the P[arty] is bound up with this conviction, that cannot be inculcated into the broad masses by the methods of scholastic pedagogy but only through revolutionary pedagogy, in other words only through the *political fact* that the R[ussian] P[arty] as a whole is convinced and is fighting in united fashion.

I am sincerely sorry that our letter was not understood by you in the first place and that, in any case, along the lines of my personal note, you did not seek to understand it better. Our letter *in its entirety* was a point-by-point criticism of the opposition groupings, not carried out in demagogic terms and, for that very reason, it was more effective and more serious. I am asking you to include this letter too in the official documentation, together with the Italian text of the letter and my personal note.[27]

Warm greetings

Antonio

Source: APC 513-1-410/28-33 with copy in AAG; handwritten on Chamber of Deputies notepaper

---

To Jul'ka

27 OCTOBER 26

Dearest Юлька,

I've received no news from you this week, either. On the 30th, that is in three days' time, I'm leaving Rome and will try to get out of the country to come to the next Enlarged Executive. I'm not sure if I'll fully succeed in this but it seems there are a number of favourable probabilities. As soon as I cross in to sovietist territory I'll send you a telegram, but this time too I don't think you should come to the station except if the weather is good and you are completely free. With all this, there's going to be a period, maybe a long one, when I won't hear from you and won't be able to write to you. But the hope of seeing all of us together is some consolation.

An embrace for you together with the babies.

Antonio

Source: AAG

To Jul'ka

4-XI-926

My dearest Юлька,

I have received your letter of 26 October. Due to an incident, I had to return to Rome and because of that received your letter and can still reply to you. In its general lines my previous letter is however confirmed.[28]

How I would like to caress you and hold your poor head close and tight. But rest assured: it isn't at all true that lots and lots of the darkest ideas have sprouted and are continuing to sprout within me. I think it's a question merely that the thoughts that come to me, given my extreme emotional loneliness, take on a schematic and cold form when I try to express them. When, like an insistent lament, they reach you, who live instead in a world of ever fresh and lively impressions, they must, as you say, have a disastrous and … terrorising effect. But you have to understand that such an effect is not reasonable, you have to try and reconstruct my states of mind in line with the reality that you know and in line with my temperament, formed as it has been in something like twenty years of loneliness as regards my family and the exercise of only my own critical and volitional faculties. Does what I am saying not seem right to you? I would really be a wretch if I didn't manage to make myself understood by you and, even under the cold outer shell of my expressions, make you feel all the immensity of my love and my calm confidence.

Maybe once again I've been clumsy. I don't want to contribute to you needing to become even stronger than you are, in order to maintain your serenity in the midst of all the events and managing in that way to dominate them.[29] I hope that by the time you read these words Del'ka will have already recovered and Ženja too, and that you will be able to await my arrival without any more serious concerns. I want to find all of you calm, maybe out of a selfish wish, out of an inexorable desire to be able to enjoy, every so often, interludes of joy. A close and tight embrace for you, любимая [ljubimaja: darling], together with the children.

Ant.

Source: AAG

APPENDIX TO CHAPTER 7

To Gramsci from Togliatti

18 OCTOBER 1926

Dearest Antonio,

The present letter is to explain, fairly briefly, my opinion on the letter from the P[olitical] B[ureau] of the PCI to the C[entral] C[ommittee] of the CP of the USSR. I am not in agreement with this letter, for a number of reasons that I am here indicating very schematically:

1. The essential fault of the letter lies in how it is formulated. The fact of the split that has taken place in the leading group of the CP of the Union is put in the foreground and only behind that does one find the problem of the correctness or otherwise of the line being followed by the majority on the C[entral] C[ommittee]. This procedure is characteristic of the way in which many comrades of the western Parties consider and judge the problems of the CP of the Union, but it does not correspond to an exact formulation of these problems. There is no doubt that the unity of the leading group of the RCP has a value that cannot be compared with that of the unity of the leading groups of other parties. This value stems from the historical task that fell to the lot of this group in the constitution of the International. However great this task was it should nevertheless not lead us to judge the questions of the RCP on the basis of a line that is different from that of principles and political

positions. The danger inherent in the position adopted in your letter is a great one, due to the fact that, probably, from now on the unity of the Leninist old guard will no longer, or only with difficulty, be realised in a continuous fashion.[30] In the past the greatest factor of this unity resided in the enormous prestige and personal authority of Lenin. This is an element for which there is no substitute. The Party line will be established through discussions and debates. Both we and the comrades of the rank-and-file must become used to keeping our nerve. And we must initiate ourselves and the Party militants into a knowledge of the Russian problems so as to be able to judge them following a line of principles and of political positions. It is this study of Russian questions, and not an appeal for the unity of the leading group, that will offer the help that the other Parties of the International must give to the RCP. What you say is therefore right as regards the need for an intervention by these parties in the conflict between the C[entral] C[ommittee] and the opposition, but this intervention can only take place in the form of a contribution, on the basis of our revolutionary experience, towards establishing and confirming the exact Leninist line in the solution of the Russian problems.

If our intervention has a different starting point, there is a danger that it will not be useful, but damaging.

2. The consequence of this mistaken starting point lies in the fact that in the first half of your letter, where in fact you outline the consequences that a split in the Russian Party (and its leadership core) may have on the western movement, you speak indifferently of all the leading Russian comrades, in other words you make no distinction between the comrades who are at the head of the C[entral] C[ommittee] and the heads of the opposition.

On page two of the pages written by Antonio the Russian comrades are invited to 'reflect and be more aware of their responsibilities'. No mention is made at all of any distinction between them.

On page 6 it is said:

> 'It is on this element especially that we believe it is our duty as internationalists to recall the attention of the most responsible comrades of the CP of the USSR. Comrades, in these last nine years of world history you have been the organisational element and driving force of the revolutionary forces of all countries.

The role you have played has no precedent in the entire history of humankind that equals it in breadth and depth. But today you are destroying your own work, you are degrading and running the risk of nullifying the leading role that the CP of the USSR had gained through the impetus of Lenin. In our opinion the violent passion of the Russian questions is making you lose sight of the international aspects of the Russian questions themselves, is making you forget that your duties as Russian militants can and must be carried out only within the framework of the interests of the international proletariat.'

Here too one cannot see even the faintest distinction. One cannot but draw the conclusion that the P[olitical] B[ureau] of the PCI considers that everyone is responsible, everyone is to be called to order.

It is true that at the end of the letter this approach is corrected. It is said that Zinov'ev, Kamenev and Trotsky are the people 'most' responsible and it is added that:

> 'we want to be sure that the majority of the C[entral] C[ommittee] of the C.P. of the U.S.S.R. does not intend to be all-conquering in the struggle and is willing to avoid excessive measures'

The expression 'we want to be sure' has a limitative value, i.e. by using it you want to say that YOU ARE NOT sure.

Now – leaving aside any consideration regarding the opportunity of intervening in the current Russian debate by attributing a small part of the blame even to the C[entral] C[ommittee], leaving aside the fact that a similar position cannot but be resolved to the TOTAL benefit of the opposition, leaving aside these considerations of appropriateness, can one claim that a small part of the blame belongs to the C[entral] C[ommittee]? I think not. To prove this one needs only to look at the attempts made before the Fourteenth Congress to reach an agreement and, what is more important, to look at the policy followed after the Fourteenth Congress, which was very careful and which cannot be accused in any way of being a policy conducted blindly in one direction. As for the internal life of the Party, the Russian Central [leadership] is no more responsible for the discussion, for the fractional activity of the opposition, for the acuteness of the crisis, etc, than we, as the Italian Executive, were responsible for the fractional activity of Bordiga, for the constitution and activity of the Liaison Committee.[31] It is beyond doubt there is a rigour in the internal life of the CP of the Union. But this must be the case. If the western Parties wanted to make a representation to the leading group to have this rigour abolished they would be committing a very grave mistake. In this case the dictatorship of the proletariat really could be compromised.

I therefore regard the first part of your letter and the concluding expressions connected with it to be politically an error. This error ruins (even in the first part) what there is of good in the letter.

Yet another observation on this point. It is only right that the foreign Parties should be worried about a sharpening of the crisis of the Russian Communist Party and it is right that they should, as far as it is in their capabilities, try to make it less sharp. It is however certain that, when one is in agreement with the Central Committee line, the best way to contribute to overcoming the crisis is to express one's support for this line with no conditions posed. If the Russian opposition had not counted on the support of some opposition groups, or on entire Parties of the International, it would not have adopted the attitude it did after the Fourteenth Congress. Experience has demonstrated that the opposition uses the slightest wavering that makes itself evident even in the judgement of groups and Parties that one knows are in agreement with the C[entral] C[ommittee].[32]

3. In the passage I have cited above on recalling the Russian comrades to their responsibilities, it is said that they are losing sight of the international aspects of the Russian questions. In claiming this you are losing sight of the fact that after the Fourteenth Congress the Russian discussion shifted from mainly Russian questions to international ones. Forgetting this fact explains why in the letter you make no mention of these international problems and this represents a third serious defect.

4. Your letter is too optimistic when it speaks of the Bolshevisation being carried out after the Fifth Congress, and it seems you are attributing the halt in the process of consolidation of the Communist Parties solely to the Russian discussion. Here too there is a limit to your judgement and an error in assessment. You have to recognise in the first place that the Bolshevik solidarity of some of the leading groups put in charge of our Parties by the Fifth Congress was of a

wholly external nature (France, Germany, Poland), and that for this reason the subsequent crises were inevitable. In the second place, then, you have to recognise that these crises are bound up, much more than with the Russian discussion, with the change in the objective situation and with its repercussion within the vanguard of the working class. The Russian crisis, too, is bound up with this change, in the same way moreover as in all the previous crises and discussions, and in particular, for example, the one which was closed by the tenth Congress and which has the closest analogy with the present one.[33]

5. The letter is too pessimistic, on the other hand, not only as regards the consequences of the Russian discussion, but in general as regards the capacities of the proletarian vanguard to understand what the line of the Russian CP is and have it understood by the working masses. For this reason you overestimate the damaging consequences of the Russian discussion within the western proletariat, and your pessimism gives the impression that you are of the opinion that the line of the Party is not wholly correct. If this line is correct and corresponds to objective conditions, we must be able to make its value understood to the masses, we must be able to keep the masses united around Russia and the Bolshevik Party, discussions notwithstanding. Through discussions and splits the Bolshevik Party succeeded in winning the leadership of the Russian proletariat. It seems to me that you now understand the historical role of the Russian Party and the Russian revolution in a purely external fashion. It is not so much the unity of the leading group (which has never been something absolute) that has made the Russian Party the organiser and driving force of the world revolutionary movement of the post-war era, as the fact that the Russian Party led the working class to the conquest of power and to the maintenance of power. Does the current line of the Party condemn it – yes or no – to failing in this, its historical task? In this way the question must be posed of the position of the Russian Party in the international workers' movement if one does not wish to fall directly into the reasoning of the opposition.

These are just some observations made hurriedly. But they are, I believe the basic ones. Let me know your thoughts on the subject.[34]

Fraternally

Source: APC 513-1-410/2-4; copy at APC 513-1-410/24-26 and partial copy in AAG; typewritten and unsigned

NOTES

1. This suggestion, in the manuscript, is omitted in Gramsci (1992).
2. Paolo Pili, a leader of the Sardinian Action Party (*Partito Sardo d'Azione*), supported dairy producers, important in the island's economy: see Gramsci's letter to his brother Carlo of 22 March 1929 in Gramsci (1994a, Vol. 1), pp253-5. Pili was elected to parliament in 1924 for the Fascists, but later broke with them. The anti-fascist Sardinians elected in 1924 included Lussu, and Mario Berlinguer, father of Enrico, general secretary of the PCI from 1972 to his death in 1984.
3. Gramsci (1992) has 'justified' instead of the correct – as here – 'judged'.
4. In Gramsci (1992) the word 'real' is omitted while the sentence has the words 'at this current political moment' instead of the correct 'faced with this policy'.
5. This reference is to southern democrats such as Giovanni Amendola and, despite the name 'social democrats', to groupings, especially in Sicily, which were actually conservative.
6. The Sardinian Action Party had held a Congress in Macomer, a town in the centre of the island, in September 1925.
7. Jul'ka and Delio, together with Evgenija, had spent from October 1925 in Italy (see Introduction). Jul'ka left Italy for Russia on 7 August 1926, and the couple's second child, Giuliano, was born in Moscow on 30 August: see Fiori (1970), pp201-6.
8. Delio had stayed behind, with Tanja and Ženja looking after him, at Trafoi in the German-speaking Alto Adige (South Tyrol) in the North East of Italy.
9. The verb here is 'to think' [of myself], not 'to feel myself' as appears in Gramsci (1992).
10. The date of these last letters is not always included on the original, and in such cases square brackets indicate the date inferred from sound evidence. For this letter the date, not present in the copies in the Rome or Moscow Archives (513-1-440/2), is deduced from those of the articles in *Il Mondo* and *L'Unità*.
11. Alfonso Leonetti, then editing *L'Unità*, wrote back to Gramsci, defending the work of his journalists and criticising the tone and content of the service note, but printed a correction from Gramsci on 19 September.
12. The letter of 15 September in which Gramsci thought it was possible, almost persuaded by Tat'jana, that twins had been born.
13. Accusations of Party full-time workers paid by 'Moscow gold' had recently been made by some Italian papers.
14. Aleksandra Kollontaj, afterwards Soviet ambassador in the Nordic countries and later rediscovered by the women's movements of the late

1960s and 1970s, was then waging a proto-feminist battle in the Comintern's women's section.

15. I.e. the covering note, sent to Togliatti, for the letter to the Central Committee of the Soviet Communist Party; these and the letter to Jul'ka, the only one bearing a date, were written all together in the Soviet Embassy in Rome.
16. The present letter is a personal one to Togliatti; 'another letter' refers to the one to Jul'ka of the same day (p367), while the 'document' is Gramsci's famous letter, written in the name of the PCI's Political Bureau, to the Central Committee of the Soviet (All-Union) Communist Party, and reproduced here immediately following this letter (p369). After consultations in Moscow with Humbert-Droz, Kuusinen, Manuil'skij and Bukharin. Togliatti wrote a response to the letter (see p383), to which Gramsci's letter of 26 October (p378) is a reply (see also Introduction).
17. The more easily legible of the two identical digitalised copies of this letter in the Archives in Rome clearly shows various underlinings in the text and lines in the margin, all in pencil and therefore not by Gramsci, who wrote the letter in pen. A comparison of the phrases and passages marked in pencil with the criticisms and direct quotes from Gramsci's letter that are made in Togliatti's reply to Gramsci from Moscow (included as an appendix to this chapter, p383) demonstrates that these pencilled additions are Togliatti's. Indeed, between the lines of Gramsci's original handwritten letter are occasional words in French pencilled in by Togliatti as a guide for the letter's immediate translation into French (APC 513-1-410/21), a language more readily understood at the Comintern. Underlining (shown as italics) in this letter is to be attributed to Togliatti, while italics combined with underlining in the present text indicates a double vertical bar ('||') in the margin, again attributable to Togliatti.
18. Through an oversight, perhaps due to haste, Gramsci writes 'Conference', which had limited powers of decision, while the event was actually a full Party Congress, which opened two weeks after this letter on 27 October.
19. The manuscript has the plural 'internazionali' – referring to newspapers and statesmen – not the singular form referring just to the bourgeoisie, as found in Gramsci (1992) and in previous English translations (Gramsci 1978b, p427, and Gramsci 1994b, p307).
20. The request was made in a letter to all sections of the International immediately following the December 1925 Fourteenth Congress of the All-Union Communist Party (Bolsheviks), as the Party named itself at the Congress.
21. 'Nepmen' was the name given to the well-off traders, speculators, etc, who had benefited from the New Economic Policy (NEP) launched at the Tenth Congress of the Russian Communist Party in 1921.
22. 'Or besieged' is added above the line.

23. 'May be' substitutes the original crossed-out 'are'.
24. A typed-up copy of this letter, with no significant variations and without underlinings, is at APC 513-1-410/16-19.
25. With near certainty this refers to the essay 'Some Aspects of the Southern Question', unfinished when Gramsci was arrested just over a fortnight after this letter.
26. 'Plan': the word used by Gramsci ('piano') may also be interpreted as a (metaphorical) geometrical 'plane'.
27. Togliatti added a handwritten note to 'Type up a copy and send copies to Italy (2 to the secretariat of the P[arty] and to Antonio); the same for the personal covering note for the first letter to Antonio'.
28. On 31 October Gramsci left Rome by train to attend the meeting of the Party Central Committee near Genoa, due to start the following day. Terracini recounts that, when Gramsci had to change trains in Milan, he was told politely but firmly by a police officer 'for your own good, go back to Rome'. This he did, saving from immediate danger the comrades waiting for him in Milan, as well as those in Genoa, but having to give up all idea of taking part in the meeting: cf Spriano (1969), pp59 and 64-5.
29. The manuscript has 'dominarli' ('dominate them', i.e. the events), not 'dominarti' ('dominate yourself') as transcribed in Gramsci (1992).
30. The 'your' used by Togliatti in 'your letter' is a plural, referring to the PCI Political Bureau, and not the personal 'you' with which Gramsci replies to Togliatti in his letter of 26 October.
31. For Bordiga and the Liaison Committee see chapter 6.
32. The word 'even' is a handwritten addition by Togliatti.
33. The 1921 Tenth Party Congress had banned both fractions and 'groupings'.
34. Here Togliatti switches from the collective plural to the singular form ('your'), thus asking directly for Gramsci's opinion, for which see the reply of 26 October.

Select Bibliography

The select bibliography lists by no means all the articles and books referred to in this volume but those, including some mentioned only in passing, which contain essential information for reconstructing the backdrop to the letters.

Carlucci, Alessandro and Caterina Balistreri (2011). 'I primi mesi di Gramsci in Russia. Giugno – agosto 1922, con Antonio Gramsci, *Saluto alla XII Conferenza panrussa del Partito Comunista Russo (bolscevico)*' ('Gramsci's first few months in Russia. June-August 1922, with Antonio Gramsci, *Greetings to the XII pan-Russian Conference of the Russian Communist Party (Bolshevik)*), in *Belfagor*, LXVI (6), pp. 645-58.

Carr, E.H. (1954). *The interregnum 1923-1924*, Macmillan: London and St Martin's: New York.

Chiara, Daniele (ed.) (1999). *Togliatti a Mosca, Gramsci a Roma*, Einaudi: Turin.

Daniels, R.V. (1960). *The conscience of the revolution: Communist opposition in Soviet Russia.* Harvard University Press: Cambridge (Mass.).

Degras, Jane (1960). *The Communist International 1919-1943. Documents, Volume 2, 1923-1928.* Oxford University Press: London.

Detti, Tommaso (1972). *Serrati e la formazione del Partito Comunista Italiano*, Editori Riuniti: Rome.

Fiori, Giuseppe (1970). *Antonio Gramsci. Life of a revolutionary* (trans. Tom Nairn of *Vita di Antonio Gramsci*, Laterza: Bari, 1966), New Left Books: London.

Frosini, Fabio and Guido Liguori (eds), (2004, third repr. 2011), *Le parole di Gramsci* (*Gramsci's words*), Carocci: Rome.

Giasi, Francesco (2009). 'Gramsci a Vienna. Annotazioni su quattro lettere inedite' ('Notes on Four Unpublished Letters') in Giasi, Francesco, Roberto Gualtieri and Silvio Pons (eds), (2009), *Pensare la politica* (*Thinking politics*), Carocci: Rome 2009, pp. 185-208.

Gramsci, Antonio (1971). *Selections from the prison notebooks*, ed. and trans. Quintin Hoare and Geoffrey Nowell Smith, Lawrence and Wishart: London.

Gramsci, Antonio (1976). *A. Gramsci Scritti 1915-1921*, ed. Sergio Caprioglio, Moizzi: Milano.

Gramsci, Antonio (1978a [1971]). *La costruzione del partito comunista 1923-1926* (*The construction of the Communist Party 1923-1926*), ed. Elsa Fubini, Einaudi: Turin.

Gramsci, Antonio (1978b). *Selections from political writings 1921-1926*, ed. and trans. Quintin Hoare, Lawrence and Wishart: London.

Gramsci, Antonio (1982). *La città futura*, ed. Sergio Caprioglio, Einaudi: Turin.

Gramsci, Antonio (1985). *Selections from cultural writings*, David Forgacs and Geoffrey Nowell Smith (eds), trans. William Q. Boelhower, Lawrence and Wishart: London.

Gramsci, Antonio (1988). *Il rivoluzionario qualificato* (*The skilled revolutionary*), ed. and introduced by Corrado Morgia, Delotti: Rome.

Gramsci, Antonio (1992). *Lettere 1908-1926*, ed. Antonio A. Santucci, Einaudi: Turin.

Gramsci, Antonio (1994a). *Letters from prison*, 2 Vols, ed. Frank Rosengarten and trans. Raymond Rosenthal, Columbia University Press: New York.

Gramsci, Antonio (1994b). *Pre-prison writings*, ed. Richard Bellamy and trans. Virginia Cox, Cambridge University Press: Cambridge.

Gramsci, Antonio (1995). *Further selections from the prison notebooks*, ed. and trans. Derek Boothman, Lawrence and Wishart: London.

Gramsci, Antonio (2009). *Epistolario I. gennaio 1906-dicembre 1922* (*Letters I. January 1906-December 1922*: National edition of the writings of Antonio Gramsci, Vol. III). Istituto della Enciclopedia Italiana Treccani: Rome.

Gramsci, Antonio (2012). *Epistolario II. gennaio-novembre 1923* (*Letters II. January-November 1923*: National edition of the writings of Antonio Gramsci, Vol. IV). Istituto della Enciclopedia Italiana Treccani: Rome.

Gramsci, Antonio, jr (2008). *La Russia di mio nonno: L'album famigliare degli Schucht.* (*My grandfather's Russia. The Schucht family album*), Italian trans. from the Russian by Andrea Lena Corritore, L'Unità / Fondazione Istituto Gramsci: Rome.

Gramsci, Antonio, jr (2010). *I miei nonni nella rivoluzione. Breve storia della famiglia russa di Antonio Gramsci* (*My grandparents in the revolution. Brief history of Antonio Gramsci's Russian family*), Il Riformista: Rome.

Gramsci, Antonio, jr (2014). *La storia di una famiglia rivoluzionaria. Antonio Gramsci e gli Schucht tra la Russia e l'Italia* (*The history of a revolutionary family. Antonio Gramsci and the Schucht family between Russia and Italy*. Editori Riuniti University Press: Rome.

Hájek, Miloš (1972). *Storia dell'Internazionale Comunista (1921-1935)* (*History of the Communist International (1921-35)*) Editori Riuniti: Rome, Italian trans. by Luciano Antonetti of *Jednotná fronta. K politické orientaci Komunistické internacionály v letech 1921-35* (*United front. On the political orientation of the Communist International 1921-35*).

Inprecorr (1922-25), Vols. 2-5. Leningrad; from 1924, Vienna.

Ives, Peter and Rocco Lacorte (eds.) (2010). *Gramsci, language and translation*, Lexington Books: Lanham.

Leonetti, Alfonso (1978). 'Un ricordo di Gramsci studente in lettere' ('A recollection of Gramsci as student of letters'), *Belfagor* XXXIII, (1), pp. 85-86.

Liguori, Guido and Pasquale Voza (eds.) (2009). *Dizionario gramsciano 1926-1937*, Carocci: Rome.

Matt, Luigi (2008). 'Aspetti linguistici delle lettere pre-carcerarie' ('Linguistic aspects of the pre-prison letters') in *Gramsci nel suo tempo* (*Gramsci in his time*), *Vol. II*, Francesco Giasi (ed.) Carocci: Rome, pp. 793-811.

Merli, Stefano (1964). 'Le origini della direzione centrista nel Partito Comunista d'Italia. Nuova documentazione sulla "svolta" nella direzione del Partito comunista d'Italia nel 1923-24', ('The origins of the centre group leadership of the Communist Party of Italy. New documentation regarding the "turning point" in the leadership of the Communist Party of Italy in 1923-24'), *Rivista storica del socialismo*, Vol. 7, no 23, pp. 513-40.

Ordine Nuovo (1976). Anastatic reprint of the original review, 1919-20 and 1924-5, Teti: Milan.

Paulesu Quercioli, Mimma (ed.1977). *Gramsci vivo nelle testimonianze dei suoi contemporanei* (*Gramsci alive in the testimonies of his contemporaries*), Feltrinelli: Milan.

Paulesu Quercioli, Mimma (ed. 1987). *Forse rimarrai lontana. Lettere a*

Iulca 1922-1937. (*Perhaps you will remain far away. Letters to Jul'ka 1922-1937*). Albatros/Editori Riuniti: Rome.

Paulesu Quercioli, Mimma (1991). *Le donne di casa Gramsci* (*The women of the Gramsci household*). Editori Riuniti: Rome (reprint ISKRA: Ghilarza 2003).

Righi, Maria Luisa (2012), 'Gramsci a Mosca tra amore e politica (1922-1923)' ('Gramsci in Moscow beteween love and politics (1922-1923)'), *Studi storici* 52 (4), 1001-1038.

Rosengarten, Frank (1984-5), 'The Gramsci-Trotsky Question (1922-1932)', *Social text*, Vol. 4 (3), No. 11, pp. 65-95.

Schirru, Giancarlo (2011). 'Antonio Gramsci studente di linguistica' in *Studi Storici* 52 (4), 925-73.

Somai, Giovanni (1979). *Gramsci a Vienna. Ricerche e documenti 1922/1924*. Argalìa: Urbino.

Spriano, Paolo (1967). *Storia del Partito Comunista. Vol. I. Da Bordiga a Gramsci* [*History of the Communist Party, Vol. I: From Bordiga to Gramsci*], Einaudi: Turin.

Spriano, Paolo (1969). *Storia del Partito Comunista. Vol. II. Gli anni della clandestinità* [*History of the Communist Party, Vol. II: The Clandestine Years*], Einaudi: Turin.

Togliatti, Palmiro (ed.) (1962). *La formazione del gruppo dirigente del partito comunista italiano 1923-1924* (*The formation of the leadership group of the Italian Communist Party 1923-1924*), Editori Riuniti: Rome.

Trotsky, Lev Davidovič. (1973) *Letteratura e rivoluzione*, Italian trans. by Vittorio Strada, Einaudi: Turin; original *Literatura i revoljucija* (Izdatel'stvo Glavpolitprosvet Krasnaya Nov': Moscow 1923; reprint Politizdat: Moscow 1991).

Vacca, Giuseppe (2012). *Vita e pensieri di Antonio Gramsci 1926-1937*, Einaudi: Turin.

Zucàro, Domenico (1957). 'Antonio Gramsci all'Università di Torino 1911-1915' ('Antonio Gramsci at the University of Turin 1911-1915') in *Società*, Vol. xiii, No. 6, pp. 1091-1111.

A note on the translation

Readers will note that some of the letters read unevenly, and there may be marked differences in style even within the same letter. Gramsci's early letters from Cagliari, for example, are typical of an adolescent who has not as yet fully mastered the niceties of written expression, and even contain grammatical errors. Their style is far removed from that of his mature writings, and an attempt has been made to reproduce these weaknesses; rough edges in the English versions of these early letters are therefore not (all) due to the translator. These letters betray both Gramsci's criticism of his father and often his anxiety, too, which sometimes leads him to make further mistakes and introduce some ambiguities of meaning; where necessary, these problems are indicated in the endnotes to the various chapters. Later on, in the letters from Moscow to the Party leadership in Italy, the occasional absence of the refined mode of expression that characterised Gramsci's journalistic output is almost certainly due to another hand at work, that of either Ersilio Ambrogi or Egidio Gennari, with whom Gramsci agreed the texts of the letters before signing them. Some of these political letters have excessively long paragraphs; when ease of reading requires it, these have been divided into more easily manageable blocks.

Due to switches from personal to political matters, sharp changes in language are found in the letters Gramsci writes to his wife, Julija Apollonovna Schucht (see the section on the Schucht family in the General Introduction). As with the letters from Sardinia, an attempt has been made to reproduce these switches. With other people, for example sympathisers outside the narrower circles of the Communist Party, or others more distant from his positions, for example Zino Zini (letter of 2 April 1924) or Giuseppe Lombardo-Radice (March 1918), his style becomes much more formal. These stylistic questions are dealt with in Matt (2008).

In many letters to Party comrades, abbreviations are used not only to save time but also space; where feasible a rendering of these is given; for example '17/11' for '17 November'; 'comp.' ('compagno') is rendered as 'com.' for 'comrade', so as to further give a direct impression of the original texts and, indeed, of the conditions under which Gramsci was working. When parties and organisations are named, they are often referred to by their initials in the original and this convention has been maintained, with the rest of the word added in editorial square brackets as an aid to the reader when useful. For pseudonyms and people often referred to solely by either first name or surname, if a guide in square brackets is not included, see the name index at the end of the book. Gramsci and his various secretaries were not always consistent in the use of capitals, the main words here being 'State' and 'Party', which are almost always capitalised, and this convention has been kept to here, especially when 'Party' refers to a Communist Party; an exception is made for the letter to Amadeo Bordiga of 18 August 1925, where the typescript consistently has a small letter. In referring to the USSR, Gramsci normally uses the adjective 'soviettista' (here rendered as 'sovietist'), which in these early days seems to emphasise the role of 'soviets' as 'councils', i.e. the system of self-management; the later 'sovietico' ('soviet') gradually took on the overtones of statehood.

Page numbers in archive copies of documents kept at the Fondazione Istituto Gramsci in Rome, used for most of this volume, refer to the current digitalised version; attention is drawn to any exceptions. In general these page numbers are different from those in Antonio A. Santucci's 1992 volume of the letters then known, which used the hand numbering of original typescript and manuscript pages, sometimes but not always corresponding to page numbers in the Comintern Archives in Moscow. The letters to Jul'ka and Evgenija, without exception handwritten and so not needing an explicit specification to this end, were consulted in Rome and when necessary also in the typed-up copies in the Comintern Archives (fascicules 513-1-095 and its near-exact copy 513-1-104); the Comintern copies often bear a note signed by Evgenija testifying that the transcription is a faithful copy of the original.

There is, as ever, a problem about words and names quoted from other languages, and on occasion Gramsci mistakes a form or gives a version corresponding to how the name sounds, rather than how it is really written. Usually these variations, e.g. 'Radich' for 'Radić' or 'Rakosci' for 'Rákosi', are corrected silently. Slav languages written in

Cyrillic present a particular problem. With minor exceptions, we adopt here the International Standards Organisation convention known as 'scientific transliteration' (very similar to the UN 1987 one), with departures from this to preserve historically well-established forms such as 'soviet' (see above), 'Bolshevik', and 'tsarism', which in the ISO convention would appear in the unfamiliar form of 'sovet', 'Bol'ševik', and 'carism' respectively. Another departure has been to transliterate the Russian guttural consonant 'x' (like the Scottish 'ch' in 'loch') as 'kh', so as to maintain the familiar form 'Bukharin', rather than 'Buxarin'; and the family name, German in origin, of Gramsci's wife is given as 'Schucht' rather than 'Šuxt' using the ISO convention, convention, while the familiar form 'Trotsky' is used rather than the ISO (and Italian) form 'Trockij'.

The letters transcribed as č, š, šč (ч,ш,щ respectively) are equivalent to the English sounds 'ch', 'sh', 'shch', while for the letter ж, ž is used rather than the 'zh' familiar from the novel and film Dr Zhivago. The letter 'я' is transliterated as 'ja' while in other conventions it appears as 'ya'; hence the Sanatorium where Gramsci spent much of the Summer and Autumn of 1922 appears as Serebrjanyj Bor ('Silver Wood'), the 'y' before the final 'j' corresponding to the 'hard vowel' ы. The letter ю is transliterated as 'ju', so the term of endearment 'любимая' which we have translated rather freely as 'darling' (rather than the etymologically nearer but rather archaic 'beloved') appears as 'ljubimaja' in the Latin alphabet, and the famous hotel where the foreign Comintern delegates lived in Moscow is the Hotel Ljuks rather than 'Lux'. Gramsci's wife's name Юлия is thus Julija, almost always found as the diminutive Юлька, i.e. Jul'ka, with the 'soft sign' (ь) transliterated as the single inverted comma ('), also found for example in Zinov'ev. Jul'ka's elder sister, Evgenija, often appears in Italian in the letters as 'Genia', which in Italian attempts to arrive at the sound of the Russian diminutive of her name, the ISO version of which ('Ženija'), is used here. Where Gramsci, as often, writes his wife's name in Cyrillic or uses terms of endearment in Cyrillic to convey his personal feelings and sentiments, a transliteration and if needed a translation follows in square brackets after the word or words.

For a general reader the only really unfamiliar form found here is probably in names containing the Russian letter ц, pronounced as 'ts' and transliterated as 'c' in the ISO system; the name Троцкий is then, as in Italian practice, 'Trockij' (with 'ий' rendered as 'ij') rather than the form 'Trotsky' normally found in English up to recently. For other well-known Bolsheviks of the era, the convention used here gives Lozovskij, Pjatnickij etc, rather than Lozovsky, Piatnitsky etc.

Finally, most but not all the letters included in this anthology have been published in various places in Italian, and sometimes discrepancies exist between the printed versions, or between these and the original manuscripts and typescripts. Attention to discrepancies and errors is drawn in the endnotes.

Note on main characters and organisations

This appendix provides a guide to the people and organisations of importance for the events dealt with in the letters, and to those who, sometimes present only in passing, were of subsequent great importance. Brief notes on others are found in the endnotes to the various chapters, or to the General Introduction, and may be found through the book's index. In Italy Mussolini, and in Russia the top-rank Bolshevik leaders, are well enough known not to need further biographical notes, but now generally less well-known Bolsheviks are included here. The two of Antonio's brothers who are of some political importance are likewise included, while other information on the Gramsci and Schucht families (including especially Julija and Evgenija) is contained in the General Introduction, the letters themselves, and their notes.

Occasionally the names of people listed will be seen in variant forms especially in non-Italian publications of the period or even later. This appendix gives the correct form of all Italian names.

PEOPLE

Ambrogi, Ersilio Founder member of the Communist Party; one of the fifteen communist parliamentary deputies in 1922. In Moscow as a Party representative on the Comintern Executive from February to November 1922, then sent to Berlin after criticism by Bordiga for haphazard methods of work in Moscow and irregular habits and lifestyle.

Amendola, Giovanni Southern liberal anti-fascist and leading member of the Aventine secession; died as a result of injuries sustained at the hands of fascist aggressors. His sons Antonio, Giorgio and Pietro all became communists, Giorgio emerging as the main leader of the right in the PCI in the mid-1960s.

Bianco, Vincenzo One of the working-class communist émigrés in Moscow; helped maintain contact between Gramsci and Jul'ka from an early date and present in the Schucht home when the *Prison Notebooks* arrived there. On behalf of the Italian Party, was a signatory to the document that in 1943 dissolved the Comintern.

Bombacci, Nicola A leading communist in the early 1920s but when, on the conclusion of a trade treaty between Italy and Soviet Russia, he argued that there were 'affinities' between fascism and communism, the PCd'I Executive forced his resignation from parliament. He went over to the fascists, maintaining that fascism was authentic communism in action, and remained with Mussolini to the end, like him being executed by the Italian partisans.

Bordiga, Amadeo Acknowledged leader of the PCd'I in its first period; criticised by Lenin in *Left-wing communism: an infantile disorder* for his policy of abstentionism from the parliamentary struggle. Party leadership passed from his left group to Gramsci's centre one in 1924 (see especially Chapters 5 and 6). He was re-elected to the PCI Central Committee at its Third Congress (Lyon, January 1926), which sanctioned Gramsci's new line, but was expelled from the Party in 1930, remaining politically inactive during the rest of the fascist period.

Chiarini, Antonio Chaim (or sometimes Cain) Mordko Haller or Heller (also known as Anton Hechelev); Polish communist who, along with Niccolini (Ljubarskij) represented the Comintern in Italy for some time from 1919. Suspicions expressed about him by PCI leaders, including Gramsci, were unfounded. Important in informing Lenin about the Italian situation, and gave favourable reports on the Turin *Ordine Nuovo* group. On his return to Moscow, he continued to influence the Comintern Executive, normally supporting Tasca's right-wing of the PCd'I.

Cocchi, Armando After a shooting incident with fascists in Bologna, went into political exile and while Gramsci was in Russia was secretary of the Italian communist organisation there.

Cocchi, Romano Catholic communist who had trained for the priesthood; expelled from the Popular Party in 1921; secretary first of all to Guido Miglioli and later on to Gramsci; journalist for various PCI publications and edited the Party journal for peasants, *Il Seme*; in the 1930s was one of the few practising catholics on the Party Central Committee; was expelled from the Party for open opposition after the Molotov-Ribbentrop agreement; died in Buchenwald.

Croce, Benedetto Italy's main twentieth-century idealist philosopher; an early influence on Gramsci who saw him as counteracting the influence of positivism. Continued to be a moral influence on younger generations but played no active role against fascism; his brand of political liberalism became increasingly more conservative with old age. His initial reviews of the post-war publication of the *Prison Letters* and *Notebooks* were positive, but was piqued by Gramsci's critique of him expressed there.

De Nicola, Enrico President of the Chamber of Deputies from 1920 until after the elections of 1924; after Italy became a Republic in 1946, provisional Head of State and, as such, was a signatory to the Constitution (December 1947).

Einaudi, Luigi Liberal economist; elected President of the Republic (1948) after the Constitution came into force.

Fortichiari, Bruno Milanese communist, on the left of the PCI; after World War II left the Party and became a leader of a left communist grouping.

Frossard, Louis-Oscar First General Secretary of the French Communist Party but differed from the Comintern on the United Front policy. Elected to the Comintern Executive at the Fourth Congress in 1922 but in 1923 resigned from the PCF secretariat and the Party, rejoining the socialist SFIO.

Gennari, Egidio Veteran socialist who, in March 1919, successfully proposed that the still united PSI should affiliate to the Comintern; the motion remained a dead letter. Founder member of the PCd'I; enjoyed great personal prestige among the rank-and-file; was important as both a leader and as a figurehead; a member of the Comintern Presidium after the Third and again after the Fourth Congress.

Giolitti, Giovanni The dominant bourgeois politician of the generation before fascism. Five times prime minister and occupant of other key ministries, famed for his cynical use of power; promoted industrial development and cautiously accepted a role for trade unions, trying to incorporate the working class into the system; his agricultural protectionism favoured the big southern landowners.

Gramsci, Carlo Four years younger than Antonio; important in liaising between Gramsci in prison and the outside world; was one of the family members who kept contact with Piero Sraffa; with Tat'jana Schucht, oversaw the question of Antonio's funeral.

Gramsci, Gennaro (Nannaro) Six years Antonio's senior; became the book-keeper for *L'Ordine Nuovo*. After Antonio's arrest, safeguarded his brother's position by not admitting to the PCd'I leaders any political difference between Antonio and the Comintern after the ultra-left turn of the latter at its Sixth Congress; a Spanish Civil War veteran.

Grieco, Ruggero Originally close to Bordiga, but moved towards the new centre group that formed in 1924, while still maintaining an autonomous position. From the mid-1920s up to his death in the 1950s, one of the PCI's main experts on agrarian and peasant questions; in the 1930s, during Togliatti's absence on Comintern business, substituted for him as PCI general secretary.

Humbert-Droz, Jules Swiss communist, formerly a protestant pastor, who followed Italian events for the Comintern closely; attended the Second (Rome) Congress of the PCd'I in February 1922 and was in Italy as Comintern representative in the months before Gramsci's return there; enjoyed a fruitful working relationship with the new PCI leadership (cf his personal letter to Gramsci of 20 August 1925: Comintern Archives, 513-1-314/82). After the Sixth Congress of the Comintern, his differences led him to join the Swiss Socialist Party of which he became general secretary.

Kolarov, Vasil Petrov A leading member of the Bulgarian Party and the Comintern, from time to time in Italy and, like Humbert-Droz, was a Comintern representative at the Second Congress of the PCd'I. Led an unsuccessful popular uprising against the fascist regime that overthrew the peasant government of Aleksandăr Stambolijski in 1923; provisional president, subsequently foreign minister and prime minister of Bulgaria in the immediate post-World War II era.

Lazzari, Costantino Veteran socialist who moved the resolution in 1914 that expelled Mussolini from the Socialist Party; secretary of the PSI in 1919 and then a leader of the Third Internationalist ('terzini') fraction of the Party but did not follow the others of this fraction into fusion with the PCI.

Leonetti, Alfonso In the centre group of the PCI with Gramsci; editor of *L'Unità* at the time of Gramsci's arrest. Later, with Ravazzoli and Tresso, one of the left anti-Stalinist opposition to the sectarian switch in Comintern policy in 1928; the three were expelled from the PCI in mid-1930 for fractional activity rather than for their political views. Went into exile in France, rejoining the PCI on his return to Italy in the politically more relaxed atmosphere of the early 1960s.

Ljubarskij, Nikolaj Markovič Under the name Carlo Niccolini, from 1919 to 1921 one of the Comintern representatives delegated to aid the formation of the Italian Party; took the position that the Communist Party should include all, or as many as possible, of those in the Socialist Party opposed to the reformist leaders.

Longo, Luigi Initially a leader of the communist students in Turin and, from the early 1920s, also of the Italian Young Communist Federation; under the name Luigi Gallo, Inspector General of the International Brigades in Spain, then deputy commander of the Partisan forces (CVL) in Italy; general secretary of the PCI for eight years, from the death of Togliatti to the election in 1972 of Enrico Berlinguer, then becoming Party President.

Lozovskij, Solomon Abramovič Best known as head (1921-39) of the Profintern, or Red International of Labour Unions, the Comintern's sister trade union organisation; a prestigious veteran Russian revolutionary, was one of the last to be tortured and executed (1952) under Stalin; rehabilitated four years later.

Maffi, Fabrizio A medic ('the poor people's doctor'); along with Ezio Riboldi the main leader of the Socialist Party 'terzini' fraction. Elected to Parliament on the joint ticket with the PCI in April 1924; during the 'fusion' between the PCI and the terzini in the wake of the V Congress of the Comintern, was nominated to the Executive Committee of the united Party.

Manuil'skij, Dmitri (sometimes seen as **Dmitro**) **Zakharovič** Under the name 'Beruzzi', was Comintern representative in Italy in spring 1923; as President of the Italian Commission at the V Comintern Congress (1924), supported the new majority line in the PCI Central Committee after Gramsci's return to Italy. Later, a key figure at the Seventh Congress of the International (1935); after World War II, Ukrainian representative at the UN General Assembly; People's Commissar, then Minister, for Foreign Affairs of the Republic (1944-52), after which he lost power.

Marabini, Anselmo A popular communist of the older generation. In 1921 presided over the founding Congress of the PCd'I at Livorno and, in 1945, over the PCI's first post-World War II Congress (the Party's Fifth Congress). In Russia from the mid-1920s until his re-entry into Italy in 1945; a leader of the International Red Aid organisation and, during the 1930s, elected to the Moscow Soviet.

Maximalists (see also 'Terzini') The Socialist Party's generically Marxist 'centrists', led by G.M. Serrati; wooed by the leadership of the Third International, up to the IV Congress of the Comintern against the wishes of Gramsci and the PCI. Many remained in the Socialist Party (PSI), but some, under Serrati's leadership, went over into the PCd'I with the terzini in mid-1924.

Miglioli, Guido A key figure for the PCI policy of social and political alliances; leader of the catholic peasant union in the Po valley, he was expelled from the Popular Party for being too far to the left; worked with the communists on agrarian issues and was elected Vice-President of the Krestintern as well as being a leader of the International Red Aid organisation.

Nenni, Pietro In this period on the right of the maximalist Socialist Party; in 1923 ousted Serrati from editorship of the Socialist Party daily *Avanti!*; was the dominant figure among the Italian socialists until the late 1960s.

Pastore, Ottavio Journalist on *L'Ordine Nuovo* and later first editor of *L'Unità*.

Pjatnickij, Osip Aronovič In the early 1920s one of the secretaries of the Comintern; head of the Comintern's International Liaison Section (OMS) and of the Comintern budget commission; arrested and shot in prison in the late 1930s but rehabilitated after the Twentieth Congress of the CPSU.

Platone, Felice Journalist and close collaborator of Gramsci's on *L'Ordine Nuovo*; member of the General Staff of the Garibaldi Brigades in Spain; best known in post-war years as the editor, under Togliatti, of the six-volume thematic edition of Gramsci's *Prison Notebooks*.

Rákosi, Mátyás Leading Hungarian communist; Comintern representative in Italy in 1922-23, then replaced by Manuil'skij; supported the right of the PCI. Was the target of much criticism from the PCI leaders; not liked or greatly esteemed by Gramsci. After World War II, was prime minister of Hungary and secretary of the merged Social Democratic and Communist Parties; responsible for much of the Stalinist terror in Hungary, but was marginalised after 1956 and, in 1962, expelled from the Party.

Ravazzoli, Paolo Aligned with Gramsci's positions; elected to the Central Committee at the PCI's III Congress; one of 'the three' expelled for fractional activity after the VI Congress of the Comintern; for a brief period close to Trotsky.

Ravera, Camilla The leading Italian woman communist of her generation and head of the women's organisation of the PCd'I; a delegate to the IV Congress of the Comintern, then becoming one of the centre group that formed in the Party under Gramsci. Like Terracini – and Romano Cocchi – expelled from the PCI for differences over the Molotov-Ribbentrop pact, and readmitted when Togliatti came back to Italy from exile. Towards the end of her life, was nominated a life senator.

Riboldi, Ezio One of the main leaders of the terzini; elected to parliament on the joint *Unità proletaria* list with the PCd'I in the 1924 election. Later stood trial with Gramsci but in 1933 was released, after a request for pardon by his wife; for this he was expelled from the Party.

Scoccimarro, Mauro Founder member of the PCd'I; member of the Executive with Gramsci on the latter's return to Italy. Arrested several times; tried and sentenced with Gramsci to twenty years; was in charge of the Party when Togliatti returned to Italy after eighteen years of exile, becoming Finance Minister (1945-47) in the short-lived governments of national unity.

Serrati, Giacinto Menotti The long-time editor of the Socialist Party daily, *Avanti!*; emerged as leader of the centrist 'maximalist' fraction of the Italian Socialist Party, hoping to bring the Party over to the Third International in its near-entirety; the target of many of Gramsci's polemics, with the better maximalists went over to the PCd'I in 1924; then headed the Party's trade union section.

Souvarine, Boris Founder member of the French Communist Party; represented it on the Comintern Executive; excluded from the PCF in 1924 and became one of the great anti-Stalinist left dissidents, albeit in disagreement with various stances of Trotsky.

Sraffa, Piero One of the twentieth century's great economists and winner (1961) of the forerunner of the Nobel Prize for economics. Initially a leader of the communist student movement in Turin, went on to work in London at the Labour Research Department before winning a university post in Italy; from there called to Cambridge by Keynes in 1927. He became Gramsci's intellectual and, along with the Comintern, financial mainstay in the prison years, providing a key link in the indirect relation, usually via Tat'jana Schucht, between Gramsci and the PCI leadership in exile, in the person of Togliatti.

Tasca, Angelo Founder member of the PCd'I, and always on its right wing; member of the *Ordine Nuovo* group of Turin but, rather than direct activity among the masses of workers and a pre-eminent role for the factory councils as the germ of a new State, favoured agreements with recognised union and party leaders, which then reflected his approach to the process of unity between the PCd'I and the PSI.

Expelled from the PCd'I in 1929, went over to the Socialists and, in 1938, was responsible for the first publication in its entirety of Gramsci's letter of October 1926 to the Central Committee of the Russian (All-Union) Party, critical of developments there.

Terracini, Umberto Member of the *Ordine Nuovo* group and a founder member of the PCd'I, frequently representing the Party in Moscow, sometimes on the Comintern Executive or Presidium. After some hesitation, joined the centre group being formed around Gramsci in 1923-24. A brilliant lawyer and main defendant of the prisoners in Gramsci's trial, he received the longest sentence of anyone. Like Camilla Ravera, opposed the Molotov-Ribbentrop pact and was expelled from the Party, being readmitted when Togliatti came back to Italy. When the Socialist Party split at the start of the Cold War, leaving the PCI as the next biggest parliamentary party after the Christian Democrats, he acceded to the Presidency of the Constituent Assembly, and together with De Nicola and the prime minister, Alcide De Gasperi, was signatory in December 1947 of the Republican Constitution. Led the PCI in the Senate in different legislatures and was nominated a life senator.

Terzini (Third Internationalists) The pro-Comintern left of the maximalist Socialist Party, less compromising than Serrati's maximalist 'centrists'. Under Fabrizio Maffi and Ezio Riboldi's leadership, the terzini fought the April 1924 election on a joint list (*Unità proletaria*) with the PCd'I, and then in the so-called 'fusion' process, united with the Party in mid-1924.

Togliatti, Palmiro Of the Turin *Ordine Nuovo* group, and always prominent in the leadership of the PCd'I; after Gramsci's arrest, succeeded him as the acknowledged main leader (usually General Secretary) of the Party. In the mid-1930s, with Georgi Dimitrov became joint secretary of the Comintern, playing a major role in the Seventh Congress that sanctioned the Popular Front policy; the main Comintern representative in the Spanish Civil War. After eighteen years exile, returned to Italy in March 1944 and re-oriented the PCI towards a policy of national anti-fascist unity. Vice-President of the Council of Ministers (Cabinet), then Minister of Justice, in governments of national unity that fell with the onset of the Cold War. Was instrumental in ensuring (together with Tat'jana Schucht and Piero Sraffa) that after Gramsci's death, his manuscript notebooks reached safety in Moscow; subsequently he oversaw publication of the *Prison Letters* (1947) and Felice Platone's thematic edition of the *Notebooks* (1948-51). Enjoyed enormous prestige among the Party rank-and-file and guided the PCI to gradually increasing popular support; died in August 1964. A life-long supporter of the Soviet Union, albeit guardedly critical then, at the end of his life, more explicitly so. In a message on the fiftieth anniversary of the founding of the PCI, György Lukács called him the 'best tactician' of the Communist International. Some choices Togliatti made were controversial, but he had very finely-tuned antennae for judging the possibilities of a given situation, both in Moscow and in Italy.

Tresso, Pietro Founder member of the PCd'I, working especially in the trade union sphere; elected to the Central Committee at the Third Congress of the PCd'I. Expelled for fractional activity in the wake of the Sixth Congress of the International; became a founder of the Fourth International and, according to his comrades, was killed by 'orthodox' communist partisans in France in 1943.

Turati, Filippo A founder of the Italian Socialist Party in 1892, and long-time parliamentary deputy, was one of the main leaders of the reformists, splitting from the maximalist Socialist Party to form the Unitary Socialist Party (October 1922); fled Italy in December 1926 after the mass arrests by the regime, dying in exile in France in 1932.

Vaillant-Couturier, Paul Prestigious French journalist and intellectual; a socialist as a result of his First World War experiences; founder member of the French Communist Party and parliamentary deputy.

Zini, Zino One of the furthest left of the older generation of Turinese intellectuals and a socialist member of the Turin city council (1906-19). At the University of Turin, taught the moral philosophy course attended by Gramsci. Became a sympathiser of the workers' council movement and was instrumental with Gramsci in setting up a Turin section of Moscow's Proletkul't movement.

ORGANISATIONS

CGL or **CGdL** General Confederation of Labour. Founded in 1906 and suppressed under fascism; resurfaced towards the end of the resistance struggle under a joint communist-socialist-catholic leadership, but broke up at the start of the Cold War into what became the communist-socialist Italian General Confederation of Labour (CGIL), the social democrat and republican UIL and the catholic CISL.

ECCI (Ispolkom) Executive Committee of the Communist International.

Krestintern The Comintern's sister organisation for peasants.

MOPR, **Rote Hilfe** and **Arbeiter Hilfe** (International Organisation for Help to Revolutionaries, Red Aid and Workers' Aid respectively). According to the period and task – help to working-class victims of capitalism or to the workers in the Soviet Union – the organisations are known under various names in the English-speaking world, such as International Red Aid, International Workers' Aid, Workers' International Relief, International Labor Defense, International Class War Prisoners Aid, etc.

OMS (Otdel Meždunarodnykh Svjazej), International Liaison Section of the Comintern, headed by Osip Pjatnickij.

PCd'I Communist Party of Italy (Partito Comunista d'Italia), the Party's name from its foundation when it split off from the Socialist Party in January 1921, until the dissolution of the Comintern in 1943, when it officially became the PCI (Partito Comunista Italiano), the name under which it was in any case widely known from its formation.

PSI (sometimes **SP**) Italian Socialist Party, founded in 1892 as the 'Partito dei Lavoratori Italiani' ('Italian Working Peoples' Party'); often in the period of his volume called the 'maximalist' Party both before and after its right wing broke away to found the unitary socialist PSU.

PSU The ultra-reformist Unitary Socialist Party, formed as a breakaway from the 'maximalist' PSI a few weeks before Mussolini was nominated prime minister in October 1922.

U9 The office headed by Gramsci in Vienna (beginning of December 1923 to mid-April 1924).

Name Index

Pseudonyms and given names are cross-referenced to the main entry giving the real name of the person; the exception is for the representatives of the International in Italy who were known at the time exclusively under their pseudonyms, which are used in these cases as the main entry. Numbers in italics indicate the use of a person's pseudonym or given name on the page in question when it occurs on its own, without the real name. Gramsci himself is listed only under his pseudonyms, Masci or Sardi

Also available from Haymarket Books

Antonio Gramsci
Selections from Cultural Writings

By Antonio Gramsci
$22

Antonio Gramsci was one of the world's most influential cultural critics; his writings on the interconnection between culture and politics fundamentally changed the way that scholars view both. Gramsci was among the first to argue that art is not the product of "men of genius" but rather of particular historical and social contexts, and he remains one of the most widely read theorists of modern culture.

Gramsci's Political Thought

By Carlos Nelson Coutinho
$28

Focusing on the central concepts of the *Prison Notebooks* and relating them to the history of modern political ideas, *Gramsci's Political Thought* demonstrates that Gramsci's ideas continue to be relevant for understanding today's world. Written by a leading Brazilian Marxist theorist, this book provides one of the most succinct and theoretically focused introductions to Gramsci's thought available in any language.

The Gramscian Moment
Philosophy, Hegemony and Marxism

By Peter D. Thomas
$36

The influence of Antonio Gramsci's thought is only exceeded by the diverse interpretations to which it has been subjected, resulting in contradictory images of "the true Gramsci." Drawing on the recent flurry of linguistic work on his *Prison Notebooks*, Thomas argues that Gramsci's significance is his distinctive position in the development of the classical Marxist tradition.